SANITY

AND INSANITY.

BY

CHARLES MERCIER, M.B.,

Lecturer on Insanity at the Westminster Hospital Medical School, and at the Medical School for Women.

WITH ILLUSTRATIONS.

LONDON:
WALTER SCOTT,
24, WARWICK LANE, PATERNOSTER ROW.
1890.

To

MY OLDEST AND BEST FRIEND,

DR. F. H. FORSHALL,

THIS BOOK IS DEDICATED IN GRATEFUL REMEMBRANCE OF

INNUMERABLE KINDNESSES RECEIVED

FROM HIM.

CONTENTS.

———o———

CHAPTER I.

CHAPTER VIII.

CHAPTER IX.

CHAPTER X.

CHAPTER XI.

CHAPTER XII.

CHAPTER XIII.

CHAPTER XIV.

CHAPTER XV.

LIST OF ILLUSTRATIONS.

————o————

PREFACE.

———o———

The other day a corn merchant consulted me about one of his children who had some nervous malady. "I took her," he said, " to Sir Omicron Pie, and " (indignantly) " he gave her bromide ! " It struck me as a fact of remarkable signifi- cance that a man who was immersed all day and all the year round in his own business, should have sufficient knowledge, and sufficient intelligent interest, in a somewhat special department of a widely different profession, to observe what particular drug was ordered for his daughter, and to form his own judgment as to the propriety of administering that drug in that case. Thirty years ago such a remark would have been impossible. Then the medical man was looked upon as an oracle, who was regarded vaguely and generally as clever or the reverse, but whose dicta were to be accepted or rejected ; not criticized. The ordinary intelligent layman gathered his notion of the professional ability of his medical adviser from general grounds, and not from critical obser- vation of particular prescriptions. Nowadays it is different. The patient and the patient's friends expect a detailed description of the precise seat and character of the disorder ; and what is more, they consider themselves quite capable of judging whether the explanation given is rational, and whether the treatment is appropriate. Medical terms are glibly used, and medical theories are freely discussed in general society, and inability to join in a medical discussion is regarded as evidence of deficiency of general culture. Society has adopted

the opinion of Melancthon : that it is disgraceful for a man
not to know the structure and composition of his own
body.

There is, however, one department of medical knowledge
to which even the most intelligent of laymen has not yet
gained access, and that is the department that deals with
insanity. With respect to this malady the great majority
of medical men are themselves in the position of laymen.
They have not studied it. It was not included in their
examinations ; it was a thing outside their curriculum—a
thing apart, having little community of nature or similarity
of character with the subjects of their professional studies.

To the outside layman—to the non-medical public,—
insanity presents itself in two somewhat contradictory
aspects. Sometimes it is to them a matter of transparent
and childlike simplicity, a thing which a person of most
ordinary intelligence—say a common juryman—is capable
of estimating with accuracy and certainty. At other times
it is viewed much as our ancestors viewed the Black Art ;—
as something mysterious and marvellous ; something super-
natural ; something to be spoken of with bated breath ;
something too full of awe to be even named explicitly. It
must then be referred to in indirect and elliptical terms,
with pursing of the lips, with raised eyebrows and shoulders,
and with shakings of the head.

Considering how common an affection insanity is ; considering that there is scarcely a family in this country that
has not had at least one of its members more or less insane ;
it is somewhat remarkable that so little should be generally
known about insanity. It is not, indeed, remarkable that
this malady is not discussed with the same freedom that
bodily diseases are talked of, for its occurrence is still looked
upon as almost a disgrace to the family in which it occurs,
and he who introduces the subject never knows whose toes
he may be treading on. Nor is it remarkable that it is not
discussed with that fulness of knowledge with which the
dyspeptic legislates on dietary, and the materfamilias on

measles ; for even amongst experts—the medical officers of asylums—the subject has hardly yet begun to be scientifically studied ; so that there is no body of knowledge for the layman to draw upon beyond a mass of more or less authentic anecdotage. The eager interest with which these anecdotes are received and repeated, shows, however, that there is much curiosity alive upon the subject, and that systematic information with regard to it will be received with avidity. The dissemination of such information can scarcely fail to do good in several ways.

In the first place, it may tend to diminish the absurd and unreasoning horror with which insane people are regarded. I have known ladies, in other respects sensible and kind-hearted, refuse to sit at table with other ladies as well-bred and well-conducted as themselves, because the latter were unsound in mind. And if it were known, as I trust it never will be known, that scarcely a week passes in which I myself do not take a party of lunatics to one or other of the London theatres, it is very probable that those excellent places of entertainment would find a serious falling-off in their receipts. How often have I not watched an unsuspecting stranger chatting and exchanging criticisms between the acts with one of my companions, little thinking that for the last hour he had been sitting between a couple of lunatics, and was at that very moment talking to one of them.

In the second place, a little familiarity with the phenomena of insanity may prevent well-meaning people from making idiots of themselves by talking of insane people *in their presence*, as if the insane possessed neither hearing, understanding, nor memory. "But does he *know* that he is in an asylum?" or, "He is not *dangerous*, is he?" a lady will ask (ladies are the chief offenders in this respect), in the hearing and in the presence of a courteous gentleman who has been doing his best to entertain her for the last half-hour. She appears to regard him as an automaton, who acts and speaks by machinery, has no feelings to be hurt, and is incapable of appreciating an insult.

Thirdly, a knowledge of the principles on which insanity should be regarded can scarcely fail to be of service to that large, and now much increased, section of the community who have to do officially, but as amateurs, with the insane. I refer to the magistrates under the new Lunacy Act, to barristers, and others. The want of knowledge of the rudiments of insanity among the general public is remarkable. I have heard a Queen's Counsel gravely tell a jury that it was against the law for a lunatic to be sent to an asylum unless he (the lunatic) was dangerous. That is, fortunately, not the law ; but there are very many people who are strongly of opinion that it ought to be the law. A very little knowledge of lunacy would alter this opinion. Apart from the fact that it is desirable to cure the insanity, and that in many cases a cure can only be attempted within an asylum ; apart from the necessity, that so often exists, of secluding a perfectly harmless lunatic in order to prevent him from squandering his means and ruining himself and his family ; apart from the desirability of restraining him from performing acts which are not dangerous, but which are disgraceful, and which he himself would, on his recovery, be loudest in blaming his friends for not preventing ; there remains the most important fact that the distinguishing feature of the insane is, not their dangerous aggressiveness, but their revolting indecency and obscenity. Of course, not all the insane are thus characterized, but a majority of them, probably a large majority, of both men and women are, or would be if freed from restraint, more shameless and filthy in their conduct than so many monkeys. It is not merely that the public must be protected from such conduct as this. They have a right, also, to be prevented from witnessing it, to be protected from the danger of witnessing it ; and it is for this reason, more than for any other, that the seclusion of the insane in asylums is necessary and right.

Lastly, a knowledge of the facts of insanity must be of service both to those who are liable to become insane and to their friends, for of this malady, more than of any other, it is true, that the earlier its beginnings are recognized, the better the chance of prevention and the more sanguine the hope of cure.

The present volume is not, however, devoted mainly, nor even largely, to a mere description of the facts of insanity. That has been done very completely by people of far longer experience, and of better powers of description, than are possessed by the writer. In this book the endeavour is made, and is made, I believe, for the first time, not so much to describe and enumerate, as to *account for* the phenomena of insanity. That certain occurrences are occasional, others common, and others invariable in insanity, all authorities are agreed ; and all are agreed, too, as to the frequent association of certain occurrences ; but so far as I know, no attempt has hitherto been made to explain either the occurrence or the association. For instance, it is an old observation that at or about the time of childbirth is a common occasion for insanity to occur in woman. It is an old observation that a melancholy turn of mind never occurs without constipation of the bowels. But why these things should be associated together, what the link may be between them, is a question which not only has never been answered, but which, as far as I know, has never been asked. It has not occurred to any one that an explanation was desirable. These, and the other phenomena of insanity, I have endeavoured to account for, in so far as explanation in the present state of our knowledge appeared possible, and as far as the space at my disposal would permit.

The usual conception that the laity have of a lunatic is somewhat as follows : He is usually raving, shouting at the top of his voice, and smashing the furniture. When not in this state, he is controlling himself, and in the plenitude of his cunning—for he is no lunatic if not cunning—he is lulling the surrounding people into a sense of false security, until he can get a convenient opportunity of cutting their throats. Instead of a hat he wears straws in his hair, speaks of himself in the third person, and talks in ingenious and complicated parables.

It is hard to relinquish a simple faith that has grown up with us from childhood, and become part of our very nature; and for my part I shall never forget the shock it was to me when I took office in an asylum containing about two thousand lunatics, to find not one single straw sticking out of a single head in the institution. So far from speaking in parables, they asked for what they wanted with simple directness, and, when they did not get it, their language was as direct and forcible as that of any sane person. Having now spent many years in daily and hourly contact with the insane, the one fact about them which continually impresses me, with more and more conviction, is the wonderfully little difference that there is between them and other people. It is not merely that the lunatic is "fed with the same food, hurt with the same weapons, subject to the same diseases, healed by the same means, warmed and cooled by the same summer and winter," as a sane person; but that in his very insanity, in the vagaries of his mind and the extravagancies of his conduct, he exhibits nothing but an exaggeration of the same peculiarities which we all possess more or less.

The reader should here be warned that the studies upon which he is about to enter are by no means easy. Every one admits that the study of mind is the highest and most difficult branch of scientific inquiry; and every biologist knows that the elucidation of morbid processes is very far more difficult than the investigation of processes in their healthy condition. When, therefore, we come to study the morbid processes of mind, we enter upon investigations of the very highest difficulty.

In writing primarily for the general reader, it will be my endeavour to study, before all things, plainness and intelligibility, and, in order to this end, it will be necessary to take nothing for granted, but to suppose that the reader comes to the study of the subject with a mind empty, swept, and garnished in so far as a knowledge of the nervous system and of the mind is concerned. I shall assume that in this regard his mind is in the condition symbolized by Locke as "a sheet of blank paper," and shall endeavour to write thereon a somewhat difficult and complicated message in a fair round text.

The great difficulty that I shall have to deal with is, however, that the paper is not blank. It is already scrabbled over with all kinds of erroneous notions; and unless they are erased I shall only be making a tangled-looking palimpsest of confused illegibility. It will be necessary, therefore, to clear the ground by eliminating as far as possible some prevailing false doctrines.

The next difficulty is in the immense extent of the subject-matter. To explain the whole of insanity requires a preliminary knowledge of neurology, psychology, and sociology, and these three sciences can scarcely be comprehended within the limits of this small volume. Something may, however, be done, if conclusions only are given, while the laborious processes by which they have been arrived at are omitted. Some of these conclusions are by no means universally accepted as yet; but space will not allow the various reasons, *pro* and *con*, to be adduced, for the reader to form his own judgment on them. Hence arises necessity for a certain dogmatism. When I am reasonably satisfied that a matter is thus and so, thus and so I shall state it to be, even if that is not the ordinarily accepted doctrine. In first acquiring knowledge, it is better for the knowledge acquired to be erroneous than indefinite. Error can be corrected, and the more definite and clean-cut the error, the easier the correction; but vague, indefinite, misty, formless notions are much worse than none at all. They give their possessor the confidence and pride of knowledge without the substance.

To render clear what is meant, an instance may be given. It is taught in this volume that in order to know anything about insanity it is necessary first to know something about sanity, and that in order to know anything about the disordered mind it is necessary to know something about

I*

the mind in health. In thus teaching, I am running directly counter to the opinion of many of my professional brethren, one of the most distinguished of whom has written books full of ridicule of this doctrine. Still, I shall proceed as if this were a reasonable course to take, and shall ask the reader to accept the doctrine as a good working hypothesis, without requiring to have the matter argued out at length.

Many of the other doctrines here advanced are in the same position of being unaccepted. The statement of the nature of insanity given in Chapter IV. was stated by me in the *Journal of Mental Science* in 1882, but I do not know that it has any adherents. The doctrine of the twofold causation of insanity is here stated for the first time. Some of the biological doctrines, *e.g.*, that of the parts taken by the male and female elements respectively in reproduction, are in the same position, as is the doctrine of the double circulation of nerve energy, that of the defect of nerve tension underlying melancholia, and many minor points. As to the majority of these doctrines, I do not claim that they are the true and correct explanation of the facts to which they are applied ; but at any rate they are explanations of some kind. Their truth or falsity may be tested by working out the consequences that they would, if true, entail, and by comparing these consequences with the facts. If the hypotheses stand this test, well and good ; if they do not, let them make way for others that are more in harmony with the facts ; but in any case it seems to me that the time has now arrived, the state of our science has now reached a point, at which some explanation of the facts of insanity has become desirable ; and that any hypothesis, even if erroneous, is a step towards the attainment of truth, and is better than a mere unorganized accumulation of facts.

Some reference should here be made to the freedom with which the sexual and reproductive functions are treated of in this volume. Such freedom is not customary in books which are not intended for the exclusive use of the medical profession ; but in this case the course taken is unavoidable.

The phenomena of insanity are dependent on, and connected with, these functions in so many ways, and with so close an intimacy, that to attempt to treat of the former without reference to the latter would render the book a mockery and an imposture. Where it has been necessary to refer to these subjects they have been treated of frankly and candidly.

For the photograph of the bearded woman, forming the frontispiece, I am indebted to my friend, Dr. Ernest White, Superintendent of the City of London Lunatic Asylum.

C. M.

HENRIETTA STREET, CAVENDISH SQUARE, W.
October, 1889.

SANITY AND INSANITY.

CHAPTER I.

THE NERVOUS SYSTEM.

IF an experienced architect had to give to an intelligent
nomad an exhaustive description of the structure of a family
mansion, he would probably find that the task before him
was threefold. He would have to describe the general
architectural scheme of the whole building, the appearance of the exterior, and the arrangement and uses of the
rooms. When this was done, he would have given but an
imperfect notion of the structure unless he explained the
shapes and ways in which the various materials—the bricks
and mortar, the stone and timber, beams, joists, rafters,
floorings and skirtings, the girders and pipes and stones
and cisterns, the panes of glass and sheets of paper—were
fashioned so as to fit into their places, and contribute to the
stability, durability, and efficiency of the edifice. Finally,
he would discover that, in addition to all this instruction, he
would be obliged to explain the nature and distinctive properties of each of these materials, so as to make clear to a
person who had never seen them the manner in which they
are fitted to the functions they severally have to perform.

As to the order in which the information should be imparted, the architect would probably find that his readiest
way would be to give first a general outline of the whole

affair, and then to proceed in detail in the inverse order of
that just given. That is to say, he would begin with the
description of the elementary constituents, and then explain
the fabrics built up by their combination.

In describing the elaborate and complicated structure of
the nervous system it will be well to follow a plan similar to
that which would naturally suggest itself in the case supposed ; and though it is unlikely that any reader will be as
ignorant of the structure of the nervous system as a Bedouin
of that of a house, yet, for the sake of completeness, it will
be well to assume a similar vacuity of information, so as to
begin at the bottom and leave nothing unexplained.

To recur for a moment to the illustration, it is obvious
that no satisfactory notion of the arrangement of a house
could be given unless the various uses of the rooms were
indicated in explanation of their shapes, sizes, positions and
fittings ; and in the same way, the shapes and positions of
the various stones and beams must account for their properties and uses. In other words, structure and function must
be dealt with together ; and with the nervous system also
this course will be found the best.

If we cast a comprehensive glance over the whole of the
animal and vegetable kingdoms, with a view to determine
the quality or property which most conspicuously and
clearly distinguishes the former from the latter, we should
probably fix on the presence or absence of purposive movement as the most characteristic distinction. It is true that,
very low down in the scale, there are rudimentary vegetable
forms with considerable powers of movement that is spontaneous, and may in some cases appear purposive ; and, in
a similar position on the other side, there are sessile and
stationary animal forms. It is true also that some of the
higher forms of vegetable life, such as the droseræ, Venus's
fly-trap, and certain of the orchids, execute movements
which undoubtedly subserve definite ends. These movements are, however, always movements of parts, often of
minute parts, and never of the organism as a whole ; and

moreover, by the wonder with which they are regarded, we are assured of their highly exceptional character, and, by the almost invariable comparison of· them to animate movements, we have brought home to us the universality with which this property of purposive movement is regarded as an attribute special and peculiar to animal life.

The apparatus by which purposive movements are actuated is the nervous system, and hence it is to the nervous system that all animals are indebted for their distinctively animate character. True it is that there are humble members of the animal kingdom which possess no nervous system, and that these animals are capable of movement, and of movements of the entire organism ; but then such movements are of a merely random character, and although they may, and do, effect certain purposes, as, for instance, the bringing of the organism into contact with food, yet these purposes are effected by the mere fact of movement, and do not necessitate movement in any specific direction, at any specific rate, or of any specific kind. Scarcely, therefore, can such movements be termed purposive.

When we raise our regard to animals capable of movements that are manifestly purposive, we find that such animals possess a manifest nervous system ; and the more definite, the more specific, the more comprehensive, the more distant, the more elaborate, the movement and the purpose for which it is undertaken, the more complex and elaborate—in other words, the more highly evolved—is the nervous system by which the movement is actuated.

The study of the properties of the nervous system resolves itself therefore mainly into a study of the means by which it actuates movements, and of those by which it directs these movements towards a definite end. I say mainly, because the nervous system has other and subsidiary functions which will be touched upon hereafter.

All movements of animals—that is to say, of animals sufficiently elevated in the scale of life to execute purposive movements—are directly actuated by muscles. In man the

general form and structure of a muscle is that of a more
or less spindle-shaped bundle of fibres, having each end
fixed into a bone. Between the two ends of the muscle
the continuity of the bone is interrupted by a joint ; so
that one end of the muscle is fixed into a bone above a joint,
and the other end into a bone below.

The peculiar and characteristic property of muscles is
their ability to contract when they are stimulated. When
a muscle is stimulated, it contracts ; that is to say, it
shortens and thickens, and this shortening and thickening
are effected with great force, so that the ends of the muscles,
and, with the ends, the bones, or whatever structures the

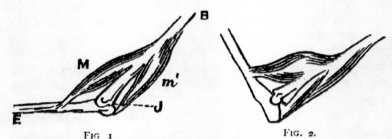

F<small>IG</small> 1   F<small>IG</small>. 2.

Diagram representing the general relation of muscles to bones. B E, bones ;
J, joints ; M M', muscles. When M contracts and M' lengthens, the
limb is bent, as in Fig 2

ends are attached to, are brought together. In this way all
bodily movements of every kind are effected, the whole of our
ability to move and act depending entirely on this property
of contraction that belongs to muscles ; the great variety of
the movements that we are able to execute, depending on
the multiplicity and variety of our joints, and the various
ways in which the muscles are disposed about them. By
far the greatest bulk of every animal is composed of muscle.
The muscles clothe the bones, and form almost the whole
mass of the limbs, besides composing the fleshy ridges on
each side of the back, the greater part of the neck, and the
walls of the great cavities of the chest and abdomen.

All these muscles are bundles of fibres, and when these fibres are examined, they are found to be themselves bundles of smaller fibres ; and these again may be separated until we find that the smallest actual fibres are all about the same thickness—all about $\frac{1}{100}$ of an inch in diameter—and that each is enclosed in a fine pellucid sheath, a mere film wrapped round it to keep it together, and that each is marked in a curious way by crossbars.

It has been said that the muscle contracts only when *stimulated*, by which is meant that the contraction takes place only when there is an impact of force upon the muscle. It appears from experiment that any force—any form of energy—will produce a contraction if it be sufficiently powerful, and if it actually get to the muscular fibres. We can make a muscle contract by striking, or pricking, or pressing, or pinching, or burning it, or by sending into it a shock of electricity. But it is found that we get no contraction unless there is an *impact*. The *continuous* application of a force is of no effect. It is only at the moment of impact that a contraction takes place ; and if we want to keep up a continuous contraction we must keep up a rapid succession of shocks of some kind or other upon the muscle.

When the muscle is in its place, playing its part in the economy of the living body, the impacts of energy which set it in action are delivered to it through the medium of the nerves. When we lift up one of the muscular masses which have been described, we find that, in addition to the firm attachment of its ends, it has a third connection with the rest of the body. At some point we shall find passing between the bundles of fibres of which the muscle consists, and entering the body of the muscle, a thread or string of greyish-white substance. If we separate the bundles of fibres to see where this string goes to, we shall find that it divides and divides again into a leash of small threads, and that one of these threads goes into every bundle of fibres. If we pursue our investi-

gations further, by means of the microscope, we shall find
that the thread in the bundle divides again into a leash of
small filaments, and that each filament becomes attached to
one of the smallest fibres of which the muscle is composed.

If we place under the microscope the point of union of
a nerve-filament with a muscle-fibre, we shall find that
the filament pierces the filmy sheath of the fibre, and
then spreads out into a branching plate, which lies on
the surface of the fibre. There is therefore the closest
possible apposition between the nerve-end and the muscle-
fibre, and in case any force were to traverse the nerve-fibre,
it would be brought to impinge in the most direct manner
possible upon the substance of the fibre of the muscle.

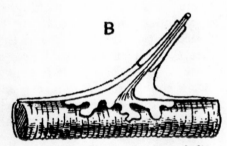

FIG. 3.—Union of nerve-end with muscle-fibre.

If we examine
again the junction of
the nerve with the
muscle-fibre, we shall
see that the former
also has its filmy
sheath, which be-
comes continuous
with that of the
latter ; and if we
trace the nerve fur-
ther and further from the muscle-fibre, we shall find that the
former, like the latter, become collected into bundles, and the
bundles into larger bundles, all bound together with the same
material that binds the muscle-fibres, until at last the bundle
becomes the considerable cord that we have already seen
entering the body of the muscle. This end of the nerve we
have traced to its destination. We have seen it dividing and
dividing until at last each ultimate filament terminates in
a plate in contact with a muscle-fibre ; but where does
the other end go ? or rather, where does this nerve come
from which thus distributes itself to the ultimate muscular
fibres ? If we trace the nerve-string, we shall find that it
goes towards the middle line of the body ; that, as it pro-

ceeds, it is joined by other strings emerging from other muscles, until quite a thick substantial cord is formed ; and if we trace this thicker cord, we shall find that it passes through a hole into a cavity which is enclosed by the bones of the skull and the spine, and here it runs into a large mass of nervous matter shaped like a tadpole, the head of the tadpole occupying the skull, and being called the brain, while the tail occupies the channel in the spine, and is called the spinal cord or spinal marrow. It is from this mass of nerve tissue that the pulses of energy emanate, which pass out along the nerves and set the muscles in action.

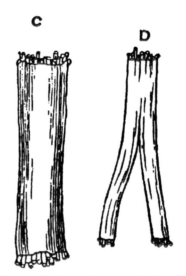

The nerves which are distributed to the muscles are, however, not the only ones which issue from the cerebro-spinal axis. Large nerve-trunks emerge from the central mass of nerve matter, and pass to the eyes, to the nose, to the tongue, to the skin, to all the internal viscera, and even to the bones ; but whatever their destination, the constitution of the nerve-trunks is the same, and their function as carriers of energy,

FIG. 4.—Portions of nerves showing the nerve-fibres bound up in bundles.

or channels for the passage of energy, is identical. There is, however, this difference in the function of nerves, that while those which go to the muscles, as well as others which go to the glands and some other organs, carry their streams of energy outwards from the great nervous masses to their branched terminations at the periphery of the body, the nerves which connect the cerebro-spinal axis with the skin and the special sense-organs carry their currents of energy from the periphery of the body inwards to the central masses of nerve-substance.

Hence it appears that, just as the body is permeated with a vast and intricate network of vessels, in which the blood is distributed from its central reservoir, the heart, through every part of the organism ; so it is permeated throughout by an equally vast and intricate system of nerves, through which energy is distributed from the central reservoirs, the great nervous masses of the brain and cord, throughout the entire organism.

The function of the nervous system is therefore to accumulate and distribute energy ; but before going into further detail let us be quite sure that we clearly apprehend what is meant by the accumulation and distribution of energy. Having definitely fixed the meaning that we attach to this phrase, we can then go on to consider how these functions can be accomplished—by what composition and structure and mode of working a tissue and a set of organs become capable of dealing with power, as another set of organs deal with matter.

FIG. 5.—Transverse section of small nerve magnified.

Recent developments of mercantile activity have rendered it much easier than it formerly was to the non-scientific reader to gain a clear notion of the storage and distribution of energy. There is in London a company whose business it is to furnish hydraulic power to its customers. From a central station is laid a branching series of pipes, which terminate in the various machines—lifts, cranes, presses, and so forth—which are required to be worked. At the central station is the pumping apparatus by which the power is accumulated, and this power is transmitted, in the form of fluid-pressure, to the point at which the application of the power is needed. It will be observed that although the power is transmitted through water-pipes, what is transmitted is not water, but water-pressure—not matter, but power. Similarly there are companies for the supply of the electric light   At the central station power is accumulated. This power passes along the wires in the form of the electric current, until it reaches the carbon filament of the lamp, at which it manifests itself to us as light.   In this case there is no transference of matter along the wire ; what passes is power only.   So closely analogous is this storage and transmission of energy to the storage and transmission of fluid, that the phraseology and nomenclature of gas lighting have been borrowed and applied to electric lighting.   These illustrations will render it easy to comprehend clearly what is meant when the brain is spoken of as an accumulator and distributor of energy, and the nerves as channels in which energy is conveyed.   It still remains to show the mechanism by which this storage and carriage are effected.

The form of energy which traverses the nerves is unique.   Accompanied by change of temperature, yet it is not heat.   Accompanied by electric changes, yet it is not electricity.   Travelling in a gelatinous semi-fluid medium, yet it is not fluid pressure, nor mere mechanical transmission.   It is *sui generis*. Although, however, it differs from every other manifestation of energy with which we are acquainted, it is evidently diffusible ; for the nerve threads in which it is transmitted are surrounded or coated with tubes of oily-looking material, whose function is, we suppose, to act as an insulator, like the coating of gutta-percha on an electric wire.   We make this supposition because we find this coating present on those portions only of the nerve fibre, from which a diffusion of the current would be manifestly disadvantageous. Where diffusion would be harmless or advantageous there is no such coating.

The circumstances which distinguish the energy that travels in the nerves from other forms of energy are, first of

A

FIG. 6.
Nerve fibre
magnified,
showing
filmy sheath
containing
insulating
material.

all, its rate of progress, nine metres per second ; and secondly, the unique fact that the current of energy is cumulative, that is to say, the further it travels the stronger it gets. A falling stone gathers, it is true, velocity, and therefore momentum, both of which become greater the further it falls ; but it does not gain energy ; for what it gains in energy of movement it loses in energy of position, as is well known.

To account for this remarkable property of the nerve current, and to explain the other phenomena of its transit, the following hypothesis has been advanced, and since it affords a satisfactory explanation of these and of the other facts of the initiation and transference of nervous energy, it may be regarded as the hypothesis which at present holds the field.

It is known that the molecules of which the gelatinous substance of the nerve fibres is composed are of an extremely complex structure, containing, it has been estimated, as many as a thousand elementary atoms each. It is supposed that these elementary atoms cohere with various degrees of closeness to the centre of gravity of the molecule. In the interior of the molecule we suppose them to be firmly compacted, and incapable of being displaced unless the molecule is completely disintegrated and decomposed. Supposing the atoms that make up the molecules to be arranged in layers, somewhat like the flakes of an onion, then the innermost layers are the most closely compacted, while as we approach the surface the texture becomes looser and looser, until the outermost layer is attached in such a way, that its stability is upset with the greatest ease. The molecule is not, however, composed merely of homogeneous layers of elementary atoms arranged around a central core. The atoms are first combined together, say, in fours and fives ; these small groups are arranged into larger groups, the larger groups into clusters of groups, until the entire molecule is a structure of much complication.

In building up an elaborate and complicated structure of any kind, force has to be employed ; energy has to be used up ; and in this particular case, as in other cases, the energy which is employed in building up the structure is converted from energy of motion into energy of position, or, as we say, it is rendered latent, and remains latent in the structure, ready to reappear and become actual when the structure is disarranged. The atoms of the molecule are bound together and retained in their position under tension. The energy which binds each of them in its position is much like that in a bent spring. When an incident force impinges on the molecule the atoms are displaced, and fall into simpler combinations ; and in suffering this displacement the energy which held them in their constrained positions is liberated, and becomes available to do work. It is transformed from energy of position into energy of motion. It is as if a number of little springs were suddenly released from their bent position. The moment the atoms have been released from their constrained positions, and the energy which held them has been set free and made available to do work, they begin to reform into their former more complex positions, to reabsorb energy and to fit themselves for another explosion upon the impact of another shock. This rebuilding of the molecule is a part of the general function of nutrition, and takes place in obedience to the same laws as regulate the building up of the whole structure of the body out of the materials of the blood.

The force set free by the falling of the outer layer of atoms into simpler combinations becomes available, as has been said, to do work ; and the first work that it finds ready to hand is the disturbance of the second layer of atoms. If sufficient energy have been liberated by the displacement of the first layer, then the more stably arranged atoms of the second layer will be displaced, and will liberate more energy, which may, if sufficient in quantity, upset the arrangement of the next layer, and so on. Remembering that the compactness and firmness of cohesion of the several layers of atoms increase as we penetrate further toward the centre, it will be seen that a layer must at length be reached which is not susceptible of disturbance, and then the discharge will cease.

By the disturbance of these several layers of atoms, a certain quantity of energy is liberated, and becomes available to do work ; and just as the energy liberated by one layer of atoms tends to disturb and evoke energy from another layer in the same molecule, so the energy liberated from one molecule impinges upon its neighbours, and tends to upset their atoms and to liberate energy from them.   In this outward as in the inward action of the liberated energy, it is helping and reinforcing the effect of the original impulse to which its own liberation was due.

The effect on the molecules of a region will therefore be similar to the effect on the atoms of a single molecule.   The first batch of molecules that is reached by a wandering force adds its quantum to the amount of free energy, and the wave, thus reinforced, breaks upon the next layer of molecules with increased intensity, disturbs them more profoundly, and gains an additional increment to its own volume.   It is thus that we account for the increase in the amount of energy that accrues with each unit of path traversed.   To use another similitude, we may compare the passage of energy along a nerve to the communication of an impulse through a row of billiard balls in contact.   When the nearest ball is struck, the impulse is communicated from one to another along the series, and the last flies off with an impulse equal to that imparted to the first.   If we suppose each ball not only to pass on the impulse it receives, but also to add to it a small impulse of its own ; and if we further suppose that the last ball parts with its energy without movement of translation, we shall have a fairly accurate diagram of the passage of a nerve-current.

So far as the *transmission* of energy is concerned, the above explanation is fairly complete.   It still remains, however, to discover the mechanism by which energy is *stored* in the great masses of nerve tissue, and liberated as required.

The supposition is that a nerve fibre is constituted of innumerable molecules of the character described, packed together in a cylinder. We may regard the mode of packing as being in rows parallel to the axis of the cylinder, or in strata transverse to the axis. The latter supposition, by which the nerve fibre is looked on as composed of a number of discs piled on one another, each disc being made up of a single layer of molecules, is the most convenient for the present purpose.

Now suppose that a nerve fibre, thus constituted, expands into a bulb or knob, similarly constituted, and similarly bounded by a coating impervious to the passing energy. What will be the result of such an arrangement? We suppose the bulb to be made up, like the fibre, of superposed discs; but instead of their diameter being uniform, as in the fibre, it increases until the greatest diameter of the bulb is reached, and then again diminishes until the bulb again merges in the fibre, and the discs resume their former diameter.[1]

A wave of energy passing along the fibre will, when it reaches the bulb, at each step—at each successive disc—impinge upon a larger number of molecules, and liberate a correspondingly larger amount of force, until the greatest diameter of the bulb is reached. If the diameter of the bulb is ten times that of the fibre, then, when the middle of the bulb is reached, the face of the advancing wave will have one hundred times the area of that in the fibre, the surface of the disc is one hundred times as large, and the number of discharging molecules is increased a hundredfold. As, in advancing through the bulb up to this point, the area of the discs has been at each step increasing, the discharge has at each step been passed on from a smaller to a larger number of molecules, and as the discharge from each molecule has therefore divided and passed on to more than one molecule, it follows that at each step the *intensity* of the discharge has diminished. But since each molecule adds something to the

[1] It is not supposed that the fibre is actually composed of separate discs in the manner described; but for the purpose of tracing the progress of a wave of energy along the fibre it is convenient to make this imaginary division into discs.

discharge, and passes it on with this added increment, it follows that the intensity will not diminish in proportion to the spread of the discharge. In its passage through the second half of the bulb the process will be reversed. The discharge now passes at each step from a larger disc to a smaller one ; from a larger number of molecules to a smaller number ; and in so doing it recovers the intensity that it lost in its passage through the first half of the bulb. The intensity of the current on emergence will therefore be equal to that on entering, plus the small increment that has been added during the passage. The volume or magnitude of the discharge will, however, have increased enormously ; for this depends on the number of molecules from which it proceeds ; and the number of molecules in a spherical bulb of ten times the diameter of a fibre will exceed the number in a length of the fibre, equal to the diameter of the bulb, in the proportion of 4,183 to 63. In other words, the discharge, in passing through a bulb of ten units in diameter, has been reinforced by the discharge of sixty-five times as many molecules as would have reinforced it in passing through a fibre one unit in diameter and ten in length, and therefore receives an increment sixty-five times as great And the time taken by the discharge to traverse the bulb will be equal to the time taken to traverse a length of fibre equal in diameter to that of the bulb, for in each there are the same number of discs, that is, of layers of molecules, to traverse. So that in the passage of a wave of energy through the bulb, sixty-five units of force will be liberated in the same time that one unit would be liberated in its passage along an equal length of fibre. The interposition, in the course of a fibre, of such a bulb as we

FIG. 7.—Diagram of the relation of a nerve-cell to nerve-fibre. In passing from B to C the discharge receives a reinforcement sixty-five times as great as in passing from A to B.

have supposed, would therefore have the effect of adding very largely to the magnitude of the discharge, and of rendering the discharge more explosive in its character.

Such bulbs as have been described are of very frequent occurrence in the nervous system. They are termed nerve-cells, and number many millions, each one, like the fibre on which it is situated, being of microscopic dimensions. For the sake of simplicity, the cell has been spoken of as situated in the course of a fibre, but more often the cells are meeting-places of three or more fibres, which again divide and ramify at a greater or less distance from the cell. A dis-

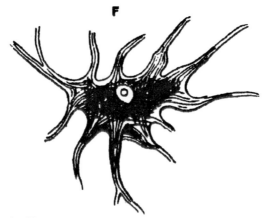

FIG. 8.—Nerve-cell connected with many fibres, highly magnified.

charge communicated to any of these distant branches will travel along the fibre until the cell is reached, when it will set up the explosive discharge already described, and the resulting ebullition of energy will make its escape by way of the various fibres into which the cell is prolonged.

From this description it will be evident that the nerve cells, constituted and acting as has been described, form veritable reservoirs of energy, storing continuously in their intervals of repose, when their component molecules are growing up into more complex and unstable aggregates, and liberating freely and copiously from time to time when stimulated by an impinging current.

Viewed in the mass, nerve tissue is found in the body in two chief forms—as nerve trunks, or, as they are usually termed, nerves, and as central masses of irregularly rounded form. The nerves are simply nerve fibres bound up together in bundles. If we follow the course of such a bundle of fibres, we find that in one direction it separates into smaller and smaller bundles, until at last the individual fibres run alone, and end either in muscle in the way already described, or in skin or in some other organ. Followed in the other direction, the bundle of fibres is found to receive other bundles, which become bound up with it, and to end at last by entering one of the central masses.

These central masses of nerve substance, constituting the brain and the spinal cord, consist of two different looking substances, called respectively white matter and grey matter, distributed in a very irregular manner, and forming very unequal portions of the nerve tissue, the former preponderating. Examined microscopically, the white matter is found to consist entirely of nerve fibres in every way similar to those of the nerve trunks. The grey matter is differently constituted. It is in the grey matter alone that the nerve cells are found, and they are found in immense numbers. In addition to the cells and ramifying between them, the grey matter contains an immense plexus or mesh of nerve fibres, which differ from the fibres of the nerve trunks and of the white matter, in having no insulating jacket. Many of them can be traced to a junction, or, rather, fusion, with a nerve cell. Others can be followed till they are found to become continuous with one of the fibres in a nerve trunk. The vast majority, however, appear to terminate in one direction, after branching again and again, in free points of great tenuity, embedded and lost in the third chief constituent of the grey matter. This third constituent, the matrix or ground substance of the grey matter, is a homogeneous jelly, in which the cells and fibres are embedded, and which is closely similar in nature to the substance of which they are composed.

The very highest importance attaches to this last and apparently insignificant ingredient of nervous matter. Regarded for a long time as serving the purely mechanical function of holding the fibres and cells in their places, it is now believed to be the matrix out of which they are formed, and the medium by which separate fibres become connected with each other.

The entire matrix of the grey matter is permeable, though with difficulty, to discharges of the same kind as travel so easily in the nerve fibres ; and these latter, as they exist in the grey matter, are regarded merely as channels of greater permeability in a similar substance which is less permeable.

When a discharge passes along a fibre thus embedded, it will remain confined to the fibre so long as the channel is of sufficient calibre to carry it ; but as the fibre diminishes in calibre, the intensity of the discharge, according to the law we have already investigated, will increase ; and when the discharge arrives at the fine-pointed end of the fibre, embedded in the slightly different matrix, the tension will have reached a very high degree, and will have become sufficient to communicate the discharge to the more stable matrix. In the matrix the discharge will travel with more difficulty. Instead of travelling in a concentrated current like water in a pipe, it will travel in a diffused wave, like the ripples on a pond, spreading wider as it gets further from the point of origin. As the wave spreads, it will at length come in contact with the pointed termination of another nerve fibre, and finding in this direction a free passage, the bulk of the discharge will become concentrated towards this point in the same way that we see water in a bath flowing from all sides towards the escape pipe. Succeeding portions of discharge escaping from the first fibre will tend to flow with more and more directness towards the point of the second fibre, until at length a definite connection has been established between the two fibres, a definite

3

channel has been bored from the one to the other, and the
fibres have become practically continuous. It is in this way,
through the intermediation of the slightly permeable ground
substance, that distinct tracts of nervous discharge are connected with one another, and the connection made structural
and permanent. Let us suppose that the discharge of one
tract of grey matter actuates one movement, say, of making
an up-stroke with the pen ; and that another tract actuates
another movement, say, of making a down-stroke. Then
the organic connection between the two tracts that has been
above described will provide for the immediate occurrence
of a down-stroke after an up-stroke, provided the energy is
not drafted off in some other direction, to some other tract
of discharge.

We have supposed that the stream of energy is flowing
in one direction across the intermediate tract of matrix from
the end of one nerve fibre to the end of another ; but it is
obvious that both these pointed ends are the ends of channels
along which streams of energy habitually flow *towards the
points*. When a connection becomes established between
the two points, it will sometimes happen, therefore, that two
opposing streams will be passing simultaneously towards the
points ; will, now that the channel is continued beyond the
points, pass on into the intermediate tract ; and will at length
meet in some intermediate position. When two opposing
streams of energy meet in this way, in the course of a
channel which is in process of becoming a fibre, there will,
of course, be a condition of very great tension set up at the
point of meeting. The energy will tend at that point very
strongly to escape into the surrounding matrix on all sides,
and at that point a bulging will tend to occur in the course
of the channel. As the same thing happens time after
time, the channel will at that point bulge more and more,
until at length a definite bulb is formed at the spot, and the
uniformity of the nerve fibre is interrupted by the interposition in its course of a nerve cell.

The disposition of these tracts of discharge with respect

to the parts of the body that they actuate, and their arrangement with respect to one another, are extraordinarily complicated, but some idea of them must be given, in order to render clear the ways in which the working of the nervous system becomes deranged in insanity and other disorders.

In passing the tall warehouses that line certain of our streets, we notice, projecting from below the roof, the arm of a crane, which is used for lifting heavy goods from the street to the upper floor. When a bale of goods has been raised by one of these cranes to the necessary height, the arm swings round on a pivot, and the bale is deposited on a projecting ledge. If we notice the man who guides this swinging movement of the crane, we observe that he holds in his hands two ropes, which pass over pulleys, one to the right, the other to the left, of the crane, and are then attached to the extremity of the arm. In guiding the crane round to the right, he pulls on the right-hand rope, and at the same time pays the left-hand rope out to the required extent. When the crane has moved far enough,. the left rope is checked, and the arm arrested at the required point. The advantage gained by the simultaneous use of the two ropes is obvious. If only one rope were used at a time, the arm could, it is true, be swung round to that side ; but the speed of its movement could not be regulated with any nicety, and the extent of the movement could not be regulated at all. The arm of the crane would either not move far enough, or it would swing round until it struck a violent blow against the side of the building.

The mechanism of the movements of the body is precisely similar to that of the movements of the crane. The vast majority of our movements are performed by the pull of the muscles on the bones, acting, like the ropes on the crane, on levers of the third order ; and in the one case, as in the other, the lever, which is moved by the pull of a force acting in one direction, is steadied by the pull of a lesser force acting in the opposite direction. There is no instance in the body of a muscle without an antagonist muscle having

a precisely opposite action ; and whenever a muscle begins
to contract and to pull upon its point of attachment,
simultaneously its antagonist starts into action, and begins
to pull in the opposite direction, so as to steady and
smoothen and regulate and check the movement produced
by the other. So that the physiological unit of movement
is a pair of antagonistic muscles. Muscles are brought into
action by the discharge of the grey matter of the central
nervous system delivered through the nerve fibres, so that
in order to produce such a duplex muscular action as is
necessary, there must be some definite and appropriate

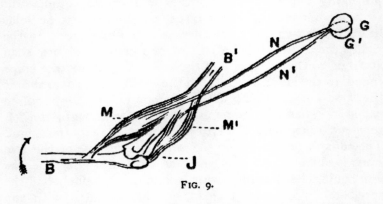

FIG. 9.

connection of a region of grey matter with the nerves
running to the muscles.

Suppose B, B' to be bones, connected by a joint at J, and
having attached to them two muscles, M and M', pulling in
opposite directions. Let G be a region of grey matter, and
N, N' nerves running from this region to the muscles. G
is a reservoir of energy which is discharged by some
impinging force whose origin we need not now inquire
into. Upon the discharge of G a head of pressure is set up
within it, and the energy presses upon all sides and seeks to
escape. If the outlets N and N' are of equal calibre, the
energy will pass out by them in equal amounts, the muscles
will be equally stimulated, will contract with equal force,

and the bone B will not move, but will become rigidly braced up in its present position. If, however, the outlet into N is larger than that into N', more energy will escape by N than by N', the muscle M will be more strongly stimulated than M', will act more forcibly, the bone B will move in the direction of the arrow, and the limb will become more bent.

If the limb is required to move in the opposite direction, it is evident that there must be another region of grey matter, connected with the muscles by other channels, having a reverse proportion to that of N, N'. Thus there will be required a separate tract of grey matter for each separate movement ; and each such tract of grey matter, so connected with muscles as to produce by its discharge a definite movement, is termed a *nerve centre*. Although each movement requires a separate centre, yet for each such centre it will not be necessary for a separate pair of channels (nerve fibres) to run to the muscles. It will be enough if the *outlets* from the centres into the nerves bear the requisite proportion, and this being secured, the outlets can empty their discharge severally into a single pair of channels common to all the centres actuating that pair of muscles. Thus, the movement of the bone B in the opposite direction to that of the arrow may be actuated by a centre G' whose outlet into N' is greater than its outlet into N.

Suppose now that it is required to bring into simultaneous action more than one pair of muscles, as indeed frequently happens in the execution of movements. In breathing, for instance, movements of the chest, abdomen and throat are executed simultaneously, and in forced breathing, as after exercise, or when there is some hindrance to the proper aeration of the blood, it becomes necessary to move simultaneously not only the chest, abdomen, and throat, but the mouth, nose, neck, and often the arms as well. We have seen that for each pair or group of antagonistic muscles operating a single movement, a separate nerve centre is necessary ; so that for the simultaneous action of several

pairs of muscles, the simultaneous action of several nerve
centres becomes necessary. How can the simultaneous
discharge of several centres be effected? One obvious
method suggests itself at once. If the centres, whose
simultaneous discharge is needed, were all connected with
another centre, then the discharge of this other common centre would set all the rest discharging simultaneously. Suppose A, B, and C to be three nerve centres
actuating the muscles of the chest, abdomen, and throat
respectively, by means of the nerves $a\,a$, $b\,b$, and $c\,c$, and
suppose that from each of these centres there goes a cord or
channel of communication to a common centre at D. Then
the discharge of D will set going simultaneously the discharges of A, B, and C, and will produce simultaneous

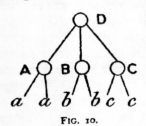

FIG. 10.

action of the three sets of antagonistic groups of muscles which these
three centres represent. Again,
the muscles of nose, neck, and
mouth might be represented in
three other centres, E, F, and
G, and these be grouped together
by a central station at H, and then
H and D connected with a still more comprehensive station
at I ; and then the discharge of I would bring about simultaneous action of the whole of the muscular apparatus
employed in forced respiration.

It is obvious that any number of muscles can be brought
into simultaneous and duly proportioned action by a similar
arrangement of duly proportioned channels proceeding from
a single centre ; and by such an apparatus even the movements of equilibration, which demand simultaneous and
duly proportioned action of almost all the muscles of the
body, can be actuated.

The majority of our acts do not, however, depend solely
on the simultaneous action of muscles. In walking, for
instance, while a number of muscles must act simultaneously
to produce each movement of each leg, yet these movements

would be of little service if they were not timed to follow one another at proper intervals. So also in writing, in speaking, and in every form of handicraft, while each movement of arm and hand is actuated by the simultaneous pull of many muscles, the conspicuous factor in the success of the operation is the nicety with which each movement follows precisely in the nick of time upon the heels of its predecessor It is obvious that no single discharge from any one centre, however comprehensive in its control over the body, will account for a *sequence* of movements,—for the occurrence of a number of movements following one another in orderly succession. Since every movement requires the discharge of a separate centre, sequences of movements

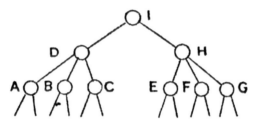

FIG. 11.

must necessitate the discharge of many centres in succession ; and each discharge must occur in its right place in the series, and at the moment at which the movement is required. However much the apparatus that we have already considered may be extended and developed, it can never assume a function of which it has not, as far as we have ascertained, acquired even the rudiment. To fit it for this new function a new factor is required.

Take as an instance the action of moving an object from one place to another. In this case the successive movements of stretching out the arm, grasping the object, moving and arresting the arm, and relinquishing the grasp, have to be made in due order. If the matter is considered, it will become apparent that to move the hand to the object, the guidance of sight is required. The same aid is needed to determine the extent to which the fingers and thumb must be separated in order to grasp the object. The amount of approximation of the digits is guided partly by sight and partly by touch, and so on of the remaining movements that go to complete the act.

Sequences of movement are regulated, then, by the guidance of the senses ; but the question is, What is the value of this expression, "guidance of the senses," when reduced to terms of nerve currents and muscular movements ? When we say that the sequence of movements is effected under the guidance of sight, we mean that the time and extent of the successive movements are determined by the impression made upon the eye by light-waves proceeding from the object and the other surrounding circumstances. The breaking of these waves on the nervous expansion at the back of the eye sets up a certain leash of discharges combined in certain ways, which start from the expanse in question and are distributed among the centres in the brain. As the hand moves toward the object, the combination of these currents changes from moment to moment as the impression made in the eye changes, and, when the hand reaches the object, the grouping of the ingoing currents is such that, when combined with those already existing, they discharge the nerve region that actuates the opening of the hand, and that movement occurs. The new impression produced by the open hand, in definite and appropriate relation to the object to be seized, combines again with the free energy existing among the centres, switches it off in a new direction, and causes it to break against and discharge the centre which actuates the closing of the hand, and so the process is continued. At every step, the occurrence of the appropriate movement at the proper time, and its cessation after it has performed its task, are determined by the leash of currents started by an impression made through some of the "avenues of sense." Hence the sequences of movements that we can perform are as infinitely various as the circumstances in which we can be placed.

CHAPTER II.

FROM the foregoing discussion two important conclusions stand out prominently. First, that while certain nerve-centres actuate movements directly, by discharging through the nerves into the muscles ; there are other centres which actuate movements indirectly by discharging into and setting in action the centres of the first order. The second conclusion is that the determination of the special direction, and of the time of starting, of a current into this or that set of muscles, is brought about by the influence of ingoing currents derived through the organs of sense from the outside world. These are the two fundamental facts in the physiological constitution of the nervous system, and as such they will require some further consideration.

It will be seen from what has been said, that the nerve-centres that are in direct communication with the muscles are comparatively few, and comprise those only which actuate the simplest movements. The vast majority of our movements are actuated indirectly by combinations of simpler movements, brought about by the action of secondary nerve-centres combining the action of the primary centres, and of tertiary and still higher orders of centres, combining the action of the secondary. The physiological constitution of the nervous centres is, therefore, it appears, a hierarchy, the members having the simplest structure and the rudest and most elementary functions being at the bottom, and being overlaid by successive layers of centres, the centres of each layer becoming more complex and elabo-

rate in structure, and actuating movements of a more complex and elaborate character.

The more elevated the position of a centre in this hierarchy,
the larger is the number of centres whose functions it controls and combines; and therefore, not only is the movement
that it actuates of a more complex and elaborate character,
but it affects a larger part of the body.   When we arrive at
the highest layers of all, we find centres which act through
a number of subordinate ranks ; which actuate movements
of the utmost delicacy, elaborateness, precision and complexity, and, most important of all, which require for their
proper performance a consensus of action of every part of
the body.

As the lowest centres act directly upon the muscles, the
movements that result from their action will be intense and
forcible ; while, as each layer of superior centres is separated
from the muscles by more and more layers of subordinate
centres, whose resistance has to be overcome before any
movement can take place, the discharge from the higher
centres will be to some extent diffused, and will reach the
muscles in a less intense and more attenuated form, and
will produce a less forcible action.

Again, while the lowest centres are directly connected
with the muscles and have but few lateral connections with
each other, the whole or nearly the whole of their discharge
will be delivered into the limited number of muscles that
they severally actuate ; the movement will invariably
follow the discharge ; there will be little lateral diffusion
of the discharge, and little tendency for other movements
to occur. In the case of the discharge of a higher centre,
however, on the one hand the interposition of intermediate
centres will tend to oppose somewhat the downward discharge into the muscles, and on the other hand the more
numerous connections with neighbouring centres will open
more avenues for the discharge to escape in other directions ;
and the combination of these two conditions will result in
a portion of the discharge being diverted into lateral

channels. If the discharge is weak, so large a portion of it may be thus drafted off that no movement at all occurs. If the discharge is powerful, the diversion by lateral channels into neighbouring centres will produce a tendency for movements of allied character and of neighbouring parts to accompany the movement directly actuated. Upon discharge of the highest centres of all, the movement, however rapid, can never exhibit the electric suddenness of the simple movements actuated by the lowest centres; it will be of a smoother and more flowing character. The side connections of these highest centres are so numerous, that the opportunities for weak discharges to pass away without producing movements will be many, and, for the same reason, the tendency for allied movements to occur will be great. As the discharge passes with ease from centre to neighbouring centre, so with ease and celerity will movement follow allied movement.

In this way, by the resistance which the inertia of the lower centres opposes to the disturbance of their equilibrium, and by the readiness with which the discharge of the higher centres can escape laterally, the action of these higher centres is to some extent dissociated from that of the lower, and from their outcome or muscular expression; but yet there is in other respects a very intimate association between the several strata. Every nerve-centre except the lowest is so connected with centres beneath it that its discharge sets up, or tends to set up, action of its subordinates; and, conversely, every nerve-centre except the highest is so connected with centres above it, that it is, or may be, set in action by their discharge. This statement expressses, however, only half of the connection that binds the several layers of centres together into an harmonious, organized whole.

In addition to its power of starting its subordinates into activity, every centre maintains, upon the centres beneath it, a constant steadying, controlling influence, by which their tendency to discharge upon the provocation of wandering forces is held in check, and their discharge is suffered only when the superior centre transmits to them its mandate. Thus each rank of centres is controlled, inhibited, and held in check by the continuous influence of its superiors, and each, in its turn, controls the rank below.

The hierarchic arrangement of the nerve-centres is therefore similar to that of the officers of an army, or the officials of a great business concern ; and, as will be seen from the above description, very closely similar. Not only does each superior rank maintain over its subordinates a constant disciplinary control, and apply to them from time to time an initiatory stimulus ; but the lower ranks have authority and control over the fewest subordinates, while the higher govern the most, until the highest centres of all control the entire organism. So, too, we have seen that the higher centres have a certain detachment from the lower, and we have now to notice another aspect of this arrangement. The highest officials of a business—say, the directors of a gas company—can absent themselves from the business for comparatively long intervals without seriously deranging the concern ; but a strike of stokers is a very serious matter. So, too, the highest nervous centres may be out of action for hours together, as in sleep or drunkenness, and yet no ill effect ensue, but if the nervous mechanism of the heart or breathing is deranged it is a very serious affair. The parallel that has been suggested between the arrangement of the nerve-centres and that of the officials of a business is, indeed, so close and so exact that it can be pursued even into minute details, and in the most various aspects of the two organizations it is found to hold good with a persistence which argues some community of origin and of nature between them. Such a community indeed exists, for both are organizations of similar materials which have grown up in obedience to the same laws, those of evolution, to serve similar ends.

So far we have considered the nervous system as the originator, regulator, and controller of the movements of the body ; but this view of its functions is unduly limited, and in order to represent truly the part that it plays, our concept requires to be extended.

The form of energy which is stored and distributed by the nervous system is, so long as it is limited to the nervous system, an affair of molecules. Only when it reaches the muscles it does become transformed into molar movement. Hence it is not surprising to find that these currents of molecular energy govern not only the molar movements of the organism, but the molecular movements also. The molecular substitution of waste and repair ; the detrition of the tissues, by use and wear, into particles which are washed away by the stream of blood that bathes all the tissues ; the rebuilding of the wasted tissues out of material furnished to them by the blood—these are processes whose activity depends on the general molecular activity of the tissue concerned. And the general molecular activity depends on the amount of molecular energy that reaches the part through its nerves. When copious streams of nervous energy are poured into a tissue they arouse whatever potentialities of action lie latent in that tissue. An egg will lie for days and weeks without undergoing any change ; but let it receive from the parent bird a continuous and copious supply of molecular energy in the shape of heat, and its latent potentialities are aroused, its molecules undergo continuous re-arrangement, and the chicken is formed. When the bird leaves the nest and the egg cools, the process is arrested. In much the same way, though with greater directness and rapidity, do the streams of nervous energy arouse the activity, whatever it may be, of the tissue into which they flow ; and in much the same way does this activity abate when the flow of the stream slackens and ebbs. On the stimulus of their nerve-supply, not only do muscle-cells and fibres contract, but gland-cells secrete or eliminate, and the elements of every tissue—bone, cartilage, ligament, membrane, skin, muscle, gland, or what not—have their molecular processes of waste and repair accelerated and invigorated. Conversely, when the nerve-currents become languid and attenuated, then the functions that they stimulate and regulate are slackened. Secretions diminish, excretion is retarded, muscular action is enfeebled, nutrition is impaired.

The control which the nerve-centres exercise over the process of nutrition is subject to the same laws as determine their influence over muscular movement ; that is to say, the lowest centres control that limited part of the organism to which their nerves are distributed ; but their connection with this limited part being direct, the control they exercise is absolute, and when their influence is withdrawn by severance of the nerves or by destruction of the centre, a profound impairment of nutrition ensues, and ensues at once. The part so deprived of its nervous supply shrivels ; it becomes profoundly altered in appearance ; the whole process of nutrition is retarded, enfeebled, and reduced to its lowest ebb. Parts may, and often do, even die and slough away. If the injury occurs while the body is growing, the growth of the part is retarded or altogether arrested, and that side remains for the rest of life smaller than the other.

If the influence of an intermediate centre is withdrawn, the effect on nutrition is different. These centres are less directly connected with the periphery than the lowest, and have, therefore, a less direct influence on nutrition. Moreover, if they are destroyed, there still remain the centres below them, which can still perform some part in regulating the nutrition of the region supplied by them, although they will perform their part less efficiently than before, and their manner of doing so will be altered by the loss of the regulating influence of their superior centre. Each intermediate centre, while less directly actuating the nutrition of the region that it controls, will yet, as in the case of movement, regulate a much larger share of the whole body than an inferior centre. When, therefore, an intermediate tract is destroyed, the effect on nutrition is not at once discernible, but after a time it becomes apparent, and is then found to affect a large area of the body. Instead of affecting a single limb, or the legs merely, it affects both arm and leg and perhaps a side of the face also. The alteration of nutrition, while it is less immediate, is also less profound, and is of a more complicated character. In lieu of a simple withering or sloughing, there is a thickening and glazing of the skin, or an inflammation of a joint, or a distortion of the nails, due to some disturbance of their nutrition.

When the destruction takes place in the highest centres of all, there is always, as in the case of the inferior centres, a disturbance of nutrition ; but in this case the obvious disturbance is still longer delayed, it is of a still more complex character, and, instead of being confined to a limb or a region, it affects the whole of the body. Owing to its less striking and less manifest character, to its tardy appearance and universal diffusion, the alteration of nutrition that accompanies disorder of the highest nervous centres is often overlooked, but in every case there will be found, if searched for, some discoloration of the skin, some excess or deficiency or alteration of the perspiration, some peculiarity in the growth of the hair or nails, some excessive appetite, indicative of defective assimilation of food, or some other evidence that the process of nutrition is not proceeding normally.

Throughout all the functions of the nervous system, therefore, and from whatever point of view these functions are regarded, the hierarchical principle prevails.

The other great principle of action which has already been alluded to is also universally prevalent. It has been shown that the " determination of the special direction and the time of starting of a nerve-current into this or that set of muscles, is brought about by the influence of the ingoing currents, derived through the organs of sense, from the outside world," and this law holds good throughout the entire range of the nervous system from the lowest centres to the highest.

To take, first, a very simple case. A closure of the eyelids can be actuated by a mechanism such as has been described, consisting of a nerve-centre representing the movement, and of nerves connecting this centre in appropriate ways with the muscles by which the movement is affected. Once set in action, such a mechanism will enable a closure of the lids to take place ; but in order to set it in action the centre must be stirred by the impact of a nerve-wave. When, therefore, an object suddenly approaches the eye, and the lids close protectively, there must be some arrangement by which the approach of the body can of itself set the centre in activity. The method by which this end is attained is very simple. The rays of light proceeding from the approaching body pass through the humours of the eye, and strike upon a nervous expansion which is spread out at the back of it, and which possesses just such a degree of instability that light waves are sufficient to produce a discharge of its elements. The discharge thus started is carried by a nerve direct to the centre, which actuates closing of the lids, and thus the movement is produced just at the time that it is needed. While the greater part of the ingoing current is absorbed in producing the discharge of this centre, a certain portion escapes, and, reinforced by part of the discharge of the centre, passes on to higher strata, where it produces effects that will be considered later on.

For the present we have to notice (1) that the complete nervous process consists of an ingoing current reaching the centre ; a discharge of the centre ; an outgoing current from the centre to the muscles ; and a fragment of discharge proceeding upwards. (2) That this nervous process is started by an impression made upon the organism from without, and ends in a muscular movement. (3) That the movement thus made is appropriate to the circumstances which produced the impression. By an appropriate movement is meant a movement which is to the advantage of the organism ; either by guarding against, or protecting itself against, or avoiding injury from the impressing circumstance ; or by gaining for the organism some benefit from the circumstance. In the above instance the process is throughout of the simplest character. The circumstance to be conformed to is simple ; the impression made on the organism is simple ; and the movement by which the organism adapts itself to the circumstance is simple.

Let us now take a somewhat more complex case. In a game of tennis, the movements of running to and striking the ball are actuated by simple nervous mechanisms actuating the muscles concerned. The direction in which the run is made is determined by the nervous currents set up by the impression made by the ball, and the direction, strength, and method of the stroke are determined by the group of impressions made by the speed and position of the ball, the shape and relations of the ground, and the positions of the adversaries. In this case, as in the last, the nervous process consists of ingoing currents reaching the centres concerned ; of discharges of the centres ; of outgoing currents from the centres to the muscles ; and of portions of discharge communicating between the centres immediately actuating the movements and higher centres. As before, the process is started by an impression made upon the organism from without, and ends in muscular movement ; and this is true also of each step in the process. As before, the movement is appropriate to the circumstances which make the impression. In the present case the impression is of a more complex character, is started by more numerous circumstances, not merely by a moving object, but by an object moving in certain definite surroundings, which contribute to the impression. The movement is of a more complex character. No longer confined to a small part of the organism it implicates the whole of it. The whole process, while similar in character to that in the previous instance, is throughout more complicated in form.

It is clear, however, that there is some other factor in producing the movements in the game of tennis beyond those that we have considered. For the same impressions that evoke the movements of the players are made upon the

4

spectators, yet in them no answering reaction is called forth.
They sit still and take no part in the game. What is the
factor that has been neglected ? It is to be found in that
hitherto unconsidered part of the nerve current which has
been spoken of as communicating between the centres
actuating the movements and centres of a higher order.
While each individual movement is started by an individual
impression, and while the movements are modified from
moment to moment by impressions momentarily arriving,
the entire series of movements is permitted by the general
removal of inhibition from the whole group of centres
immediately concerned,—an inhibition actuated, as already
described, by centres of a higher order, and loosened by an
alteration in their mode of action.

At this point we are again confronted with the problem of
initiation. What influence is it that starts these higher
centres into action, and causes them to remove from their
inferiors their inhibitory influence ? Again the same solution
applies. It is the arrival of impressions from without, it is
the meeting of the players and the arrangement made
among them for the playing of the game. In this case also
there is an impression from without upon the organism ;
there is the discharge of a nerve tract ; and there is the
issue of this discharge in the liberation of movement. But
in this case we observe a new element introduced into the
reaction. In the previous cases the reaction was direct and
was immediate. In the present case the reaction is indirect,
is delayed, and is prolonged. Such, we have already discovered, are the characteristics of the action of centres of
the higher ranks.

When we rise once more to actions of a much more complicated character, to acts such as, for instance, the entering
upon a lawsuit, we find the same general law holds good.
It is the impression made upon the organism by the whole
of the circumstances of the case,—the suffering of injury, the
refusal of redress, the ability to produce witnesses, the
existence of documentary evidence, the advice of trusted

counsellors,—that starts the process ; which in this case is much more complicated, much more delayed, much more prolonged, but which is still at every step guided and modified by impressions arriving from without.

The current that passes upward from the lower centres has been spoken of, in the first and second examples, as the remainder of the ingoing current started by the impression —the remainder that is left over after the reacting centre has been started,—but this account is not quite complete. What passes upward to the superior centres is a current compounded of the ingoing current and of a portion of the discharge of the inferior centre. So that the impression received by the superior centre, in the first case, is not merely that produced by a body approaching the eye, but also that produced by a discharge of the centre actuating closure of the lids. This centre therefore discharges in two directions. Its downward discharge produces a closure of the lids, and the remnant of the discharge, which passes upward, acts as an ingoing impressing current, and conveys to the superior centres intelligence, as it were, that the lids are closing.

Similarly, every discharge of an inferior motor centre is mirrored in the superior centres, which are thus rendered *au fait* of all the actions of their subordinates.

From what has been said it will be seen that the organization of the nervous system is an intricate arrangement of centres, disposed in layers subordinate to each other, each layer being in communication, more or less directly, with the sense organs, and so with the outside world, from which it receives its initiating impulses ; and each being in communication also with the muscles, to which it issues its mandates.

It has been shown how a centre may discharge so faintly that the resulting current has not sufficient impetus to reach the muscles, but although the discharge produces no movement, it is not without effect. It spreads where it can, and produces some effect on neighbouring centres. It may be that a centre is discharged by an ingoing current, but that its discharge is not of sufficient moment to produce an

immediate muscular reaction. Although, however, it produces no effect in a downward direction, it may pass upward,
and on reaching the higher layer it may, since higher centres
are more unstable than lower, produce a discharge which
does reach the muscles, and in this way a simple impression
may bring about a widespread reaction. It is to be noted,
however, that the current which starts the effectual discharge
is derived, not from the simple impression alone, but from
the centre first discharged by this simple impression. It is
a much more complex affair. It contains elements from the
ingoing current, and elements of discharge whose usual
destination is outwardly. It is, to speak technically, a
a sensori-motor process. The lowermost centre, which first
receives the ingoing current, is the recipient, not of this
particular impression alone, but of many impressions continually arriving from the same special-sense organ. By
these continually arriving currents its constitution and the
arrangement of its elements have been moulded originally,
and modified from time to time. Hence the discharge that
it emits, and that starts the action of the superior centre,
while initiated by the particular impression, represents not
that impression only, but many allied impressions ; and
represents not impressions only, but the simple movement by
which these simple impressions may be directly responded
to. Thus the entire leash of currents that starts the action
of the superior centre is a very complex affair, and hence it
appears that, just as the lower centres perform, on the motor
side, as it were the menial work of the higher, receiving
their mandates in general, and carrying them out in detail,
with the aid of impressions from without ; so on the ingoing
or sensory side, the lower centres combine and elaborate the
impressions received, before transmitting them to the higher.
The impressions received by the lowest centres of all are
simple currents transmitted direct from the sense-organs by
which they are received ; the impressions received by centres
of a higher rank are impressions not only of what has acted
on us from the outside world, but of simple ways in which

the organism can react on the outside world. Each higher rank of centres receives impressions from below, of still more complicated and intricate nature.

We find, therefore, that every action of the nervous system, from the lowest and simplest to the highest and most complex, consists of four parts—the ingoing current, the discharge, and the outgoing current, with the addendum of the communicating currents between the centre immediately concerned and its superiors. We find that not only do the centres become, in proportion to their position in the scale of elevation, more complicated in their structure and more diverse in their communications with neighbouring centres, but that both the currents they emit and the currents they receive become continually more complicated in their composition.

We have seen that in that part of the nervous system which regulates the molecular processes of nutrition the hierarchical arrangement prevails with quite as rigorous a sway as in that which regulates the molar movements of the limbs and body ; we have now to notice that the other principle—the sensori-motor principle, or the principle of flow and return of energy, also obtains equally throughout both divisions of the nervous system.

When food is introduced into the stomach, the local stimulus produces at once a local reaction, and the lining of the stomach pours out a fluid which acts upon and digests the food. This immediate reaction is analogous to the immediate reaction of the blink of the eye which follows a local stimulus to the other system of nerves. At the same time, however, the contact of the food produces a discharge of the sensory nerves which have their endings in the mucous lining of the stomach. The current is carried by the nerves to centres of low rank, which discharge downward into the muscular wall of the stomach and produce movements by which the food is turned over and churned about. In this case, therefore, as in the other, there is (1) an inward current started by a stimulus on the nerve ends, and going to a nerve centre ; (2) a discharge of the centre; (3) an outgoing current from the centre to muscles, producing movement; and there is also (4) a residuum of current passing from the centre upward to a higher centre, and indicating to the higher region what is going on below. To the higher centre this upward current acts as an inward or stimulating current, and produces therein a discharge of which the main part, as before, goes outward, and a residuum goes to a higher centre still. The reflexed or outgoing part of the current acts as a relaxor of the blood vessels, and allows more blood to go to the stomach to supply the needs of the local glands, which are now actively at work, pouring out their digestive juice ; part, too, goes to the neighbouring portion of the intestine, which gets into readiness to begin secreting and to receive and deal with the food passed on from the stomach. Another part goes to the liver and stimulates its cells into activity.

The upward-going portion reaches a still higher centre, and produces effects that are still more diffused and still more indirect to the original stimulus of the food on the stomach.

The contact of food with the stomach is of course not the only stimulus which provokes this upward-going current. Not only does contact of a foreign body with the skin set up a current in the local nerves which passes upward to the highest regions of the brain, but the soaking of a solution of food material through the mucous membrane of the mouth produces, when the solution comes into contact with the nerve-endings, a similar current. In this latter case the process which acts upon the nerves is wholly molecular. Similarly, every molecular change throughout every part of the body gives rise to an alteration of the nerve currents, and sends an alteration up through the series of nerve centres to the highest. The nerve currents which are originated in the organs of sense by light waves, sound waves, chemical changes in the mucous membrane of tongue or nose, are not always passing. They are intermitted, and arise only occasionally. But in the body at large, the processes of nutrition and decay, of waste and repair, of secretion and elimination, are always at work, and hence the currents which these processes originate in the nerves are always passing upwards to the brain. As the processes are always at work, and as they are under all circumstances controlled and regulated by the molecular currents which flow into them through the nerves, it follows that not·only are the ingoing currents which they originate always passing, but the outgoing currents from the regulating nerve centres to the working tissues are always passing.

Thus there is in the body a double circulation of nerve energy just as there is a double circulation of blood. From the heart to the body at large, and from the body at large back to the heart, flows the greater or systemic circulation, and from the heart to the lungs, and from the lungs back to the heart, flows the minor or pulmonary circulation. Similarly from the sense organs and the skin to the brain, and from the brain back to the muscles, flows the greater circulation of nerve energy, by which the movements of the body are adapted to circumstances in the outside world ; and from the viscera and the body at large to the brain, and from the brain back to the viscera and other organs, flows the lesser circulation, by which activity of function is adapted to bodily needs.

It has been mentioned above that the higher centres are more unstable than the lower. Their equilibrium is more readily disturbed, their discharge more readily evoked, their communications and connections more readily extended and modified than those of the lower. It remains to explain this most important difference in their mode of action.

When a new mode of action is originated—when a novel adjustment is made to circumstances—when the organism reacts in a new manner to impressions made upon it, there must occur some new combination of nerve elements to produce the new combination of movements. The new combination of nerve elements is affected in the way already indicated when treating of the matrix or ground substance of the grey matter. Either a new set of circumstances impresses the organism, in which case a new combination of nerve currents sets inward ; or an old set of circumstances impresses the organism, in a new way, in which case the old combination of nerve currents receives a new addition on its way upward, which alters its arrangement and direction. In either case, the higher centres are impressed in a way that is new, and the consequence is, that instead of the usual centres being discharged in the usual ways, the currents are drafted off into new directions. But it has already been shown that the channels in which currents frequently pass, are channels which have become, from the effect of this frequent passage, scoured out to an appropriate calibre, and able to carry the accustomed currents without leakage ; while the irruption of a voluminous current into by-paths and unaccustomed channels results in its escape from the formed channels into the ground substance, and the excavation of new passages therein. When, therefore, new circumstances impress us, or when old circumstances impress us in new ways, there is a tendency for the nerve currents in the higher centres to break their bounds and to escape in new directions. Whether the tendency becomes an actuality or no, will depend on whether the new element in the incoming current is of sufficient intensity, and whether the ground substance is easily enough permeable. Supposing, however, that these conditions are favourable, and that the current does overflow, it will find its way, in some new direction, to a centre that has not hitherto been in the habit of acting with the centre from whence the discharge comes. (For, if it had habitually so acted, a formed channel would already exist between them.) The consequence will be that these two centres, not hitherto associated in action, will act together—in other words, a new combination of nerve centres will be formed, and their combined action will result in a new mode of reaction—in new movements, or a new course of conduct.

The repetition of the impression will bring about a repetition of the action, and with each such repetition of the passage of the current in the new direction, the new channel, which conveys the current from one centre to the other, will be enlarged, and rendered more patent and definite, in the way already described ; until the connection between the two centres becomes thoroughly organized, and the course of action habitual. The more and more often the combined action is repeated, the more thorough and complete becomes the union between the two centres, and the less and less readily does the combination of their action admit of interference from centres outside of them. By the mere force of repetition and of the definite organization which repetition brings about, novel acts become habitual ; habitual acts become automatic ; and automatic acts become reflex. The differences between these several degrees of consolidation are thus marked. An act is habitual when it occurs with perfect facility, but yet requires the guidance and direction of higher centres for its performance. An act is automatic when it has become so far organized that the mechanism which actuates it is complete in itself, and, given the necessary impression, the action occurs without any guidance or regulation from higher centres. Such are the acts of walking, the fingering of musical instruments, the manipulation in many handicrafts, the movement of the lips and tongue in speaking. All these movements occur with a celerity and an accuracy which indicates thorough organization ; all of them can be performed without direct guidance from the higher centres, or while the higher centres are otherwise employed—while, as we say, we are "thinking of something else " ; and any direct interference of the higher centres—any undue attention to the movements tends to spoil their facility and accuracy. Lastly, when organization is complete, movements become reflex ; that is to say, not only do they occur on the occurrence of their appropriate stimulus, but they occur necessarily. The nerve-channel is so completely formed in itself, and the neighbouring currents are so built out, that when once the process is started, it goes on to completion as a matter of necessity, and no action of the higher centres can interfere to prevent or alter it. Such movements are those of blinking, of swallowing, of coughing, and the like.

Several implications and consequences of this property of mere repetition to bring about the organization of a nervous process demand our notice.

It has been seen how, as the channel between the newly-connected centres becomes more permeable, the ease with which they act together is increased. Thus repetition produces *facility* of action. How true this is, the whole experience of education teaches us.

It has also been seen that, as the channel becomes wider and more permeable, there is less lateral diffusion of the current. The new channel becomes by degrees able to take up and transmit the whole of the current, and those portions which at first spread here and there, and aroused the activity of neighbouring centres, are absorbed. The effect of these wandering currents was to produce, along with the new combination of movements, a number of superfluous movements, such as those of the tongue and face that we see in children learning to write ; such as are seen in the straggling, disordered, and excessive movements exhibited by the novice in playing tennis, in fencing, skating, and in every other complicated exercise. As efficiency increases by practice, these superfluous movements disappear, and in nothing does the play of the expert appear more remarkable than in the slight apparent exertion with which he attains success.

The effect of repetition in producing a fixed organization, and so shutting off partly or entirely the influence of superior centres, has already been referred to ; but it is obvious that this effect will only be produced when the action is at each repetition free from such interference. If at each repetition the action is modified, then will the tendency to modification become organized along with the rest of the mechanism, and the result will be an arrangement like that which actuates the movements of walking, for instance, in which the stage of automatism has been reached, not only by the fundamental to and fro movements of the legs, but also by the various modifications rendered necessary by inequalities in the ground, obstacles, hills, turnings, and so forth.

Hitherto, for the sake of simplicity, the new channel between the two centres has been spoken of as a single channel, but this of course is far from being the case. It is a complicated leash of channels. And the communication spoken of as established between two centres, is actually made between many. To go back to our account of the way in which the communication is first established. A leash of ingoing currents disposed in a novel arrangement disturbs a centre, or group of centres, in a new way, and produces a discharge in a new direction. The discharge thus started travels in a complicated mesh of channels, which are, *ex hypothesi*, unaccustomed to carry a discharge of this volume. The discharge, therefore, escapes into the ground substance, and forms new connections in the way already described. Having got a clear idea of the process in its simplest form, we may now go on to note that the escape of the discharge into the ground substance will take place not at one point only, but at many ; and the communication opened up will be with not one centre only, but with several. The general result will be, in short, that after proceeding for a certain distance in established channels, the discharge will break out in several directions and form new communications with several centres. The point at which the discharge breaks out will therefore become the point of meeting of several complex groups of channels, converging from several directions. In the course of the general activity of the nervous system, discharges will frequently pass along one or another of these channels, and often along more than one at a time, towards the point of meeting. But when two currents passing along the same fibre in opposite directions, meet, the point of meeting tends to become an enlargement—to grow into a cell. And where, as in this case, many fibres meet in a plexus within a given area, there will be many points of meeting of opposing currents—there will ensue a formation of many cells. The point, or rather the area, of the meeting of these various groups of channels will, in short, develop into a nerve centre.

Now notice the connections of this new centre, thus formed. It is a meeting-place for the channels of egress of several centres, each of these channels having a complexity of composition representing that of the centre from which it issues. The meeting of these channels, of such a complexity, produces a mesh of much greater complexity—of complexity, roughly speaking, equal to the sum of the complexities of the components. This mesh becomes in course of time a centre, and, as a centre, retains nearly all its original complexity. So that the new centre is far more complex in composition than any of the old ones.

When the new centre discharges, the discharge, carried simultaneously by all the contributing channels to all the contributing centres, will arouse the activity of all these centres ; and hence, whatever activities the contributing centres represented, the new centre will represent them all. If each of the contributing centres represented activity of a part of the body, the new centre will represent activity of all these parts. If the contributing centres represented various modes of activity of the whole body, the new centre will represent all these modes.

The connections of the new centre being with the contributing centres only, any influence it may have on the muscles can be exerted only through the contributing centres. Its connection with the muscles is therefore less direct or immediate than theirs.

In every respect the new centre, as compared with the old or contributing centres, has the qualities which have already been described as characteristic of *higher* centres, and hence we arrive at the general conclusions, that the higher centres are of more recent formation than the lower, and that as the experiences of life accumulate, as new circumstances from time to time impress the organism, and as old circumstances impress the organism in new ways, new strata of nerve centres are continually being laid down on the top of the old. The entire nervous system is continually breaking out on its upper surface into growths of greater and greater complexity and elaborateness. Each outgrowth is no sooner completed than it is dominated by a still loftier growth. Each stratum is no sooner laid down than it is submerged beneath one still more recent.

We have seen how little a channel that is in course of formation differs from the matrix out of which it is formed. And we have seen how little a nerve-cell that is swelling in the course of a fibre is distinguished from the matrix from which it is separated. It is obvious that, at their early stages, it will take but a slight disturbing influence to derange the formative process that is going on ; and that a disturbance that would have no appreciable effect on the fully formed fibre protected by its insulating jacket, or on the mature cell fixed in its organization, might altogether destroy the slight difference existing between the nascent fibre or cell, and the ground substance from which it was becoming differentiated. It will be obvious, too, that disturbing agencies acting on nerve centres will produce effects of magnitude inversely proportional to the age of the centre. The youngest centres, which, as we have seen, are also the most complex and the most elaborate, and the highest in every sense, will be the first to be affected by the disturbance. As the disturbance increases, they will be more and more deranged, and at the same time the derangement will spread deeper and deeper, to centres that are older and more fully fixed in organization. The highest centres will be affected first and most, the lowest last and least, the intermediate centres intermediately.

If we notice the effect of a late frost upon the vegetation of the garden, we see that it is the youngest shoots and the newly opening leaves that are most severely affected—that are blackened and shrivelled by its effects. The old leaves, whose fibres have become fully developed, and whose structure is fully organized and fixed are not injured. Should the frost be more severe, we shall find that not only are the young leaves killed, but the old ones also suffer more or less severely. The woody trunks, however, are uninjured, for in a week or two they begin again to push out their buds and show their unimpaired vitality. Should the frost be of extreme severity, the whole tree may perish. Now notice that, say in the case of the peach, the flowers, the parts that are earliest attacked and soonest succumb to the slightest adverse influence, are the most highly elaborate part of the tree, and fulfil the most complex and far-reaching function. The leaves, which are the next to suffer, are the next in elaborateness of organization,[1] and next in the complexity and general elevation of the functions that they fulfil, while the last part of the tree to suffer is the wood, which is not only the oldest and the most fixedly organized, but subserves also the simplest and most fundamental functions.

[1] Flowers and leaves are not commonly seen on the peach at the same time, but the simile is sufficiently accurate for the present purpose.

CHAPTER III.

THE MIND.

So far we have considered the living organism as a mechanism, accumulating energy and expending it in movement ; receiving impressions from the outside world, and responding to them by adapted actions : but we have not yet dealt with the phenomena of mind, nor have we found how mental phenomena are related to the working of this elaborate nervous mechanism.

The relation of mind to nervous processes is very peculiar, and since it is, in fact, very different from that which is vaguely current, and, I will not say accepted, but assumed, by many who have not studied the matter, it will be necessary for the reader to rid himself as far as possible of all the preconceived notions of the matter, and to begin its consideration afresh with a perfectly open mind.

In the first place, he must discard altogether the notion that mind can work upon, or influence, or produce changes in, the nervous system, or in matter of any kind, however arranged ; and, in the second place, he must rid himself of the idea that any nervous process, or any movement, or rearrangement of material particles, can ever, under any circumstances, be transformed into a mental phenomenon—into an idea, or a feeling, or any other state or condition of mind. That such transference of the mental into the material is possible, and even, that it is usual and normal, is an assumption made not only daily and hourly by the laity in ordinary conversation, but also with intolerable frequence by writers on psychology who ought to know better. We find their works peppered all over with terms that imply that the states and movements of matter are convertible into states and processes of mind. One writer speaks of memories being stored up in the brain-cells. Another explains how an ingoing current undergoes a " peculiar metabolic " change, becomes " animalized, intellectualized," and finally is transformed into an idea ; which is much as if a beefsteak were put into a sausage-machine, where it would undergo a peculiar metabolic change, and emerge as a sonata. One eminent writer suggests that the brain contains a substance intermediate between mind and matter, which partakes of the nature of both without being exclusively either. Imagine a thing which is partly an iron bar and partly a smell of paint, without being exclusively either ! It is frequent to find the mind spoken of as a form of brain-energy. One person who writes on psychology says that the brain secretes ideas as the liver secretes bile. Such terms and phrases as " psycho-motor centres," "ideo-motor processes," "sensations changing into movements," are exceedingly common ; while commonest and worst of all is the prevalent opinion, expressed or implied, that above the material part of the brain, somewhere in the skull cavity, there sits a little deity who sends his orders out this way and that, and by some mysterious but easy process produces all the movements of the body. He plays on the centres of the brain as a performer plays on the key-board of the piano, and produces just such combinations and successions of movements as he pleases, untrammelled by natural laws. This being is variously named, according to the predilections of the writer, some calling him the Will, others the Ego, others again the Conscious Personality, others the Soul ; while yet others split him up into several beings, and with the natural tendency of anthropomorphism, not only let them make common cause against their unfortunate servant, the body, but set them fighting among themselves. The whole doctrine is a survival in slightly altered form of the old superstition of demoniacal possession.

It is very obvious that if the brain is made up, as we know it to be, entirely of cells, fibres, and ground substance, with the necessary framework of connective tissue, blood vessels, and so forth ; and if the processes going on in this structure are limited, as we know them to be, to molar and molecular movements ; there is neither room, nor need, nor possibility for any interference of mental conditions with these movements of material particles. Reduce the affair to its simplest expression, and see how it looks, not when spoken of vaguely in general terms, but when closely examined and brought to a focus.

You come in from a walk on a hot summer day feeling very thirsty. You see a glass of water on the table and you drink it. To what were due those movements of stretching out the hand, grasping the tumbler, and lifting it to the mouth ? To the *feeling* of thirst, you say, and to the *desire* for water to quench it. Well, the actual movement we have seen to be actuated by the discharge of a nerve centre, under the guidance of impressions arising from without, that is to say, of nerve-currents running inward from the eyes, and upon the initiation of a discharge descending from higher centres. Now, at what point in this series of processes does the influence of the feeling or the desire come in ? Does it alter the discharge of the nerve-centre, or does it bring this discharge about ? We know what the discharge is. It is a liberation of energy due to a rearrangement of molecules—due to the falling of the molecules into simpler combinations. Take a feeling of thirst and drive it against the molecules so as to upset their equilibrium ; or take a desire for water and knock it against the nerve centre. You cannot. Can you interpose a feeling of thirst, or a desire for water, in the course either of the current running from the eye to the centre, or of the current running from the centre to the muscles ? These currents, as we call them, are, as we know, merely a succession of changes communicated from molecule to molecule. Take a feeling of thirst and push it between two molecules. You cannot. But, you will say, these are not stages at which

5

the mental process comes in.   There is a fourth element.
There is the current descending from the higher centre
which initiates the action of the centre actuating the movement of reaching for and grasping the glass.   The feeling of
thirst, the desire for water, precedes the movement.   It is in
these higher centres whose action also precedes the movement, that the feelings produce their effects.   Well, mount
as high as you like, whatever part of the brain you explore,
you will find nothing but cells, fibres, and ground substance,
and all alike are reducible to molecules—to molecules
differently arranged and moving in different ways.   Take any
one of these molecules, or any combination of them, that you
please.   Twist them and turn them about as you like, combine them into what groups of utmost complexity you can
conceive, when all is done, have you produced anything that
has the appearance of a feeling of thirst, or of a desire for
water ?   Or notice their movements, and say whether there
is anything in them that resembles feeling—not that appears
to be prompted by feeling, but that itself resembles thirst or
desire.   If there be no such movement, then create one,
imagine one, attempt to conceive some molecular movement
which shall resemble a feeling, a desire, or an idea.   The
thing is impossible.   It is not merely impossible—that is a
feeble term to express our impotence—it is inconceivable.
Not only is it not now possible, but it is manifest that under
no circumstances, after no lapse of time, by no future extension of our knowledge or of our intelligence, will such a thing
ever become possible.   The movements of matter and the
phenomena of mind are separated by a fathomless abyss.
Betwixt the one and the other there is a great gulf fixed, and
neither can matter act upon or induce changes in mind, nor
can mind act on or induce changes in matter.

    At this point I shall probably find myself bereft of my
reader's sympathy and concurrence.   " What ! " he will say,
" mind not act upon matter !   How is it then that I lift my
hand to my head when I will to do so ? how is it that a
sudden fright makes me turn pale ? how does anxiety dry

my mouth ? why does an amusing thought cause laughter ? how is it that faith undoubtedly cures bodily diseases ? whence is the tendency for every thought to translate itself into action ? whence the outward expression of every emotion ? The whole daily and hourly experience of life is dead against your first statement ; and as to matter not acting upon mind, if I am struck do I not feel pain ; if I lose blood do I not feel dizzy ; if I drink enough brandy do I not lose my senses ; if I take opium do I not fall asleep ? The whole proposition is monstrous."

Well, so it seems at first blush, but a complete explanation is contained in the difference between the words *post* and *propter*. It is not denied that the events occur in the order stated, but the inference drawn from their succession is not the same.

The true connection between nervous and mental phenomena is believed to be this : that when, in the course of its circuit which we have so often traced, from the organs of sense to the muscles, a nerve current reaches the highest centres, and sets them in action, then this activity of the highest nervous centres is attended, we cannot say why or how, by a mental state. Every alteration of nervous tension in these upper centres is attended by a variation in the mental processes. Every fluctuation of nerve currents in this way and in that, has an accompaniment in a variation of mental states strictly in correspondence with it. The one set of changes takes place in the nervous system, and is an affair of molecules and discharges and nerve currents. The other set of changes takes place in the mind, and is an affair of ideas and feelings and volitions. The one set of changes accompanies the other set of changes invariably and instantly, just as the movements of the shadow accompany the movements of the man. But the mental changes can no more influence or alter the nervous changes, than the shadow can move the man ; and the nervous system, or the body which contains it, can no more act independently and directly upon the mind than the man can pick up his shadow and

throw it away. The influence of the body is limited to the
changes that it brings about in the working of the higher
nervous centres ; and when such a change is produced, a
change of mental processes takes place simultaneously, just
as a change of attitude of the body is accompanied by a
change of shape of the shadow. But to suppose that an
action on the body can influence the mind without changing
the nervous centres, is like supposing that a man can alter
the shape of his shadow without moving his body.

As on the sensory or ingoing side, so on the motor or outgoing side ; the mental state does not arise save only when
the nervous process is set a-going. When a certain nerve-
centre discharges, it stimulates certain muscles in such a way
as to produce a movement of the arm. That is the bodily
process. Simultaneously with this discharge of the nerve
centre, and with this movement of the arm, an idea of
moving the arm arises in the mind. The shadow of the
bodily movement is thrown upon the screen of the mind,
and we know that we are moving. The idea of the movement is not in the centre ; it is not in the cells ; nor in the
fibres. It is not entangled in any material process ; nor does
it exist in any place. When the centre energizes, the idea
arises, and that is all we know. It may happen, and this is
most important, that the discharge of the centre is not sufficiently powerful to reach the muscles, and that consequently
no actual movement occurs ; but, nevertheless, if the discharge takes place, its mental shadow is formed, and still we
have an idea of the movement, though no movement take
place. When the discharge is powerful and the movement
actual, the mental shadow is vivid, and the mental state is
that of *willing* the movement and of *feeling* that we are
moving. When the discharge is faint and the movement
does not occur, the mental shadow is a mere penumbra ; the
mental state is that, not of willing the movement, but of
thinking of the movement.

A German physiologist has said that there is no thought
without phosphorus. He might as well have said that

there is no thought without carbon, no thought without oxygen, without nitrogen, or without any one of the numerous elements which enter into the molecular constitution of the nervous system. The complete expression is that there is, *no thought*, or rather no mental condition, *without a nervous process*. There is no mental condition—no thought, and no feeling—which is not the mental shadow, or equivalent, or obverse, or accompaniment, of some process, some discharge, some disturbance of tension, or some molecular rearrangement in the nervous centres.

This is the secret of the connection between body and mind. When a violent impression is made upon the body, when the body is struck, or pinched, or cut, or torn, a current of great intensity rushes to the highest nervous centres, and produces in them a violent commotion. This violent molecular commotion in the highest nervous centres has its mental counterpart in a violent commotion of the mind, which we call pain. When brandy or opium is absorbed from the stomach into the blood, and poured by the blood upon the highest nervous centres, it benumbs their action, it stills the vibrations of the molecules, it clogs the groups of molecules into clusters of inert particles. Molecules so poisoned can no longer fulfil their functions ; they are unable to transmit discharges. Their forces are locked up and unable to escape. The busy commotion of the centres subsides into stillness. The centres no longer discharge. Since there is no discharge, there can be no mental accompaniment, and consequently states of mind cease to exist. As the stillness settles down on the molecular activity of the centres, so, simultaneously, consciousness fades into unconsciousness.

On the motor side the difficulty will be greater of persuading the reader that his oldest and most cherished notions of bodily activity are mistaken. If there is anything certain in life, it would appear to be that we move our limbs and speak our thoughts by an effort of will ; and that in this case, undoubtedly, the mental process is not only the forerunner, but the actual cause of the bodily movement. It is not so however. The high pressure and constant widespread activity of our highest centres, during our waking hours, have for their mental image a complex state of consciousness, which is, for the time being, our conscious or mental self. So long as this activity is equally and widely diffused, and is everywhere of moderate intensity, so long we are wakeful, but bodily inactive. Let, however, a concentration of energy take place in any particular region, so that this region is aroused into preponderant activity, and immediately the bodily movement actuated by that region begins. Now, since every molecular change in these superior nervous regions has its own special and characteristic mental shadow, it will easily be imagined that so marked and conspicuous and important a process, as the concentration of energy in a limited area, will have a similarly marked and conspicuous and important mental accompaniment. The particular condition of mind that accompanies this process is termed *Willing ;* and the exercise of will, which appears to be the cause of bodily movements, is in reality the mental shadow of the particular nervous process which really is the cause.

It has been said that mental phenomena accompany the action of the higher centres only, and it remains to explain this peculiar difference between the higher centres and the lower. Let us first, however, establish the fact.

It has been shown how the occurrence of a new mode of action means the establishment of a new centre, and how the newest centres are always added on the surface while the oldest are also the lowest. When a new mode of action is initiated, when a thing is done for the first time, when we first begin to learn a new accomplishment, a new poem, a new handicraft, the process is not only slower and more difficult than on subsequent repetition, but it is also attended by a more vivid consciousness. It requires, as we say, a greater mental effort. It has a much more conspicuous mental accompaniment. With each repetition, the action not only becomes easier and more rapid, but it is attended with less mental effort. When, for instance, we first attempt to commit a passage to memory, we read it through, and then lifting the eyes from the page we repeat the words, conscious of a certain mental effort in doing so. Presently there comes a hitch, we have forgotten the context. The next word is wanting. A powerful mental effort is made, and the word is recalled. The next time the passage is repeated, the hitch again occurs, but this time the recall is made with less effort—the mental accomplishment is less vivid. With each repetition, not only is the difficulty less, but the whole mental accompaniment is reduced. At first the passage made a powerful impression upon us by the appropriateness with which a great thought was clothed in beautiful words. But by continual repetition the beauty of the words strikes us less vividly ; and the grandeur of the thought makes less impression upon us. The enthusiasm which the passage at first inspired, declines by degrees into a mild commendation. If the process is still continued, and the passage is repeated again and again, it is found that after innumerable repetitions, not only does the emotion at first inspired fail to arise, not only do the words flow glibly off the tongue, while at the very time we utter them we may be thinking of something else, but at length we cease to attend to the sense of the words at all ; and we may find that continual and repeated efforts are required to enable us to follow with our minds the sense of the words that we utter so readily. Take the case of a liturgy, and let any one who has habitually used the same form of words Sunday after Sunday for years together, say if it is possible to keep the attention from wandering while the words are being uttered. Or take the case of grace said daily at meals. Who is there who has habitually used the same form of words for years that can without effort pay any attention to the thought the words express ? Again, the child learning to read, or the novice learning a musical instrument, finds at first that the correct articulation of each word, and the correct sounding of each note, requires his whole attention, and is attended by a separate and definite mental effort. But after years of practice it becomes a matter of course to read without paying the smallest attention to the articulation of the words, all the mental accompaniment being that of the sense they convey. And similarly, the practised musician never thinks what note he has to play, but is conscious solely of the sounds produced. It is the same in every handicraft, and what is true of every handicraft is true of every course of conduct. When we first determine to pursue a new course of conduct, the mental effort is considerable; we have, as we say, to make up our minds. But not only is it easier —attended with less mental exertion, with less vivid consciousness—to take that course again, but it becomes easier also to break through our routine of conduct in other directions.

Not only is it the new course which requires the greatest mental effort to enter upon ; not only is it the novel experience which most vividly impresses us, but, as might be expected, the more novelty there is in the act or the experience, the more widely it differs from previous acts and previous experiences, the more vivid is the mental accompaniment. Policemen, who are accustomed to spend their lives on their feet, with their hands idle, find it difficult to learn work which requires the use of the fingers. Women who are accustomed to work with the fingers are extremely awkward in exercises requiring the use of the arm, such as throwing a ball, playing billiards, and so forth. To learn such exercises they have to pay great attention. The newer experience has the more vivid mental accompaniment. A man accustomed to the outdoor existence and scanty society of country life, finds, when he spends a week or two in town, his interest and attention far more keenly and constantly on the alert than the citizen ; and, conversely, the latter, removed to the country, is aroused and excited by experiences which to his country friend present no interest, and who accounts for his lack of interest by the explanation that he is accustomed to them.

That novelty is attractive is proverbial, but we find the

truth is wider than this, the fact being that we are conscious only of what is new. Of course we are conscious of the landscape that we see from our windows, though we may have seen it every day for fifty years, but, for all that, we are conscious of it only because it is *relatively* new, because it is a change from the object last looked at, because our eyes range over it and we see its parts differently. If we were to keep our eyes continuously fixed on one point of it for a sufficient length of time, we should cease to be conscious of it.

Since states of mind are but the obverse side, or, as I have termed them, the shadows, of nervous processes, it was to be expected that repetition, which has so great an effect on nervous processes, should have an effect equally great on mental states ; and this we find to be the fact. The law is that a new nervous process is attended by the most vivid mental state ; and that the more unlike the nervous process is to previous processes, the more vivid is the mental state that accompanies it. With nervous processes we have seen that continual repetition brings about complete organization —organization so complete that a very small incentive is required to start the process, and by starting the process to set the movement going. We have seen how new acts become habitual, habitual acts automatic, and automatic acts reflex. We have now to notice that as the nervous mechanism subsides through these several stages from a nascent to a complete state of organization, so the mental accompaniment, at first vivid, becomes fainter and fainter, until, when the latter stages are reached, it altogether disappears. When an act has become habitual, it has so little mental accompaniment that as we put our watch down on the dressing-table we may be uncertain whether, the instant before, we wound it up or not. It has so little mental accompaniment that on meeting a carriage in the road we draw the near rein to the required extent with scarcely a consciousness —a thought—of what we are doing. When the act becomes automatic, and still more when it becomes reflex, there is no

appreciable mental accompaniment to the discharge of the
centre that actuates the movement ; though there may be
a mental accompaniment to the movement itself, obtained
in other ways. For instance, the fixed mechanism which
actuates such movements as sneezing or swallowing is not
only cut off from the influence of the highest centres, so that
no amount of focussing or concentration of energy there—
no effort, as we say, of will—can produce them ; but the
action of these mechanisms is attended by no mental manifestation. We know that we are sneezing, and that we have
sneezed, by intelligence arriving from the periphery ; but
the instant before the sneeze happens, we cannot say when
it will happen, or even that it will take place at all.

Hence it appears, since the most fixedly and completely
organized centres are the lowest, and the most recent and
least organized are the highest, that the mental accompaniment of the nervous discharge gradually increases
in vividness from the lowest centres to the highest.
Quite at the bottom are the mechanisms actuating
directly the movements of the heart and other viscera,
which are in health absolutely void of mental accompaniment ; above these are the mechanisms for breathing,
swallowing, and other reflex actions ; and with their activity
a faint glimmering of consciousness is occasionally perceptible. Above these again are layer upon layer of
mechanisms actuating automatic and habitual acts of every
degree of fixity ; and with their action appears a certain
amount of consciousness, broadening from a mere glimmer
at the bottom, through an ever-lightening twilight, to full
dawn at the top. The action of the highest centres is
accompanied by the broad daylight of wakeful consciousness,
and the occasional concentration of energy in particular
tracts, and the vigorous and energetic discharge of these
tracts from time to time, are accompanied by mental states
of exceptional vividness, which, in comparison with the usual
more quiescent condition of consciousness, may be likened
to bursts of sunshine on a cloudy day.

The preceding sentence introduces to our notice another factor in the nervous process that influences the vividness of the accompanying mental state. The latter depends greatly indeed upon the novelty, but it depends also in large measure upon the *intensity* of the nervous process. When the nervous process is feeble, the mental accompaniment is faint; when the nervous process is forcible, the mental accompaniment is vivid. An instance of this has already been given. It was stated that when the arm is moved, the nervous process actuating the movement has for its mental accompaniment an idea of the movement; and that when the same nervous process occurred, but with an intensity insufficient to produce a movement, there was still an idea of the movement, but the idea was faint in proportion to the lessened activity of the nerve centre. It is the same on the sensory side. If I look at the lawn in front of me, the impression carried through the eyes to the higher centres rouses the activity of a certain nervous region, and this activity has for its mental shadow a feeling of green in the mind. If I lower my eyes again to the paper I can still think of the green lawn—I can still have in my mind, though in a much less vivid degree, the feeling of green— and I know that, for this feeling to arise, there must be activity of the same nerve-region as before. This time, as the activity is much less energetic, so the feeling is correspondingly less vivid.

The difference between a central nervous process set in motion directly by an impression from without, and a similar process originated by the far less intense stimulus of an internally initiated current, is considerable; and the difference in vividness of the two states of mind, the difference between the colour that we say we see and the colour that we say we remember or imagine is correspondingly great. But there are minor differences of vividness in the mental states, corresponding with minor differences in the activity of the nervous process. Thus if, while I am looking at the grass, the sun shines out, a more powerful impression is

made upon the eye, a more energetic discharge of the
nervous centre is evoked, and a more vivid feeling of green
arises in the mind; and, generally, the vividness of the
mental state varies directly as the intensity of the impression
that evokes the nervous process, and therefore varies as the
intensity of that process itself.

There are also intrinsic causes of difference in the activity
of the nervous process. When the tide of nervous energy
is at its height, as when the body is in robust health, and
after the recuperation of sleep, and before the daily expenditure has become considerable, the discharge of the highest
nervous centres is, *cæteris paribus*, of greater activity than
towards the close of day, when the tide is ebbing and the
expenditure of the day has left the nerve cells depleted of
much of their store of energy. Hence we find that, in the
morning, the same impression evokes a more vivid mental
condition than in the evening. We find that the morning
is the time to work out difficult problems, to appreciate fine
shades of difference, to commit things to memory, and,
generally, to perform those tasks in which the maximum
of mental exertion is required on the minimum of impression from without. In the evening a stronger stimulus is
needed to produce a mental condition of equivalent intensity,
and hence we find the evening devoted to those occupations
in which the main element is the impression given from
without. The evening is the time at which we enjoy lis-
tening to music, witnessing spectacular displays, and receiving in other ways powerful impressions on the senses.

The same law—that the vividness of the mental condition
depends on the activity of the nervous process—is exemplified in the fact that in states of great excitement, when
the activity of the highest centres is at its maximum, impressions produce effects out of all proportion to their magnitude, and to the mental states which, on common occasions,
accompany them. Thus it is commonly said that a position
of great danger calls forth all a man's faculties ; the fact
being that the state of excitement in which he is—the state

of high tension of his nervous system—enables new combinations of centres to be effected, which the ordinary nervous tide would be insufficient to accomplish ; just as we see that an extraordinarily high tide in the Thames will not only overflow, but will break down barriers which are a sufficient defence against ordinary tides. These new combinations are, *ex hypothesi*, of greater novelty than usual, and hence on that account have a more vivid mental accompaniment ; but this is not all. The ordinary processes, such as are in daily and hourly working, are all intensified, and their accompanying mental states share in the intensification. It is a common observation that in moments of great danger, great anxiety, great excitement of any kind, the mind acquires an extraordinary wakefulness, and the entire scene, in which the individual is placed, impresses itself to the minutest detail upon him, with an intensity which becomes painful. Dickens has described in the trial of Fagin a mental experience which most people have undergone in some degree.[1] In such cases there is of course no increase

---

[1] "He looked up into the gallery again. Some of the people were eating, some fanning themselves with handkerchiefs ; for the crowded place was very hot. There was one young man sketching his face in a little note-book. He wondered whether it was like him, and looked on when the artist broke his pencil-point and made another one with his knife, as an idle spectator might have done.

"In the same way when he turned his eyes towards the judge, his mind began to busy itself with the fashion of his dress, and what it cost, and how he put it on. There was an old fat gentleman on the bench, too, who had gone out, some half-an-hour before, and now come back. He wondered within himself whether this man had been to get his dinner, what he had had, and where he had had it ; and pursued this train of careless thought until some new object caught his eye and roused another.

"Not that, all this time, his mind was for an instant free from one oppressing, overwhelming sense of the grave that opened at his feet ; it was ever present to him, but in a vague and general way, and he could not fix his thoughts upon it. Thus even when he trembled and turned burning hot at the idea of speedy death, he fell to counting the iron spikes before him, and wondering how the head of one had been broken off, and whether they would mend it or leave it as it was."

This vivid description well portrays the elevation of sub-conscious into wholly-conscious states under the influence of great excitement.

in the strength of the impression that is made. The circumstances are the same, and their action on the organism is the same as usual, but the increased tension of the nervous system causes an exaggerated acti n n the receipt of an ordinary impression, and this exa␣gerated nerv us action has for its accompaniment an exaggeratɛd mental con lition.

Upon the novelty and upon the activity of the nervous process, depend, therefore, the degree of consciousness with which the nervous process shall be accompanied. It is pɪ - bable that, upon consideration, this expression may be yet further simplified, and that the mental accompaniment may be found to depend upon a single fact r in the nervous process. For we have seen that the distinction between a new and an old nervous process is that, while the latter proceeds in old-established, well-worn channels, thoroughly organized, fixed in character, and of calibre adapted to the volume of the current they have to carry; the former proce ls in channels that are new, that are but little differentiatcd from the ground substance in which they ɪun, that are but faintly and inefficiently divided from thiꜱ ground substance, that are but slightly organized, and therefore easily modified, and that are insufficient in calibre to contain the whole volume of the current. The essential difference between the old process and the new is that the former proceeds in established channels, while the latter proceeds partly in the ground substance. The essential difference between the feeble process and the vigorous process is that the former entirely proceeds in established channels, while the latter breaks their bounds and escapes into the ground substance. Hence it is probable that the common factor in the two conditions is that which determines the common accompaniment, and that the factor in the nervous process on which the concomitant occurrence of consciousness depends, is the passage of the nerve current through the ground substance of the grey matter.

Such being the condition upon which consciousness in

general depends, it remains to show what are the variations, or special modes, or characters in the nervous process, upon which depend the various manifestations of consciousness which we know by the names of Memory, Thought, Reason, Will, Imagination, Emotion, and so forth. In order to do this effectually, it will be necessary to give first a brief account of the general constitution of mind and the nature of the various faculties of which it consists.

If we look into our own minds and observe what goes on there, we shall find that the entire content or factors of consciousness fall into two groups. When I glance from the green lawn in front of me to the blue sky above, I am conscious of a feeling of green, of a feeling of blue, and of a change from one feeling to the other. When I hear two notes struck in succession on the piano, I am conscious first of one sound, then of the other, and of the change from one to the other. The door opens and a blast of cold air enters. From the feeling of warmth that I had a moment ago, I now become conscious of a feeling of cold, and distinct from each is the consciousness of the change from one to the other. In thinking over the events of yesterday I recall the feeling of disappointment that I had when a friend failed to keep an appointment, and the feeling of pleasure that arose when I received a letter from him bearing good news, and I am aware of a change from the feeling of disappointment to the feeling of pleasure. In thinking of the case that I saw this morning, the recollection of the various symptoms that it presented forms a highly complex state of mind ; and in passing from this recollection to the recollection of other cases, I am aware successively of several highly complex states of mind, and of the changes from state to state. The same factors are present in all conditions of consciousness. When the silence is broken by a knock at the door, I hear the knock, I have a feeling of noise, and at the same time become conscious of the change from silence to noise, and from noise to silence. When I open my eyes after sleep, I am aware of the feelings of light and colour, and of the change from darkness to light. Similarly, when I wake out of sleep, I am conscious of many vivid feelings, and of the change from a consciousness of but few faint feelings, such as I had during sleep, to the waking consciousness of many vivid ones. Throughout the whole of conscious life we know of but two factors—states of mind, and changes from one state to another.

If the matter is considered, it will be found, not only that there can be no change of consciousness without a state from which, and an adjoining state to which, the change is made ; but also that there can be no state of consciousness which is not bounded by changes. Not only does the constant procession of thoughts, which we find ever passing through our minds, necessitate the change from one state of consciousness to another ; but, if we try to maintain one state of mind unchanged, we are unable to do so. In noticing the simplest thing, we are continually passing from the observation of its form to that of its colour, from its colour to its position, from its position to its surroundings, from its entirety to its parts. If we wilfully determine to fix our attention on one of these factors to the exclusion of others, and if we succeed in doing so, then the intercalated mental states refer to something else, to other similar objects, to other similar occasions on which we made similar attempts, to things wholly unconnected with the object before us—to yesterday's weather or to to-morrow's excursion. What is true of states of mind which we voluntarily bring up, is true of states of mind impressed upon us from without. The continuous roar of a cataract, the continuous clacking of a mill, the continuous rumbling of carts through the streets, become at length inaudible to those who live beside them and are never free from their influence. Originally they were almost continually audible, the feeling of sound obtruding itself continually into the series of mental states. As it became more accustomed, it intruded less and less often, until at last attention must be specially directed to it for it to be heard. But if now the noise suddenly ceases, if the mill is stopped, or the traffic is diverted for the repair of the road, this change is at once responded to by a change in consciousness. Not only is the sudden accession of silence felt, but in being felt it brings a knowledge, till then obscured and unnoticed, of the sound which preceded it.

These two conditions, therefore,—states of mind and changes of state—compose the entire content of consciousness, and each of them is indispensable to consciousness; without either of them consciousness could not exist.

If we examine each factor separately, we find that while in one respect they are similar, in other respects they are very different. They are similar in this, that although they are here called differently, states and changes of state, yet upon ultimate analysis a change from one state of mind to another is itself a state for the moment for which it lasts. Their differences, however, are much more marked. States of mind are infinitely various, various in kind, various in complexity, various in intensity, infinite in number; some being crude sensations, as of colour or sound or touch; others emotions, as hope, and joy, and fear—vexation, anxiety, and sympathy; others, again, are recollections, as of a particular room or landscape, at a particular time, under a particular aspect; others are theories and hypotheses of various kinds; indeed, the whole bulk of our consciousness is made up of states of mind; the changes of state can be but the dividing lines which separate the states from one another.

Changes of state, or, as we may hereafter term them, relations between states, differ from the states themselves in being but two in number. The change may be from one state of mind to a different state, as from a feeling of blue to a feeling of red, or from a recollection of a poem to a feeling of anger, or from the percept of a running rabbit to the concept of a gun, or from the percept of a rod of a certain length to the percept of a rod of a different length, or from the percept of an article of a certain quality or price to that of an article of a different quality or price, or from a

6

certain conceived method of dealing with circumstances to
a different method. Or the change may be from one state
of mind to a similar state, as from a feeling of blue to a
feeling of the same shade, or from a percept of a certain
area or length, to that of a similar area or length, or from
the percept of an article of certain quality or price to the
concept of other articles of the same quality or price, and so
forth. The fact is, that there are only two possible changes
from one state of mind to another, one to a similar, the
other to a different state of mind. Thus our notion of the
contents of consciousness becomes somewhat more detailed.
Consciousness consists of successive states of mind, and of
changes from one state to another ; of conscious states, and
conscious likenesses and differences between states ; of
states, and of relations of likeness and difference between
them. The states of mind are called *feelings*, and the relations between them are called *thoughts*, and out of feelings
and thoughts all consciousness is made up.

We have next to notice that while mind is made up of
both feelings and thoughts, and while there can be no
feeling without thought, and no thought without feeling,
yet feeling and thought are rarely or never equally predominant in consciousness. One element or the other
preponderates.

Let us take a very simple case. Take the case of the
feelings of sound and their allied thoughts. A musical note,
followed by another note, arouses, as we have seen, three
conscious states. There is first a feeling of sound ; then
another feeling of sound ; and in addition to these two
feelings there is a consciousness of the likeness or unlikeness
between them ; of the sameness or difference of pitch, or
of loudness, or of timbre. So long as consciousness is
occupied with this or that sound, so long there is feeling
pure and simple ; but directly we become aware that this
note is louder than that, or that that is shriller than this—
directly we attend, not to the feelings themselves, but to
the relation between them—we are forming a *judgment*.

The attitude of feeling has passed into the attitude of thought. It is clear that neither the feeling nor the thought can exist alone. In every state of consciousness there is both feeling and thought, but the two are never equally prominent in consciousness. The varying condition of consciousness, in which the limiting terms and the relation between them alternately rise into prominence, may be represented by F r F and f R f. Now, if the two notes are struck simultaneously, a new state of consciousness arises, differing from each of the three previous states. It is a state compounded of the two feelings *and of the relation* between them. When a note and its third, or fifth, or octave, are struck simultaneously, we are aware of two sounds and of a difference in pitch between them. Yet the three states of consciousness are blended so intimately, that the chord affects us as a single sound. The three states have become consolidated into one. The single state thus formed can enter as a unit into relation with other mental states. It can behave in every way as a simple feeling. It is, in fact, a compound feeling. Suppose one such chord to be followed by another, then, precisely as in the simpler case, there is a feeling, followed by another feeling and separated by a relation ; and just as in the previous case, the feeling or the relation may chiefly occupy consciousness—may be the prominent component of the conscious state. If we are affected chiefly by the pleasing or harsh sound of the chords, the conscious state is one mainly of feeling. If we notice chiefly the similarity or difference in loudness, or pitch, or harmony of the two chords, the conscious state is one mainly of thought. The symbols representing the two states of consciousness would be (F r F) r (F r F) where the element of feeling is conspicuous and the relational element insignificant ; and (f r f) R (f r f) where the relation between the chords is conspicuous and the element of feeling neglected.

But these are not the only relations that can be established between the two chords. Consciousness may be occupied with the comparison of the *interval* between the first pair of notes and the interval between the second. The interval between the first pair may be a third, and that between the second pair may be a fifth, and consciousness may be occupied with the difference between these two intervals. But each of these two intervals is itself a relation between the pitch of one note and the pitch of another ; so that consciousness is occupied, not with a relation between feelings, as in the previous cases, but with a *relation between relations*. In graphic form the symbol for such a state of consciousness would be $(f \text{ R } f)$ R $(f \text{ R } f)$.

We may imagine each of the terms of this relation to be composed of the feelings aroused by chords of three or more notes ; each additional note adding to the complexity of the feeling, each more complex feeling adding to the complexity of the state of mind which, together with another feeling and a relation, it constitutes ; and each such state of mind being capable, when consolidated into a single feeling, of entering into relation with yet another feeling, and so constituting a state of consciousness of still higher complexity. When to differences of pitch, loudness, and number of simultaneous sounds, are added differences in the succession of sounds ; the states of mind, the feelings into which they are consolidated, and the higher and higher orders of states into which they become combined, reach a very great degree of complexity ; and when to these differences are added differences of timbre, by the employment of different instruments, the complexity of the states of consciousness is still further increased. Yet, even if the content of consciousness is the comparative merits of two operas, each executed by a full orchestra, each consisting of many parts, each performed by many vocalists, each occupying two or three hours in its performance ; it is easy to see that the *judgment* arrived at as to their merits is precisely the same in form as the judgment of the superiority in harmony of one chord to another ; and that the form of the content of consciousness is still R. In the one case as in the other there is a relation between two terms. In the one case the terms are extremely simple, in the other they are extremely complex, but the judgment still consists in the establishment of a relation between two terms.

Such being the universal form of all thought, it remains to compare the mental process with the process in the highest nervous centres of which the former is the shadow, and see if these two have any features in common. In examining the way in which the nervous centres act, we found that at the turning point at which the ingoing current from the sense organs is reflected as the outgoing current to the muscles, there is interposed, in the lowest levels of the series, a patch of grey matter at which the current is reflected and by which it is reinforced. But at the highest levels we found a duplication of the patch of grey matter. The ingoing current is received by one centre, which then transmits its discharge to another centre, whose activity sets the muscles in action. The process in the highest centres is therefore threefold. There is the discharge of a centre, the passage of the discharge through channels, and the discharge of a second centre. And it is this activity which is accompanied by consciousness, whose form, as we have already seen, is similarly threefold. Hence it is a natural inference that the feelings are the mental accompaniments of discharges of grey matter, while the relations between the feelings are the mental accompaniments of the passage of the discharge through channels from one centre to another. This inference will appear the more justifiable when we remember that it is the passage of the discharge through the channels that brings into relation the discharges of the two centres.

Feelings, therefore, accompany discharges of grey matter. Thoughts accompany the passage of discharges from centre to centre. Feelings are intense when discharges are vigorous ; are voluminous when discharges are widespread ; and are complex when the discharging centres are complex in structure. Thoughts are similarly complex when the channels in which the discharge travels are numerous and intricate ; are vivid when the discharge is of high tension ;

and are more intense, the less permeable the channels in which the discharge flows.

When thought is complex and novel, it is termed imagination ; and the conditions in the nervous system that are active during imagination will be gathered from what has gone before.

Memory is the recurrence of a mental state that has occurred before. It is, on the bodily side, the revivescence of a nervous process that has previously been active. It is obvious that this physical process may occur both in centre and in channels, and so we can remember both feelings and thoughts. It has been already shown how repetition of a nervous process acts in rendering the process more facile and more rapid, and how, as facility and rapidity of the nervous process increase, the mental accompaniment diminishes ; and thus we are prepared to find, not only that the more often a thing has been repeated, the better we remember it, but that the more perfectly it is remembered, the less effort—the less consciousness—we have of its remembrance ; until, when memory becomes perfect, it ceases to become conscious — we cease to consider it memory. Thus, I remember with effort the name of the person to whom I was introduced yesterday ; I remember without difficulty the name of my friend of a year's standing ; but it would be inappropriate to say that I remember that the name of this thing on the plate before me is bread. Similarly, I remember with effort the way to tie a turk's head ; I remember more readily, how to make a clove hitch ; but it would be inappropriate to say that I remember how to tie a knot. Thus conscious memory fades and merges into unconscious memory, and the more perfect the memory is, the less of consciousness accompanies it. When memory is looked at from this point of view, as, on the physical side, the repetition of a nervous process that has occurred before, and, on the mental side, the conscious accompaniment of this process where it has a conscious accompaniment ; the scope and meaning of the term become considerably extended, and a community of origin and of nature is found to exist between processes that are at first sight widely different. All automatic actions—the movement of the legs in walking, of the fingers in writing, of the lips and tongue in speaking—are actions whose memory has become perfect, and therefore unconscious. The movement of the newly-hatched chick, in pecking at food a few hours after birth, has been called a remembrance. It is said that the chick remembers how its parents pecked ; and this statement, at first sight fanciful, is, if we adopt this view of memory, almost accurate. For the chick inherits a fully formed nervous structure, which, when set in action, produces the movement of pecking. Such a structure can have been formed in the ancestral fowls only by continual repetitions of the act ; repetitions that were at first accompanied by conscious memories, and subsequently became automatic. In the newly-hatched chick the movement is evidently preceded by hesitation, it is at first tentative and imperfect, and only after repetition attains its perfect precision. Every one of the acts is, however, actuated by the repetition or revivescence or recurrence of a nervous process, and is therefore, on the physical side, a case of remembrance ; and no one can doubt, who has seen the hesitation, the deliberation, and the manifest tentativeness of the first few pecks, that they are accompanied by consciousness—by conscious states, which are, in such a case, memories. In the same way, the vast bulk of the content of our consciousness at any time consists of memories. The judgments that we continually and sub-consciously form of the distances of all objects that we see around us, are made up of the memories cf the amount of stretching or reaching, or of the number of steps, or of the time taken to traverse, the intermediate distance between us and objects similarly related to us, on innumerable previous occasions. The similarly sub-conscious instant judgments that we continually form of the direction of objects, is similarly constituted of memories of the direction of efforts made to reach objects

similarly placed with reference to ourselves, and similarly
appearing. Our ideas of the solidity, of the hardness and
softness, roughness and smoothness of bodies, are similarly
made up of memories of the sensations that we have had in
handling bodies of similar appearance and surface. It is the
same with more complex judgments. Our decision as to the
probable qualities of a horse, is made up of memories of the
qualities of horses having similar points ; we decide as to the
healthiness of a house by memories of the salubrity of
other houses similarly situated ; and as to the prudence of a
line of conduct, by memories of the consequences of other
lines of conduct previously pursued. Similarly again on the
bodily side, the skill with which we perform any operation,
depends upon the accuracy with which we remember the
amount of previous efforts and their results, and on the
precision with which we reproduce them. But to reproduce
an action is to have over again an activity of the same
nervous process which produced it before—that is, to
remember the action. From every point of view, then, we
see the importance of memory. Of fully conscious memory,
which is the early repetition of a newly formed nervous
process, accompanied by vivid consciousness ; of sub-
conscious memory, which is the repetition, after very many
times, of a well-organized nervous process, accompanied by
faint consciousness ; and of unconscious memory, which is
the repetition after innumerable times, of a completely
organized nervous process, unaccompanied by any consciousness.

As has been so often said, a nervous process, once
established, tends to occur again. But this is not all.
Since each of these higher nervous processes consists
of the discharge of one centre, the passage of the discharge through channels, and the discharge of a second
centre, it follows that whenever the first centre discharges
again, there is a tendency for the discharge of the second
centre again to follow ; and this tendency is strong in proportion to the strength of the original discharge between

centre and centre, and to the number of times the discharge has passed from one to the other. Or if, instead of regarding the bodily process, we look to the mental accompaniment, the statement will be, that when one state of mind has been connected by a relation with another state, then, whenever the first state recurs, there will be a tendency for the second state to follow it in similar relation ; and this tendency will be strong in proportion to the vividness of the consciousness on its first occurrence, and to the number of times that the succession has been repeated. This tendency of states of consciousness, previously associated, to follow one another again, is what is known as the Law of Association, which has many important implications. It is, as is evident, merely the law of memory stated over again, but stated in this way it leads us to conclusions which would have been less readily reached from the former basis.

Whenever the occurrence of one state of mind drags after it into consciousness another state, in the relation in which they have previously occurred, there is a remembrance, a case of memory ; but in some such cases we give another name to the process. Outside the window at which I am writing there is a spray of foliage dancing in the sunshine. The sight of it—the appearance of the leaves and the aerial roots that bristle along the stem—produces in me a definite state of consciousness, and this state is instantly followed by the idea of the sound "ivy," with which it has so often been connected before. I remember instantly that the name of the plant is "ivy." But I do not call it a remembrance. I say that I "perceive" that the spray is a spray of ivy. Yet if we consider we shall see that to perceive that the spray is ivy implies much more than merely to remember that its name is ivy. For when we remember the name, there is so far an end to the mental process ; but when we perceive that the plant is ivy, we imply that it has all the qualities and attributes that we have found by experience that other pieces of ivy possess. We imply that it has the power of attaching itself by its aerial roots, that it is evergreen, that it has flowers and fruit of certain appearance, that it has a certain smell, taste, and manner of growth. The attribution of all these qualities to the spray before us are all so many remembrances of previous experiences of plants of similar appearance ; and we call the recollection, in a more or less definite and vivid manner, of all these various attributes, coupled with the appearance of the spray before us, the "perception" that the spray is a branch of ivy. If, however, I take my eyes off the spray and begin to write a description of its shining, pointed leaves, its appearance, and its other qualities, I no longer call my consciousness of all these qualities, even though the qualities are in every respect identical with those I thought of before, a "perception" of the ivy. I say now that I remember. I am writing the description from memory. Wherein, then, lies the difference between the percept and the remembrance ? Clearly it lies in the fact that, in the case of the remembrance, all the states of consciousness answering to the attributes of the plant are of the dim, faint, inconspicuous order. In the case of the percept, some of them were of the vivid, bright, conspicuous order of feelings that we get when an object is actually *presented* to our senses, and which are therefore called "presentative" feelings. The difference between a percept and a remembrance is, therefore, that in the former a remembered feeling, or a group of remembered feelings, follows a feeling or group of feelings, some of which are actually presented, and follows them in consequence of having previously been related to them, either in their faint or their vivid forms ; while in the case of the memory, both terms consist exclusively of faint, remembered, or representative feelings. In the percept the form of consciousness is (f..f) R $(f^1.f^2.f^3..$ &c.). In the memory the form is $(f.f)$ R $(f^1.f^2.f^3..$ &c.).

Such being the nature of perception and of memory, it remains to show the nature of reasoning, the third form of thought. It has already been shown how large a part memory plays in the formation of judgments, but for all that, judgment or reasoning forms a faculty of mind very distinct from memory and perception. The difference is, that while in memory and in perception the process is a revival in consciousness of a relation that has been established previously, in reasoning two terms are brought together for the first time, and a new relation is established. Thus, as I watch the spray of ivy swaying up and down in the wind, I am impressed by its flexibility. I remember from previous experience its toughness, and the idea occurs to me that it may be used as a withy to bind up bundles of sticks. Here is a process of reasoning. The display of flexibility that I see in the ivy, and the toughness that the flexibility drags after it into my consciousness, are combined and brought newly into relation with the memory of a need, which impressed me yesterday, for some substance possessing flexibility and toughness. The two states of mind had never been approximated before. Now, for the first time, I become aware that (the qualities of this spray) are like (the qualities of a withy), and the idea of using it as a withy arises in the mind. This assimilation of the qualities of the spray to those of a withy is neither a memory nor a percept. It is a judgment, an act of reasoning, and its differentia from memories and percepts lies in the fact that the two terms are newly brought into relation. The likeness of the qualities has never been noticed before, and the establishment of this relation of likeness is a ratiocination. Both in memory and in perception there is merely the revival of a relation previously established. Whether I am looking at the spray when I form the opinion, or whether the remembered flexibility and toughness of the spray arouse the remembrance of similar qualities in the withy, does not affect the form of the mental process. It is obvious that whether one or both terms of the relation are presented to the senses, or whether both are remembered, makes no difference to the *novelty* of the relation, which is the circumstance that determines its nature as a ratiocination. Every process of reasoning is the same in form—is the establishment of a new relation—and the difference between different judgments depends first on the complexity of, or the number of memories in, the two terms that are thus newly brought into relation ; and secondly, on the degree of novelty of the relation.

That the process of reasoning advances with the complexity of the terms united, needs but little insistence. To conclude that the properties of ivy are appropriate to fit it for a binding material is a less elaborate judgment than to conclude that the qualities of a certain man will fit him to hold a certain position ; and it is less elaborate because the qualities needed in a binding material are few and simple, and the terms of the new relation, which consist of a consciousness, presented or remembered, of these few and simple qualities, are likewise simple. But the qualities necessary to fit a man for a certain position are many and complex, and the state of consciousness in which these many and complex qualities are imagined, and inferred, and remembered, and brought into proximity, is likewise complex. To conclude that an expedition composed of many men and animals will be successful, is to bring into a precisely similar relation a pair of terms, each of which is very far more complex ; and the judgment formed is still more elaborate.

The novelty of the new relation is a far more important element in the constitution of the judgment ; on it depending the *originality* of the conclusion that is formed. By the novelty of the relation is meant the wideness of separation that has previously existed between the two terms that are now brought together ; or, to put it otherwise, the general dissimilarity of the things that are now seen to be alike, or the general similarity of the things between which a distinction is now drawn.

When I see in front of my window a yew tree with whose appearance I am familiar, and recognize it as the yew tree that I have so often seen before, the process of recognition is a process of remembrance, as has already been explained. The same appearance that was before presented arouses the memory of the same qualities that have been found in experience associated with that appearance. At the same time that I recognize the familiar appearance of the tree in its accustomed place, I notice that it is, in horticultural phrase, " breaking "—that the new branches and young leaves are beginning to start from the buds. The tree is therefore not precisely the same—does not present precisely the same appearance as formerly, but the difference is so trifling that the process of cognizing it to be the same tree as has hitherto occupied the position does not rise to the level of a judgment. It is still a percept, although the first term in the relation—(this group of appearances) is like (this group of remembrances)—contains new elements, elements of difference. The terms brought together in this relation are, in short, not precisely the same as the terms of any previous relation, but they are so very nearly the same—the relation has so little novelty—that the thought is called a percept or remembrance, and not a judgment. We perceive or remember that the object before us is our old acquaintance ; we do not reason that it is.

In my walk through the country yesterday I came across another tree, having the same habit of growth, form, and colour of branch and leaf, the same phyllotaxis, the same toughness and elasticity of bough as this tree with which I am familiar. The familiar appearances aroused at once in consciousness the familiar name, and I knew it was a yew tree. Here the relation in the mind was (the appearance of this tree) is like (the remembrance of yew trees). In the first term of the relation there was a good deal that was novel. I had never seen before a tree having precisely the same shape, spreading in precisely the same way, growing to precisely the same height and breadth ; but these elements of novelty were insignificant beside the familiar elements—the mode of branching and the character of the trunk and leafage. It was not the particular shape, height, and mode of spread that aroused in me the consciousness that it was a yew tree, it was the familiar and more general qualities ; so that, although the first term of the relation contained much that was novel, it also contained much that was old ; and it was the old elements, not the new, that conspicuously entered into the relation. Hence the thought was a percept or memory, and not a judgment. It was, however, less obviously a percept than the previous instance. It partook more of the nature of reasoning, and less of the nature of memory, to say that this tree, which I have never seen before, is a certain kind of tree, than to identify this other tree as the same that I have for long been familiar with.

Being interested in trees, I notice, as I go round my garden, that certain characters in leafage and fruitage of the yew are similar to those of the cedar, the fir, the cypress, and other trees, and the whole group of trees exhibiting these characters are associated in my mind as members of one family to which a collective name may be given. In this case the dissimilarities of the things between which a likeness is traced are much more numerous and more marked than in the previous cases. The differences of height, of size, of shape, and of general mode of branching are very great. The leafage and fruitage, which are the appearances assimilated, are by no means closely similar. Both leaves and fruits differ in size, in colour, in surface, in shape, in consistence, and in smell. The leaves are alike only in having no stalks, being long, narrow, and closely set, and the fruits in being cones. In this case, then, in which likenesses are seen among things having many and conspicuous differences, the process of thought is undoubtedly a judgment. It will be noticed that while the differences are conspicuous and numerous, the likenesses are widely pervading.

To group together all conifers in one natural order is more characteristically a judgment than to group together two yews as trees of the same species, because the establishment of a likeness amongst conifers is a more novel process than the establishment of a likeness between two yews ; and the process is more novel because the likeness between the several conifers was less conspicuous than that between the two yews, and the differences more marked. So that, as before said, the elevation of the reasoning depends on its novelty, that is on the number and conspicuousness of the differences between the things which are seen to be alike, and the number and conspicuousness of the resemblances between the things which are seen to be different.

To discriminate between a healthy person and a sick person does not require a very powerful effort of reasoning; the unlikeness being manifest, patent, and unmistakable. Among barbarous people there is no discrimination between one illness and another. If a man is ill, he is ill. The degrees and kinds of disability which the illness produces are not distinguished, and the remedy is much the same in all cases. With the increase of experience and knowledge it becomes recognized that there is more than one way of being ill, more than one kind of illness. It is seen that while all cases of illness are alike in that they produce disability, there are some illnesses that produce total disability for exertion, and that in these illnesses the patient's skin is hot and dry, he is thirsty, he rapidly wastes away, and his progress to death or recovery is rapid. This discrimination of fever from other illnesses is a higher effort of reasoning than the discrimination of sick from healthy people, and it is higher because the things perceived to be different are less conspicuously unlike. As time goes on, and the study of disease progresses, it is noticed that in some cases fever is preceded by a wound or injury, while in others there is no such antecedent. Hence the division of fevers into traumatic and idiopathic. Observation of idiopathic fevers shows that some of them are accompanied by the appearance of a rash on the skin, while others are not. This further discrimination of difference between things generally alike is a further advance in knowledge, and is achieved by an effort of reasoning which is of higher character than that required in the previous cases, and is higher because the difference perceived is less conspicuous, and the things perceived to be different have more numerous points of resemblance. The separation of eruptive fevers into small-pox, measles, scarlatina, typhus, &c., is a still further advance of the same process, is a higher effort of reasoning, and owes its estimation as a more elevated process to the same circumstance. Many years after typhus fever has been known and studied some cases of it are found to have a somewhat different appearance, and to run a somewhat different course from others. A long course of observation establishes the fact that under the name of typhus fever have been included two different maladies, having different courses, symptoms, and lesions, and hence arises the division into typhus and typhoid, a still higher example of reasoning power ; and finally, further study has discriminated several varieties of typhoid fever—abortive typhoid, anubulatory typhoid, typhoid with meningitis, and so forth. In each of these cases the advance of knowledge from the simple recognition of the broadest, most conspicuous difference between health and illness to the fine distinctions between different varieties of a highly special malady, has been by discrimination—by the discernment of differences between things at first sight alike—by establishing a new relation (of unlikeness) between things heretofore grouped together as alike. And at each step the display of intelligence—the quality of the reasoning—has been considered superior, according as the similarities between the things seen to be different are numerous, conspicuous, and close.

In practice, the two processes of discerning likenesses and discriminating differences are not carried on separately. It is obvious that in grouping together the coniferæ as having certain qualities of leafage and fruitage in common, we at the same time separate them as a group from the remaining bulk of trees and shrubs. If all plants had these peculiarities, it would not occur to us to separate the few that have been enumerated, and there would be no basis for such separation. At the same time that we group all conifers together because of their underlying likenesses pervading throughout conspicuous differences, we separate them from all other shrubs and trees because of their underlying differences of fruit and leaf prevailing in spite of the conspicuous similarities of height, size, shape, mode of growth, branching, &c.

Similarly, in dividing traumatic from idiopathic fevers, we are aware, not only of the difference between cases of the one and cases of the other, but at the same time we are impressed with the fact that all cases of traumatic fever resemble one another in being preceded by wounds, while all cases of idiopathic fever resemble one another in having no such antecedent. The same rule holds in every case. We cannot discern similarities without at the same time being aware of differences, nor trace differences without noting similarities. The whole process of thought is a rhythm between the two attitudes. Each is complementary of the other. In each the reasoning becomes more refined the more complex the aggregate of things between which the relation of likeness or unlikeness is traced ; and in each the grade of reasoning rises with the novelty of the new relation. It is higher the more numerous, the more conspicuous, the more various are the differences between the things seen to be similar, and it is higher the more close, the more striking, and the more multitudinous the likenesses among things seen to be different.

Although the two processes thus proceed together in perpetual alternation, yet they are not often equally developed in the same person. The power of discerning a fundamental likeness between things superficially different is by no means always proportioned to the power of discerning differences between things superficially alike, and, according as the one or the other preponderates, the cast of the mind differs. If we study the likeness between this plant and that, and by means of likenesses group the plants together into species, genera, orders, families, &c., the process is synthetic. If, on the other hand, we begin with plants as a whole and divide them by discerning their differences, the process is one of analysis.

In practice, as has been seen, the grouping of things and their division naturally proceed simultaneously ; but none the less is it true that the leading characteristic of the synthetic mind is the faculty of discerning fundamental similarities underlying conspicuous differences, while the distinguishing faculty of the analytic mind is that of perceiving fine shades of difference in things generally similar.

It is obvious from what has been said, that the leading trait in the scientific mind is the discernment of differences. To take an instance. The observation of the apparent diurnal movement of the sun round the earth, is the observation of differences of position of the sun with respect to the earth ; and similarly that of the annual movement of the sun among the stars is the observation of smaller differences of position. The next advance of knowledge is the observation that these differences of position are assumed with different velocities ; and the next, that these differences of velocity are accompanied by differences in the apparent size of the sun ; from the likeness of which to similar cases of moving bodies whose distance we can measure, it is concluded that at different times the sun is at different distances from us. Hence the inference of the ellipticity of the apparent movement of the sun, that is, of the earth's orbit. Next it is observed that the variation, or range of difference of the apparent velocity is different from the variation of the distances. Here, then, is observed a difference between differences, and thence we conclude an actual variation in the velocity of the sun's movement. In the same way the observed difference in longitude from time to time of the whole body of stars shows us the precession of the equinoxes, and a still finer difference in longitude and right ascension of the stars, occurring over shorter periods, demonstrates the occurrence of nutation. The whole advance in knowledge is a succession of discriminations of difference, with here and there a tracing of resemblance. The fact that some plants stand upright by their own sturdiness, while others are dependent on extraneous aid for their support, is apparent to the most ordinary observer. A gardener, from closer observation, knows that of the latter class some support themselves by means of tendrils, while others, without that special means of prehension, gain support by twining their stems and branches among trees of more robust growth. Botanists know that of tendrils there are many kinds, some being furnished with suckers to stick to their supporters, others with hooks to cling, while others again depend for a fast hold merely upon their power of twisting on themselves. Again, some tendrils are modified leaves, others are modified stipules, others modified parts of leaves, others modified branches, others modified flower peduncles. In every instance the discovery of the origin of the tendril marked an advance in knowledge and was the observation of a new difference. The one quality before all others which science demands, which is characteristic of all scientific work, and which advances with the advance of science, is *exactness ;* and exactness is nothing but the discrimination and exclusion of small differences. The farmer who weighs his cattle on a weigh-bridge and sells by actual weight is more scientific than he who guesses at their weight by their apppearance ; and he is more scientific because more exact, because the possible error is . less, because the difference between the estimated weight and the actual weight is smaller. From the weigh-bridge, which discriminates only between pounds, to the chemical balance which discriminates between minute fractions of a grain, the advance is continuous, and he is deemed the more scientific who deals with the finest differences. Weighing and measuring are at the root of all science ; and weighing and measuring are but means of discrimination of differences between weights and sizes. No branch of knowledge is entitled to be called a science until means have been devised of measuring its subject-matter, and every advance in the science is an advance in accuracy of measurement. The invention of the thermometer was the foundation of the science of thermology, and every advance in the science has depended on an improvement in thermo-metrics.   Not until means of measuring the volume and intensity of electric currents had been devised, did electricity advance from the position of a toy to be the subject-matter of a science.   The difference between the rude estimates of the ordinary mechanic and the scientific calculations of the engineer, are represented by the difference between the two-foot rule of the one, and the complicated machine by which the other measures differences of one two-millionth of an inch.

While the observation of the facts of science is for the most part a discrimination of differences, the organization of these facts into knowledge is, for the most part, an assimilation of resemblances.   That the difference in velocity of the sun's apparent movement is accompanied by differences in its apparent size, is a fact of observation and a discrimination of differences ; but the inference that the sun moves at different distances from us, is an assimilation of this group of differences to other like groups of phenomena in which the distances have been found to be different ; as, for instance, to the case that when a man's apparent size is great and his rate of movement across the field of vision rapid, he is nearer to us than when his apparent size is less and his speed across the field of vision slower.   Similarly, the description of the various forms, textures, surfaces, and mode of growth of leaves are facts of observation, and are discriminations of difference ; while the recognition of whorls of leaves in the parts of the flower, is an assimilation of resemblances.

Just as the leading feature in the scientific mind is its intellectual keenness, shown by the ability to discriminate differences, so the leading feature in the mind of the poet is not its intellectual power, but the volume, the profundity, the vastness of the feelings by which it is agitated.   Feelings of this character, powerful though they be, are in their nature vague, formless, and indefinite ; and hence poetic writings are rich in power and poor in precision.   What purely intellectual, as distinguished from emotional, power the poet possesses, is antithetical in nature to that of the man of science. It is not the ability to perceive differences between things that are superficially similar, but the ability to perceive resemblances between things apparently unlike. It was Goethe, a poet, it will be remembered, who perceived the similarity of the bones of the skull to the vertebræ, and of the petals of the flower to leaves, and thus cast a new light upon morphology. Here the things between which a resemblance had to be perceived were so widely different that the ordinary scientific mind was unequal to the task, and the poetic faculty was needed for its accomplishment. If we seek to identify the special quality in poetic writing which most widely distinguishes it from prose, it will be found in the abundant use of simile and metaphor—that is to say, in the abundant likenesses that are traced between things superficially and widely different. The poetic fancy is nothing but this faculty of seeing likenesses between widely different things.

It still remains to examine the nature of Will—a knotty problem which has given rise to innumerable and bitter controversies. By Will is meant the feeling that precedes action. To recur to a former illustration, I may think of moving my hand in a certain way, or I may actually so move it. In the former case there is, as we have already seen, a faint excitation or discharge of the same region that in the latter case discharges more strongly. In the former case I think of moving the hand, in the latter I Will to move it, and it moves. It is evident that since the nervous processes differ in nothing but intensity, the mental processes can differ in nothing but intensity, and hence to will a movement is to think very intensely of that movement. Proofs of this proposition are found in the phenomena of muscle-reading. The muscle-reader is able to discover movements thought of by the subject; and he discovers them by holding the hand of the subject—by observing trifling movements or stresses, *i.e.*, tendencies to movement, of hand, arm, and fingers. So that when we think of moving,

which is an incipient form of willing movement, we actually
do excite in incipient form the movements we think of.
Add to the intensity of the nervous process, and the movement, from being incipient, becomes actual ; the mental
accompaniment, from being a thought, becomes a volition.
The volition appears, it is true, not to accompany, but to
precede the movement ; and actually does precede it by a
short time—by the time necessary for the nervous discharge
to travel from the centre of whose activity the volition is
the mental shadow, to the muscles whose activity appears to
be a consequence of the volition.   But the feeling that
immediately precedes a bodily movement is not the only
feeling that we call a volition.   We give the same title to
the process of " making up the mind " to pursue some
prolonged and complicated course of action.   When, for
instance, we finally decide to bring an action at law, we say
we Will do it ; and we recognize the decision as a volition,
although it does not immediately precede action—although,
for instance, we may not write the letter of instructions to
the solicitor for days.   In order to discover the community
of nature between this process and the simpler case of
moving the arm, we must recall the nature of the nervous
processes on which they severally depend.   When I determine or Will to move my arm, what is the nature of the
nervous process ?   We have already seen that it is the discharge of a nervous centre, but we must go behind this and
ask why it is this particular centre that now discharges.   The
answer is that there is impressed upon the organism from
without, in the way already shown, the need for activity ;
and this impression arouses general nascent activity of the
whole nervous system.   The impress is more specific.   It
calls for activity of the arm ; and throughout the whole
region of grey matter in which movements of the arm are
represented, the nascent activity is intensified.   Now, but
one movement of the arm can take place at a time.   Among
these nascent activities, all of which are striving, as it were,
to become actual and to produce movement, there is a

struggle for preponderance ;—a struggle which is evidenced outwardly in the bracing up of the muscles preparatory to exertion. At length, owing to the nature of the impression, and to the direction of paths previously traversed by currents in circumstances somewhat similar, one of these struggling centres gains the preponderance. The fittest survives ; the tension among the bursting centres is relieved by the discharge of one of them ; and thus the nervous accompaniment of volition is not merely a discharge of a single centre, but a discharge which follows a struggle for preponderance, and marks the triumph of one of the conflicting factors. Hence this feeling arises not only when actual movement follows this successful struggle, but arises also in a somewhat modified form when a similar struggle takes place on a higher plane of nervous action, and terminates in the preponderance of one of the struggling activities, without that activity finding immediate expression. In other words, volition or Willing comes to be the feeling which accompanies the termination of a struggle among nascent activities by the preponderance of one, just as Hesitation is the feeling that corresponds with the duration of the struggle.

In connection with the Will, the vexed question of Freewill must be touched upon. If it is asked whether I am free to do this thing, the first question manifestly is, What is this I, that is free or not free ? What, in other words, is the nature of the conscious ego ? We have already seen that consciousness accompanies the activity of nervous processes ; that the newer processes are accompanied by more vivid consciousness, the older by less vivid consciousness, and the oldest by no consciousness at all. The scene of greatest activity among our nervous processes is continually shifting from one centre to another, and from one region to another ; and, correspondingly, our consciousness is continually changing. We have from moment to moment a succession of thoughts and feelings. As the brain becomes modified by use, growing in one direction and perhaps wasting in another ; as new channels are opened, new con-

nections made, new centres erected, in some regions ; while
in other regions disused channels are closing and disused
centres decaying ; so, day by day and year by year, the general
scope and locality of the greatest nervous activity alters,
and so, day by day and year by year, the general consciousness changes, and we find that we no longer feel and think
as we used. New interests are aroused, new pursuits
followed, new thoughts absorb us, while old ones fade and
disappear. Throughout all changes, however, we feel that
something has persisted. Although I have changed, I still
feel that throughout there has been an " I," and the same
" I " has been changing—that there has been throughout a
substratum which has not changed or has changed but little.
A fortiori, throughout the changing consciousness of a day,
through all the succession of different thoughts, feelings,
and volitions, there has been a persistent somewhat that
has thought, felt, and willed. Although the procession of
figures, of pictures, of shadows, across the screen of consciousness has been incessantly changing, the screen has
remained throughout, inconspicuous but essential. If, then,
our conscious personality at any moment is but the sum of
all the states of consciousness, of all the thoughts and feelings,
vivid and faint, that exist at that moment, what are the
states that thus persist ?

The answer to this is as follows. Our consciousness, our
" self-consciousness," our " conscious personality," our " ego"
at any moment is but the sum of all our thoughts and feelings,
vivid and faint, at that moment. But these co-existent states
of consciousness are very numerous and complicated. The
nervous processes, of which they are the mental shadow,
are kept in activity by the continuous arrival of currents
from without, and respond by continuous discharges that
escape outward. Now, when a current arrives from without,
the discharge of the tract that receives it has a mental
accompaniment. And when a current escapes outwards the
discharge of the tract that emits it has a mental accompaniment. Thus are we kept aware of what is acting on us and

of the ways in which we are reacting. But in addition to this continual flux and reflux of currents to and from the outside world, there is, as we have seen, another tide, an internal circulation of energy, which also contributes to the general activity of the nervous centres. Not only through the sense organs do we receive impacts of energy from the outside world, but from every part of our own bodies currents are continually flowing into the central reservoirs of the nervous system ; and from all the nervous regions, from the highest to the lowest, discharges are continually being distributed to every recess, nook, and corner of our own organization.

What is true of the apparatus which keeps us in communication with the outside world is true also of this interior apparatus of energy-distribution. Every wave of energy that arrives from the viscera, the muscles, or any part of the interior of the body, and washes on the shore of the central nervous masses, produces there a discharge, which has, vivid or faint, some mental accompaniment. And every discharge that starts from the great nervous centres to be distributed in the interior of the body has also, vivid or faint, its mental shadow. Hence is consciousness composed not only of feelings and thoughts referring to the outside world, but beneath these there is a vast body of other feelings and other thoughts referring to what is going on in the interior of our own organism. Now, from the nature of things it will appear that since the internal bodily processes are, as a rule, same and continually repeated, the mental accompaniment will, from the laws already investigated, as a rule be faint and inconspicuous. But since the currents arriving from the interior of the body are continuous and same, they will tend to modify continuously, and in the same direction, the other currents arriving from without the body ; and hence on them will depend what we term the " disposition " of the individual. Since the currents thus internally initiated and internally distributed are of enormous volume, their potentiality of altering the other currents will be great ; and when

disordered, their effect will be very important. It is
notorious that although in health we are unconscious of the
action of, for instance, the stomach, yet the way in which
that organ performs its functions makes all the difference to
us of happiness or misery. Lastly, since these currents are
continuous, whatever consciousness they have as their
accompaniment will be continuous, however subdued, however inconspicuous, however eclipsed by the more vivid and
definite consciousness arising from commerce with the outside
world. Moreover, while the definite, vivid consciousnesses
arising from commerce with externals is continually changing,
and changing through a very wide range of variation, that
which arises from the internal circulation is subject normally
to changes which are few, which are slow, and which are
slight, and thus, so far as consciousness can be, it is from
moment to moment unchanging. It is little liable to change.
It is a rhythmical succession of slow and slight changes of a
process which is itself voluminous and vast. Hence the
consciousness, while faint, is continuous and is voluminous.
And it is always present. The feelings of sight disappear
when we shut our eyes. Often we receive no impression
through the ears, the nose, the tongue. But the currents
from within our own body are always arriving. Waking or
sleeping they never cease. According as the impressions
arriving from without are numerous, powerful, and definite,
this sub-consciousness, this cœnæsthesis, subsides yet more into
obscurity and is forgotten ; but when the avenues of sense are
closed, or when we are in darkness and in silence and in inactivity, then emerge into a less obscure twilight these
feelings of what is going on within us, this consciousness of
our bodily operations. Who has not found, when lying
wakeful in the darkness and silence of night, that his heart
beats with, it appears, preternatural vigour ; that in this foot
or that arm there are sensations which must surely portend
disease; that a burning here or a chilliness there are felt with
an intensity which is never experienced in the daytime ?
The changes of these processes, though slight, will still be

sufficient to secure that some consciousness shall attach to their working, and their great volume will secure that whatever feelings attach to their operation, shall be, if not vivid, voluminous and pervading.

The conscious personality, or conscious ego, is, then, the sum of all the states of consciousness at one time existing, of which some—externally initiated— are vivid, definite, for the most part intense, and subject to frequent and sudden changes, while others—internally initiated—are faint, indefinite and voluminous, and change slowly and seldom. Hence it comes to pass that the former series of changes are regarded as imposed upon the latter as figures upon a background ; the latter are looked upon as the permanent, persistent being *of which* the former are changes. When a new feeling is superposed on the existing mass of consciousness, as when I hear a sudden sound, a change takes place in the externally-connected series of consciousness, but there is no corresponding change in the internally-connected series. This internally-connected series, bound up as it is in experience with changes in my body, continuous as it is, and little subject to change, I identify in an especial manner with myself, and I speak of the conspicuous change in the one series, superposed on the unaltered subordinate series, as a change occurring *to me*, when I should say it is a change occurring *in me*—in my consciousness. Similarly, when an outgoing current is discharged from a superior centre and eventuates in a movement, there is a change in the definite conspicuous series of consciousness, with no considerable corresponding change in the more fundamental series, and again the temporary state is superposed on the permanent state which is specially identified with the ego, and I say that "I willed" the movement, that the volition was effected by me, when I should say that it occurred *in me*— in my consciousness. In other words, when a volition is made, there is a change in consciousness. The whole complex group of feelings and thoughts changes and gives way to another group. Of this complexus which thus changes, there are two parts, one subordinate, inconspicuous, voluminous, and pervading, which changes little ; and one prominent, definite, intense, and limited, which changes much. Hence it comes to be considered that the more enduring portion *produces* the change in the more transient ; whereas the fact is that the change is the product of conditions to which both moieties of consciousness are subject. It is the mental shadow of a change of nervous processes, a change brought about in the way already indicated, by impressions arriving from *both* sources, acting upon a specially constituted structure, and liberating energy in special directions.

The totality of consciousness is then made up of two parts— one corresponding with impressions made by, and actions made upon, the outside world; the other corresponding with currents arriving from, and discharges distributed to, the interior of the body itself. The former constitutes our consciousness of the world at large, the latter our consciousness of self. Or, as sometimes expressed, the former is object-consciousness, the latter is subject-consciousness.[1] Another term for this latter moiety of consciousness is the "cœnæsthesis." Whatever it is called, the inferior moiety of consciousness is to us a matter of immense importance, since it is the seat of by far the major portion of our experiences of pleasure and pain.

That what is termed " bodily pain"—that is to say, pain arising from some actual lesion or physical injury to the body—is the mental shadow of a disturbance in the central mass of grey substance, due to intense currents arriving through the nerves from the injured part, does not need demonstration. Apart from acute pains, there are the feelings of illness, of malaise, of langour, of misery, which accompany changes of injurious character that are wider spread and slower in their operation—such changes as inflammations, derangements of function, &c. All such feelings manifestly belong to the cœnæsthesis, and being

---

[1] These terms are, however, used also in a very different sense—the former, to express action of the organism on the environment ; the latter, action of the environment on the organism.

general and unlocalized in character, they stand out distinct from the "pains" proper. In addition to these general feelings accompanying general disorder, there are some which are more specialized according to the part affected. If we exclude the special sense organs, the skin and the muscles and bones, whose nervous afflux and reflux corresponds with changes in the moiety of consciousness with which we are not now dealing, there remain, roughly speaking, but four groups of viscera as sources and receptacles of the nerve currents which correspond with the cœnæsthesis. These are the heart, the lungs, the digestive organs, and the genito-urinary organs ; and a morbid change occurring in either of these groups imparts a special character to the nervous currents proceeding from it, and is attended by a special modification in the cœnæsthesis. Thus, the special alteration of consciousness that attends disease of the heart is a tendency to anxiety—to active terror. When the lungs are diseased it is said that there is a tendency for the cast of mind to become joyous, and it is certain that the apprehension of danger and sense of ill-being are often insignificant in comparison with the gravity of the disease. Affections of the bowels are invariably attended by mental depression, by melancholy and wretchedness more or less acute and profound, and this is the case whether or no the patient recognizes that he suffers from such a disorder. In affections of the genito-urinary apparatus, in addition to the feeling of illness common to all maladies, there is an irritability of temper, and often an hypochondriacal attention to the disease, which is peculiar to disorders of this class.

While, however, it is to nerve currents internally arising and internally distributed that we are indebted for those variations of nervous discharge in the central masses that have all these varieties of pains and miseries for their mental accompaniments, it is to currents of the same class that we owe that condition of nerve pressure which has for its mental side the feeling of well-being that we experience in

robust health and vigour, and which is the foundation, if
not the immediate occasion, of all our feelings of happiness.
All conditions of pain are conditions of low nerve pressure,
and especially in those massive and voluminous and unlocalized forms of pain which we call depression and misery
and unhappiness, the tension in the nerve centres is slack
and feeble. When, however, all the organs are acting
normally, smoothly, and vigorously, then the currents they
transmit to the centre are full and powerful, the return
currents evoked are full and powerful, the reverberation of
these powerful discharges spreads through the whole nervous
system and evokes a heightened tension, and this tension is
sustained and increased by the efficient nutrition provided
to the whole nervous system by a body of viscera working
actively and harmoniously. Our general disposition of mind
to happiness or the reverse depends, then, primarily on the
molecular tension throughout the lesser or visceral circulation
of nervous energy ; overflow of spirits and sense of well-
being being high in proportion as the tension is great, and
vice versâ. The degree of tension depends primarily on the
constitution of the individual nervous system, as vigorous or
the reverse ; secondarily, on the smooth and healthy action
of the viscera, determining incoming and outgoing discharges of normal vigour ; and thirdly, on the efficiency
of the nutrition of the nervous system as effected by
these viscera. These being the foundations in the cœnæsthesis of a sense of well-being, it only remains that the other
portion of consciousness, answering to our commerce with
the outside world, to be free of painful elements, for us to
experience a general feeling of contentment and satisfaction ;
and should there be in this other moiety of consciousness
elements of positive pleasure, our mental condition will rise
from mere contentment to active enjoyment and delight.

That our pleasures depend in some degree upon the
nature of our commerce with the world outside us, as
harmonious and successful or the reverse, needs no demonstration ; nor does the dependence of our happiness on the

healthy state of our viscera and organism generally need insistence. As to the dependence of our sense of well-being upon the degree of tension of the nervous energy, it is evident that if it so depends, then variations in the tension will be accompanied by variations in the feeling of well-being. That such variations do occur, and occur in correspondence, needs but little exposition. Diurnal tides in the nervous energy are familiar to every one but the most vigorous and the least observant. Daily experience shows us that on first waking in the morning we are lethargic, that we have little tendency to move, and less to rise, and that with this lethargic condition, indicative of low nervous tension, there is a certain want of buoyancy in the mind; small difficulties seem great, great difficulties insuperable. In a short time the tide of energy rises, we bounce out of bed, dress, and get to work, and in the early part of the forenoon reach at once our condition of greatest activity of body, and our condition of greatest hopefulness, confidence, and cheerfulness of mind. As night closes in, the bodily energy diminishes ; we are less inclined to exertion, and more to repose, and at the same time the buoyant confidence of the morning diminishes, and we become more cautious, less adventurous. As the hours wear on, the bodily activity becomes less and less ; with fatigue comes, if not actual depression, at least soberness and want of enterprise, and when the small hours of the morning are reached the tide of energy is at its lowest ebb. If we wake between three and four in the morning, how different do our surroundings and prospects seem to what they were at noon ! Difficulties that then were trifling now appear insuperable ; odd sensations that in the turmoil of the day were unperceived, unnoticed, now not only become startlingly prominent, but appear to be alarming forebodings of serious, nay, fatal disease. For us the sun has indeed gone down, and the darkness without and within fills us with " baleful visions of eternal woe, and desolation dire." Presently we fall asleep, the nervous system recuperates, tension is restored, the tide of energy rises, and when we rise in the morning the host of vampires has fled with the night.

With longer periodicity than the diurnal tides, recur times of days or weeks duration when the bodily activity is great, when strenuous exertion is not only pleasurable but an imperious necessity, when pleasures are appreciated with a keener zest, when difficulties are met with determined obstinacy, and reverses fail to produce depression ; and alternating with these periods are times of lethargy and weariness—times when strenuous exertion is a laborious effort, when obstacles dismay and failures dishearten. In each case the general mental state of happiness or depression corresponds with the bodily capability of exertion, and with the general indications of high or low nervous tension. Lastly, the difference between the restless, boisterous activity of youth, with its insensibility to fatigue and its rapid recuperation after exhaustion, and the phlegmatic repose of age, so readily fatigued and so long in recovering, corresponds with the difference between the proverbial hopefulness of the one, which looks forwards on a roseate world, and the equally proverbial placidity of the other, which looks backwards on a world dyed with the grey tint of experience ; and each owes its respective qualities, both bodily and mental, to the condition of the nervous tension, high in the one and low in the other.

CHAPTER III.

THE difficulty of precisely defining the nature of insanity, or of saying precisely what insanity is, has been recognized, not only by every writer on the subject, but by all those who have had to deal practically with the insane, whether medical men, judges, or legislators. A very high legal authority—Lord Justice Blackburn—giving evidence before a select committee of the House of Commons, said—" I have read every definition which I could meet with, and never was satisfied with one of them, and have endeavoured in vain to make one satisfactory to myself. I verily believe that it is not in human power to do it." Very high medical authorities—Dr. Bucknill and Dr. Hack Tuke—in their great work on psychological medicine, say—" We believe it to be impracticable to propose any definition entirely free from objection, which shall comprise every form of mental disorder. Every definition hitherto proposed has failed either to include all the conditions under which insanity exists or to exclude all in which it does not, and the more laboriously the definition is constructed the more decided is usually the failure."[1]

---

[1] As a sample of the proposals that have been made to define insanity, the following, by an American writer, may be instanced : "Insanity is either the inability of the individual to correctly register and reproduce impressions (and conceptions based on these) in sufficient number and intensity to serve as guides to actions in harmony with the individual's age, circumstances, and surroundings, and to limit himself to the registration as subjective realities of impressions transmitted by the peripheral organs of

The most authoritative definitions are of course those which are propounded by the law ; and it is, for scientific purposes, unfortunate that the law lays down three widely-different definitions of what it recognizes as insanity. In criminal cases the legal test of insanity is the knowledge of right and wrong ; that is to say, a criminal is considered to have been sane when he committed his crime if " he then knew the nature and quality of the act, and that it was wrong." So that conversely a person is insane if he does an act whose nature and quality (whatever that may mean) he does not know, or if, knowing the nature and quality of his act, he does not know whether it is right or wrong.

In testamentary cases the requirement of the law is different. Here the nature and quality, the rightness or wrongness of the act, are not considered. A testator is considered to be sane if he is "of sound mind, memory, and understanding ;" and conversely he is insane if his mind, his memory, or his understanding is unsound. In this case the question of the knowledge of the nature and quality, or of the rightness or wrongness of the act, does not arise.

In a third class of cases a third test, different from both of the preceding, is required by the law, and this class is the more important because in it alone is the question of the sanity or insanity of a person *directly* raised. In criminal cases the issue is raised quasi-incidentally, and much evidence bearing on the question is often excluded by the forms of legal procedure. In testamentary cases the issue is the validity of an instrument executed by the person, and the question of his sanity arises again quasi-incidentally. But in an inquisition in lunacy the actual issue placed before the jury is—Is the subject of this inquisition sane or insane ? And

sensation ; or the failure to properly co-ordinate such impressions and to thereon frame logical conclusions and actions : these inabilities and failures being in every instance considered as excluding the ordinary influence of sleep, trance, somnambulism, the common manifestations of general neuroses, such as epilepsy, hysteria, and chorea, of febrile delirium, coma, acute intoxications, intense mental preoccupation, and the ordinary effects of nervous shock and injury."

to the test applied by an inquisition more importance therefore attaches. This test is as follows: *Is the patient incapable of managing himself and his affairs?* It will be
seen that this test is very widely different and of very far
more comprehensive scope than either of the others. In
both the previous cases the jury have to get, as it were,
inside the man's mind, and to guess as best they may at what
was the condition of his consciousness on a certain date.
They have to determine what he then knew, what he
thought, what was the state, and what the validity, of his
memory and his judgment. Now it is obvious that there is
only one person who can possibly know the state of a man's
memory, of his knowledge, and of his judgments—and that
person is the man himself. Whatever we know about the
interior of other people's consciousness, we know only by
inference—by judging from their actions what the condition
of their consciousness is likely to be ; supposing that actions
are in them accompanied by states of consciousness similar
to those which in us accompany like actions of our own.
As a matter of fact, we know by daily experience that like
actions may be preceded and accompanied by very different
states of consciousness ; or, as we say, that similar conduct
may be prompted by very different motives ; so that our
knowledge of the state of other people's consciousness is not
only inferential, but uncertain. In the third class of cases,
however, the subject-matter of the investigation is very
different. In an inquisition in lunacy the jury have to
determine whether the person is capable of managing himself and his affairs ; and this they can do by immediate
inference from observation of whether he *does* manage himself and his affairs capably. In this case there is no question
of getting into a man's mind, and observing the feelings and
thoughts that are passing therein. Here we have only to
look to his *conduct*, which is open to our direct observation.

In propounding this test the law has recognized and supplied an omission which has vitiated and spoilt every
medical definition of insanity that has ever been proposed.

Not only do the laity regard insanity as a disorder of the mind, but all the numerous medical definitions of insanity— and every writer on the subject has proposed at least one— however much they may differ in other respects, agree in this—that they regard insanity solely as a mental disorder. This is the first misconception of which the student of insanity has to rid himself. Insanity is always regarded as a disorder of the mind. It is not so.

Of course, disorder of mind is always present in insanity, and salt is always present in sea-water; but sea-water is a different thing from table-salt, and insanity is a different thing from mental disorder. There are many disorders of the mind which are not insane. Here is a person who, when you show him a red light, has a feeling not of red, but of grey. The agent which should arouse one feeling arouses another. His feelings are disordered. But we do not call him insane, we say he is colour-blind. Here is another person who, on the approach of a migraine, sees in front of him a little ring of colour revolving. Wherever he turns he sees between him and the nearest object this little moving coloured ring. He has a feeling of colour which has no external origin; he perceives an object where no object exists; he has a disorder of feeling and a disorder of perception; his mind is disordered, but he is not insane. A man calls on me with a little bill. I look at it, and see that the amount is 13s. 6d. I count out the money and give it to him, when he surprises me by stating that the amount should be 15s. 6d. I look at the bill, and there, sure enough, the figure which I took to be a 3 is plainly a 5. There can be no doubt about it, I have made a mistake. The figures are plainly written, the light is good, my eyesight is unimpaired. I can only apologize, and in doing so say, "I certainly thought the amount was 13s. 6d." Here, then, was an erroneous perception. The process of perception, which is of course a mental process, was disordered. There was disorder of mind; but there was no insanity. The foregoing instances are very simple; but feeling and thought, when they reach much higher levels, are still susceptible of disorder, without such disorder being necessarily insane. A man comes home from business after a worrying and anxious day, and on sitting down to dinner finds the soup smoked, the fish stale, and the joint tough. After dinner he discovers that a paper which he left on his table in the morning has been mislaid, and this occurrence evokes an outbreak of temper altogether out of proportion to the event. He becomes extremely angry, and this intense feeling of anger is quite out of proportion to the trivial circumstance which aroused it. In other words, the process of feeling is disordered, so that feelings are no longer in proportion to circumstances ; and this disorder of feeling is a disorder of mind, but it is not insanity. That the outbreak of anger is a disorder of mind, and is an approach to insanity, is seen by the old saying, *Ira furor brevis est;* that it is not actual insanity, is of course. A farmer travelling in a new district sees a crop which is new to him flourishing luxuriantly, and finds that it is easy of cultivation and extremely profitable. He goes home and introduces it upon his own land, with the hope of realizing handsome profits, but the result is failure and loss. He has neglected to take into consideration the difference between the two localities in soil, climate, and position, and this neglect to consider important factors in the problem before him was a defect in his process of reasoning. The reasoning, by which he arrived at the conclusion that the crop would be profitable to him, was defective ; the mental process was disordered. But this defect or disorder of mind was not insanity. Clearly, then, disorder of mind, including disorder both of thought and of feeling, both in their lower and higher manifestations, may exist without insanity.

Not only may disorder of mind exist without insanity, but in insanity there is much besides disorder of mind. Suppose that you see a man reading, or walking, or eating his dinner, or doing any act you please, and doing it normally and in the customary manner; that man may be deeply and hopelessly insane, but you, seeing him *act* normally, do not suspect his insanity for a moment. If he reads aloud, and reads the same sentence over and over again in a loud, aggressive tone of voice; or if he skips and dances along the road with his boots off and his coat turned inside out ; or if he tries to feed himself through his ears instead of his mouth ; you recognize at once that he is insane; but you do not form your judgment on the ground of what is passing in his *mind*—of anything that he thinks or feels. It does not occur to you to suspend your judgment until you have investigated the motives which induce him to act in this manner. The fact that he does so is evidence enough. That is to say, you ground your judgment of his insanity not on what he thinks or feels but on what he *does;* not upon inferred disorder of mind, but on perceived disorder of conduct. It has happened that many people have been troubled by hallucinations. Mrs. A——, the lady whose case has become celebrated by the report of Sir David Brewster, frequently saw a spectral cat, and heard unspoken voices, her mind being therefore distinctly disordered ; but since her conduct was in every respect normal, the question of insanity did not arise. It has happened in attacks of *petit mal*, that a man suddenly becomes entirely unconscious ; and while in this unconscious condition will walk for a considerable distance, will climb over stiles, get through gates, avoid passing carts, and even answer when spoken to; and so long as he conducts himself normally, no question of insanity arises in the minds of the bystanders, although his mind is for the time being absolutely annulled. If, however, his conduct should, during this period of unconsciousness, become abnormal—if, for instance, he should, as such patients often do, begin to undress himself in the middle of the road in broad daylight, and on being remonstrated with break out into extreme violence, he would at once be considered insane ; and he would be so considered although his mind were altogether absent, and could scarcely therefore be called disordered.

Even when we avowedly ground our judgment of insanity upon mental disorder—upon, for instance, the existence of a delusion—we really and indeed actually ground it upon conduct ; for only by conduct can mind be known. Suppose the delusion is known to us by the patient's description, and that we learn it by conversation with him, still conversation is but oral conduct. Putting this view aside, however, it is not from mere oral description that we should conclude that a person suffered from an insane delusion. We should not regard its existence as proved until we had the evidence of overt acts. A man might assure us repeatedly and day after day that he was Emperor of China, but if he con- ducted his business successfully, and if his conduct towards his servants, his family, his friends, and all his surroundings, was normal and proper, we should never consider him insane. But if he were to go to town with a yellow silk umbrella, we should begin to look on him with suspicion ; and if he were to send yellow buttons to distinguished strangers as a mark of distinction and favour, we should no longer doubt that he suffered from insane delusion. Here, again, the test of insanity is not mental condition, but conduct.

If we consider the matter in the light of what has been said in the previous chapters, we shall see that it is in fact impossible for mind alone to be disordered. For feelings and thoughts, mental states and mental processes, are but the shadows or accompaniments of nervous states and nervous procesess ; and since no mental change can occur save as the shadow or accompaniment of a nervous change, so à fortiori no mental disorder can occur except as the shadow or accompaniment of a nervous disorder. Whenever, therefore, there is disorder of mind, there must be disorder of nervous processes—of those processes which have a mental accompani- ment—that is to say, of those which are highest. But the highest nervous processses are those which regulate the movements of the body with respect to the circumstances in the outside world—are, in fact, those which actuate conduct. Hence, when these highest nervous processes are disordered, not only must mind be disordered, but conduct must be disordered also. While, therefore, we find from observation, that as a matter of fact disorder of mind is not the only deviation from the normal in insanity, on the other hand we find from the principles already laid down, that mental disorder cannot exist alone, but must always be accompanied by disorder of nervous processes, and disorder of conduct. We have already seen that the essential and necessary factor in insanity is disorder of conduct, and we have seen, too, that in insanity disorder of mind is always present ; and the co-existence of these two disorders implies and necessitates disorder of those highest nervous processes which actuate the one and accompany the other ; so that any expression which indicates the true and full nature of insanity, must be one which will include and sum up these three disorders, and express them in a single proposition.

Movements of the body as a whole have been spoken of as equivalent to conduct, but this equation of terms is only provisional and approximate. A more accurate expression must now be submitted. Conduct may mean—*i.e.*, our affairs may be conducted by—movements very much less than those of the whole body—by a shrug, a smile, a wink ; nay, by the very absence and suppression of movement ; and there are movements of the whole body—such, for instance, as yawns and convulsions—which cannot be considered conduct. We may, indeed, substitute for conduct, as has been done in the earlier part of the book, the phrase "purposive movement," and so far be accurate ; but then will at once arise the question, How purposive ? What is meant by a purposive action and a purpose ?

The answer is this : those actions are considered to be purposive, those movements are considered to belong to conduct, *by which the individual adapts himself to the circumstances which surround him.* Such movements must always concern, if they do not always involve, the entire organism ; and thus differ from movements of parts of the body with reference to one another, and without reference to surrounding circumstances, which belong to the domain of physiology, and do not concern the psychologist. The same movement may, under different circumstances, belong to the one or to the other category. For instance, the closing of the eyelids, which serves to keep the surface of the eye lubricated and clean, is as purely physiological a movement as that of the jaws in mastication, of the gullet in swallowing, or of the stomach in digestion. All these movements are, in a sense, purposive, since each subserves an end, but none are intelligent, and none belong to conduct ; the reason being that each has direct reference to such conditions only as are included entirely within the precincts of the organism itself. None of them is a direct adaptation to surrounding circumstances. But when the eyelids close in answer to the stimulus of a too brilliant light, the affair is a very different one. The movement is now an adaptation to conditions— the existence of a bright light — altogether outside the organism itself ; and now, instead of being a mere vegetative movement, it is an intelligent movement ; instead of being a purely physiological affair, it has come into the region of conduct ; and its consideration belongs to the psychologist. When the lids are lowered to avoid a searching gaze, the case is again a movement in adaptation to circumstances. The circumstances to which the movement is adapted are now of a far more complex character ; instead of merely the existence of a simple luminous body, there is the existence of a being like ourselves, whom we credit with certain knowledge, certain motives, certain abilities to discern our feelings and the state of our mind from our looks, and so forth, and in answer in adaptation to this complex of attributes in the object outside of us, the movement is made. The movement is a direct adaptation to circumstances outside of us, and is therefore an intelligent movement, and a part of conduct.

In the foregoing cases the immediate adjustment of the individual to surroundings of different degrees of complexity has been effected by similar simple movements. It is evident that there are all degrees of complexity in the circumstances outside of us that have to be met and dealt with, and similarly there are all degrees of elaborateness in the acts by which we meet and deal with circumstances ; and the rule is that the complexity of the circumstances dealt with is reflected in the elaborateness of the conduct by which the individual adjusts himself to them. Thus, to step over a fallen trunk that lies across our path is a very simple act, by which we adapt ourselves to a very simple circumstance. To nurse a parliamentary constituency by buying lands and houses, subscribing to local isocieties, clubs and charities, promoting local undertakings, speaking at local meetings, and ingratiating oneself with the local population, is an immensely elaborate series of acts adapted to an immensely complex combination of circumstances. However simple or complicated the circumstances, and however simple or elaborate the acts by which they are dealt with, the same law obtains throughout, viz., every movement that forms a part of conduct, every act that can be considered intelligent, is an adaptation of the organism to surrounding circumstances, or, briefly put, *conduct is the adjustment of the organism to its environment.* Consequently, erroneous conduct is an error in the adjustment of the organism to its environment, and disordered conduct is disorder of this adjustment. If, in stepping over the fallen trunk, I do not lift the foot high enough, but trip and fall, the act is not accurately adjusted to the circumstances. There is failure of the adjustment. And if the candidate for parliament takes a course on some burning question which alienates the suffrages of a large party in the constituency, and thus loses him the election, there is similarly a failure in the accuracy of the adjustment of his acts to his circumstances.

If this be the nature of conduct, then it follows that feeling, which is the motive of conduct, and thought or intelligence, of which conduct is the external expression, must also bear some definite relation to the circumstances in which the organism exists and acts, or, as we say, to its environment. Let us see what these relations are.

When I have a feeling of warmth, I have a certain state of consciousness, or, more accurately, my consciousness includes a certain state. Now this mental state is simultaneous with the action upon me of ethereal waves permeating my environment and beating on my body. As long as the action of the waves on me lasts, the feeling lasts. The feeling corresponds with the action in duration. The greater the amplitude of the waves, and the more intense their action on me, the warmer I feel, the more intense is the feeling. The state of consciousness corresponds with the action in intensity. If the feeling arises from getting into a warm bath, it is of greater volume than if it arises from putting merely a hand or a limb in the water ; and the larger the surface acted on, the greater the mass of the feeling. The state of consciousness corresponds with the action in volume. In duration, in intensity and in volume, in every respect, that is to say, in which they are comparable, the state in the organism corresponds with the action upon it of the agent in the environment. When I have a feeling of anger, this feeling is a state in me which is aroused by the action, actual or incipient, of some external antagonistic agent upon me. Whereas the feeling of warmth corresponded *directly* with the action of the ethereal waves, being simultaneous with the duration of their action, and varying directly with their intensity and volume ; the feeling of anger corresponds only indirectly with the action of the antagonistic agent, for it may arise while that action is impending, before it has become actual, or while it is going on, or after it has ceased. It may arise in correspondence with an action which never actually takes place, but is threatened only. This indirectness of the correspondence of the state in the organism with the action upon it, involves a difference in the rank of the feeling, which is not, as in the previous case, a simple sensation, but an emotion. Although, however, the correspondence is indirect, it is maintained. So long as the action of the agent on me is antagonistic, so long the feeling is one of anger ; but if the action alters and becomes beneficent, the feeling alters and becomes kindly. That is to say, the quality of the feeling corresponds with the quality of the action. Again, if the antagonism is but slight, the feeling is slight; if the one is intense, the other also is intense. The feeling corresponds with the action in intensity. In quality and in amount the state in the organism corresponds with the action upon it of an agent in the environment. When I have a feeling of freedom, this feeling is a state in me which is aroused by the experience of lack of restraint to my own actions. The quality of the feeling (freedom) depends on the quality (unrestrainedness) of my actions. The amount of the feeling depends on the degree to which restraint is lacking. Both in quality and in amount, the feeling corresponds with the action of the organism on the environment. Similarly, every case of feeling is the occurrence of a state in the organism in correspondence with an interacti n between the organism and its environment.

Although, however, feeling always *corresponds* with an interaction, yet it is not always *adjusted* to the interaction with which it corresponds. The feeling of cold, which I now experience, corresponds with a diminution of amplitude of the ethereal waves that are breaking on the surface of my body, and is intense in proportion to the diminution of amplitude. The feeling is adjusted to the action with which it corresponds. But suppose that the feeling of cold attends the shivering fit which marks the invasion of blood-poisoning. So far from the amplitude of the heat-waves that break upon me being diminished, it remains the same, or may actually be increasing. Here, then, an alteration of feeling corresponds with an unaltered action. The feeling is unadjusted to the action with which it corresponds. Again, so long as my feeling of anger corresponds with the relation of antagonism to me on the part of some agent in the world outside, so long it both corresponds and is adjusted. But if the agent which I take to be antagonistic is not antagonistic at all; if I have been misled by appearances and by false reports, to believe in an antagonism which does not exist; then the feeling of anger is no longer adjusted to the action with which it corresponds. Again, my feeling of freedom corresponds with the unrestrainedness of my actions. But suppose that while I have been writing, some lover of mischief has quietly locked the door upon me. The feeling of freedom corresponds with a relation that no longer exists. It corresponds, but is unadjusted. When feeling is erroneous, therefore, there is a lack or a failure of adjustment of states in the organism to the circumstances with which they correspond; and when feeling is disordered there is disorder of the adjustment of the organism to its environment.

The correspondence of thoughts with things is a little more complicated than that of feelings with actions. Thought, we already know, is a relation between feelings, and hence, as each feeling has its corresponding circumstance in the environment, we may expect to find that thought corresponds with a relation between circumstances.

When I perceive that this object before me is a horse, there recurs in consciousness, as has already been fully explained, the relation, previously established, between (this group of presented mental states, of colour, shape, size, movement, &c.), and (this other group of remembered states —the sound "horse" and the remembrance of the many qualities that I have found in experience that horses possess). This relation of proximity or cohesion between the two groups of mental states, is the thought, the internal process, the mental relation. Now what has to be observed is that this internal relation corresponds with an external relation, with a relation of co-existence between the qualities corresponding with these mental states. While the internal relation is (this group of presented states) coheres with (that group of memories), the relation in the environment is (this group of qualities—solidity, colour, shape, size, movement, &c.) co-exists with (that group of qualities—the ability to wear harness, draw carriages, eat corn, &c., and the attachment of the name horse).   To put the matter in a clearer form, the mental relation, the thought alone, is—

Mental state.	*Relation.*	*Mental state.*
(This group of presented states)	coheres with	(That group of memories).

while the state of things that we now have to consider, when we are dealing with mental processes, no longer in their simplicity, but in correspondence with circumstances, is—

Internal relation.		*External relation.*
These mental states cohere with Those mental states. }	corresponds with {	This group of qualities co-exists with That group of qualities.

What is true of percepts is evidently true of memories in general, of which percepts are but a variety ; the difference being that in memories proper both the mental terms are purely represented or revived in thought, while in percepts one term contains presented feelings or sensations.   The general formula for all percepts and memories will be—

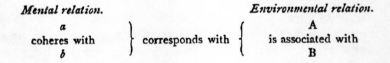

Mental relation.		*Environmental relation.*
a coheres with b }	corresponds with {	A is associated with B

In other words : when one group of mental states coheres with another, so that the occurrence of the one drags the other after it into consciousness, it is because the qualities of something in the outside world which acted on us and aroused the first state, were associated with other qualities, which immediately afterwards acted on us and aroused the second state.   The first state of mind corresponded with the first set of qualities, the second state with the second set ; and the relation of contiguity or cohesion between the two states of mind corresponded with the relation of association, of co-existence, or sequence, between the two sets of qualities.

We have already seen how two nervous processes that have followed one another before, tend to follow one another again ; and how two states of mind that have before followed one another tend to follow one another again ; and we now see that this tendency to follow one another—this cohesion—between the states of mind, corresponds with an association of the qualities of some object which the states of mind reflect.

The case of reasoning is a little different from that of memory. Reasoning, we have seen, consists in observing likenesses and differences. That is the internal process. From the present point of view, reasoning is the establishment of likenesses and differences among mental states, *in correspondence with likenesses and differences between the things that these mental states represent.* For instance, if I reason that the strike of miners is likely to raise the price of coal, the mental process is (those memories of sequences—of former strikes being followed by raised prices) is like (this concept of a sequence—this strike being followed by raised prices). Expanded into terms of correspondence with circumstances, the judgment becomes—

Mental relation.		*Environmental relation.*
These memories of sequences are like This concept of a sequence	corresponds with	Those sequences of events are like This sequence of events.

Here a new relation is established between two groups of mental states, each of them corresponding with groups of circumstances that have not before been thought of together. The bringing together of these mental states is a process of reasoning, and gives rise to a relation of likeness between the mental states, corresponding to the relation of likeness between the circumstances to which the mental states refer.

In every case of thought, therefore, whether of perception, remembrance, or reasoning, there is a correspondence between the internal and the external, between a relation in the organism and a relation in the environment. We have now

to notice that in thought, as in feeling, the internal term
may be adjusted or unadjusted to the external term with which
it corresponds.

This animal, which on a casual glance I perceived to be a
horse, surprises me by the character of its whinny, and on
looking at it again I see that it is not a horse, but a mule.
At the first glance the precepts of form, colour, &c., dragged
into consciousness and cohered with memories of equine
qualities which the mule did not possess. So that the
internal relation of cohesion between presented states and
remembered states, corresponded to an external relation
of *non*-coexistence between the group of qualities presented
and the group inferred. The internal relation was not
adjusted to the external relation with which it corresponded.
Graphically, the state of affairs would be represented thus—

Mental relation.		*Environmental relation.*
This group of presented states	corresponds	This group of qualities
coheres with	with, but is	does *not* coexist with
This group of memories	unadjusted to	This other group of qualities.

It will be observed that as thought is the correspondence of
internal with external relations, so, when thought is erroneous,
it is the internal *relation* alone that fails to correspond with
the external. Each term of the internal relation, considered
separately, not only corresponds with, but is adjusted to, an
environmental circumstance. The group of presented
mental states—the ideas of form, colour, size, distance, &c.,
of an object, are in correct adjusted correspondence with the
actual form, colour, size, and distance of the object. The
memories of equine qualities do correctly represent the
actual qualities that pertain to horses. What is erroneous
is not the occurrence of these mental states in correspondence
with the qualities that they severally refer to, but their
occurrence in that particular *relation* of · cohesion, representing and implying a corresponding *relation* of co-existence,
which does not in fact exist, between the observed object and
equine characteristics.

The case of memory does not need to be separately considered, and we may go on at once to consider how, in the case of reasoning, the internal relation may fail in its adjustment to the circumstances with which it corresponds. If, in reasoning that the strike of miners is likely to result in a rise in the price of coal, I omit to notice that when a rise in prices has followed previous strikes, the masters had conceded an increase of wages to the men ; while in the present case the men had struck against a reduction of wages, to which they had eventually been obliged to submit ; it is obvious that the mental relation is unadjusted to the external relation with which it corresponds ; or, graphically—

Mental relation.		*Environmental relation.*
These memories of sequences are *like* This concept of sequence.	corresponds with, but is unadjusted to	Those sequences of events are *unlike* This sequence of events.

From the foregoing examination of Conduct, Feeling, and Thought, it appears that each of them can be reduced to the common terms of adjustment of the organism to its surroundings. Conduct is the adjustment of the acts of the organism to the circumstances in which it is placed. Feeling is the adjustment of states in the organism to interactions between the organism and its surroundings. Thought is the adjustment of relations in the organism to relations in the surroundings. Each is a phase or a factor or a means in this adjustment ; and hence we arrive at a comprehensive statement of the function of the highest nervous regions, whose outcome is Conduct, and whose concomitants are Feeling and Thought. If we predicate that the function of these highest nerve regions is the adjustment of the organism to its surroundings, we have evidently obtained the expression of which we were in search, which will include and sum up disorders of these highest centres, disorders of Conduct and disorders of Mind in a single comprehensive expression. They are all included and implied in *disorders of the adjust-*

9

ment of the individual to his surroundings, or *of the organism to its environment.*

Although in thus expressing the nature of insanity we have made a great advance upon the views which regard it as a disorder of mind only or of conduct only, yet the expression is not yet perfect, for in its present form it will include the whole category of mistakes, failures, abnormal sensations, erroneous remembrances, and invalid reasonings which we have already illustrated so copiously. Each of these is in its own way a failure—a disorder—of the adjustment of the organism to its environment ; and it therefore becomes necessary to find a limitation of this expression, which shall exclude such failures of the adjustment as are of the nature of mistakes, and are consistent with sanity, and shall include those disorders only which are insane. Such a limitation is not difficult to find.

Here is a locked door, and here is the key which should unlock it. The attempt to unlock the door is made, and fails. What are the possible sources of failure ? The defect may be in the key. It may be broken ; the pipe may be obstructed ; or the wards may be worn away. Or the defect may be in the lock. The tumbler may be broken ; or the lever bent ; or a screw may have got loose and fallen among the works ; or its parts may be glued together by rust. In either case, whether key or lock is in fault, the attempt at unlocking fails. But there is a third source of possible failure. The *process* of unlocking may be at fault. The key may be so inserted in the lock that the peg of the latter, instead of running into the pipe of the key, runs alongside of it. Or the key may not be pushed home, and so fail to turn. Or the lock may be a reversed one, and the key may be turned in the wrong direction. In either case, the attempt to unlock the door will fail ; and it will fail, not because of any defect in key or lock, but because the *process* of unlocking is wrongly conducted.

What is true of this very simple case of the adjustment of one thing to another, is true also of the very complex case of the adjustment of the organism to its environment. The adjustment may fail because the organism is damaged or inefficient ; or because the environment exhibits conditions which the organism is not competent to deal with ; or, which is virtually the same thing, because the environmental conditions are imperfectly known. In either case the adjustment fails from fault of one or other of the things which have to be adjusted. It is either the lock or the key which is at fault. But if the environment presents no conditions but those which the normal organism is capable of coping with ; and if the organism is physically capable, and yet fails to adjust itself to its environment ; then the failure is due, not to the insufficiency or fault of this or that factor in the adjustment, but to disorder of the *process* itself of adjustment ; and this is the disorder which constitutes insanity.

If a man is deaf, and fails to hear the approach of a carriage, which, in consequence of his non-avoidance, knocks him down, there is a failure in the adjustment of acts to circumstances. The failure of the adjustment is due, however, to the fault of the organism. Had he been aware of the approach of the carriage, he would have avoided it, and have shown thereby that the *process* of adjustment was unimpaired. In this case the defect is in the key. Or if he is aware of his danger, but gets knocked down and injured because, being infirm, he does not move quickly enough to get out of the way, there is again a failure of adjustment of acts to circumstances ; but here again the failure is due to fault, not in the process of adjustment, but in one of the factors or terms that have to be adjusted. The efforts that the invalid makes to get out of the way prove clearly that the *process* is intact. It is the organism that is at fault. The defect is again in the key. If, on the other hand, his hearing is normally acute and his movements sufficiently active, but yet he fails to get warning of the approach of the carriage because, for instance, snow is on the ground and silences the sound of its approach, or because some intervening vehicle that he had to avoid

obstructed his view and obscured his warnings of danger,
then, in such cases, it is clear that what is at fault is the
condition of things in the environment, which renders it
impossible for him to make the due and necessary adjustment of acts to ends. The fault is in the lock. But suppose
that none of these defects or obstacles are present, and yet
the adjustment fails. Suppose that the man is of normal
strength and vigour, and his sight and hearing are acute ;
and suppose that the carriage is driving towards him along
a clear and unobstructed road ; suppose that neither factor
in the adjustment, neither organism nor environment, is
defective or at fault ; and suppose that, notwithstanding
these favourable conditions, the man walks in the middle
of the road, gazes vacantly at the approaching carriage, fails
to get out of the way, and gets knocked down and run over.
In such a case the fault is neither in the organism nor in
the environment, neither in key nor lock. What is defective
is the *process* of adjusting the one to the other; and in such
a case the condition is one of insanity.

Or take a somewhat more elaborate case. A merchant
has despatched to him a telegram stating that a fleet, laden
with the commodity in which he deals, has been lost in a
tornado, and that no more supplies of that commodity will
be forthcoming for a year. To adjust himself to this altered
state of circumstances it is evident that he ought to buy
every pound of that commodity that he can lay his hands on.
Suppose he fails to do this. The failure may arise from one
of three causes. The telegram may fail to reach him ; or,
having reached him, it may have been altered in transmission so as to convey the impression that the fleet is not
lost but doubled ; or the intelligence may have reached
others first, and every scrap of the merchandize may have
already been taken off the market. In either case he fails
to buy. His acts are not adjusted to his circumstances ;
there is failure of adjustment ; but the cause of the failure
is in the circumstances. The defect is in the lock, and no
question of insanity arises. On the other hand, the tele-

gram may be properly worded, and may reach him in time, but he has forgotten the cypher, and cannot read it ; or he is stricken with illness and cannot attend to it. In such cases the failure in the adjustment is due to defect in the organism. The fault is in the key, and in such cases the question of insanity does not arise. But if he receives and reads the telegram in its true sense, and if there is plenty of stock on the market, and if he yet goes into the market and sells a bear, then it is manifest that the fault is now neither in the environment nor in the organism, neither in lock nor key, but in the *process* of adjustment of the one to the other; and now it is evident that the act is an insane one.

What is true of the adjustment of the acts of the organism to circumstances in the environment is true also of the adjustment of states in the organism to interactions between it and the environment ; it is disorder of the *process* of adjustment that constitutes insanity. Suppose that a man shouts to attract my attention, and I fail to hear him because I am deaf ; in such a case there is action of an agent upon the organism without the occurrence of a corresponding feeling. There is a failure of adjustment of the organism to the environment, and the cause of the failure is defect in the organism. The key is at fault. But if from the state of the atmosphere his voice fails to reach me, although he is pretty near and shouts loudly, then again there is failure, and the failure is due to defect in the environment. The lock is at fault. But if he shouts a friendly greeting and I hear words of objurgation and abuse, then the defect is neither in organism nor environment, but in the process of adjusting the state in the one to the action of the other, and then the defect is an insane one.

Or suppose that I have a feeling of anger. There are four possible conditions under which such a feeling may arise. The anger may be aroused by the antagonistic action of some person towards me ; and if the amount of feeling is duly proportioned to the degree of antagonism, the con-

dition of things is perfectly normal. But suppose it is not
normal. Suppose that the feeling of anger is aroused by
a relation or attitude, which is not antagonistic, of some
person towards me. Then, as before, there are three al-
ternatives. Although the action of the person towards me
be not antagonistic, yet I may have been brought by mis-
leading appearances and false reports to believe that it is
so. The impression coming upon me from my surroundings
is such as would be produced by antagonism in the agent,
and hence arises the corresponding feeling ; the cause of
the non-adjustment of the feeling to the action being therefore in the environment. The lock is out of order. Or the
action may not have been antagonistic, but friendly, as,
for instance, if a man's housemaid tidies up his papers
in his absence ; but if he has been harassed in business,
if he has had an unsavoury dinner, and if, above all,
he is suffering from dyspepsia, the action may provoke an
outburst of anger quite out of proportion to—unadjusted
to—the circumstances. In such a case the disproportion
of the feeling to the circumstances is owing to defect in the
organism. The individual is abnormally irritable, and
undue emotion is provoked by a trifling offence. But in
such a case what happens ? The next morning, after a good
night's rest and a good breakfast, the anger has disappeared.
The man recognizes that it was in excess of the occasion ;
he laughs it off, and withdraws the notice of dismissal that
he had given to his servant the night before. In other
words, *the feeling is readjusted to the circumstances*, and
this very readjustment shows that the *process* of adjusting
must be unaffected. In neither of these cases, in which
the environment alone, or the organism alone, is affected,
does the question of insanity arise. But suppose that the
next morning the feeling is not readjusted to the circumstances. Suppose that the anger is as hot as ever, and that
the sentence of dismissal is confirmed. Suppose that the
servant is not only sent away, but sent away without a
character, and that she is followed to her home by abusive

letters. Clearly in such a case we should say that the man was mad, and we should say so because, not only was his feeling of anger disproportionate—unadjusted—to the circumstances in which it occurred, but it was *incapable of readjustment.* It did not cool down with time and reflection. And this incapability of readjustment proves that the *process* of adjusting feelings to circumstances was disordered.

The same test as applies to conduct and to feeling determines the sanity or insanity of thought. When I think that the bill shown to me amounts to 13s. 6d. instead of 15s. 6d., the error, as in the previous cases, may have one of three sources. It may be that my sight is defective, so that I cannot distinguish the difference between the figures ; or it may be that the glance I gave was too cursory to give me a clear view ; in which cases the defect is due to the organism. Or it may be that the figures are indistinctly written, and the 5 is made so like a 3 as to mislead ; in which case the environment is at fault. Or it may be that neither organism nor environment is defective, but that the process of perception is wrongly conducted. In the latter case the test of insanity is the possibility of rectifying the error. If my sight is good, and the figures are clearly written, and yet upon attentive examination I still maintain that the amount is 13s. 6d., then there is only one explanation—I am suffering under an illusion. The process of adjusting internal relations to external relations is disordered, and the illusion is outside the pale of sanity.

As with perception, so with memory. If I remember the name of this flower as coriopsis when, as a matter of fact, its name is calliopsis, the error may have one of three sources. It may be that my hearing is defective and I did not catch the name as it was pronounced, in which case the organism is at fault ; or it may be that the gardener was uncertain in his pronunciation, and laying emphasis on the last two syllables slurred over the first so as to mislead me, in which case the environment is at fault. Or it may be that I heard and understood distinctly at the time that the name was calliopsis, but that now the name is revived differently as coriopsis, in which case there is a failure in the adjustment of the internal relation to the external relation. But if, on referring to my authority and being corrected, I accept the right name, the faulty relation is readjusted, thus showing that the *process* of adjustment is intact. While if, on the other hand, in spite of the assurances of the gardener and the bystanders, I maintain that the name given to me was coriopsis, I must be suffering under a delusion.

In the case of reasoning the same law obtains. If I maintain that the strike of miners must be followed by a rise in price of coal, the circumstances of the strike being similar in all respects to the circumstances of previous strikes which have been followed by enhanced prices, the process is normal, and if a rise in prices actually ensues, it affords proof that the relation between ideas was properly adjusted to the relation between circumstances. But if I reason that the strike will be followed by an advance in prices when, as a matter of fact, it is followed by a fall, there are, as in each of the other cases, three possible sources of error. The defect may be in the organism. I may have omitted to note that the strike has failed, and that the men have gone in again at the old rates ; but if this omission is brought under my notice, and I rectify the error and so alter the internal relation as to bring it into adjustment with external —if, that is to say, I predict, on getting possession of this new datum, that there will be no rise in prices—then the process of adjustment is normally affected, and so establishes its own validity. Or the defect may be in the environment. The newspaper report may affirm that the masters have given way to the men, when, as a matter of fact, the men have given way to the masters. When, however, the real state of the case becomes known, the readjustment is made, the prediction altered, and again the process of making the adjustment is seen to be intact. But suppose that the strike has been against a reduction of wages, and suppose that it has failed, and the men have had to submit to the reduction ;

and suppose that there is no counterbalancing circumstance giving an upward tendency to prices. If now, knowing all this, I still maintain that, since other strikes were followed by enhanced prices, this strike must result in a similar rise, it is manifest that the limits of the normal are exceeded. Even when in possession of the necessary data I am unable to make the correction necessary to bring the internal relation between ideas into adjustment with the external relation between circumstances. It is the *process* of making this adjustment which is disordered, and the defect is now an insane one.

Whatever form or phase we take of the adjustment of the organism to its environment, we find that still the same rule prevails. So long as a failure in the adjustment is due to defect in the organism or in the environment, so long it amounts merely to a mistake ; but if the failure is due to defect in the process of adjustment, then it amounts to insanity; and this is true whether the disorder is of conduct, of the simpler forms of feeling known as sensation, of the more complex forms of feeling known as emotion, or of any of the three forms of thought—perception, memory, or reasoning.

If this be the true doctrine of the nature of insanity, then it has certain consequences and corollaries which have to be considered.

Before we can tell whether the process of adjustment is disordered, we must first discover whether, as a fact, the adjustment is defective. If it be defective, we have then to determine whether the defect is in the organism, the environment, or the process of adjustment of the one to the other. But the first question to determine is, Is there defect in the adjustment of this individual to his surroundings ? If we find a defect we may then go on to discover the source of it.

To decide whether a plug is suited to fit a hole we must notice the size and shape and material of the plug, and the size and shape and material of the hole also. A round plug will not fit a square hole ; a brass plug, of however excellent workmanship, would not suitably fill up a hole in a silk dress ; nor would a plug of salt be suitable to stop up a hole in a cistern. So, too, in deciding whether a man is suited to a certain position we have to consider not only the qualities of the man, but the requirements of the position, and only when both have been considered can we say whether or no the one is suited to the other. In the same way we cannot determine whether or no there is any defect in the adjustment of a person to his surroundings, until we have examined not only the person himself, but his surroundings also. Feelings, thoughts, and conduct, that are very unsuitable to one set of surroundings, may be perfectly in accordance with the fitness of another set ; and that may be sanity in one set of circumstances which in another would be insanity. A few instances will make the matter clearer. Suppose that a man sits still all day and shouts incessantly at the top of his voice. Under ordinary circumstances such conduct would be insane ; but if the man has fallen into a pit and broken his leg, such conduct would be the best method of attracting attention and leading to his rescue ; it would be the normal and proper means of adapting himself to his circumstances. Or take the case of a man who jumps out of a second-floor window into the street beneath ; such an act is, under ordinary circumstances, unquestionably insane. But if the house is in flames behind him, and the firemen below are holding a sheet to catch him, the act gives him the best chance of preserving his life. It is the normal and proper means of adjusting himself to his circumstances, and so is sane conduct. A man who is unable to count above five, who walks about naked, *coram populo*, adorning his person only with feathers and tawdry ornaments, would ordinarily be called insane ; but if he has a black skin, and lives on the banks of the Congo, he is considered an average specimen of normal humanity. These are extreme cases, but the necessity of taking account of a man's surroundings before pronouncing him insane is equally imperative in every case that comes before us. In corroboration of this view, which I advanced in the *Journal of Mental Science* some years ago, Dr. Wilks, upon seeing the article, recorded the following cases :—

" A gentleman, holding a good position in a Government office, broke down in health, and his medical man sought the advice of two or three physicians as to the line of treatment which should be pursued. The consultants were informed by his attendant that, according to the patient's own view of his case, it was not so much office work as domestic anxiety and worry which had crushed him ; for he had long suspected the unfaithfulness of his wife, and had even seen gentlemen in his house. This statement his medical attendant regarded as a sad exposition of the patient's mental condition, and in consequence looked on him as bordering on insanity. This view the consultants accepted, as they were informed that all the gentleman's suspicions were groundless. He was sent away into the country and was ordered to be rigidly watched. He did not live long, and after his death it came out most unmistakably that his wife had been unfaithful to him, and that gentlemen had been admitted even into her husband's house."

" In a case which some time ago came before a legal tribunal, in which there was reasonable question of insanity, one witness in favour of insanity candidly told me that he at once assented to the proposition when he was a witness of the unusual circumstances in which the patient was placed, which were these :—He was a gentleman of good position and fortune, lodging in an obscure part of London, unknown to his family, his only acquaintance being those belonging to the house in which he lived. The whole procedure was so unnatural and unusual that, when his children discovered him, there was no difficulty in getting him pronounced insane. A friend of the gentleman, however, who knew him well, was most indignant at the imputation, and afforded an explanation of his conduct by saying that his wife was dead, his daughter had run away, and his two sons were so impoverishing him by calls upon his purse, that he had no other resource than to escape and hide himself, in order to avoid these importunities.''

"Another case was that of a gentleman who was pronounced insane by myself and four other medical men. The patient was living in the suburbs of London, and had long been known to me by name and by sight. He lived in a detached house, with a large garden, having carriages and servants and all the appurtenances of a well-to-do man. He was reported as being very rich. I was asked one day to visit him professionally. I met two medical men, general practitioners in the neighbourhood, who informed me that for some weeks he had taken to his bed, refused food, had grown very thin, had sleepless nights, and declared that he should not live until Christmas. My visit was in the autumn. He had fallen, they said, into a state of melancholy, and was suffering from fearful delusions; he was constantly talking of his wickedness, of the dreadful future which awaited him hereafter, should he by any possibility escape a felon's doom in this world. He was constantly asking if the police had arrived to lodge him in gaol. I then went upstairs to see him, and after condoling with him and expressing my regret to see him in this unhappy state of mind, suggested what could be done to turn his thoughts into a happier channel. He answered that it was of no use talking to him, that he should not live long, that he never knew when morning broke whether before night he would not be in prison. In this way he continued to talk, reasoning was of no avail, and so I left him. Two other physicians had pronounced the case to be one of melancholia. We inquired carefully of his wife as to any circumstances which might have thrown him into this distressing state of mind, but could hear of none. A few weeks afterwards a relative of his called upon and informed me that the patient had been trustee for some orphans, that he had for many years been appropriating the funds to himself, and that when the time arrived when he knew that the crash must come, he broke down, being perfectly unable to meet the shock, took to his bed, and fell into a state of despair. He had been guilty of gross frauds, and every word he said about his own wickedness was correct, and it was only too true that at any moment the police might have entered his house and carried him off to gaol, where he would have spent his remaining years in infamy. To save this disgrace an arrangement was made to refund the purloined money as far as possible, and when this was settled he left his bed, and lived nearly three years afterwards."

The second corollary that follows from the doctrine that insanity is a disorder of the process of adjustment of the organism to the environment, is this, that where there is a failure in the adjustment the test of sanity is the *corrigibility* of the defect. If the process of adjustment is not disordered the want of adjustment will be recognized, and attempts at readjustment made, and if neither organism nor environment be at fault the readjustment will be effected, and the organism again be brought into harmony with its circumstances ; but if the *process* be disordered, the lack of adjustment will not be recognized, and then no attempt at readjustment is made, or if made is unsuccessful. The truth of this proposition has already been incidentally illustrated in the previous pages, but its importance demands some further notice. A feeling of anger is, as has been said, the normal state that arises in the organism upon cognizance of an antagonistic agent in the environment. Suppose, for instance, that an Irish land-agent, after a scene with some of his tenants, has stones thrown into his window, and sees the defaulting tenant outside. He experiences a feeling of anger, which is the natural and normal result of the action. In the evening, as he is sitting writing, he again hears stone after stone thrown against his window, and the feeling of anger revives and is intensified. Examination is made, however, and it is found that the noise attributed to the striking of stones against the window is really due to the knocking against it of the branch of a tree swayed by the wind. Now to bring the organism into adjustment with the circumstances the feeling of anger against the tenant should disappear. If it does so, well and good. But suppose that it does not, suppose that it remains at height in spite of this discovery, then the feeling—the state in the organism—is unadjusted to the circumstances. If, however, upon second thoughts, and on the remonstrance of friends, the man can be made to see that his anger is unreasonable, and to suppress it, the failure in adjustment is corrected, the process of adjustment, at first lacking, is re-established, and the question of sanity does not arise. But if, in spite of clearest demonstration, he retains his anger against the tenant because of the tapping of the branch of the tree against the window, the matter has clearly gone beyond the domain of sanity.

Again,, if a woman, as in the case of Mrs. A——, sees a spectral cat, and recognizes that the appearance has no corresponding substance in the environment, although perception is disordered, insomuch that she sees a cat where no cat exists, yet the fact that she can *correct* this perception by appeal to experience, and so bring her inner conviction that there is no cat, into adjustment to the outer circumstance that no cat is there, proves that the process of producing adjustment is unaffected, and establishes her sanity. If, however, she actually believes that the spectral cat is real, and cannot be convinced by tactual experience that no cat is there, the inability to *correct* the hallucination proves her to be insane.

If a man of wealth and substance takes it into his head that he is miserably poor, that he has no right to his splendid house and fine equipages, and that his inevitable destination is the workhouse, his friends will probably try to convince him of his error by affording him proofs of the prosperity of his affairs. They will take him to his bank and get the manager to certify to his balance there. He will reply that however great his balance, it is nothing to his liabilities. They will enumerate his investments and point out their stability and remunerativeness. To no purpose ; he replies that they are but a drop in the ocean of his responsibilities. They take him to his counting-house, get an accountant to examine his books and certify to his complete solvency and sound position. Again to no purpose. The actuary is incompetent ; the books are falsified ; accountant, friends, partners and clerks are in a conspiracy to deceive and befool him. Since the *process* of adjustment of himself to his surroundings is disordered, he cannot *correct* his false opinions, and the incorrigibility of his opinions constitutes them delusions.

Hence we see the futility of attempting to argue an insane person out of his delusions. If they were removable by argument they would not be delusions. It is because the process of correcting opinions, and bringing them into accordance with circumstances, is disordered, that he holds the delusions ; and so long as this process is disordered, it matters not how clearly the circumstances may be presented, the adjustment is still impossible. If the lack or failure of adjustment were due to the want of definiteness of the circumstances, if, in short, it were the environmental factor in the adjustment that were at fault, then the case would be different ; then the clarifying and defining of this term would restore the adjustment to the normal ; but since the defect is in the *process*, no improvement in the terms is any help. It is no use oiling the lock if the key is still turned the wrong way.

It is the same with conduct. Insane conduct cannot be corrected. Here is a patient who is possessed by a puck-like spirit of mischief. He cannot refrain from burning, breaking, destroying or throwing away everything that he can get into his possession. The one thing that he is passion-ately fond of is smoking. Yet he will smash a new pipe into fragments, well knowing that he thereby deprives himself for several days of his favourite pursuit. He is vain of his appearance, and was delighted at being given a new umbrella ; but on his way home he dropped behind to throw it over a hedge without being seen. No amount of punishment that might be inflicted on him would correct these habits, and their incorrigibility constitutes their insanity. Understand, it is not said that the habits cannot be *cured*. Cure the insanity and you do away with the conduct. But so long as the insanity exists, so long no motive that can be held out to him will induce him to abandon the conduct. Here, again, is a man of boundless wealth and generous disposition, who cannot dine at a friend's house without stealing the spoons. The value of the spoons is nothing to him. The disgrace of discovery would overwhelm him and his family with shame and consternation. A man of acute intellect and sound judgment, no one could appreciate more fully than he the consequences of his conduct ; yet he cannot correct it.

It is not said that the conduct of the insane cannot be influenced by the ordinary motives of reward and punishment which influence and regulate the conduct of the sane. Unquestionably it can. But the conduct of the insane is not necessarily insane conduct. Most insane persons have a large sphere of conduct in which they are comparatively, perhaps absolutely, sane ; and this portion of their conduct is regulated in the same way as that of sane people. Only the insane portion of their conduct is incorrigible ; and so long and so far as they are insane, the incorrigibility of this portion of their conduct is absolute. In one ward of an asylum of which I had charge there used to occur a number of unaccountable black eyes. The attendants were frequently cautioned, and frequently changed, and yet the black eyes occurred, and were usually found on those patients who were too feeble to protect themselves and too demented to give an account of how they received them. At length among the admissions was a little quiet under-sized Irishman, who was placed in this ward, and the next day a patient, G. S., who had been zealous in endeavouring to discover the source of the black eyes, received from the new admission a tremendous thrashing. His explanation was that the attack was unprovoked, but the Irishman asserted that G. S. had hit him in the eye, and he, being an ex-pugilist and a former light-weight champion, had promptly retaliated. The result was, that from that day no more black eyes appeared in that ward. There was no doubt that the source of them was G. S., and the fact that they ceased after he had been punished proved that, in this respect, his conduct was not insane, but was merely the gratification of the bullying and savage instincts of a low and brutal nature. No amount of punishment would alter the really insane portion of his conduct.

In this distinction between sane and insane conduct, as apart from the sanity or insanity of the actor, we have evidently the key to the employment of punishment in the discipline of asylums. There are some who say, and say with justice, that it is as cruel and unreasonable to punish a lunatic as to punish a person for his dreams. On the other hand, those who have practical experience of the insane, know that in maintaining discipline among them punishment is frequently employed, and is frequently effectual. The discrepancy is reconciled when we remember that the conduct of insane persons is not all insane. It may be that only the highest and most elaborate and most difficult of the adjustments to surroundings are disordered, while all adjustments of inferior rank are normally carried out, and the process of effecting them intact. In such a case punishment would be effectual in restraining conduct in all its lower divisions, while its higher manifestations would be totally uninfluenced. These cases, in which only the very topmost strata of nervous arrangements are touched by disorder, are just those which produce the greatest bewilderment in the minds of the laity, who hold on the one hand that it is wrong to detain such cases in asylums, and on the other that they are cases in which punishment is imperatively called for. It is easy to understand that in insanity, that is with disorder of the highest nervous arrangements, the very lowest nervous arrangements may be unaffected, and that, for instance, the movements of the

heart and those of breathing may be perfectly well performed ; that the middle layers of nervous arrangements
may be healthy, that the limbs may be unparalyzed and the
movements of walking and of handicraft normally and
efficiently performed ; all this is readily recognized and
admitted. But it is by no means so easy to grasp the fact
that all the subsidiary nervous functions up to those immediately beneath the very highest may be normally and
well performed, while the highest arrangements of all are
completely out of gear and inefficient. An insane person
may not only be in vigorous physical health, may not only
have his purely vegetative functions, worked by the lowest
nervous arrangements, in good order ; may not only be an
efficient artizan, a skilful billiard or cricket player, that is,
may not only have his middle nervous arrangements working
efficiently ; but he may be an amusing and intelligent companion, be able to conduct himself well in society, may be
able to transact business, and to perform passably well the
elevated mental operations required in the exercise of an
intellectual profession ; but for all that, his highest processes
of all may be disordered, and he may, in a limited but complicated sphere of action, be insane. He may be able to
conduct successfully the erection of a church, but yet be
unable to conduct himself towards his wife and family as a
sane man. Such cases are a perennial source of wonder to
the laity, but it is evident upon reflection that it is not
more wonderful that there may be disorder of the highest
nervous arrangements without disorder of those *immediately*
below them, than that it may exist without disorder of
those *considerably* below them.

Out of the observation that the disorder in insanity may
be limited to a thin stratum at the top of the nervous
arrangements, and therefore to a small but elevated part of
the whole sphere of conduct, has arisen a common and silly
saying that all people are insane on some point. The argument seems to be that since in some cases of insanity the disorder is limited to but a small portion of conduct, feeling, and

thought, therefore in every person there is some small portion which is disordered : an argument which, when stated in plain terms, is seen to be an absurd *non sequitur*. The facts that every one makes mistakes, that every one fails sometimes in effecting perfect adjustment of himself to his circumstances in the general domains of thought, feeling, and conduct, either from carelessness, or from defect in organism, or from difficulty in circumstances, has nothing to do with the question. It is as absurd to say that every one is insane " on some point " as to say that every one's digestion is disordered on some point. No doubt there are for every man circumstances to which he cannot adjust himself, just as there are for every man things which he cannot digest ; but the fact that he cannot adjust himself to his circumstances is of itself no more a proof of insanity than the fact that he cannot digest tenpenny nails is of itself a proof of disordered digestion. Such a saying is like that of Fabatus, who held that seafaring men are all mad. " The ship is mad, for it never stands still ; the mariners are mad to expose themselves to such imminent dangers ; the waters are raging mad, in perpetual motion ; the winds are as mad as the rest—they know not whence they come nor whither they go ; and those are maddest of all that go to sea ; for one fool at home they find forty abroad." " He was a madman that said it, and thou peradventure as mad to read it."

Nevertheless, in this, as in most sayings that have obtained a wide prevalence, there is a glimmering of truth ; and the truth which it seeks to express is, not that every one is insane " on some point "—by which I presume is meant to some extent—but that every one is insane *at some time.* This last proposition, if not absolutely true, is very nearly so. There are times in the lives of all of us when thoughts are experienced, when feelings are felt, when acts are done, that can only be accounted for as due to temporary derangement. On some of these occasions we are not aware of any special cause for the disorder of the highest nervous centres which we experience ; on others the cause is apparent and the

existence of the disorder unquestionable.   Such occasions
are those of intoxication with alcohol, ether, chloroform,
opium, and other drugs ; such are the occurrence of delirium
in fevers and other forms of blood-poisoning, in starvation,
in hæmorrhage, &c. ; such are the disorders, often trivial,
sometimes grave, of conduct and mind which occur in great
fatigue, after prolonged sleeplessness, &c.   Few persons live
to maturity without the occurrence of some one or other of
these occasions in the course of their lives, and consequently
of few persons can it be said that throughout the whole of
their lives they were perfectly sane ; but as stated thus, the
proposition that every one has his insane moments becomes
at once intelligible and probable, which cannot be said of
the proposition for which it has been substituted.

There is yet another corollary that may be drawn from
the doctrine of the nature of insanity as here stated.   If
insanity be a disorder of the process of adjustment of the
organism to its environment, or of self to surroundings, and
if this disorder may be limited to a thin stratum at the top
of the nervous arrangements, then it follows that although a
person may be insane so long as he is in surroundings of
such complexity as to demand the use of his highest faculties—
that is, of those which are disordered—yet, if he be placed in
an environment of simpler character, in which no call is
made for the exercise of his highest faculties, but all the
requirements of his simpler surroundings can be met by the
exercise of his less elevated faculties, to which the disorder
has not extended, then to that simpler environment he is
able to adjust himself, and in those simpler surroundings he
is virtually not insane.   To a stranger going for the first
time through a large lunatic asylum, the most astonishing
circumstance is the apparent sanity of a large proportion of
its inmates.   And the sanity is in many cases more than
apparent ; it is real, so long as the individual is retained in
those simple surroundings.   Having proved himself unable
to perform the necessary adjustments required by the larger
surroundings of the outside world, he is here provided with

a set of surroundings to which little effort on his part is needed to adjust himself, for they are already artificially *adjusted to him.*

The burden and stress of earning his living, temptation to drink, opportunities for immorality, incitements to theft, provocations to rage, he is here carefully shielded from, and no call being made upon his highest faculties, which alone are disordered, no insanity shows itself. No opportunity being given him to further extend the deteriorative process by drink and other means, it remains at its high level, and the lower and simpler processes, which alone he now needs, remain intact. But send this tranquil, orderly, sedate individual out into the world again, and in a fortnight he will come back to the asylum, a raving maniac.

So far we have arrived at two definite conclusions with regard to the nature of insanity:—1. That it is a disorder of the adjustment of self to surroundings; and—2. That the seat of the physical disorder is in the highest nerve arrangements, whose function it is to effect this adjustment. It will be remembered that the circulation of energy in the nervous system has been described as twofold ; that there is a minor circulation of energy to and fro between the brain and the viscera, and a major circulation to and fro from the sense-organs to the brain, and from the brain back to the muscles. Furthermore, it has been shown that the central or cerebral portion of the one circulation has for its mental accompaniment the consciousness of self, and that the central portion of the other has for its mental accompaniment the consciousness of surroundings. Hence it will appear that in the highest nervous arrangements, in the supreme strata of the nervous system, in which self is brought into relation with surroundings, factors of both these circulations are present. There the most highly elaborated streams of energy, proceeding from the visceral and nutritive processes, are received, and the most highly elaborated discharges for the regulation of these processes are initiated. There, too, are received the currents from eye, ear, nose, tongue, palate, and skin ;

and there are originated the currents to the muscles by which movements are made in adaptation to impressions from without. But these two sets of processes must not be regarded as carried on separately. The function of the highest nerve-regions we have seen to be the adjustment of self to surroundings. In them, therefore, not only are represented the actions of surroundings and the reactions upon surroundings, but self also is represented, and is brought into relation with these actions and reactions.

When there is disorder of these highest nervous arrangements, there is disorder of the central portion of the *major* circulation of nerve energy. The impressions received from the eye, ear, &c., are received and responded to by muscular movements, but they are wrongly received or wrongly responded to, or both. There is disorder of the adjustment of one to the other. Similarly, when these highest arrangements are disordered, there is disorder also of the central portion of the *minor* circulation of nerve energy. The impressions arriving from the viscera, and from the nutritive processes at large, are received and are responded to by the emission of regulating streams of energy, but they are wrongly received, or wrongly responded to, or both. Hence it happens that, whenever the highest nervous arrangements are disordered, not only is there disorder of conduct and disorder of that part of consciousness which corresponds with conduct, but there is also disorder of the visceral and nutritive processes throughout the body, and there is disorder of the other moiety of consciousness—the consciousness of self—which is the mental reflection of these processes.

In every case of insanity the nutrition of the whole body is disordered ; it may be that the disorder is but slight and inconspicuous, but disorder more or less there always is. Since any disorder in the nutrition of the internal parts of the body would not be directly observable, and, moreover, would not always be of sufficient magnitude to affect function conspicuously, and so enable us to estimate it, it is to the exterior of the body—to the skin and its appendages—that we usually have to look for evidence of nutritive disorder in insanity ; and here it is usually conspicuous enough to be discovered. There is, as might be expected, a parallelism between the insanity and the disorder of the skin. In mild and slight cases of insanity the disorder is inconspicuous ; in chronic and severe cases it is usually very marked. The skin is dry and harsh, the hair staring and refractory, the nails ridged and furrowed ; or the skin is unduly moist and sweaty, the epidermis is shed abundantly, the odour is often strong and extremely offensive. The colour of the skin is often altered, and becomes dusky and earthy. The alteration of hair and nails is often extreme and peculiar. I have known the nails on both fingers and toes to be actually shed after an attack of acute mania ; and the harsh, bristling, erect condition of the hair often causes it to assume extraordinary positions, and to impart a weird and impressive character to the face. Eminent alienists—Dr. Hack Tuke, and Sir James Crichton Browne—have remarked alternations of the state, and even of the colour, of the hair, corresponding to alternations in the mental condition. These alterations in the colour of the hair and skin in insanity may usefully be compared with the alterations that take place in violent emotions ; the cause—a disturbance in the highest nervous centres—being the same in both. In the latter class of cases the disturbance, though transitory, is usually more sudden and intense, and hence the changes that it produces are more conspicuous. The familiar observation of the hair turning grey in grief and in great anxiety is a case in point. Doubts are sometimes expressed as to the accuracy of this observation, but there are cases on record which place it beyond a doubt. Numerous cases have been recorded of the hair turning grey in a single night, but the following, related by Staff-Surgeon D. P. Parry, is even more remarkable. "On February 19, 1858, a prisoner in the S. of Oude was brought before the authorities for examination. Divested of his uniform, and stripped completely naked, he was surrounded by soldiers, and then first apparently became alive to the dangers of his position. He trembled violently, intense horror and despair were depicted on his countenance, and, although he answered the questions addressed to him, he seemed almost stupefied with fear ; while actually under observation, within the space of half-an-hour, his hair became grey on every portion of his head, it having been, when first seen by us, the glossy jet black of the Bengalee, aged about 24. The attention of the bystanders was first attracted by the sergeant, whose prisoner he was, exclaiming, ' He is turning grey ! ' and I, with several persons, watched the process. Gradually, but decidedly, the change went on, and a uniform greyish colour was completed within the period named." It is interesting to note that not the hair only, but the skin also may change colour as the result of a violent nerve storm, accompanied by a violent emotion. In the *Journal Encylopédique* is related the case of a man who had, after being very angry, an apoplectic attack, which ended in paralysis of the right side, and at the same time this side of his body became completely yellow, not except-ing even the right half of his nose. During the first French Revolution a woman was condemned to death by the Parisian mob, and the lantern (the instrument of execution) was actually let down at her feet. She was reprieved, however. Shortly afterward her colour began to change, and in a few days she became as dark as a moderately dark negro. She died in 1819, aged seventy-five, more than thirty years after, her skin remaining dark until her death. Laycock relates the case of a young lady, aged sixteen, who met a man in the dark who insulted and greatly terrified her. In the morning her eyelids were yellow. The colour gradually extended for eight days, until her face was covered ; then the yellow deepened into black. Eight days afterwards the arms began to turn yellow, and became slowly black. The colour remained for four months, at the end of which time she rapidly recovered.

In 1761 a Parisian lady of high rank (a duchess) suffered much anxiety and grief, two of her children dying while her husband was away at the wars. After excessive weeping her eyelids became discoloured, as if painted black, and this colour extended over the cheeks in patches. She recovered, and some time after her remaining child fell ill. Her forehead then became reddish brown, and finally quite black, the colour extending gradually until the whole face was black. Eventually the colour disappeared.

From these examples it is evident that every commotion in the highest nerve-regions has an effect upon nutrition, and that in some cases the effect of such a commotion is very conspicuous. We have next to notice the complementary facts, that every disorder of the lesser or visceral circulation of nerve-energy, involves an alteration in the consciousness of self, and that, while a local disorder in the peripheral portion of the circulation involves but a slight alteration in the self-consciousness, the alteration of consciousness becomes more pronounced and more decided the more widespread the disorder of the visceral circulation, and the more nearly the disorder invades the highest nerve-regions.

When the entire visceral circulation is affected by an increase or a diminution of the tension of the nerve-energy, then of course the section of the circulation included in the highest nerve-regions is similarly and continuously affected ; and under such circumstances the feeling of well-being is heightened or lowered in proportion to the increase or diminution of the nerve-tension. When this alteration of tension of the nerve-energy is unaccompanied by disorder of the highest nerve-regions, there is simple alteration of the sense of well-being, without other alteration of mind. The individual feels happy or miserable without the occurrence of external changes to make him so, and without being able to account for the feeling. When the portion of the highest nerve-regions which directly receives and redistributes these visceral currents is disordered, then there is disorder of the appreciation of self. The self-consciousness is altered. The individual believes himself to be different, to be possessed, to be dead, to be unnatural, to be double, and so forth. This disorder of the appreciation of self may be accompanied by either heightened or diminished tension of nerve-energy, and therefore by feelings either of satisfaction or of misery. The function of the highest nerve-regions, it will be remembered, is not merely the representation of self, but the adjustment of self to surroundings ; and hence, when these highest centres are disordered, it can but rarely happen—it is scarcely possible—that the disorder can be so localized as to be limited to the appreciation of self. When the appreciation of self is disordered, there is always some amount of mal-adjustment of self to surroundings ; so that when a man believes himself to be different, or unnatural, or dead, these disorders, referring primarily to the appreciation of self, are always accompanied by disorder of conduct of some extent.

Thus we arrive at last at a complete statement of the nature of insanity. Insanity, we find, is a disorder of the adjustment of self to surroundings. This adjustment of self to surroundings is effected by the highest of all the nervous arrangements, and the central and primary factor in insanity is the disorder of these arrangements. Dependent on this central disorder are other disorders :—1. Conduct, which it is the function of the highest nervous arrangements to actuate, is disordered ; and—2. Consciousness, which accompanies the working of the highest nervous arrangements, is disordered. Regarded in one light, according as it accompanies discharges from cells or currents in fibres, consciousness is divisible into feelings and thoughts ; and according as discharges in cells or currents in fibres are mainly affected, the disorder is mainly disorder of feeling or disorder of thought. Regarded in another light, according as it accompanies activity of that portion of the highest nervous arrangements which is the supreme development of the visceral circulation of nerve-energy, or as it accompanies that portion which is the supreme development of the major or sense-muscle circulation of nerve-energy, consciousness is divisible into consciousness of self and consciousness of the relation of self to surroundings; and according as the one or the other region of the highest nervous arrangements is mainly affected, the disorder is mainly disorder of the consciousness of self, or disorder of the consciousness of the relation of self to surroundings.

In every case of insanity there are present all the three factors—disorder of the highest nerve arrangements, disorder of conduct, and disorder of consciousness; and in every case the disorder of consciousness includes disorder of thought and of feeling, of self-consciousness and of consciousness of the relation of self to surroundings. In no two cases, however, are these various factors combined in quite the same way, and thus no two cases precisely resemble one another. On the way in which they are combined depends the form which the insanity assumes.

CHAPTER V.

Heredity.

INSANITY is, in mathematical terms, a function of two variables. That is to say, there are two factors, and only two, in its causation ; and these factors are complementary. Both enter into the causation of every case of insanity, and the stronger the influence of one factor, the less of the other factor is needed to produce the result. These two factors are, in brief, heredity and stress. It has been explained that, in order to work efficiently, the nervous system should have in a high degree a certain form of instability—an instability which allows of ready and free rearrangement of the atoms of its molecules, with easy and copious liberation of the energy accumulated in them. So long as this rearrangement proceeds without actual decomposition of the molecule, the process remains within the limits of the normal ; but it is easy to see that this form of instability has a certain relationship to another form—a form in which the disturbance of the molecules does not stop short at rearrangement, but goes on to partial or even to total decomposition. Since a certain degree of instability of the first form is an essential to nervous action, and necessarily exists in every possessor of a nervous system, and since this form of instability is related, more or less closely, to the second form, it is obvious that some tendency to the second form of instability exists in every individual. The amount or strength of the tendency varies with each individual, but in every one it exists to some degree.

It is manifest that the amount of disturbance that is necessary to upset any orderly arrangement depends entirely on the stability of the arrangement. When the component parts of a structure are firmly compacted together, a violent disturbance will be necessary to upset or disintegrate the structure ; and when the cohesion between the component parts is but feeble, the structure will be liable to disintegration from disturbances of a much less pronounced and less violent character. A jerry-built villa is liable to be blown down by a storm of wind, but nothing short of an earthquake will destroy a well-constructed mansion.

Now insanity is a disorder of the highest nervous centres ; that is to say, a derangement of the structure of these centres, and this derangement of structure will be produced by slight disturbances where the structure is loosely compacted and the instability great ; while in cases in which the structure is well and soundly constituted and of firm stability, it will require a violent disturbance to upset its equilibrium. Hence we find that, according to the opening statement, insanity is a function of two variables. It needs for its production a certain instability of nerve-tissue, and the incidence of a certain disturbance. When the instability of tissue is great, a small disturbance will suffice. When the instability is small, a violent disturbance is necessary. But for every individual, as for every wooden beam, there is a breaking-point. If you load a beam with sufficient weight, a certain weight will be found, varying with the strength of the beam, at which the beam will break ; and if you subject a man to stress, a certain stress will be found, varying with the stability of his nervous system, at which the man will become insane. Hence, to determine the causes of insanity, we have to find, first the factors which tend to initial stability or instability of the highest nervous arrangements ; and, second, the nature and severity of the stresses to which these arrangements are subject.

The fact that the majority of people do not become, or do not remain, insane, indicates that they possess a nervous organization of sufficient stability to withstand such stresses as they are subject to. And the minority who become or remain insane, are endowed with a nervous organization which is either more easily upset, or is subject to stress of greater severity. As a matter of fact the factor which is chiefly and most often at fault is the nervous organization. Although, as has been said, there is an intensity of stress which will permanently upset even the most stably constituted nervous system, yet stresses of this extreme severity are so rare in human experience, that in practice a person of normal and average nervous constitution will not be driven mad by any of the ordinary vicissitudes of life. And since, in the vast majority of cases of insanity, we find that the occasion of the disorder was some stress of but medium intensity, we may be quite sure that in all such cases the important factor in the production of the insanity is not the magnitude of the disturbance, but the fragility of the arrangements on which the disturbance breaks.

The stability or instability of a person's highest nervous arrangements depends primarily and chiefly upon inheritance. Every man is the outcome and the product of his ancestry ; and this is true not only of the broad and fundamental characters by which he is animal, by which he is human, by which he is national, by which he betrays the country and the family from which he proceeds ; but extends to the trivial and minutely trivial characters by which he is distinguished from other individuals of his own race, country, and family. Doubtless every man is to some extent moulded into conformity with cirumstances by the influence of circumstances upon him ; but the small amount of new character that circumstances can produce in any individual, in comparison with the characters transmitted to him by his ancestry, may be gathered from the length of time that circumstances can act upon him, in comparison with the aggregate length of time during which the long line of his ancestry have been subject to modification by circumstances. Doubtless if we take a seedling plant, and if, while it is young, and its tissues plastic, and its potentialities undeveloped, we subject it to certain conditions of life, we can modify the arrangement and alter the stability of its most elaborate and highly-organized parts—of its flowers and fruit ; and doubtless, also, if we subject a child to certain conditions of life, we may in the same way modify the arrangement and alter the stability of its most elaborate and most highly-organized parts—of its highest nervous centres ; but the fact remains that, for the great majority of people, the question of the stability or instability of their highest nervous arrangements resolves itself into a question of the kind and degree of organization that they have inherited from their ancestry. To ascertain, then, the influence of the first factor in the production of insanity, it will be necessary to give a brief account of the laws of heredity.

The laws of heredity are two : the Law of Inheritance, and the Law of Sanguinity. Both of them are important in connection with the causation of insanity.

The Law of Inheritance is simple, and is easily stated and understood. It is that *the offspring tend to inherit every attribute of the parents*, or that every attribute of the parents tends to appear in the offspring, and will appear unless some counteracting influence prevents. Doubtless there are many cases in which attributes of the parents fail to appear in the offspring, but these are not exceptions to the law. The laws of nature know of no exception, and when apparent exceptions occur, it is either because the laws are acting in ways not understood, or because of the interference and counteraction of other laws. The rising of a balloon is not an exception to the law of gravity, it is an illustration of the law acting in an unusual way.

That the law is true of the general and broad outlines of structure and function is universally accepted—is, indeed, a truism. Men do not gather grapes of thorns, nor figs of thistles. "That wheat produces wheat—that existing oxen have descended from ancestral oxen—that every unfolding organism eventually takes the form of the class, order, genus, and species from which it sprang, is a fact which, by force of repetition, has acquired in our minds almost the aspect of necessity." But that the same law is true of the smaller attributes, down to the most trivial details of structure and function, is not so generally admitted, and is even widely disbelieved. Every now and then, however, we meet with conspicuous instances of the operation of the law in matters of small moment, which serve to fix our attention, and demonstrate the constancy of its working. Peculiarities in gait, in gesture, and general bearing, are often inherited ; a case in point being that in which a father had the trick of sleeping on the back with the right leg crossed over the left, and whose daughter, while an infant in the cradle, assumed the same attitude in sleep. It is notorious also that there are family similarities in handwriting as strong and as frequent as family similarities of features ; and this is the more important from the present point of view, since a peculiarity of handwriting depends upon an arrangement of nerve-tissue that must be extremely delicate, extremely elaborate, subtle, slight, diffused, and yet precise. In comparison with such a quality of nervous arrangements, the peculiarity of tissue organization which underlies insanity is gross indeed ; and hence if the one is transmissible by inheritance we may be quite sure that the other may be. That the children of insane parents are apt to inherit a tendency to insanity is what might be expected, and is a well-established fact ; the existence of insanity in other members of the family being ascertained to exist is more than twenty per cent. of the patients admitted into asylums in this country. But this direct inheritance of insanity is by no means the only way in which the first law of heredity influences the tendency to insanity. What is inherited from an insane person is not insanity itself, it is an undue instability of nervous organization ; and hence, whenever there is undue instability of nervous organization in the progenitors, there will be liability to insanity in the offspring.[1]

Thus, among the most conspicuous instances and evidences of undue instability of organization of the higher nervous centres, is epilepsy. Epilepsy is a sudden and excessive discharge of nerve elements, beginning usually in the highest regions ; and the undue and abnormal instability of nerve elements, which epilepsy displays, may be transmitted by inheritance to the offspring. But in the offspring this instability may not exhibit itself as epilepsy. It may be that, instead of a liability to sudden and excessive discharges, there is a liability to excessive and disorderly discharges of much more gradual character, and the same essential defect which in the parent caused epilepsy may in the offspring underlie insanity. The links between epilepsy and insanity form, in fact, a continuous chain, as will be shown hereafter, and the peculiarities of brain-tissue which underlie them are allied. In the same way the hysterical parent may have children who become insane, the nervous organization which allows of the one disturbance being virtually the same as that which allows of the other. So with people who are highly eccentric, extremely passionate, or who give other evidence of defect in the organization of the highest nervous arrangements. Such defects are so nearly allied to that which underlies insanity, that it is as natural for the parents who show one of these defects to have children who exhibit another, as it is for a piebald rabbit to have offspring whose piebald markings are of different shape and extent from those of the parent.

---

[1] By liability to insanity is here meant liability to become insane under the operation of stresses, such as would not produce insanity in the average or normal man. As has already been shown, every one is liable to become insane on the incidence of a stress that is sufficiently severe.

While, however, the existence of instability in the highest nervous arrangements of the parents undoubtedly facilitates, or, more accurately, increases the chances of, the occurrence of insanity in the offspring, it by no means necessarily follows that the children of such parents will become insane ; nor, on the other hand, are the children of those, whose nervous arrangements are of normal stability, by any means exempt from developing such a character of nervous tissue as may involve their breakdown into insanity under the strain of ordinary circumstances. The reasons of these exceptions to the operation of direct inheritance from parent to child we have now to discover, and they will be found in those influences which have already been alluded to as interfering with or modifying the first law of heredity. Briefly stated, these influences are as follow :—

An attribute which appeared in the parent at a certain time of life tends to appear in the offspring at a corresponding time of life. The successive stages in the development of every organism present abundant instances of this rule. The embryo resembles the embryo of the parent at a corresponding age, and the successive characters assumed at successive stages appear at the same age in the new being as in the old. Thus the caterpillar emerges from the egg, undergoes repeated moults, changes into a chrysalis, and then into a moth ; and each of these changes occurs at an age corresponding with that at which it appeared in the parents. Similarly the youth finds his voice breaking and his moustache budding at about the same age at which the same changes took place in his father ; and later on he grows stout, his hair turns grey, his skin becomes wrinkled, and his gait shambling at ages corresponding with those in which the same changes appeared in his parents. The same rule holds good with attributes which appear *de novo* in the parents. In the family of Le Compte blindness was inherited through three generations, and no less than twenty-seven children and grandchildren were all affected at about the same age. This rule is true also of insanity, and many cases have been recorded. Piorry tells of a family every member of which became insane at the age of forty. Esquirol relates a case in which the grandfather, father, and son all committed suicide when in or near their fiftieth year. Dr. Savage says he has known several instances in which the family inheritance was a tendency to pass into weak-mindedness with melancholy at a certain period of life. This principle may evidently account for some instances of absence of insanity in the children of insane persons. They may not arrive at the time of life at which the insanity would have occurred.

When the same attribute appears in several generations, but is not congenital (that is, present at birth), it may appear at an earlier age in each successive generation. For instance, gout is rarely met with under thirty years of age, except in hereditary cases ; and the stronger the hereditary tendency to gout, the more generations of gouty ancestors he has had, the earlier in life is he liable to the disease. The same is true of cancer, of goitre, and of some other maladies ; thus in one family the grandmother became blind at thirty-five, her daughter at nineteen, and three grandchildren at thirteen and eleven. Cases have been recorded showing a similar advance in the inheritance of insanity, and it is obvious that where such an advance takes place the insanity is becoming more and more strongly established in that stock with each successive generation. On the other hand, in any case in which the insanity appeared at a later age in successive generations, it might be fairly argued that the disease was dying out.

Attributes pertaining to one parent (especially those appearing late in life, when the reproductive function is active) tend to be reproduced in the offspring of that sex only. Thus universally the secondary sexual characters, the beard, the more massive frame, the deeper voice, are transmitted from the male parent to the male offspring ; while the smooth features, the smaller bones and muscles, the shriller voice, the large breasts and long hair are transmitted from mother to daughter only. Besides these trite instances there are many others. The hæmorrhagic diathesis is often transmitted to males alone. In some families the tendency to bleed is so strong that scarcely a single male arrives at maturity, while the females are not at all affected. In the Lambert family, known as the "porcupine men," the skin disease was transmitted to four generations, and was strictly limited to the male sex, seven sisters in one of these generations being free. Colour-blindness is much commoner in males than in females, but in one instance, in which it first appeared in a female, it was transmitted through five generations to thirteen individuals, every one of whom was a female. The influence of this principle also will evidently account for the absence of insanity in some members of families, the offspring of a sane and insane parent.

Curiously enough, the opposite of the last proposition is also true, and sometimes attributes pertaining to one parent are transmitted to the offspring of the opposite sex only; a further explanation of the non-inheritance of insanity. A remarkable instance will be given further on, under the head of Reversion, as occurring in the hæmorrhagic diathesis.

Attributes peculiar to one parent may be most apparent at one period of the life of the offspring, and those of the other at another. Girou states that calves, the offspring of a red and a black parent, are not unfrequently born red, and subsequently become black. Darwin crossed several white hens with a black cock, and many of the chickens were during the first year perfectly white, but acquired during the second year black feathers; on the other hand, some of the chickens which at first were black became in the second year piebald with white. The operation of this influence may explain the occurrence of outbreaks of insanity that are apparently causeless.

From the possession by the offspring of one attribute peculiar to one parent, we may infer the possession of other attributes peculiar to the same parent. Thus, I crossed an albino mouse with a common brown mouse. Of a litter of six, two were albinoes and inherited, with the colouring, the tameness and gentleness of the mother, while the other four inherited from the father, not only their brown colour, but their activity and untameable wildness of disposition. Moreau, indeed, asserts, but as it seems to me on entirely insufficient evidence, that in the case of inherited insanity, the facial characters tend to be inherited from the parent from whom the insanity was *not* derived. Sedgwick says that "there is a definite connection between the development of the ear and the different forms of insanity, and both the form of the ear and the insanity may be hereditary."

LATENCY AND REVERSION. Among the most remarkable of the many remarkable occurrences of heredity are the complementary phenomena known as Latency and Reversion. When an attribute exists in an individual, is absent in his offspring, and reappears in the third or some subsequent generation, it is said to be *latent* in those generations in which it does not appear ; and the individual in whom it at length appears is said to *revert*, in so far as that attribute is concerned, to the ancestor in whom it was present.

For instance, a grandfather has six digits on each hand ; his children are normally constituted, but his grandchildren have, like himself, supernumerary digits. In such a case the grandchildren are said to revert to the grandfather, and the attribute of possessing supernumerary digits is said to be latent in the intermediate generation. Instances of latency and reversion are very common in every class of organisms. The following highly characteristic examples are given by Darwin : "A pointer bitch produced seven puppies ; four were marked with blue and white, which is so unusual a colour with pointers that she was thought to have played false with one of the greyhounds, and the whole litter was condemned ; but the gamekeeper was permitted to preserve one as a curiosity. Two years afterwards a friend of the owner saw the young dog, and declared that

he was the image of his old pointer bitch Sappho, the only
blue and white pointer of pure descent he had ever seen.
This led to close inquiry, and it was proved that he was the
great-great-grandson of Sappho." In another instance a
calf reproduced accurately the very peculiar markings and
colouring of its great-great-great-great-grandmother, all the
intervening generations having been black.

In the human race instances of reversion in peculiar
attributes are not easily proved, for the obvious reason that
we have not the same facilities for observing a number of
generations, but reversion is certainly active. It is seen in
the inheritance from the maternal grandfather of diseases
peculiar to the male sex. For instance, it is common in the
transmission of the hæmorrhagic diathesis for the children
of the affected individual to escape altogether; all the
children of the sons and the female children of the daughters
also escape; but the sons of the daughters are affected. A
very striking instance of reversion of both physical and
mental characteristics, and one evidently reproduced from
experience, is described by Hawthorne in "The House with
the Seven Gables."

Reversion is seen, not only in the transmission of isolated
and peculiar attributes, but in the re-assumption, after a
longer or shorter series of generations in which the race
has been modified, of the aggregate of general characters
exhibited by the original race before the modification took
place. For instance, the domestic pig may, and does under
certain circumstances, revert to the characters of the wild
boar; the highly modified and specialized breeds of the
domestic fowl may revert to, and assume the characters of,
the ancestral *gallus bankiva*, the wild form from whence
they all originally descended; the offspring of the grotesque
fancy pigeons may father themselves on the blue rock, the
remote wild ancestor of all the domestic pigeons.

Since all the other peculiarities of working of the principle
of inheritance display themselves as well in the human race
as in lower organisms, it is natural to expect this peculiarity

also to appear among men, and there is no doubt that it does so. It is not merely that we find occasionally a man who manifests the ungovernable ferocity, and the delight in inflicting suffering for the mere gratification of experiencing the emotion of power while so doing, which he derives, after the intervention of many generations of milder minds, from his raptorial ancestors ; but that, after some temporary deviation, there is a return to conformity with the general type of organization of the race. The tendency for the developing organism to unfold after one particular manner and in conformity with one general type, has been fixed by transmission through so many generations, has required such force of momentum in its long descent, that the perhaps local and temporary influences which produced in the parent a deviation from the type, are overborne in the offspring by the steady, enduring, massive pressure of its race-heredity. The whole weight of race-heredity comes down upon the developing organism, and forces it with irresistible stress into the old grooves and channels of development, despite the nearer but feebler influence of immediate parentage, which tends to divert it into some new direction. Thus, when a gardener has with utmost pains and skill produced a new variety, of plant-form, he is often exasperated to find that in spite of all his exertions, a portion, a large proportion, the majority, it may be the whole of his seedlings will revert to the original form from which he bred ; and that, if he would perpetuate his stock, he must do so by layers, or grafts, or cuttings. The accumulated momentum of the developmental forces, descending through many generations, bears down all opposition to their progress in the wonted direction. Although the newly-acquired qualities may be for a time more conspicuous, yet underlying them are always the massive race qualities, which, in proportion to the number of generations through which they have passed, tend to reassert themselves and reappear.

It is doubtless in obedience to this principle that insanity so often fails to appear in the descendants, immediate and remote, of the insane. Indeed, were there not a natural tendency for insanity to die out and disappear, it is doubtful whether there would be a single sane individual left to turn the key on the rest of his race ; for it is as difficult to find a family without at least one insane member, as to find a litter of pigs without a tony, or tithe pig. Hence the undoubted importance of inheritance in the production of insanity should never arouse undue alarm in the minds of those who know of the existence of insanity in their near relatives ; for the influences which act upon this factor in its production are so numerous, and so enormously complex, that it by no means follows that even the most direct heredity will be successful in producing the result ; and if they knew the family circumstances of their sanest and soberest friends, they would be astonished to find how large a proportion of them come of a stock that gives more or less evidence of insanity.

The influence of reversion is unfortunately not wholly beneficial, however ; for although in many cases it helps in the process of breeding out insanity, in some it is a direct factor in its production. The children of the insane, like the children of bleeders, may altogether escape the malady ; but in the one case as in the other, the grandchildren may revert to the qualities of their grand-parents. Where several generations have intervened, and the occurrence of insanity in the progenitor has been forgotten, the appearance of insanity in perhaps but one member of a large family may be inexplicable ; but if inquiry were made, and the evidence in existence, it would be found to be a sporadic case of reversion.

The operation of reversion sometimes produces curious results. Occasionally, under certain conditions, an individual of one sex will assume many of the characters of the opposite sex, the reversion being to its ancestors of this sex. It is well known that a large number of female birds, when old or diseased, or when operated on, assume many or all of the secondary male characters of their species. A duck ten years old has been known to assume the perfect winter and summer plumage of a drake. A hen which had ceased laying has assumed the plumage, spurs, voice, and warlike disposition of a cock ; and the same thing occurs, *mutatis mutandis*, with the other sex. It is important to notice that not only structural peculiarities, but habits, such as that of incubation, and mental qualities, such as courage, are among the characters which may be lost and gained in this manner. The influence of this form of reversion, which also occurs in the human race, upon the production of insanity, is shown in two ways. In the first place such changes are attended by, and are evidence of, an internal revolution in the general organization analogous to that which takes place at puberty, when the secondary characters of sex are first assumed. The inversion of sex cannot take place without a commotion analogous to that of the assumption of sex ; and this change takes its place, therefore, among the stresses which will hereafter be considered as determining causes of insanity. In the second place, this peculiar form of reversion is sometimes accompanied by the production of long-lost characters peculiar to some distant ancestral form. Such a reversion, if it take place in a man or woman, and if it be to some cast of mind and habits peculiar to an ancestor sufficiently remote, that is, to a form of life adapted to widely different surroundings, may itself constitute insanity in the individual in whom it appears. When a hen assumes, at its climacteric, the plumage and characters of a cock, it may at the same time revert to the common and remote parent of all domestic fowls, and the characters it assumes may be that of the male of the *gallus bankiva;* and when a woman at her climacteric assumes, as some women do, the beard, the diminished mammæ and the deep voice and other characters of a man, she may at the same time revert as to habits and mental qualities to some remote feral or semi-feral ancestor of man, and may in consequence exhibit such inability to adapt herself to civilized surroundings as constitutes actual insanity. There is in every asylum a certain number of bearded and bass-voiced women, whose insanity is usually of very intractable type ; and I have had under care at the same time, two men, whose hairless faces, large mammæ and shrill voices betokened an assumption of the secondary characters of the other sex, and whose insanity was notably intractable.

In connection with the subject of reversion falls to be considered the remarkable peculiarity of heredity called *prepotence*. Such attributes as are common to both parents, and are alike in both, will tend to be accurately reproduced in the offspring ; but where the parents possess contrary or contradictory attributes, the offspring cannot inherit from both, and among these qualities there will be, as it were, a struggle for preponderance, for possession of, or precedence in the offspring. The quality which obtains the mastery, and succeeds in reappearing in the offspring, is termed *prepotent* over the other. Cases frequently occur in which the tendency of a certain quality to appear in the offspring is very strong ; and in such cases this tendency is hereditary, and the quality is transmitted with certainty through many generations. This tendency to " breed true " is an instance of the *prepotency* of the quality in question. Like the other manifestations and modifications of the first law of heredity, this of prepotence appears to be very capricious in its application. Some qualities, such as certain colours, are strongly prepotent in some animals, and not at all in others, or may be prepotently transmitted by one sex and not by the other. Occasionally the characters first imported into a race by a single ancestor will appear in generation after generation of that race with ineradicable persistency. The prepotence of the Napoleonic features is a case in point. They have been transmitted with surprisingly little variation from some common ancestor of Napoleon Buonaparte and his brothers, to at least the fourth generation. The Bourbon nose appeared so persistently in the family as to be notorious. The features of the Austrian Emperors have been markedly similar from generation to generation ; and in all these cases the marriage, in each generation, of the men with women of a different stock, has been insufficient to disturb the powerful prepotent tendency of the features of the father to reappear in the offspring.

The causes of prepotency are obscure, there being but one circumstance which can be pointed to as of unequivocal influence in enforcing it ; and this is the union of a parent, in whom a quality is present and strongly marked, with one in whom the same quality is latent ; in whom, that is to say, there is an hereditary tendency to assume that quality, but without actual assumption of it. "Thus we have reason to believe that there is a latent tendency in all horses to be dun-coloured and striped ; and when a horse of this kind is crossed with one of any other colour, it is said that the offspring are almost sure to be striped. All pigeons have a tendency to become slaty blue, with certain characteristic marks, and it is known that, when a bird thus coloured is crossed with one of any other colour, it is most difficult afterwards to eradicate the blue tint."

If we consider this question of prepotency in connection with insanity, we shall be able to discover two very valuable rules for practical guidance. In the first place, if it appears that insanity has become prepotent in a family, then the most stringent measures ought to be adopted to prevent the marriage of the members of that family, and to avoid the transmission of so terrible an inheritance. In the second place, if there is in a family a tendency to insanity, without that tendency having the force and certainty of prepotence, then, while not interdicting the marriage of its members, the greatest precautions should be taken that they do not marry into families in which a similar tendency exists, for if they do, it is probable that insanity will appear in their offspring.

CHAPTER VI.

THE CAUSES OF INSANITY.

The Second Law of Heredity.

THE second law of heredity, which I have called the Law of Sanguinity, is likewise an important factor in the production of insanity, and requires the more notice here, since, so far as I know, it has not hitherto received any attention in this regard. The following is the best expression of the law that I have been able to construct :—

There are certain limits, on the one hand of similarity, and on the other of dissimilarity, between two individuals, between which limits only can the union of those individuals be fertile ; and in proportion as these limits are approached, the offspring deteriorates.

Put in a somewhat less accurate but more intelligible form, the law will run thus : *There is a certain degree of dissimilarity (sanguinity) between parents, which is most favourable for the production of well-organized offspring ; and parents who are more similar (consanguine), or more dissimilar (exsanguine), will have offspring (if any) whose organization will be inferior in proportion to the distance of the parents from the most favourable point.* In order to make the matter quite clear, let us put it in graphic form.

Suppose the line MM^1 to represent a series of males, and FF^1 a series of females, and suppose that the amount of similarity between the individuals of the one series and those of the other to be indicated by the distance between the lines; thus, m^1, is very closely similar to f^1; m^2 and f^2 are more unlike, while m^6 and f^6 are extremely dissimilar to each other. Now suppose that each male marries the female in the corresponding position of the other series, then the marriages between SS and DD will produce the best offspring. Marriages between SS and ss, and between DD and dd, will produce offspring of inferior organization, and the nearer the pairs of individuals to the lines ss or dd respectively, the more will the organization of the offspring be impaired. Finally marriages of pairs between ss and MF, and of pairs between dd and M^1F^1 will be sterile : no offspring will be produced.

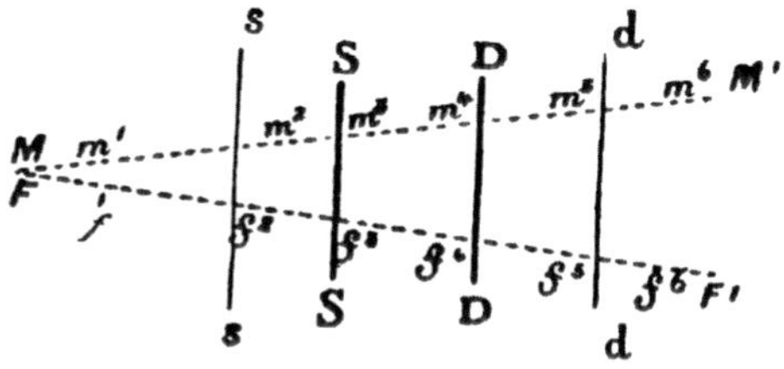

FIG. 12.

Let us take the case of similarity or consanguinity first. Starting from the point of similarity which is the most favourable for the production of well-organized offspring, we find, as the closeness of similarity between the parents increases, that the offspring deteriorates more and more ; and when a certain degree of closeness of similarity is reached, offspring ceases to be produced. By similarity is not meant here merely blood relationship as generally understood. Closeness of blood-relationship is necessary to that closeness of similarity which is here spoken of, but does not necessarily imply such similarity. While there cannot be close similarity without close blood-relationship, there may be close blood-relationship without close physio-logical similarity—similarity of constitution. If two brothers inherit very strongly the character of one of their parents,

say their father, and if each of these brothers transmits
prepotently these paternal qualities to his children, then
the cousins thus produced will have not only a close relationship in blood, but a close similarity of constitution ; and if
they marry, their offspring will be likely to be imperfect.
If, however, one of the brothers inherits strongly from the
father, while the other reverts or throws back to the
maternal great-grandfather ; and if the children of one brother
inherit mainly from their father, while the qualities of the

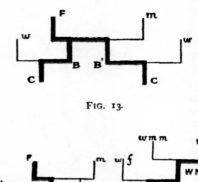

FIG. 13.

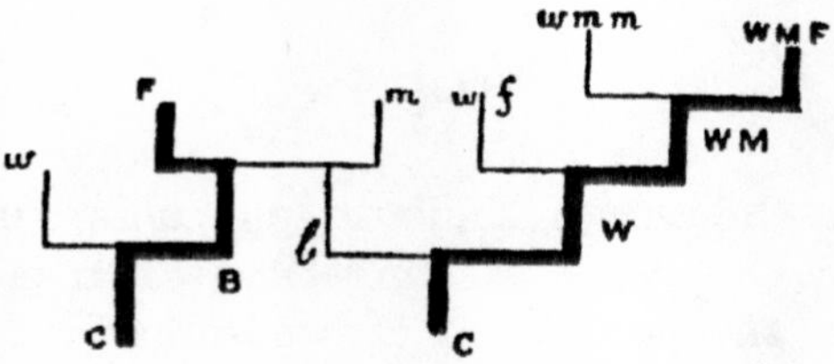

FIG. 14.

mother are prepotent in the children of the other, then it
is evident that although the blood-relationship is as close as
in the former pair of cousins, yet since these cousins are
virtually derived from different stocks, they have a wide
dissimilarity of constitution, and their offspring are not likely
to be imperfect. Graphically represented, the two cases
will be as above :—

The heavy line shows in each case the course of the main
stream of qualities ; and it will be seen that while the one

pair of cousins derive the main elements in their constitu·
tions from the same source, the others get theirs from widely
different origins, and hence are constituted much more
dissimilarly.

In these considerations an explanation is to be found of
the varying conclusions that have been reached by those
who have studied the marriage of near kin. There is a
popular feeling that marriages of cousins are apt to produce
ill consequences ; and, here and there, instances are adduced
in which ill consequences, in the shape of imperfect and
deteriorated offspring, have unquestionably followed ; yet
those who have made the most careful and copious and
laborious observations of the marriages of cousins, have concluded that, on the whole, very little ill effect is traceable. If
we consider how small is the number of cases in which cousins
inherit very strongly from one common grand-parent, and
the still smaller number in which the cousins so inheriting
marry, we shall see why it is that in the aggregate of cases
of marriage of cousins, ill effects so seldom follow. And if
we remember that every now and then among the marriages
of cousins there will occur one between cousins thus closely
allied, not only in blood-relationship, but in physiological
character and constitution, we shall see how it is that
conspicuous instances of ill effect will sometimes occur, and
will tend to bring into unwarranted discredit all marriages
between cousins. The true doctrine would seem to be that
such marriages are to be strongly discouraged when the
cousins are alike, and when there is a taint of madness or
any other hereditary disorder in the common family ; but that
under ordinary circumstances they may be undertaken with
impunity.

It is true that the testimony of breeders of stock is over-
whelmingly strong as to the evil effects of inbreeding, but
then, inbreeding when applied to animals means far more
than a simple union of cousins. It is admitted on all hands
that it is the effect of *continued* inbreeding that is detri-
mental, and the union of a pair of cousins would certainly

not come under this description. "Manifest evil," says
Darwin, " does not follow from pairing the nearest relations
for two, three, and even four generations." When the inbreeding is pushed sufficiently far, the deterioration of the
offspring is certain, and the ultimate extinction of the race
inevitable. About this there can be no doubt. No fact
could rest on more secure foundations ; but this degree of
inbreeding never happens in the human race, and is only
approached by the rare cases of marriage of cousins who
have both inherited prepotently from a common ancestor.
It is easy to form genealogical trees of the Bourbons of
Spain, or the Ptolemies, and to display an amount of
inbreeding that appears at first sight appalling. There we
find marriages, not only of first cousins, of first cousins the
children of first cousins, of uncle with niece, of brother and
sister, of brother and sister the children of brother and
sister, but of relatives of even closer degrees of propinquity.
Such inbreeding, extreme as it appears in the human race,
would not be considered very extreme in the case of the
lower animals. If we take the genealogical trees and
arrange them in a slightly different manner, so as to bring
into prominence not only the amount of inbreeding, but also
the points at which new blood has been introduced, it will
become apparent that even in the case of the Ptolemies—the
most extreme case of inbreeding of man on record—there is
no instance of absence of a cross with an entirely new stock
for more than four generations. Compare this with the
case of Mr. Wright's pigs. He crossed the same boar with
his own daughter, grand-daughter, great-grand-daughter,
and so on for seven generations. The result was that in
many cases the offspring failed to breed ; in others they
produced few that lived ; and of the latter many were idiotic,
without sense even to suck, and when attempting to move
could not walk straight. That the result was due to inbreeding is shown by the fact that, when paired with other
boars, these sows produced large litters of healthy pigs. But
the fact to observe is that these ill effects were not produced

until the closest possible form of inbreeding had been continued for six or seven generations ; and there is reason to believe that in the human race the ill effect of inbreeding would not appear so soon as in the lower animals, whose lives are shorter and whose conditions of existence are far more uniform.

The fact of most importance to carry forward from this discussion is the *character* of the defect that arises from inbreeding. The offspring of an inbred race are feeble. When a mental defect arises, that defect is of the nature of idiocy, not of the more active forms of insanity. The testimony of all breeders of stock is unanimous that the qualities which are deteriorated by inbreeding are vigour and robustness ; and the lack of vigour and robustness is the physical counterpart, as it is the physical accompaniment, of weakness of mind ; and when lack of vigour and robustness of mind and body are pushed to excess, the case is one of idiocy.

Now take the case of the dissimilarity or ex-sanguinity of parents. That a certain minimum of dissimilarity between the parents is necessary for the production of any offspring is only another way of stating what has just been said. If parents who are closely inbred fail to breed, the reason is that they are not dissimilar enough. A certain minimum of dissimilarity there must be between them, or their union will not be fertile. As this minimum is increased—as the dissimilarity between the parents widens and increases, their offspring become larger and more vigorous ; better developed and better organized ; exceeding, when a certain degree of dissimilarity has been reached, either of the parents in their organization. With a still further increase of the dissimilarity of the parents, the offspring begins to deteriorate ; but the deterioration is of a totally different kind, in a totally different direction from that arising from a too great similarity between the parents. The offspring remain vigorous, robust, and well developed, but they are wanting in fertility. They breed seldom or not at all. When the dissimilarity reaches a still further point, this sterility rises from the second generation to the first. No offspring is produced. Individuals so dissimilar are sterile *inter se*.

The testimony of all who have had experience in this matter is quite unanimous, and innumerable cases of the most convincing character have been recorded. The benefit of introducing "new blood" has become proverbial. Whenever a stock has become deteriorated by inbreeding, a cross with a distinct race *invariably* produces a sudden increase in their size and vigour. The case of the pigs already mentioned is an example. When the race was deteriorating from being bred in, the union of the offspring of these too-similar parents with an animal of different race—with a more dissimilar form—produced offspring both abundant and healthy. A race of fighting cocks which had been inbred until they lost their disposition to fight, and stood to be cut up without making any resistance, and were so reduced in size as to be disqualified for the best prizes, regained, on being crossed with a new stock, their former courage and weight. All breeders of stock, whether of horses, oxen, pigs, dogs, or other animals, or of fowls, pigeons, or other birds, who desire to gain size, vigour, and hardihood in their stock, avoid inbreeding with the utmost care, and depend for the production of the qualities they desire, largely upon frequent crossing with distinct strains. On the other hand, when breeding for specific qualities, for particular markings or shape in dogs, for length of ear in rabbits, for colour, shape, and milking qualities in cattle, for peculiarities of feather, face, bearing, or habit in fowls or pigeons, the tendency is to breed closely in those particular strains in which these qualities are strongly marked ; and the consequence is that it has been remarked that " the same amateur seldom long maintains the superiority of his birds " ; for, all being of the same stock, it becomes essential, in order to maintain the necessary hardihood, to introduce a bird of another strain, and in this way, while hardihood is gained, the special qualities of beak, or feather, or what not, are deteriorated.

Sir John Sebright declares that by breeding in and in he has actually seen the offspring of strong spaniels degenerate into weak and diminutive lap-dogs. The most incontrovertible evidence, however, is that of money value, and it is a well-established principle among all breeders of stock, that for the purposes of the butcher and the cook, that is to say for size, weight, and early maturity, the value of cross-bred animals is indisputably greater than that of pure stock. The beneficial effect of crossing varieties of fruit-yielding plants has been described by experienced gardeners as "astonishing."

In all the foregoing cases the dissimilarity between the parents is not very great, and in all cases in which the dissimilarity reaches, without exceeding, a certain indefinable limit, the offspring benefits, and becomes a better organism than either of its parents. When, however, the dissimilarity between the parents is still further increased, the offspring begins to deteriorate. Instead of deteriorating in size and vigour, as occurs when the parents become more alike, the offspring exhibits a falling off in fertility. As its parents increase and widen in their unlikeness to each other, its offspring—the grand-children of these parents—become fewer and fewer, and at length cease to be produced. The sterility of mules and of hybrids generally is a sufficiently well-proved and notorious fact. It has been proved that among certain plants, a series can be formed, of species of gradually increasing dissimilarity, from pairs which, when crossed, yield fewer and fewer seeds, to species which never produce a single seed, but yet are affected by the pollen of other species, for the germen swells; and so on to pairs so divergent that not even this effect is produced.

With the diminution of fertility resulting from the union of too-dissimilar forms, we are not, in seeking the causation of insanity, concerned; but the other effect—the increase of size, vigour and hardihood—resulting from the union of sufficiently dissimilar parents, concerns us nearly. Before considering the bearing of these facts on the production of insanity, it will, however, be necessary to mention two incidental effects which result from the union of rather widely dissimilar forms.

The first of these is the production of reversion, which is a frequent result of cross-breeding. Darwin gives many wonderful instances of this occurrence, which he was himself the first to establish. He selected long-established pure breeds of fowls in which there was not a trace of red, yet in several of the mongrels this colour appeared, and one magnificent bird, the offspring of a black Spanish cock and a white silk hen, was coloured almost exactly like the wild *gallus bankiva*, the remote ancestor of both. " All who know anything of the breeding of poultry will admit that tens of thousands of pure Spanish and pure white silk fowls might have been reared without the appearance of a red feather," and would agree that hundreds, and perhaps thousands of generations must have intervened between the wild bird and the remote descendant which so resembled it. Again, some breeds of fowls have lost the instinct of incubation, yet when two such breeds are crossed, the instinct reappears, and the mongrel sits with remarkable steadiness. Professor Jaeger crossed the Japanese, or masked pig, with the common German breed, and the offspring were intermediate in character. He then re-crossed these mongrels with the pure Japanese, and in the litter thus produced one of the young resembled in all its characters a wild pig.

The second of the incidental effects of crossing is this : when a domesticated animal is crossed with a distinct species, whether this is a domesticated or only a tamed animal, the hybrids are often wild to a remarkable degree. This has been noticed in the cases of pigs, goats, ducks, cattle, fowls, and other animals. Mules, it is true, are not at all wild, but they are notorious for obstinacy and vice. These facts, Darwin goes on to say, " remind us of the statements so frequently made by travellers in all parts of the world on the degraded state and savage disposition of crossed races of man." Livingstone remarks that half-castes are much more cruel than Portuguese. An inhabitant remarked to Livingstone, "God made the white men, and God made the black men, but the devil made the half-castes."

There is yet one other phenomenon in procreation which requires notice before we can draw from all the facts the inferences that will show us the bearing of the second law of inheritance on the production of insanity. This is the phenomenon of parthenogenesis. It is commonly supposed that the ovum does not begin to live until the male element acts upon it, and imparts life to it; but this is an error. In all organisms the ovum undergoes a certain amount of development before the male element reaches it. The ovum of mammalia, while still in the ovary, enlarges and developes. The nucleus divides, and portions of it are expelled as the "polar globules." When the ovum escapes from the ovary, a further change in the direction of development takes place; but if impregnation does not now occur, the changes proceed no further, development ceases and the ovum perishes. If, however, the ovum comes in contact with the male element, a fresh start is made, an enormous impetus is given to the process already begun, and under the propulsion of the impetus so given, the ovum passes through the prodigious series of changes involved in the process of unfolding from a simple cell to the marvellously complex and elaborate structure of the adult organism. The factor imported into the process by the male element is of the nature of an *impetus*, and on the magnitude of this impetus depends the length of time during which development shall be continued, and the extent to which it shall proceed.

The next step in the development of the ovum after the impregnation, is the "segmentation of the yolk," or the spontaneous division of the cell substance first into two, then into four, then into eight, and so on into very many small portions. This segmentation does not usually take place in the

mammalian ovum unless and until the ovum is impregnated
by the male element ; but in many of the lower animals,
and in some mammals, the development of the unimpregnated ovum does proceed thus far, and segmentation
takes place even without impregnation.   There are again
other cases, among the lower animals, in which the development of the unimpregnated ovum goes beyond the mere
segmentation of the yolk, and proceeds as far as the formation
of an imperfect embryo.   Yet again it happens occasionally
in some insects, *e.g.*, some moths, that not only are eggs laid
without concourse with the male, but a small proportion of
these eggs actually hatch, and develop into living caterpillars.
Some of these caterpillars develop into moths, in every
respect resembling their single parent.   This phenomenon
of parthenogenesis, or asexual or unisexual generation, which
happens occasionally and exceptionally in the higher insects,
becomes in some of the lower insects almost the rule.   That
is to say, there are certain low forms of insect life—
aphides—in which offspring, living and vigorous offspring,
are habitually produced without concourse with the male.
Hence it appears that, apart from the impetus communicated
by the male element, the female element alone possesses a
certain momentum in the same direction, a momentum
which is always present in some degree, and will always
carry the process of development to a greater or less distance,
and which is sometimes even sufficient to carry it far enough
to produce a perfect offspring.

Although, however, the female possesses this intrinsic
momentum, yet in the vast majority of cases the momentum
is insufficient of itself to carry the development far enough
to produce perfect offspring ; and even in the extreme cases
in which this effect is produced, the female influence alone
is not sufficient to carry on the process indefinitely.   The
caterpillars which are derived from a virgin mother, cannot,
on reaching their adult stature as moths, lay fertile eggs
without the assistance of the male.   Aphides can produce
one, or two, or several, generations of virgin mothers, but

unless the aid of the male is at length evoked to give a new impetus to the process of development, the momentum, existing in the female line only, dies away, and no offspring is produced.

It is next to be noticed that the vigour of the impetus given to the process of development by the union of the male element with the ovum, varies in different cases. In the first place, the larger the *number* of male elements that act on the ovum, the more vigorous is the impulse given to the process of development. Naudin fertilized a flower with three grains of pollen, and succeeded perfectly. He then fertilized twelve flowers with two grains each, and reared but a single seed. With one grain each he had to fertilize seventeen flowers before a seed was produced. These two latter seeds produced plants which never attained their proper dimensions, and bore flowers of remarkably small size.[1]

In the second place the more *vigorous* the male element, the greater is the impulse given to the process of development. It is a commonplace among all breeders of stock of whatever kind, that for the production of the finest offspring, the healthiest and most vigorous males must be used as stock getters. The rule amongst breeders of such prize poultry as need size as a condition of success, is to discard the male birds after their first year of service.

In the third place, the more *different* the male element is from the female, the greater the impulse given to the process of development, providing that the elements are sufficiently similar for union to take place at all. The momentum in the direction of development which the ovum possesses, does not, it is evident, depend on the size of the ovum, for the minute ova of aphides possess a momentum which carries them further than the much larger ova of birds. Hence, supposing we were able to increase the size of the ova by the addition of more *matter* from the maternal

[1] It is now believed that in animals a single spermatozoon only unites with the ovum.

organism, there is no reason to suppose that we should thereby be storing in the ovum an addition to the developmental *energy*, or enabling the ovum to proceed farther in the path of development without help from the impulse of the male. If, instead of an increase in the original size of the ovum, the latter were to be increased by the addition to it, after it had been formed, of new matter of similar constitution from the mother form, there is no reason to think that the developmental impulse would be increased thereby. Supposing that the new matter were added in the form of particles similar to the male elements, but derived from the mother, formed in the ovary alongside of the ovum, still they would give to the ovum no accession of energy in the direction of development. In order to produce such an accession of energy there must be some *difference* between the matter composing the ovum, and the matter that is added to and unites with it ; hence the universal necessity for sexual intercourse. When the male element, without being indentical with the female, is yet very closely similar, derived not indeed from the mother, but from an organism of very closely similar constitution, the impulse given to the process of development, although considerable, is yet not sufficient to carry that process so far as to produce completely developed offspring. Hence in cases of inbreeding the offspring are defective, and they are defective in just such ways as indicate that the process of development has come to an end prematurely. For what will happen when the developmental process is wanting in vigour ? The greater the initial impetus given to a rolling ball or a flying arrow, the further the ball will roll, or the arrow will fly, before the retarding influence of friction brings the movement to a stay. And the greater the initial impetus given to the germ of an organism, the further the organism will proceed in development before the impetus is spent and the retarding influence of opposing forces brings the process to a standstill. Of the results and signs of the progress of development the most conspicuous is increase of size. From the microscopic germ, having a diameter of one two-hundreth of an inch or less, to the adult individual of between five and six feet in stature, the progress is continuous ; and the stronger the original impetus given to the developmental process, the further this process will be carried in this particular, and the greater will be the size attained by the adult animal. Hence we find that in breeding for size, the invariable practice is to avoid inbreeding and to maintain a succession of crosses with new blood ; and conversely, we find that the result of inbreeding, which diminishes the vigour of the initial impetus, is to deteriorate the offspring in size.

If two balls are set rolling along the ground one after the other in the same track, but the second with an impetus less than the first, the result will be, of course, that the first ball will travel farthest. The difference between the progress of the two balls will scarcely be perceptible in the early part of their course, the velocities at starting, though different, will not be conspicuously different, and the directions will be the same. When two-thirds or three-fourths of the course is run, however, and the balls have slackened in speed, and their momentum is diminished, it will happen that trifling irregularities in the ground, which were not sufficient to influence the course of the bowls in the early part of their career, when velocity was high and momentum great, will produce sensible deviations in the line of direction. Since the momentum of the second ball is less than that of the first, these deviations will set in at an earlier period in the course of the second ball, and the general results of its diminished impetus will be, first, that it will not travel so far, that the last part of its career will be deficient, and second, that the deviation of its course from a straight line will set in sooner ; it will be more easily diverted from its course.

Similarly in the case of a developing organism. That organism, which receives the weaker impetus, will differ from this which receives the stronger impetus, in several ways. It will not pass through the early stages of its development quite so fast as the more vigorous germ, but the difference in the rapidity of development will not be conspicuous until a comparatively advanced stage is reached ; and then it will be seen that the one organism is continuing strongly and vigorously to develop, while the development of the other is coming to a standstill.   Just as it is the last part of the career of the slower ball which is deficient, so it is the last stages in the development of the less vigorous germ which fail to be traversed.   What are the last stages of development ?   If we watch the germ through the process of its evolution into the adult organism, we find that first there is an indication of difference between the head and the body, then appears the spine—the foundation of the skeleton— then the heart, the intestinal canal, the lungs, the limbs, and so on.   The several organs and systems grow, develop, and eventually become complete, reaching their final stage at very different periods of life, some attaining completion long before birth, others being incomplete until adult age is reached.   So in the plant raised from seed—the first things to develop are the radicle and plumule, then the leaves, then the stem, and last of all the flower and fruit ; which latter mark the attainment of adult age by the plant.   Now the flower of the human organism is the highest portion of the nervous system.   This is the region in which development attains its supremest height.   All the rest of the body is but, as it were, the foundation of, and preparation for, the highest nervous regions.   The body is but a house for them to live in, an apparatus for them to act through, an organization for them to control.   They are the culmination and climax of the process of development.   Hence, if development is not carried far enough, if it fails to reach its latest stages, if its forces are spent ere its full course is run, the part whose development will fail to be attained will be the highest nervous regions.   And what is the evidence ?   The evidence is that in close inbreeding not only do the late offspring of such inbreeding fail to reach the full size and stature of their race, but the highest nervous regions fail to attain the development normal to that class of organism. They are idiotic. The inbred fighting cocks stand to be cut up without making any resistance. The inbred pigs have not sense even to suck.

Here we have to notice that not all idiots, indeed but few idiots, owe their deficient development to inbreeding; but nevertheless all cases of idiocy, and of congenital imbecility, which is a lesser degree of idiocy, owe their defect to the weakness of the original impetus with which the germ started on its career of development. There are, then, other sources of weakness of impetus besides the too great similarity between the germ cell and the sperm cell. What these sources are we have already seen in part. The insufficient impetus given by the male element may be due to its own inherent weakness—a weakness which may in some cases be due to and measured by the constitutional weakness or ill health of the male parent. In other cases a man who is healthy and constitutionally strong in other respects, may yet be unable to procreate healthy and vigorous children; and if his children are stunted and feeble, it will be likely that they will also be deficient in intellect. In other cases again, the failure in vigour that occurs with advancing life, and which weighs on the procreative function with at least as heavy a stress as upon the other functions, may be the cause of the lack of vigour in the impetus that is given to the germ. Hence children, who are born late in the life of the parents, are seldom as intellectual as those born at the period of greatest vigour; and when all the children are defective, those who are born latest are most defective. Dr. Clouston records a most instructive case of a lady, herself upon the borderland of insanity, who had fourteen children. "The first four of these were fairly healthy, and are still living; then came the subject of the present note (a certified lunatic) . . . and after her came nine children, all of whom are now dead. The elder ones lived longest; and then, as the mother grew in years, the strain on her became greater, the duration of the life of her offspring shortened."

Or the insufficient impetus may, as we have seen, be due to an insufficiency in the *number* of male elements which reach and unite with the ovum. Here again the fault may be in the male, who produces elements in insufficient quantity, or it may be that a sufficient quantity is produced, but from some accidental cause, enough do not reach the ovum to give the requisite impulse to the developmental process, and this may account for the occasional occurrence of a single case of idiocy in a family of otherwise vigorous and healthy children.

Again, the insufficient impetus may be due to some unsuitability of the male to the female element. What the cause or nature of the unsuitability may be we do not know, but it is a well-ascertained fact that females, which were either previously or subsequently proved to be fertile, have failed to breed with particular males, also of undoubted fertility. Instances have been observed with horses, cattle, pigs, foxhounds and other dogs, and pigeons. Now if we suppose the unsuitability or incompatibility of the male to the female to be somewhat less in degree, so that some offspring would be produced ; but to still exist, so that the impetus given to the germ would be insufficient to produce perfect offspring, we should have another cause for the production of idiocy.

The defect in the vigour of the developmental impetus need not necessarily be in the male element, nor in the unsuitability of the male element, from too great similarity or difference or other cause, to the female ; it may lie in the defective vigour of the germ itself. We have seen how every germ has of itself a certain tendency to develop, and how in some cases this tendency is carried to actual completion, and to the production of offspring without help from the male. Ordinarily the additional impetus imparted by the union of the male element is required to carry the process to completion, and ordinarily this impetus is sufficient. But it may happen that the germ itself is of so sluggish a nature, and contains within itself so feeble a capacity for development, that not even the impetus given by the union of abundance of suitable and vigorous male elements is sufficient to give it the necessary start, and the process comes to a premature close, with the result that the offspring is idiotic.

Any condition of impaired vigour in the female, present at the time of conception, may be a cause of this defect of energy in the germ. Thus we find that the children born at the extreme end of the child-bearing period are seldom of great bodily or mental vigour, and that when a woman has suffered during her pregnancy from an exhausting disease, the child may be idiotic.

If idiocy and imbecility be, as is here asserted, due to a premature cessation of the process of development, then we should expect to find in idiots and in imbeciles other evidence, if other evidence there be, of this premature cessation. It has already been shown that one other effect of the early failure of the process of development will be the inaptitude of the individual in whom it so fails to attain the full size and stature of his race; and it is an indisputable fact that the vast majority of idiots and imbeciles are stunted and undersized.

Although this is the rule, it is not an absolute rule; imbeciles being occasionally of normal stature and proportions; and it is notorious that giants are almost always persons of feeble intellect, while many men of undoubted genius have been of diminutive stature; so that some factor in the causation of feebleness of mind, which accounts for such cases, must have been hitherto overlooked. The factor in question seems to be this : Between mere growth, that is to say, increase of size, and development, or increase in elaborateness and complexity, there is a certain antagonism, so that growth in size proceeds partly at the expense of increase in elaborateness, and *vice versâ*. It requires a genetic impulse of very unusual vigour to produce an organism of more than average size, which also carries the last and most elaborate stages of organization to a more than average extent. Plants which grow very luxuriantly, and attain an

unusual size, sometimes do not flower. European vegetables in the hot climate of India grow to rampant excess ;
and in order to make them yield seed it has been found
necessary to reduce this excess of growth, by cutting and
mutilating the roots or stems. Fruit-trees which are
" making too much wood " are always regarded unfavour-
ably by gardeners, for they never bear much fruit. The
highest nerve regions have already been shown to be the
highest and last outcome of human development, the
supreme climax of the unfolding of the organism, and to
be in this respect comparable to the flower and fruit of
plants. From this point of view, the feeble intellect, often
found in persons of abnormal size, becomes explicable ; and
the small stature of many of the men of great genius, whose
names live in history, likewise receives an explanation. We
have to suppose that up to a certain point growth and
development proceed *pari passu*, but that at length the one
gains a preponderance over the other and increases at its
expense. If we train a fruit-tree into what gardeners call a
" double oblique cordon," that is to say, into such a form
that it has two main branches of equal size, and growing in
a slanting direction at equal angles with the horizontal,
there is no difficulty in maintaining the equality between
the size of the branches, as long as the angles at which they
grow are equal. But if we allow one branch to grow more
erect than the other, it at once begins to preponderate in
size. It is not merely that the more upright branch grows
more quickly, but that it diverts to its own use sap that
should have flowed to the other branch, and thus retards
the growth of that other. Both depend for their nourishment on a common supply ; and the more of this supply is
appropriated by the one, the less remains at the service of
the other. Similarly there are two branches to the evolution of the human organism :—growth, and elaboration, both
drawing from a common source the energy which keeps
them going. If either process appropriates to its own use
more than a just moiety of energy, it will increase, not

merely faster than the other, but at the expense of the other ; and by as much as the one exceeds the standard which it would have attained had the forces been equally apportioned, by so much the other falls short of that standard.

Original or congenital deficiency of intellect, which, when extreme, is called idiocy, when less in degree but still very decided, is called imbecility, and when of still less degree is termed weakness of mind, is always due to a premature cessation of the process of development, from which results an absence of the last results of the developmental process— the highest of all the nerve regions. This premature cessation of development depends, in the great majority of cases, on a defect in the original impulse with which the process started, the effect of which is that the process dies out before it is completed. In a few cases, however, it happens that the original impulse was sufficient, but that an undue share of the energy so derived has gone to produce mere increase of size, leaving too small a remainder to carry the process of development to completion. Such are the conclusions to which we are brought by a study of the results of inbreeding. Let us now turn to the converse aspect of the case and trace the results of the union of widely dissimilar parents.

It has been shown that the vigour of the impetus, which the ovum receives from the union of the male element, depends in part upon the degree to which the male element differs from the female ; and it has been further shown that there are other factors which make for or against an energetic start of the developmental process. These other factors are, as we have already seen, inherent vigour of the female, and of the male elements, number of the latter, and suitability of the latter to the former, both in degree of difference and in other unknown particulars. Granted that the circumstances are favourable, and that the germ receives a vigorous impulse to start it on its course of development, we have next to notice that the vigour of the impulse may exhibit itself in different ways. To recur to our simile of the rolling ball. Let us suppose that two bowls of equal size are started rolling along a lawn ; and let us suppose that one ball is of solid *lignum vitæ*, and the other is of hollow india-rubber. The result will be that, if the velocities are duly proportioned and the lawn is smooth, both balls will travel about the same distance and in a direct line ; but if the lawn is lumpy with worm-casts and tufts of grass, the heavy ball will crush the obstacles and hold its own course in spite of them, while the light one will, especially towards the end of its course when its velocity is diminishing, be diverted from the straight direction by each irregularity that it strikes against, and will come to rest at a greater or less distance from the direct line of propulsion. There is a similar set of conditions influencing the progress of organisms along the path of development ; for while some progress steadily in the straightforward direction of the general course of development common to the race, others, although developing to an equal extent, going equally far in the elaborateness and completeness of their development, attaining an equal degree of ability, yet diverge in new directions, exhibit their ability in different ways, or even swerve so far out of the usual line as to exhibit eccentricities of conduct which amount to actual insanity.

What the precise conditions are which make this difference in the course of development it is not yet possible to say, but undoubtedly one most important factor is the *rate* at which the development takes place. The extent to which development proceeds—the height that it attains—depends upon the vigour of the initial impetus that is given to the process ; and consequently two individuals receiving impetus of equal magnitude will proceed equally far and attain an equal elaborateness of development. But although they attain equal heights of development, they may not attain these equal heights in equal times. One may develop rapidly, and attain completion while the other is still immature, while the other may tardily, and after a long interval, reach the same degree of perfection ; and the results of the two processes, which are of equal extent, will differ greatly according to the velocity with which they have been conducted.

When a carpenter is making some common rough article to serve a temporary purpose, such as a packing-case or a crate, or when he is making a structure which is not intended to bear stress of weather or to be exposed to the destructive agency of wet and frost, such as rafters or flooring, he uses some soft wood, such as deal or pine, the product of a quickly-growing tree. But when he is making some object which is meant to last, such as cabinet work or ornamental carving, or when he is making an article like a gate-post or a paling, which is to be exposed to the vicissitudes of the weather, and the rotting agency of wet and frost alternating with drought, he uses the hardest and toughest woods that he can get—mahogany, teak, and oak, the product of trees of the slowest growth. He finds, in short, that the product which results from the longer, slower, and more gradual process, is more stable and of longer endurance than that which is produced more rapidly. The gourd which springs up from a seed, covers yards of ground with its foliage, flowers, and fruits, all within a couple of months, withers in a single night, and rots indistinguishably into the earth in a few weeks. The iron-wood, whose annual growth is scarcely appreciable, and which takes a century to mature, is so hard as to turn the edge of steel tools, and is virtually almost indestructible. So the horse, which arrives at full stature and maturity at five years of age, is senile at twenty ; man, who requires twenty years to reach maturity, often retains his vigour till eighty, and the elephant, which does not attain its full growth till thirty, lives considerably more than a century. It is the same with other things—with all things. The business which has existed for long, and has been handed down from father to son for generations, survives the panics which ruin the firms of yesterday. "Light come, light go" has become a proverb, indicating the ease with which for-

13

tunes rapidly accumulated are rapidly dispersed. The jerry-built house, which is run up in three months, is scarcely complete before it begins to decay ; while the house which is soundly built is also built slowly. The construction of the plans is a slower process. The concrete foundations are allowed time to consolidate before the superstructure is raised upon them ; the wood has been allowed time to season before it is used ; the bricks have been burnt slowly to get them uniformly hardened ; the mortar is allowed time to set before weights are placed on it ; the paint is allowed time to dry before another coat is applied. The newspaper article which is forgotten five minutes after it is read, was scribbled off at high pressure in a few minutes while the printer's devil was waiting for copy ; the book which lasts for generations and is read by posterity, is the result of the labour and thought of years. The more slowly glass is annealed, the less brittle it becomes. To get vegetables tender and succulent it is necessary to grow them on rapidly ; those that are slow in growing are always tough and stringy. When the Oklahoma territory was first colonized by the United States, a town grew up in a single night—a town with its drinking-bars, post-office, newspaper, and bank complete. In a week the town was gone, its shanties ruined, and its streets desolate. Such things do not happen in an old country. An English hamlet of but a dozen houses remains year after year, decade after decade, century after century ; for it has grown gradually to be what it is. As to changes in the weather, it has passed into a proverb that "Long foretold, long last ; short notice, soon past." Throughout the whole universe both of nature and of art, the law is always true, that "the slow alone shall last, and the gradual only endure." It would be strange indeed if in one isolated province of nature this law, otherwise universal, did not obtain, and if those highest nervous regions which have developed rapidly, and attained completion by leaps and bounds, were not more unstable, and more easily disordered and disintegrated, than those which have attained maturity by a more gradual process. As a matter of fact it is found that in this, as in other provinces of nature, the law holds good.

When we increase the rate at which the development of an organism proceeds, the results of the development are less stable, are more easily varied and disordered than when development proceeds more slowly. Thus we find that domesticated animals, in which the capacity to mature early has been implanted by cross-breeding, and carefully nursed by selection, are far more prone to vary, are less uniform in character, resemble one another far less closely than wild animals of the same species whose development is more gradual ; and we find, moreover, that domesticated animals are more subject to disease than wild ones. The tendency of precocious children to die young has become a matter of notoriety. But the most frequent and most conspicuous result of an undue rapidity of development, and especially of the last stages of development, is unstability of the highest nervous arrangements. We have seen that a certain degree of instability is essential to the constitution of the nervous system, and without this instability it cannot act. Hence it will naturally happen that when the organism as a whole is less stably constituted than usual, the increase of instability will be especially marked in that tissue which is normally less stable than the rest. If the nervous system, and especially its highest regions, be more than usually unstable, what will be the result ? Broadly speaking, the results will be as follows.

The normal instability being increased, the normal discharges will take place on less provocation than in more stably constituted individuals. Reaction will take place on slighter impressions. Hence we find that cross-bred animals, which are distinguished on the one hand by early maturity, that is to say by rapid development, are distinguished also by their wildness. "Thus the Earl of Powis formerly imported some thoroughly domesticated humped cattle from India, and crossed them with English breeds, which belong

to a distinct species ; and his agent remarked to me, without
any question having been asked, how oddly wild the cross-
bred animals were." "Sir F. Darwin crossed a sow of the
latter [Chinese domesticated] breed with a wild Alpine boar
which had become extremely tame, but the young, though
having half-domesticated blood in their veins, were extremely
wild in confinement." "Captain Hutton, in India, crossed
a tame goat with a wild one from the Himalayas, and he
remarked to me how surprisingly wild the offspring were."
The same peculiarity has been noticed in pheasants, fowls,
ducks, finches, and other animals.[1] Now the character which
distinguishes wild animals from tame ones is their much
more energetic reaction to slight impressions. The snapping
of a twig, a distant footstep, a whiff of scent from an animal
passing far away, is enough to make the wild animal start
up on the alert, to put every muscle in his body in a state of
tension in readiness for instant flight, or to scare him into
headlong activity. The tame animal, on the other hand, will
bear to be approached, spoken to, patted, scratched, and
punched without being roused out of his sluggish contentment.

Not only will the more rapidly developed, and therefore
more unstable, organism react to slighter impressions than
the slower growing and more stable individual, but to impressions of the same intensity the former will react more
vigorously. Hence they will be generally of greater activity,
capable of stronger, more rapid, and more sustained movement than the stably constituted organism. The wildness
of crossed species, which is from one point of view a reaction to slighter impressions, is from another point of view
a more vigorous reaction to impressions of equal intensity.
The crossing of varieties and races and "strains" produces
invariably, with the increase of size and the earlier maturity,
on which we have already insisted, an increase of *vigour* in

---

[1] Darwin, "Variation of Animals and Plants under Domestication,"
1875, vol. ii. p. 19.

the offspring ; that is to say, an increase in the energy of their reaction to impressions.

From our present point of view, the most important result of an undue rapidity of the process of development is the structural instability of the tissues so developed. When the highest nerve regions attain completion very early in life as the result of an unduly rapid development, they will be unduly liable to derangement upon slight provocation ; and hence we find that very precocious children are very liable to nervous disorders ; and that such individuals, on attaining adult age, are very liable to insanity. "There be some," says Bacon, "have an over early ripeness in their years, which fadeth betimes."

There is yet another aspect of this subject that has to be considered. Height of intelligence depends in the main upon height of development ; but one element in high intelligence is the readiness with which the higher regions of the nerve tissue undergo rearrangement. The more easily new combinations of cells and fibres are formed, the more readily new channels can be excavated in the grey matter, the greater the facility with which rearrangements and recombinations are effected, the more easily can new courses of conduct and new modes of thought be originated, and the more complex are the reactions that the individual can effect upon his circumstances. Now this readiness to undergo rearrangement is, of course, in other terms, mobility or instability of the nerve tissue, and, as such, is greatly favoured by rapidity of development. Rapidity of development, as it is a factor in the production of insanity, is also therefore a factor in the production of high intelligence, and thus there is a sound scientific basis for the saying of Dryden that—

> " Great wits to madness sure are near allied,
> And thin partitions do their bounds divide."

Hence we shall expect to find that those individuals who develop rapidly will as a rule be more intelligent than those who develop slowly, and this we find to be the case ; for, as

a rule, it is undoubted that the intelligent child makes the
clever man and the backward child the dull man. The rule
is of course not without exceptions, for, as we have already
seen, height of intelligence depends essentially on extent of
development, and the more rapid process of development
does not necessarily proceed further than the slower one.
Hence we sometimes come across an individual who was dull
in childhood and youth, and developed later in life a high
degree of intelligence. In such individuals the intelligence
will be of very stable and enduring character.

On every hand we have evidence of the truth of our main
proposition, that the more rapid the development of the
highest nervous centres, the less stable is the result. We
have now to notice that this instability may reach so high a
degree as to surpass the limits of the normal. The reaction
to impressions may be so vigorous as to be manifestly in
excess : conduct may become outrageous. Or, to put it
more accurately, a certain amount of decomposition of the
nerve tissue we have seen to be necessary for the performance
of the function of that tissue. This decomposition is in
normal organisms prevented, by the inherent stability of
their tissue, from occurring in excess. But, when the tissues
are unduly unstable, and the check on its progress is
diminished, it may easily take place in such excess as to
produce actual disorganization of the highest nervous
regions ; which disorganization is, as we have seen, the
physical defect which underlies insanity. Doubtless it sometimes, though rarely, happens that an organism developes
with great rapidity and yet presents no evidence or no
striking evidence of instability ; but this may be accounted
for by its possession of what, for want of a better term, I
must call momentum. We have already seen how the
heavy ball, from its greater momentum presses steadily
forwards when the light one, proceeding at even a higher
velocity, is diverted from its course ; and similarly a railway
train that is to travel at a very high speed is made very
heavy. If it is too light it will be apt to run off the line.

There seems to be some analogous property in developing organisms which enables those which possess it in a high degree to proceed straight onward in spite of a high velocity, while those in which it is wanting are easily diverted from their course.

The conclusions at which we arrive with regard to the bearing of the second law of inheritance upon the production of insanity are therefore these :—

1. When the germ starts upon its course of development with an insufficient impetus, the development of the organism in general, and the highest nervous regions in particular, will be incomplete ; and this incompleteness, when slight, will show itself as feebleness of mind, when considerable as imbecility, and when extreme as idiocy. A still greater defect in the impetus will result in the non-production of living offspring.

2. When the impetus given to the germ is such that development proceeds with undue speed, the later stages will be apt to be faulty, and the organism so developed will be unstable, and will be prone to insanity.

CHAPTER VII.

THE CAUSES OF INSANITY (*Continued*).

Direct Stress.

IT was said at the outset of the preceding chapter that
every individual has his breaking-point ; that is to say, that
if you subject him to sufficient stress he will become insane.
The amount of stress that his highest nerve regions will be
able to bear before breaking down, depends on the stability
of constitution which he has derived from his parentage and
ancestry, as already considered. It now remains to consider
the complementary factor, and to enumerate and describe
the various stresses to which men and women are subject,
and which make for the production of insanity.

The stresses which act on and tend to disorder the
highest nerve regions are divisible, first, into the direct and
the indirect ; the former being produced by the action of
some noxious agent immediately upon the centres themselves,
the latter by agents acting on the peripheral ends of the
nerves, and setting up currents, which break upon the
highest nerve regions, and by some abnormal element of
volume or intensity, so act on these regions as to produce
disorder in them.

The direct stresses arise either from the direct application
of mechanical violence by blows on the head, or from inflammation of the brain itself, or the parts immediately
adjacent, as in meningitis, or from pressure by the rupture
of a blood-vessel, and the escape of blood into the rigid
chamber of the skull, or from the pressure of a tumour, or

from actual destruction by the ploughing-up of the brain tissue by a blood-clot, or by the encroachment of a tumour, or from the influence on the highest nerve regions of some alteration in the blood which bathes them. It is easy to understand how readily a structure of such extreme delicacy and sensitiveness as that of the highest nerve regions, can have its action altered and disordered by any alteration of deleterious character in the composition of the blood in which it lies, and, as it were, soaks.

The indirect stresses are of two 'kinds : first, those in which the agent is some commotion in the organism itself, acting on the visceral nerves and producing an alteration in those internally initiated currents whose wash upon the shore of the highest centres we have already discovered to be the foundation of the cœnæsthesis. Such internal commotions may be either general, accompanying some change which affects the whole of the body, such as those which takes place at puberty, at the climacteric, and in pregnancy ; or it may be a local affair, some local lesion, an ulcer of stomach or intestine, or tuberculosis of lung, or disease of bladder or other organ.

Lastly, there are the stresses of external origin, those produced by agents or events in the environment acting on the highest nerve regions through the ordinary channels of the special senses, the ingoing nerves and the lower and intermediary centres. Such are the so-called moral causes of insanity, adverse circumstances, worries, anxieties, and troubles of various kinds.

The direct stresses differ from the indirect mainly in this, that from the character of their action, from the immediateness of their application to the highest nerve regions, their effect is so powerful, that no nervous system, however stably constituted, can resist them. While no indirect stress of ordinary intensity can produce insanity by its action on a nervous system of normal stability ; and while it is doubtful whether an indirect stress, of however great intensity, can produce insanity, unless the nervous system on which it acts

is predisposed, by inherited instability of constitution, to
become disordered ; there is no nervous system, however
soundly or stably constituted, which is able to withstand the
influence of a direct stress of even moderate severity. It
takes a harder knock on the head to stun one man than to
stun another ; but if you only hit hard enough, you can
stun the strongest and sturdiest man alive.

The first of the direct stresses that has to be considered
is that of blows on the head. Wounds of localized portions
of the brain we need not consider, for their effect is local,
and any general symptoms of involvement of a large area
arise as a consequence of the secondary effect of inflammation,
which will be considered subsequently. At present we are
concerned with those blows only, which are widely distributed, and have a general effect, such as are inflicted by
heavy and blunt instruments, or such as result from falls.
The effect of such a blow is, of course, to produce a violent
shake of the whole contents of the skull. The brain is
knocked against its bony case, and the several parts of the
brain, firmly and carefully as they are tied and fixed in their
several positions, are violently jolted against one another.
The local effects, the bruising, the effusion of small patches
of blood, we may neglect, and may confine ourselves to the
general effect of such a shake on the constitution of the
nerve centres. The effect will be, that not only is the mass
of the brain shaken about ; not only are the hemispheres,
convolutions, and great masses of grey and white matter
jolted and banged against each other, but the molecules also,
the fine particular structures of the brain, are shaken up,
jolted against one another, and displaced.

We have already seen how the oldest and most fundamental arrangements of the nervous tissue are also the
most completely organized ; that is to say, the most firmly
and compactly fixed in their places, while the newest
are retained in position by the weakest and slenderest
ties. Hence, if the brain is subjected to a general shake,
the most recently organized portions will suffer most,

and the oldest and most firmly compacted will suffer least. Now the most recently organized portions of the brain are those whose action is accompanied by consciousness; the oldest have no such accompaniment, and the middle portion has a dim, partial, or twilight consciousness attending its action. Hence if the blow on the head is very severe indeed, the resulting commotion will be so great that even the most firmly compacted arrangements will be disorganized, the nervous arrangements which actuate the heart's movements will be broken up, the heart will cease to act, and the man will drop dead. If the blow is less severe, so as to derange the upper and middle areas, while leaving the lower capable of acting, the man will live on, but since that portion of the brain whose action has a conscious accompaniment is out of gear and out of action, consciousness will cease. The man will be stunned. At the same time that the conscious accompaniment of their action is abolished, the results of the action of these centres—their functions—will also be abolished, and their functions are to actuate conduct and movements generally, so that conduct and movement will be annulled at the same time that consciousness is lost. Observe, not *because* consciousness is lost, but at the same time and for the same reason. If the blow is still less severe, so as to derange considerably only the topmost of the nervous centres, consciousness will not be altogether lost. Much will be lost indeed, but some will be retained. A twilight consciousness of more or less intensity will remain, and the man will be dazed and confused, but not insensible. Correspondingly, conduct and movements will not be abolished, but they will be disordered. The sufferer will not fall senseless and motionless, but he will stagger and grope about, bewildered.

The molecules which have been thus shaken up and disturbed will gradually, as time elapses, tend to return, and will in great measure return to their former positions. Here again see the advantage of a mobile equilibrium. Stick the point of a teetotum into the ground, and it will stand upright, but now give it a knock, and over it goes, never to rise again. But set the teetotum spinning, and again it stands upright, not quite so steadily, but still it stands. Now give it a knock and see what happens. A much slighter knock suffices now to disturb its equilibrium, and make it sway about ; but when it has been knocked out of the perpendicular, it returns to it again and again. It may be depresssed until its stem becomes actually horizontal, and still it won't fall. The same advantages are gained by the mobile equilibrium in which the nervous molecules are arranged. They are more easily knocked out of their places than those of a bit of iron, it is true, but when you have made a dent in the iron it remains for ever, and does not tend of itself to fill up ; while the nervous molecules, when they have been displaced, tend, unless they have been altogether dislocated, to return to their old positions. It is natural that those which have been more deeply organized, more firmly compacted in their places, should have been displaced to the least extent, and should be the first to regain their old positions. So that we find breathing recovers first, then, as consciousness begins to glimmer, the simple movements become possible, the patient groans when disturbed, and opens his eyes when questioned. Then the daylight of consciousness broadens and brightens, the man begins to be aware of where he is, to recognize his surroundings, to stir uneasily on his couch and to move his arms. Then he is able to get up and stagger about, and his mind has returned in great part, but he is still confused and dazed ; and at length he becomes completely conscious and capable once more.

The tendency of the molecules to return to their old places depends, as we have seen, on the strength of the tie which binds them there. This tie depends in every one on the completeness of the organization of the particular nervous arrangement, that is to say on the length of time it has been in existence and the number of times it has been in action. But in some people and in some brains the

strength of this tie is stronger than in others. Some
nervous systems are stable and others unstable. Hence the
tendency of the molecules to return to their places will vary
in different people, in some being strong and in others weak.
In either case those arrangements will be the last to return
and will find the most difficulty in returning, will be most
prone not to return at all, which are the newest, and therefore the least completely organized, and the least firmly
settled in their new positions. A blow on a strong and
stable brain may stun, and then, as the molecules, after their
shake, return to their old positions, and consciousness
returns, it may be found that the very last and newest of
all the arrangements, those into which the molecules have
fallen during the few minutes or hours preceding the blow,
fail to return to their places. They were shaken completely
out of their orbits and have failed to return to the arrangement, new and frail and unorganized as it was, in which
they existed just before the accident occurred. In such a
case the patient will lose, with the nervous arrangement
that events produced in him, the memory of the events.
He will remember everything that happened up to a certain
time before the accident, a time sufficient to allow the new
arrangements, produced by the action of passing events, to
consolidate and settle ; but those nervous arrangements of
more recent production will be hopelessly lost.

The same blow falling upon a brain whose arrangements
were less stable, whose molecules were retained in their
orbits by a less powerful attraction, might easily produce a
more profound disorganization. In such a case certain of
the arrangements might be retained to a high level and
others lost to a comparatively low one, some might be completely disorganized, others disarranged in various degrees.
So that when some order was restored ; when the excessive
and hyperbolic swing of the molecules produced by the
blow had settled down into a gyration more nearly approaching the normal ; when such of the higher centres as were
not completely disorganized resumed their function ; and

such as were injured and altered had resumed what function they were capable of ; it would be found that the state of that person's consciousness was now completely different from what it had been before ; it would be found that the same circumstances acting on the altered structure would evoke an altered reaction, that the damaged and defective structure was no longer capable of acting normally. If the damage were local and were confined to a low level in the nervous hierarchy, then there would be paralysis without insanity ; but if it were more general and more diffused over the higher regions, then the result of the blow would be to produce insanity ; and thus are explained those cases of insanity whose origin is directly traumatic.

Next to blows we may consider a frequent consequence of blows—inflammation. Acute inflammation of the brain-substance itself, is very rare. Practically, the only acute inflammation within the skull with which we are acquainted, is that which affects the membranes. The whole of the surface of the brain is covered by a filmy cobweb-like membrane which dips down into all the hollows and grooves between the convolutions, and carries the blood-vessels for the supply of the grey matter which lies on the surface of the brain. Now this grey matter on the surface is the seat of the highest nerve regions, and hence when the membrane which lies in actual contact with it is inflamed, it can readily be understood that the highest nerve regions must suffer severely in structure and in action.

Inflammation of the membranes of the brain is not usually attended by active insanity, never by intelligent insanity. The invasion of the disease being gradual, and its area widespread, the conditions, which are necessary for the occurrence of active insanity, do not exist, and active insanity does not occur. There is, however, a condition of hebetude, dullness, and inactivity, which is the equivalent of dementia ; which is, in fact, a dementia of sudden origin and rapid course. This hebetude quickly deepens into stupor ; and the stupor passes in a few days into coma ; showing that the disorder takes the classical course of involving the nerve centres and regions in their order from above downwards, and thus is assimilated in its main features to insanity, although, since the bodily disorders are so much more prominent, it is not looked upon clinically as a case of disorder of mind. It is necessary to guard against being misled by superficial differences, and against failure to recognize the identity of fundamental nature that exists between maladies that are usually treated by different methods, and regarded from different points of view. An inflammatory process in the membranes and superficial parts of the brain, if widespread and intense, will rapidly and completely obliterate the functions of the nerve tissue to a considerable depth, and so will produce a condition of stupor, deepening into coma. The same process, if more limited and less acute, will act more slowly. An interval will elapse between the removal of the highest centres and that of those beneath them. During this interval the centres beneath the highest will be free to act without the control of their superiors, and such uncontrolled action will show itself in delirium. Hence, in meningitis delirium is common. If now the factors are slightly rearranged ; if the process is still less intense ; if the mode of invasion of the disease is of such a character that but a thin paring, as it were, is taken off the highest regions of the brain, and the immediately subjacent area not only overacts, but overacts very strenuously and energetically, then the symptoms exhibited will not be those of stupor, as in the first case, nor of a quiet and busy delirium as in the second case, but there will be a violent outburst of intense excitement, which will take the form of acute delirious mania. The one patient will be treated at home or will find ready admission into a general hospital, and will come under the care of a general physician ; the other will be taken to a lunatic asylum, and come under the care of an alienist. The two cases will be studied by different people from different points of view, and will be described in different books ; and hence their real identity of nature will be obscured and overlooked ; it is necessary, therefore, the more strongly to insist that the maladies are in reality but different phases and manifestations of the same disorder. The backward condition of our knowledge of the pathology of insanity is owing, beyond all doubt, in the main to the dissociation of its study from that of the pathology of those other disorders of the nervous system which come under the notice of the general physician and the surgeon.

The stresses that are produced by increase of the normal intracranial pressure, whether this increase of pressure be due to hæmorrhage, or to the encroachment of a tumour, or to the formation of an abscess, or to other cause, need not detain us long ; for it is found, as a matter of experience, that such increase of pressure never produces active insanity. The effect of pressure is to obliterate the cerebral functions without this obliteration having much complementary over-action as an accompaniment. The loss of function is felt, according to rule, first and most in the highest regions, and spreads, according to the same rule, gradually downward to the lowest. Hence the first effect of increased pressure is dulness of mind and inactivity of body ; and as the pressure increases, the dulness deepens and passes into stupor, and the inactivity increases to paralysis. Then the stupor deepens and passes into coma, and the paralysis becomes universal, so that the apoplectic state is reached ; lastly, the coma ends in death by failure of breathing, in the classical order. Whatever over-action there is, takes place on a low level ; signs of over-activity of the higher regions, such as delirium or mania, are never exhibited in cases of simple intracranial pressure ; but the absence of these signs of overaction, and the conspicuousness of the bodily defects and disorders, must not blind us to the fact that the effect of this form of stress is to produce a gradual obliteration of both mind and conduct, which is fundamentally the same process as, when spread out thin and extending over years instead of hours, goes by the name of dementia, and lands its exhibitors in lunatic asylums.

The next form of stress—that which arises from alterations in the character of the blood which bathes, nourishes, and clarifies the nervous system—is of a less violent and brutal character than those hitherto considered ; but, on the other hand, its operation is of the most direct description, it is applied in the most immediate and intimate manner to the nervous elements, and its effect is proportionately immediate and great. It is obvious that any alteration in the constitution of the blood must at once affect the character of the nutriment supplied to the higher nerve regions, must affect the capacity of the blood to carry from these regions their waste material, and so must be liable to interfere with and alter their working. As a matter of fact, we find that every alteration in the blood is at once responded to by a modification in the action of the nervous system—a modification which is, of course, most marked in the highest regions of the system.

Take first the simplest alteration, a mere defect in the blood supply, consequent on a copious hæmorrhage. If a man receives a severe wound, and rapidly loses a large quantity of blood, what is the result ? The result is that he faints. He falls to the ground unconscious and void of spontaneous movement. Consciousness and conduct are simultaneously abolished ; and the abolition of consciousness and conduct means the abolition of the function of the whole of the nervous hierarchy down to a low level of rank. Or suppose that the blood, instead of being suddenly diminished in quantity by hæmorrhage, simply ceases to circulate, by failure of the heart's action. The result is the same—fainting or syncope follows at once ; the nerve centres cease to act.

Now suppose that the blood is deteriorated in quality, is thinner and more watery than normal, is in fact diluted, as occurs in anæmia ; then it will happen that the nerve centres, while nourished to a certain extent, are not well nourished. Their pabulum is supplied to them in a too dilute and attenuated form, and their nourishment, and therefore their function, suffers in consequence. Their action in such circumstances is feeble, anergic, sluggish. If we observe a person suffering from anæmia, we see in the pallid and transparent complexion, in the pearly hue of the white of the eye, and in the pale colour of the lips, evidence of the poverty and thinness of the blood ; and such persons, we notice, are inactive ; they are indisposed to exertion, it is difficult to rouse them to full working order, and difficult to maintain them in full activity. Their movements are sluggish, feeble, and unsustained. If we turn from conduct, and seek evidence of the state of their minds, we find evidence of a corresponding condition. They are never bright in intellect. If previously of alert and active mind, they become slow of thought and feeble in expression. Often they will sit for long, inactive, with dropped hands, gazing at vacancy. Rouse them up and ask them what they are thinking of, and they will appear to wake and come to the surface, and will answer " Nothing ; " and this is, no doubt, approximately true. For the time, consciousness, without being altogether in abeyance, was wanting in force, and vividness, and brightness. It was clouded over. In this condition of dulled activity of mind and body, a dulness which affects only the highest regions ; which does not affect the ordinary and habitual adjustments to circum-stances ; which does not prevent, although it renders more difficult and laborious, the formation of new adjustments ;— we see just that amount of diminution in the activity of the highest nerve regions which might be expected to result from a deterioration in the quality of the pabulum supplied to them.

In close alliance with these more trifling and more tem-porary cases of damage to the function of the highest nerve region from loss or poverty of blood, are other cases in which, from reinforcement of other unfavourable conditions, the damage is more severe and more lasting. When a large quantity of blood is rapidly lost, as when a large artery is wounded, the patient not only faints, but often he has a convulsion. That is to say, the higher nerve centres cease to act, and this cessation of action produces universal paralysis, and is accompanied by loss of consciousness, so that the patient falls down and becomes insensible. But it may happen, if the blood is lost with slightly less rapidity, or if the nervous system is naturally slightly more unstable than usual, that, instead of the whole functions of the brain being lost at once, their loss, though rapid, it may be very rapid, is yet sufficiently gradual for a certain order to be exhibited. When the loss takes place in any order, it is the highest faculties that are first lost ; and throughout the nervous system the function of control, restraint, or inhibition, is always higher than that of initiation or activity, since, as we have seen, the restraint is always exercised by a centre of higher rank than that which actuates the movement. Hence, if the abolition of function is extremely rapid, all the centres will be affected nearly simultaneously, and instead of the highest centres being completely lost before the second rank is attacked, and the second completely abolished before the third suffers, it will happen that all the centres will nearly simultaneously lose first their highest function, and then all will lose their lower function, the highest centres preceding the lower in their loss by only a small interval. The result of the sudden and nearly simultaneous loss of their highest function—inhibition—by a large number of centres, will be the sudden and excessive overaction of a large number of centres, the outward expression of which will be a universal convulsion.

From an attack of convulsion to an outbreak of mania is but a short step. We have but to imagine the removal of control to be confined to the higher centres instead of being universal, and to be of more gradual character ; and the consequent overaction to take place in those centres only which are just below the highest instead of throughout the hierarchy, and to be of more gradual character also ;

and the outward manifestation will be, not a convulsion, but an outbreak of mania. Hence we may expect to find that when the influence acting on the nervous system is not of the sudden and extreme character, the abrupt arrest of nourishment, produced by a great and rapid loss of blood, but is of more deliberate and gradual onset, the result will be an outbreak of mania. Hence we find that when people are dying by inches from the effect of slow and small but prolonged hæmorrhages, the last stages are attended by delirium. Hence in death from starvation maniacal delirium usually occurs before the close.

It may be that the blood is of sufficiently good quality, and sufficiently rich in nutritive materials, but that it does not reach the highest nerve regions in sufficient quantity; and in such cases the result will be the same as if it were deteriorated in quality by loss or starvation. It must be remembered that the highest nerve regions are the last to be formed; they are the structures of latest growth; and not only is their intrinsic composition less perfectly organized, and on that account more liable to disturbance than the inferior regions; but their blood supply also is inferior in the stability of its arrangements. In the first place they are in point of distance the furthest from the heart, the centre of propulsion of the circulation, and hence any defect in the propelling power of the heart will be most felt by them. In the second place, being of comparatively recent formation, their blood vessels will not be so thoroughly well formed and organized into adaptation with their requirements as those of older tissues. Hence, on both grounds, any defect in the vigour of the circulation will make itself most conspicuously apparent in the highest nerve regions. In much the same way, the water supply to a new house will be more likely to fail than that to an older one, on account of defects of workmanship and miscalculations as to the quantity required at particular places. When the house has been inhabited for some time, any irregularities and defects will have become apparent, and will have been rectified. If the house is not only new, but is situated furthest of all from the pumping station, then it is evident that any weakness in the pumps will be most severely felt in the house that is furthest away. For these reasons we may expect that not only in conditions in which the blood is deteriorated in quality, but also in diseases in which, from failure of the propelling power of the heart, or from some obstacle to the free passage of the blood from the heart to the brain, or from some diversion of large quantities of blood in other directions, the amount of blood that passes through the highest nerve regions is reduced in quantity, in such cases evidence of disorder of mind and conduct will always be present; and when the blood supply is greatly diminished, the disorder of mind and conduct will become sufficiently conspicuous and sufficiently great to amount to insanity. Hence in the latter stages of valvular disease of the heart, delirium is a frequent occurrence; in inflammation of the heart, pericarditis and endocarditis, it occasionally occurs. In severe attacks of bronchitis, when there is evidence from the blueness of the lips and other signs that the blood is passing through the head in small quantity and slowly, some hebetude and lack of animation is always present; confusion of mind is common; and delirium is of occasional occurrence.

Any stress which, acting on a brain of normal stability, will give rise to hebetude, confusion of mind, and light or transient delirium, will, if it acts upon a brain of less than normal stability, produce the same effects in a more exaggerated form, and thus produce insanity. Hence it is found that while in every case of heart disease, when circulation at length fails, signs of disorder or defect of mind and conduct become apparent, there is a certain proportion of cases of heart disease in which the disorder of mind and conduct amounts to actual insanity; and these are the cases in which the defective circulation passes through an unusually unstable brain. Many cases have been recorded in which the delirium that so commonly attends pericarditis lasted not for a few hours, or with intermissions and remissions for a few days, but for weeks and months.

From stresses arising from loss of blood, from deterioration in the quality of the blood, and from sluggish or defective circulation of the blood, the transition is easy to those which are due to the presence in the blood of some new and deleterious agent or ingredient—some poison. When we remember how free and copious is the supply of blood to the nervous tissue ; how large and numerous are the vessels that supply the brain ; how marvellously delicate and attenuated the walls of the small capillary vessels in which the blood is distributed among the nerve elements ; how these elements are fairly bathed and soaked in the current of blood ; we shall recognize how direct and powerful may be the influence on these elements of any foreign substance that may find its way into the blood ; and that when this foreign substance is one which has a special and peculiar affinity for the nerve tissue, and is absorbed and assimilated by it with ease and even avidity, how extremely powerful is the stress that is in this way brought to bear. Moreover, when we remember how easily the blood absorbs these poisons ; how many of them there are ; how they may gain access to the blood, not only in the food and drink through the stomach, and in the air through the lungs ; but that some, when once introduced into the blood, may be reinforced and invigorated by their own multiplication ; and that others arise actually within the body itself, by disintegration of its own tissues, or by the aberration of its own processes ;—when we bear all this in mind, we shall understand the frequency with which stresses of this kind are brought to bear on the nervous system, and the commonness of the occurrence of disorders of mind and conduct that are owing to this cause.

The number of the deleterious substances which act through the blood upon the nerve elements is large, as has been said, and for the purpose of enumeration it will be advisable to divide them according to their source of origin.

Among those which arise within the body are carbonic acid, which accumulates in the blood when from any cause it is imperfectly aerated. This happens in suffocation from mechanical causes, such as strangulation, or from occlusion of the windpipe by tumours from without, or growths from within ; from diseases of the lungs, which prevent the blood that passes through them from coming in contact with the air, and from diseases of the heart and disorders of the circulation which reduce the quantity of blood that passes through the lungs, and so gets a chance of being aerated. Other poisons of internal origin are those of uræmia, which accumulates when the kidneys are not acting freely to separate from the blood, and discard from the body, those effete matters which it is their function to separate ; those which remain and accumulate in the blood when the skin fails to perform its functions ; and the diabetic sugar which passes into the blood in such vast quantities in certain disorders of the liver. In this group must come also the poison which is absorbed into the blood from a seat of inflammation.

The group of poisons that find their way into the body through the medium of the air, and which, after their admission, increase and multiply exceedingly, are those of the specific fevers—the poisons of small-pox, scarlet fever, measles, typhus, and the rest. Others, which gain entrance in the same way, but do not subsequently increase, are noxious vapours—coal gas, carbonic acid, carbonic oxide, foul and unwholesome odours of all kinds.

Of the poisons which get into the blood by way of the stomach, the most important, because the most frequent, is alcohol ; which, from its frequency, from the ease with which the dose may be graduated, from its diffusibility, and the consequent rapidity and certainty of its action, affords by far the most favourable opportunities for studying the stresses of this order, and may be taken as the type and example of them all. The other poisons of this group are innumerable. They include the whole of the vegetable narcotic poisons, opium and its constituents, belladonna, hemlock, henbane, Indian hemp, stramonium, haschish, and many others.

Of the poisons which are carried to the nervous system in the blood, some have a special power of selecting, as it were, certain parts of the nervous system, and of acting on those parts alone, or at any rate with greatly preponderant activity. Thus, the poisons of hemlock and curare appear to act on the endings of the nerves, just where they join the muscles, and on no other part. Strychnia acts on the spinal cord with intense energy, but does not perceptibly affect other portions of the nervous system. With poisons acting in these ways we are not concerned. The whole group of narcotics, however, including alcohol, act on the nervous system after the classical manner so often indicated, and remove the functions of the centres in their order from above downwards. The other poisons—the noxious gases, the poisons of fevers, the waste products of the bodily processes, all follow the same rule and act in the same way. Although, however, they follow generally the same rule, and act generally in the same way, yet among these also there are certain differences in the mode of action, depending, perhaps, in part on differences of affinity—preferences— for certain parts of the higher nerve regions, from which it happens that the delirium produced by one particular agent is of one type, and that produced by another of another. Thus the delirium of most fevers, and that of chronic alcoholism—delirium tremens—has gained the title of a " busy delirium." The patient, with earnest and preoccupied manner, is fumbling and searching and meddling incessantly with the things about him. In belladonna poisoning, on the other hand, the delirium is of a joyous cast. These differences are slight, however, in comparison with the general uniformity of the symptoms produced by the action of the different stresses of this class, all of which produce a gradual degradation of mind and conduct, with more or less of the complementary overaction on a lower level, which commonly accompanies this degradation.

There are many who will object to the inclusion of delirium among the forms of insanity, and an instance has been given of a definition or description of insanity laboriously constructed so as explicitly to exclude the delirium of fevers, of poisoning, and of injury, from the denotation of insanity. Although of course, from a clinical point of view, the transient delirium of fever must be differently regarded and differently treated from the prolonged delirium of insanity; yet, looking at them scientifically, that is to say, looking at their fundamental and important similarities and differences, it is abundantly manifest that the former are comprehensive, numerous, important, and pervading, while the latter are limited, few, trivial, and partial. The little eddy of circling air, which is just sufficient to give a spiral movement to the dust and leaves by the roadside, is superficially a very different affair from the cyclone which uproots a forest and devastates a province; but surely both belong equally to the science of meteorology, the laws of being and action are the same in both, and the one can be fully understood only by being considered in connection with the other. When France declares war against Prussia, because Prussia has exercised an undue influence in European politics, the action is superficially different from that of Styles hitting Noakes in the eye because Noakes has taken more than his fair share of beer out of the mug; but to the student of human motive and action, the two affairs are fundamentally similar, and the observation of each throws light on the occurrence of the other. It seems to me that insanity can never be studied profitably so long as the purview of the alienist is limited to those cases which are either consigned to, or are fit for, the interior of a lunatic asylum. There is nothing new under the sun, and in particular nothing wholly novel ever occurs in the bodily processes. Morbid action is not novel action. It is not a new mode or way of working which has been suddenly introduced among the bodily processes, as a new process of dyeing or printing is introduced into a cotton

factory. Morbid action of every kind is nothing but the
exaggeration of normal action.   When morbid action occurs,
it does not mean that an entirely new element has been
added to the bodily processes ; it merely means that some
process which was always present, always active, and always
took its share in the economy of the body, has either failed
to maintain its due activity, or has taken on a phase of
activity in excess.   What is true of all other morbid manifestations is true also of insanity.   The disorders of mind
and of conduct which constitute insanity are not evidence
of the introduction of some entirely new method of working
into the bodily processes ; they are evidence merely of some
exaggeration—some defect or excess, or combination of
defect and excess—in the normal working of the nerve
tissues.

If this be so, and surely every one nowadays will admit
that it is so, then will become apparent the urgent
necessity of noticing the nature and peculiarities of these
departures from the normal, not so much when they are full-
blown and developed to excess, as in their first beginnings,
in their earliest stages, when the departure from the normal
is slightest, when the particular processes in which the
disorder begins are most easily identified, and the nature
and direction of the departure most obvious.

Darwin has left on record the despair that he felt, on
contemplating some phase of animal life in all the marvellous elaborateness of its full development, of ever being able
to account for its origin, or to indicate the steps by which it
had arrived at its completion.   In endeavouring to trace the
origin of the magnificent ocelli on the train of the peacock,
" the first species of Polyplectron which I examined " he says,
" almost made me give up the search."   " Granting whatever instincts you please, it seems at first quite inconceivable
how they [hive bees] can make all the necessary angles and
planes, or even perceive when they are correctly made."
In the case of insect-communities he finds, among many
others, " one special difficulty which at first appeared to me

insuperable, and actually fatal to the whole theory" of natural selection. In all these cases the difficulties were at length surmounted, and the mode of origin and the laws of relationship were at length discovered ; and by what means ? "Let us look," he says, "to the great principle of gradation, and see whether Nature does not reveal to us her method of work." And in the principle of gradation he finds revealed the mode in which these marvellous developments have been attained. He finds that the single ocellus on the feather of the peacock has an indentation at the lower end. In *P. maccalense* he finds an ocellus with indentations both above and below. In *P. hardwickii* he finds two ocelli side by side and confluent in the middle. In *P. chinquis* he finds two side by side and converging, though not touching ; and in other forms he finds marks graduating from the perfect ocellus to the ordinary bars and stripes which are so common on the plumage of birds. So amongst bees he finds a series, at one end of which " we have bumble bees which use their old cocoons to hold honey, sometimes adding to them short tubes of wax, and likewise making separate and very irregular rounded cells of wax. At the other end of the series we have the cells of the hive bee, placed in a double layer ; each cell, as is well known, is an hexagonal prism, with the basal edges of its six sides bevelled so as to join an inverted pyramid of three rhombs. These rhombs have certain angles, and the three which form the pyramidal base of a single cell on one side of the comb enter into the composition of the bases of three adjoining cells on the opposite side." Here we have highly elaborate, bizarre, and extraordinary manifestations of life, accounted for and explained by tracing the gradual steps of their development from ordinary forms ; and similarly we may well despair of being ever able to account for the elaborate, bizarre, and extraordinary manifestations of insanity, so long as we confine our attention to instances of the full-blown malady. It is only when we trace the gradual aberration of mind and conduct from the normal, that we shall be able to account for and explain the more exaggerated and striking cases of insanity ; and attention must be paid quite as much to the initial and intermediate stages as to the fully developed malady. Hence, although no one would think of placing in a lunatic asylum a person suffering from the? delirium of fever, yet the different mode of treatment, the pronounced bodily malady, and the directly assignable causation, must not blind us to the substantial identity of ordinary febrile delirium and ordinary non-febrile delirium.

As if to emphasize this doctrine and clench the matter, it occasionally happens that the delirium of fever occurs in an unusually intense and exaggerated form, while the bodily symptoms are but slightly pronounced. In such cases the fever may be overlooked, and the prominence of the disorder of mind and conduct may be such as to necessitate, or at least excuse, the despatch of the patient to an asylum ; and cases are occasionally admitted to these institutions as cases of lunacy, which subsequently turn out to be merely exaggerations of febrile delirium. I have seen cases, of apparently ordinary mania, which turned out to be cases of typhoid fever, of typhus, small-pox, and scarlet fever, with unusually prominent delirium.

It has been said, in introducing the subject of direct stresses, that from their character, their effect is so powerful that no nervous system, however stably constituted, is able to resist them. However thoroughly a man's brain may be organized, a blow on the head will stun him if it be sufficiently severe ; and similarly, however stably and well his nerve molecules may be arranged, the direct action of a poison, circulating in the blood which bathes them, will suffice to upset their arrangement, provided that the dose of the poison is large enough. It is obvious, however, that the magnitude of the dose that is necessary will depend on the amount of stability of the structure on which it acts ; so that here again we are brought into contact with the law of the causation of insanity as originally expressed. It is a function of two variables—heredity and stress. The more of predisposition by heredity exists in a brain, the weaker the stress necessary to derange it ; and conversely, the more stable the inherited structure of the brain, the stronger the influence that must be brought to bear on it in order to produce disarrangement. Hence we find, that the amount of delirium produced by a poison in the blood, varies both with the character of the person and with the amount of the poison. Some persons can be made drunk by a glass of sherry ; in others, half a gallon of whiskey is required to produce the same effect. Only give a man enough alcohol and he must get drunk. And with the same person, the more drink you give him, the drunker he gets. Different people, it is true, display the effects of drunkenness in different ways, but this is a matter concerning the forms of insanity, and will be dealt with presently.

The last of the direct stresses that we have to consider is also one of the most frequent, and, like all stresses of this nature, is one of considerable potency ; it is sleeplessness. The necessity of complete rest at short intervals for the higher nerve regions is imperative and absolute. During wakefulness the drain of energy from these regions is continuous, and unless they are allowed the opportunity, which is given them during sleep, of recouping themselves of this energy, they will fail to act ; and not only will they fail to act, but as the drain of energy goes on they will break down and become disorganized. Since energy is stored by the building up of atoms into complex arrangements, and since energy is liberated by the falling of these atoms into arrangements of greater simplicity, it is evident that a continuous drain of energy will result in the displacement of the atoms to such an extent that the integrity of the molecule is invaded and its structure disorganized.

The conditions to which sleeplessness may be due are various, and include anything which prevents the cerebral molecules from subsiding into inactivity. The ease with which this subsidence takes place varies naturally in different individuals, some being from childhood bad sleepers, and others by nature somnolent. Some, when sleep is obtained, are habitually light, and others habitually heavy sleepers. Of the conditions which favour or retard the natural tendency of the nerve molecules to repose, some are external to the organism and others are within it.

The external conditions which favour sleep are those which tend to reduce the total of impressions made upon the organism. All such impressions set up nerve currents, which break in waves upon the higher nerve regions, and tend to keep them in a state of activity. Hence sleep naturally takes place at that period of the day at which such impressions are least numerous and forcible ; and hence, when it is desired to favour the access of sleep, these impressions are as far as possible minimized. The blinds are drawn and the shutters shut, to exclude the influence of light waves on the eye. Silence is secured as far as is practicable. The body is so disposed on a soft couch that a minimum of acute feelings of contact are aroused. In a high temperature nervous activity is more readily evoked than in a low temperature, and hence we fall asleep more readily when we are cool than when we are hot.

The internal conditions which favour sleep are, generally, those that tend to produce quiescence of nerve molecules ; and *vice versâ*. Fatigue, by exhausting the molecules of their store of energy, renders, as already explained, their response to stimuli less active, less energetic, less ready ; and hence conduces towards sleep. Activity of the nerve molecules requires a copious supply of blood to the brain, and *vice versâ*. Hence after meals, when a large draught of blood is switched off to the abdomen to serve the purposes of digestion, drowsiness is the normal condition. Hence we see that the rule among the lower animals is—after food, sleep. Hence we find the custom among civilized men of administering a dose of strong coffee after dinner to counteract the naturally soporose effect of the meal. Hence we find that, with children especially, whose digestion is rapid, the best soporific is a hearty supper.

As with nerve currents originated by external impressions, so with currents started by internal processes, an undue intensity will keep the molecules of the higher nerve regions in activity, and so prevent sleep. Hence painful bodily processes are efficient sleep preventers ; and hence any process which, without causing pain, is of undue activity, will prevent sleep. The mental attitude of attention corresponds, upon the bodily side, with an exaggerated activity of the higher nerve regions, and hence sleep and attention are mutually exclusive. If the attention is actively aroused and maintained, sleep becomes impossible ; and hence the sleeplessness of anxiety, for anxiety is but a strained attention upon an impending disaster.

Lastly, the nervous system is, as we have seen, literally a creature of habit—depends for its existence and organization upon habit, and therefore we shall not be surprised to find in any of its functions that habit assumes a dominant influence. In the occurrence of sleep the influence of habit is very powerful. At the time at which we are in the habit of going to sleep, we become drowsy. At the time at which we are in the habit of waking, we wake. The night watch-man, who has formed the habit of sleeping by day, becomes naturally drowsy in the morning and wakeful at night. The sailor who has habituated himself to intervals of four hours' rest with four hours' activity, finds that his periods of wakefulness and drowsiness come to correspond naturally with his hours of duty and of rest. A slothful man acquires little by little the habit of prolonging his hours of sleep far beyond the average, and beyond his requirements ; and similarly it is quite possible, and is not very infrequent, for a person whose nerve molecules are naturally indisposed to quiescence, to contract a vicious habit of wakefulness that is often extremely difficult to overcome.

Whatever its cause, persistent sleeplessness is a condition which is highly favourable to the development of insanity, and in most acute attacks of insanity sleeplessness is a prominent feature. Doubtless the insomnia of incipient or early insanity is to some extent a symptom and a result of the morbid process in the brain, which underlies the insanity ; but none the less does it assist and reinforce the process to which it is primarily due. As a matter of clinical experience, we find that in acute outbreaks of insanity that are accompanied by sleeplessness, the induction of sleep is usually followed by improvement in the insanity ; while cases in which insanity has become developed without the accompaniment of insomnia, are as a rule less hopeful.

CHAPTER VIII.

THE CAUSES OF INSANITY (*Continued*).

Indirect Stress of Internal Origin.

INDIRECT stresses are of two kinds, as has been said : those in which the agent is some commotion in the organism itself, and those in which it is a commotion in the environment. In either case the stress is applied, not directly to the highest nerve regions, but indirectly, through the medium of the afferent or in-going nerves ; to the visceral or systemic nerves in the first case, and to the nerves of special sense in the second. The stress applied at the peripheral end of the nerve is in either case communicated, through the nerve and the intermediate centres, to the highest nerve regions, and there produces its effect.

Of the first kind of indirect stresses—those of internal origin—there are, as already stated, two orders, one arising from general commotions pervading the whole organism, and the other from local commotions directly affecting parts only of the organism. The general commotions are those occasions of widespread and virtually universal turmoil, which accompany the great and fundamental changes of constitution that occur from time to time in the natural progress of life. Such is the commotion—the internal revolution—that takes place at puberty. Such are the changes of the climacteric, of marriage, pregnancy, and child-birth. Other general internal commotions are those por-duced by, and accompanying, fevers and other general or "constitutional" bodily maladies.

Of these internal commotions, the first in order, and perhaps the most important, is that of puberty. It is at this stage of life that the process of development is subjected to its first severe strain. The organism, which has hitherto been travelling at a rapid pace along a smooth and even path of development, almost suddenly comes upon a piece of difficult country, and, in travelling rapidly over the rough ground, it is liable to upset. How great is the internal commotion that accompanies the evolution of the sexual characters, and the attainment of the powers of reproduction, may be to some extent inferred from an enumeration of the changes that then take place. The individual diverges from the neutral condition of childhood, and takes on the distinctive characters of his or her sex. In the male, in addition to the rapid development of the sexual organs, the frame fills out, the bones become thicker and more solid, the general outline squarer, more rugged, and more manly. The voice changes, owing to the development of the structures of the throat, and the beard buds and sprouts. These changes in the body at large are mirrored in the higher nerve regions. In their development also a new start is made. New desires, new passions, new emotions come into being ; not only the bodily organization, but the mental organization also, undergoes a revolution. This new development is made with comparative rapidity. The emotions and desires of freedom, of acquisition of property, of power, of self-reliance, dignity, sympathy, and so forth, are of slow growth, and develop with the development of the organism at large. But the emotions and desires of love are, with the concomitant bodily changes, developed at a certain time of life with great rapidity. Now, all rapid development is, as we have seen, more or less unstable development ; and the period during which this rapid development is taking place is a period of more than usual instability. We may compare it to the condition of a country which is undergoing an internal revolution. At such a time an invasion would have far more chance of success than when a firm and stable power was settled in the government ; and when the human organism is undergoing the revolution of puberty, ordinary stresses, which at other times would be innocuous, are apt to have disastrous effects. If the general political condition of the country be unstable, then the effect of a revolution may be to produce prolonged or permanent anarchy, as we see in some of the South American republics ; and if the general constitution of the individual be primarily unstable, the effect of the revolution of puberty may be to produce insanity of more or less permanent character.

If such be the effect of the access of puberty in the male, in whom the revolution is comparatively slight and comparatively prolonged, we may be sure that in the female, in whom the change is far more rapid in progress and of a far more momentous character, the commotion will be more tumultuous and attended with greater disturbance. Whereas in man the attainment of maturity is gradual, and the changes of puberty are spread over many years, in woman the evolution takes place very rapidly, and the individual "passes at a bound, as it were, from childhood to womanhood," the change in her between the ages of fourteen and eighteen being as complete as in man between fifteen and five-and-twenty. In woman, too, the changes are greater. The organs which subserve the function of reproduction, and which pass at puberty from a rudimentary and dormant condition to full development and activity, are more numerous, and occupy thereafter a more conspicuous and more important position and function in her economy than in the case of man. The mental changes that accompany puberty in the female are also greater and more momentous than in the male. In the one the character develops ; in the other it is revolutionized. The access of activity, both general and special, that accrues to both sexes at this period of life, finds means of outlet and satisfaction in very different direction and degree in each. In man at this period not only does the special activity find ready outlet, since to him belongs by ancient and prescriptive custom the initiation of the overtures of love ; but at the same period of life he is usually provided with abundant outlets for the general activities of his nature, which then receive so marked an accession to their vigour.   It is at this time that he relinquishes the preparatory process of education, and enters on the more serious and important business of life. It is at this time that he joins a profession, or a house of business, or enters on that walk of life from which in future he is to gain his livelihood.   He emerges from his larval condition and takes on the full functions of manhood.   He begins to earn his own living ; he becomes a member of society, a citizen, a social unit.   Whatever activities are left unsatisfied and unabsorbed when his work is done, and the serious and necessary business of earning his livelihood is completed for the day, find easy and abundant outlet in a hundred different fields.   He can have assigned to him military or quasi-military duties ; he can undertake athletic exercises. Volunteering or cycling, or rowing or cricket, becomes, in a secondary degree, the business of his life.   He can enter freely into clubs and societies of various kinds, can take up a special study or pursuit, a science or an art, and find in such pursuits channels of escape for the activities which are so vigorously and copiously generated within him.

With women, matters are very different.   The special activity that originates at puberty, and craves for expression, cannot in them find spontaneous outlet.   They must wait until occasion arises.   They may indeed, and do, give their love unsought, but they may not give it expression until it has been required of them ; and the activity which can find no expression is unsatisfied.   Unlike their brothers, they have not those copious and multitudinous channels of outlet for their general activities, which, if freely utilized, draft off such large quantities of activity, lower the nervous tension generally, and so not only diminish the sexual craving, but provide a safety valve for the escape of the nervous energy, and obviate the likelihood of a dangerous accumulation. For all these reasons—the greater magnitude and greater rapidity of the change, and the much smaller outlet for the increased activities—the access of puberty in woman is a period of far greater strain, of more tumultuous revolution, of more enhanced liability to disorder, than in man.

That the gravamen of the liability to disorder will lie with special intensity on the higher regions of the nervous system, is apparent from several considerations. The alteration in the cœnæsthesis, due to the virtual addition of several new and important viscera to the organism, is itself a source of, and a provocation to, disorder ; for the nervous system has, during the previous years of life, become accustomed to act under the influence of a certain set of incoming currents. Any large and sudden addition to these incoming currents must of necessity produce disturbance, and until the nervous system becomes equilibrated to the new conditions acting upon it, the disturbance will be apt to increase into disorder. At the same time that these new forces are acting on it through the nerves, the brain is itself undergoing rapid and widespread change. New emotions, new passions, new cravings, a whole set of new feelings, are being added to the mental constitution ; and this means, as we already know, that new developments must be rapidly taking place in the higher regions of the brain ; for no change can take place in the shadow, mind, without a corresponding change having taken place in the substance, brain. So that these alterations in the cœnæsthesis, these new and disturbing forces, are acting on a material which is itself undergoing extensive and rapid changes, and is therefore, as before shown, more easily deranged. The access of puberty is, therefore, in all women a time of danger, and so powerful are the disturbing elements that at that time act on the constitution of the higher nerve regions, that few women pass through this period of their development without manifesting signs of disorder of those regions. Thus, at this period, more or less decided manifestations of hysteria are the rule. The girls who fail to exhibit some hysterical symptom at puberty are few indeed. In hysteria there is disorder of mind, that

is, of thought, or feeling, or both ; and there is disorder of
conduct.   Hence hysteria is closely allied to insanity, is in
fact a slight or temporary manifestation of the phenomena
which, if more decided or more prolonged, become unquestionable ordinary insanity.   At the same time hysteria
is not, like anæmia, and like drunkenness in all its manifestations, merely a temporary insanity due to a temporary
cause.   The nervous disturbance in hysteria may, it is true,
affect the higher centres only, and then, indeed, are presented
the phenomena of a slight or temporary insanity.   In such
cases there is marked disorder of conduct, there is undue
emotional instability, that is to say, the signs of emotion—
laughing, crying, &c.—are exhibited in marked and emphatic
fashion on occasions which should not normally evoke much
emotion.   The manifestations of emotion may be so extreme
as to be manifestly out of proportion, not only to the
occasion in which they occur, but to any occasion.   Laughter
may continue till the laugher is completely exhausted, or
even may merge into general convulsions.   Activity is
usually defective.   The patient is sluggish, slow, languid,
and anergic ; sometimes persistently, sometimes with intervals of eager, feverish, and shortlived activity.   Often the
activity is so defective that the patient takes to her bed and
remains there, without the justification of any bodily ailment.
In addition to mere excess or defect of activity, or of alternation of defect and excess, conduct may, and usually does, in
high-level hysteria, exhibit other disorders of more permanent
and more complex character.   The disorder may be slight,
may merely consist in little eccentricities, in alterations of
dress a little too pronounced, in too marked a preference for
little secrets and mysteries, or in a newly-developed fancy
for teasing and annoying other people.   Occasionally, however, these disorders of conduct exhibit themselves in much
graver form.   The eccentricities may develop into conduct
so bizarre as to be manifestly insane.   The alterations of
dress may take the form of wearing crowns and tawdry
ornaments, and be associated with delusions of grandeur.

The inclination to possess secrets and to make mysteries may lead to the perpetration of impostures of the most extraordinary kind. One girl will go for weeks without bodily sustenance, another will go for weeks without an action of the bowels, another will exhibit stigmata—bleeding points on the hands, feet, and side, in imitation of the five wounds of Christ. Others will simulate pregnancy; others will pretend to be blind, deaf, dumb, or to be able to speak only in a whisper. An hysterical girl will have "more diseases than two-and-fifty horses." The most serious manifestation of disordered conduct in hysteria is, however, the development of the appetite for teasing—for giving pain and annoyance to others. When this is developed in excess, it results in nothing short of murder, and very numerous cases have occurred of apparently motiveless murders committed by young girls about the age of puberty. The victims are usually young children, these being obviously the only class of persons whose death can be compassed by direct violence by young girls; and from the time of the celebrated Road murder by Constance Kent, cases have from time to time been reported of the murder of young children without discernible motive, and in a very cold-blooded manner. When such a murder is committed, and is committed in secresy, and with precautions against discovery which are absent in ordinary homicide by the insane, it is invariably found that the murderer is a young girl.

The circumstances that commonly differentiate hysteria from insanity are that, while in hysteria conduct is disordered, the disorder of intelligence which enters so largely into our concept of insanity is usually inconspicuous; and secondly, that there often exists in hysteria some bodily malady or quasi-malady, whose prominence obscures and eclipses the manifestations of disorder of mind and conduct. The factor that most clearly and decisively differentiates the two will be subsequently considered.

Although in hysteria disorder of mind is often inconspicuous, yet it is always present. It is notorious how

tumultuous and stormy are the manifestations of emotion ;
the exaggerated laughter, ending in exhaustion, or it may
be in actual convulsion ; the excessive accessions of weeping,
disproportionate to the occasions on which they occur ; the
gusts of anger ; the fits of sulks ; the frequent attitude of
suspicion. . All these manifestations, undue and excessive as
they are, indicate amounts or phases of feeling that are not
adjusted to the circumstances in which they occur,—that are
disordered.

The chief disorders of feeling that occur in hysteria do
not, however, find a place under any of the foregoing
headings. They are of a more subtle character, and one
almost peculiar, if not to the malady, at any rate to the time
of life and the class of persons in whom the malady is most
prone to occur. We have seen that the main characteristic
of the bodily changes that occur at puberty is the addition
of new viscera and new functions ; and the characteristic of
the change in the working of the nervous system is a great
and rapid addition to the contribution made to the general
volume of the nervous currents by that portion which comes
from the viscera. And the reception of the nerve currents
from the viscera—the representation of the body itself in the
higher nerve regions—is the foundation or physical side of
the cœnæsthesis :—the obscure, underlying, but fundamental
portion of consciousness which constitutes the " ego," the
" conscious personality," the consciousness of self, as distinguished from the consciousness of surroundings. In young
children this self-consciousness exists in rudimentary form
only. Almost the whole of their consciousness is concerned
with things around them. With the workings of their own
minds, and the effects of their surroundings on themselves,
they are but little concerned. So completely externalized
are their thoughts that even in speaking of themselves they
will speak in the third person. A child comes to his mother
and says, not "I have hurt myself," but " Baby has hurt
himself." He will say, not " Give it to me," but " Give it
to Jacky." And in using these expressions he indicates

that the distinction between the conscious self and the world around is not yet thoroughly appreciated. As the body develops, and as mind develops with the body, the " ego " comes more into prominence, and soon attains complete differentiation from the world at large ; and when, at puberty, a large and sudden addition is made to the cœnæsthesis, the consciousness of self swells and increases to dimensions that easily, and in many cases, become excessive. The consciousness of the surroundings, of the world they live in, and of the scenes and events that are going on in it, is no longer the predominant and almost sole constituent in consciousness. In concomitance with the increase in volume and alteration in the constitution of the nerve currents poured in from the interior of the body, arise elements in the constitution of consciousness that are new, and that for a while are dominant. No longer concerned entirely with circumstances and events in the outside world, consciousness becomes largely engaged with these new constituents, which have reference to what is passing within the organism. New feelings, feelings of change, strange, unaccustomed sensations, arise and prevail. The new nerve currents to which this extension of consciousness is due, have, in marked degree, the characters of the visceral currents to which attention has already been drawn ; that is to say, they are voluminous ; they are continuous ; their variations are not sudden cessations and recommencements, but are in waves of slow rise, progress, and decline. Moreover, voluminous and powerful as they are, they are diffused and widespread. Their limitations in space, like their limitations in time, are vague, wanting in definiteness and precision. In all these respects the feelings which are their conscious accompaniments resemble the nerve currents. The new elements, which at puberty become added to the general consciousness ; the new feelings, yearnings, desires, cravings ; are, like the new nerve currents, powerful, voluminous, pervading, continuous ; and, like them, are vague, formless, indefinite. They do not indicate their origin ;

they do not proclaim their nature ; the organism, disturbed and restless under this strange addition to its forces, is puzzled as to the direction in which the new activities should find their outlet. At this time " strange thoughts that we do not understand are stirring in our hearts. Voices are calling us to some great effort, to some mighty work. But we do not comprehend their meaning yet, and the hidden echoes within us that would reply, are struggling, inarticulate and dumb." Then comes some association, some contact, with a more or less appropriate individual of the other sex. At once the pent-up current of emotion bursts its bounds. As some liquid, filled to saturation with a dissolved salt, remains yet liquid and formless, with every particle crammed with solid matter in solution, and so remains indefinitely, yearning and craving, as it were, to yield up the new matter of which it is full, and yet failing for want of occasion and incitement to do so ; so the adolescent boy or girl remains with his or her nature bursting with emotion, which cannot, in the absence of occasion and of an object, find expression. Now if we drop into the solution a crystal of the salt, immediately the liquid yields up its dissolved contents. At once the salt separates out of solution, and clusters about, and coheres to, the foreign body, in a copious deposit of regular geometrical crystals. The formless fluctuating liquid is transformed into a fixed solid of definite shape and firm consistence. So if we bring the boy or girl, replete with formless emotion, into contact with an appropriate individual of the other sex, immediately the vague indefinite yearnings settle down upon, and cluster about, this provocative agent, in the definite shape of a more or less firmly cohesive affection. It has been said, and truly said, that falling in love is a revelation. It is so ; for at once the meaning and significance of the new cravings and yearnings becomes apparent. They were the expression in consciousness of the new powers that had become added to the organism ; and till the nature of these new powers was known, the meaning of the new elements in consciousness remained obscure.

It has been said that the occasion of this crystallization of the saturated consciousness is the contact with an appropriate individual, and to this the rejoinder will be that the individual is often not appropriate; and this is true; but the main statement holds good all the same. It is found that the readiest way to make a saturated solution deposit in crystals, is to drop into it a crystal of the same salt; but if no such crystal be handy, one of some other salt will do; and if no crystal be obtainable, then any rough substance or any angular solid will suffice to precipitate the crystalline deposit. The facts are, that there is the salt craving to escape from the solution, and in default of a cognate, similar, and appropriate substance to adhere to, it will deposit itself on anything that gives it a plausible excuse to do so; and similarly in the adolescent, there is a body of emotion craving to escape, and in default of sufficient opportunity of pouring itself out upon an appropriate object, a most inappropriate one will often be chosen. It may appear that when opportunities are equal the choice will not always fall on the most appropriate; but then it must be remembered that we are dealing with animate and imaginative beings, and that the being with whom a person falls in love exists only in the imagination of the lover. The lover falls in love, not with his adored object as she exists, but with the imaginary attributes with which he invests her. The lady who told her lover that he was in love with certain attributes was so far correct, but her statement was not complete, insomuch that she omitted to state that the attributes were for the most part imaginary. The lover's answer, it will be remembered, was "Damn your attributes, madam, I know nothing of your attributes;" and in this the poor man was doubtless, in his own belief, correct.

It may happen, however, that no object, which even the wild and rampant imagination of the lover can invest with sufficiently attractive attributes, presents itself to the replete emotional condition of the adolescent; and when this is the case, we have an analogy to the saturated solution to which no point for precipitation is offered. In the latter case, what happens is this : that for a longer or shorter time no precipitation occurs, but at last a slow and diffused crystallization takes place on the walls of the containing vessel. Upon the periphery, the outskirts of its environment, the contained matter is deposited in diffused form, but never with the rapidity nor the copiousness with which it is thrown down on an appropriate object. In the human being to whom no direct and single outlet is given for the escape of the emotions of puberty, there occurs for a time no such escape at all. Then, after a time of suffering, the pent-up emotion tardily leaks away in less concentrated intensity and in more numerous directions, and seeks usually the most remote and least definite occasions for display. The vague, voluminous, and powerful feelings which, if afforded means to do so, settle down and concentrate on a single object, in affection, find their expression, if this object be wanting, in less direct ways and more diffused form. They take the shape of religious emotion, and expression for them is found in observance of ceremonial and in devotion to a ritual.

To understand this curious connection between sexual and religious emotion, a connection which has long been recognized, but never accounted for, it is necessary to consider the fundamental nature of both. As will be shown more fully in the next chapter, the fundamental quality of the sexual emotion is the willingness, nay, more, the desire, the craving, to sacrifice self. The production of offspring can only be effected by a sacrifice on the part of the parent ; a sacrifice of corporeal substance ; a sacrifice of part of the life ; a sacrifice of part of the means of living. The sexual emotion includes, as an integral, fundamental, and preponderating element in its constitution, the desire for self-sacrifice.

The same element is an important constituent of religious emotion, and lies at the root of all religious observance. The propitiation of a Deity is, in all religions, made by sacrifice of one kind or another. In the primitive religion of savage races the sacrifice is of food, of weapons, or clothing. In the higher religions of civilized men the sacrifice is of land, or money, or time, or work. The peer who contributes a plot of land as a site for a church is stirred by the same motive as the shepherd who offers a yoke of oxen as a burnt-offering. The Nazarite who, under the obligation of a vow, suffers the inconvenience of an unshorn head, is precisely comparable with the monk who, under a similar obligation, suffers the inconvenience of a shorn one. In every case, religious observance means sacrifice of some kind, and the more severe, the more complete, the more absorbing the sacrifice, the more complete is the propitiation considered, the more satisfactory the religious observance.

In this common ground of self-sacrifice both the religious and the sexual emotions have their origin; and in their further development they maintain a close resemblance in their voluminous nature, and, previous to the crystallization of which we have spoken, in the vagueness of their characterization. The community of their origin and the similarity of their nature allow easily of the transformation of the one emotion into the other, and hence the self-denial and self-abnegation that would have been joyously and proudly incurred in the service of a lover, are incurred with equal or greater fervour, though in other forms, in the service of a church which stands vicariously in the lover's place. That emotion which fails to find a point of concentration and deposit in a single individual, diffuses itself over a wide area, and is expressed in acts of benevolence and philanthropy; but in such acts the element of self-sacrifice must enter, or the emotion is unsatisfied, and its expression incomplete. Hence we find that that benevolence which is founded upon religious emotion, and derives its more distant origin from sexual emotion, always shows itself in ways which involve sacrifice of self. While the simply benevolent man will give his money, his time, and labour freely to charitable purposes, without diminishing his means of enjoyment by more than this expenditure necessarily involves ; the man who is religiously benevolent must add to his expenditure of money, time, and work, certain other sacrifices, which are made, not with the object of benefiting others, but simply for the sake of sacrificing himself.   He or she—for this form of emotion is commoner in women—must undergo fatiguing labours, must abstain from social and other pleasures, and last, but not least, must assume unbecoming forms of dress.

This last curious and common outcome of a state of life in which the sexual emotions are unsatisfied, is easily explicable.   Ornaments, throughout the entire scale of the animal kingdom, are assumed and developed for the purpose of attracting the opposite sex, and have no other origin or reason of existence.   In mankind, dress subserves this function first and most.   Among savage races the first rudiments of costume are assumed with a view, not to protection from the weather, nor to decency, but for decorative purposes only ; and, in the most civilized and cultured of men and women, a very large proportion of the care, labour, and money that are expended on dress, are expended for decorative purposes, and have for their more or less immediate motive the attraction of the opposite sex.

This prominence and importance of dress, from a sexual point of view, must be taken together with the law that when activities fail to find their natural and legitimate outlet, and when they therefore escape in new and unaccustomed ways, and under influences that are to some extent abnormal, such activities tend to escape disorderly.   Having, for want of natural outlet, failed for some time to find expression, the activity has become pent up, has accumulated a head of pressure ; and hence, when outlet in a new direction is at last found, it is apt to escape explosively, tumultuously, and in excess.   Hence it is that so many of these activities which begin at puberty, and which are erring and mistaken manifestations of a normal sexual instinct, find expressions that are bizarre and excessive. Among the activities which then become prominent, that of self-sacrifice is the most predominant and important; and having regard to the intimate association of ornament with the sexual function, it is not surprising that the self-sacrifice should be exhibited with special prominence in connection with the ornamental properties of dress; nor that, when the activity of self-sacrifice becomes disordered and excessive, a studious repulsiveness should be substituted for the normal attractiveness of costume.

Hence we find that the self-sacrificial vagaries of the rejected lover and of the religious devotee, own a common origin and nature. The hook and spiky kennel of the fakir, the pillar of St. Simeon Stylites, the flagellum of the monk, the sombre garments of the nun, the silence of the Trappists, the defiantly hideous costume of the hallelujah lass, and the mortified sobriety of the district visitor, have at bottom the same origin as the rags of Cardenio, the cage of Don Quixote de la Mancha, and the yellow stockings and crossed garters of Malvolio.

It is during the inactive period, when the activities are accumulating, and before they have found even their limited and modified expression, that disorders are most prone to occur. This is the hysterical period. Here is a head of pressure established, an accumulation of energies struggling to escape, and finding no outlet. What will happen? Until the safety valve rises, and outlet of some kind is found, there will be evidence of the accumulation and presence in excess of vague, indefinite, diffused, powerful feelings belonging to the consciousness of self. The consciousness of self will be the predominant element instead of the subordinate moiety of consciousness. Events and circumstances will be viewed in their relation, not to each other, but to self. Self-consciousness is magnified—exaggerated to abnormal dimensions. Since, *ex hypothesi*, definite outlet for the activities is not found, and since the vague diffused nature of the emotions themselves does not

admit of definite expression, save by expenditure on an
object, the evidence of the existence of the emotion will be
of the vaguest and most general character ; but since the
emotions are powerful, and pervading, and continuous, the
expression will be emphatic and frequent. What are the
most general and most emphatic modes of expression of
emotion ? Laughing and weeping. Normally, they are
the expression of emotions roused by the experience of
circumstances, of some ludicrous or painful situation in
which the individual is placed ; but in these cases the tide
of emotion is already at flood, without the provocation of
external circumstances, and in these cases, therefore, the
expression of emotion takes place without provocation, or
on provocation that is insignificant and altogether out of
proportion to the display made. And the expression is
excessive, not merely to the occasion for which it occurs,
but to any occasion. Unprovoked laughter and unprovoked
weeping are most common manifestations of adolescent
development. At the same time other evidences of
exaggerated self-consciousness become apparent. Nothing
marks more conspicuously and emphatically the change
from the child to the woman, than the easy, spontaneous,
unconstrained, unstudied, unself-conscious gaze, aspect, and
attitude of the one ; and the restrained, considered, deliberate,
self-attentive regards and movements of the other. The
one intent upon the external object, and that only ; the
other making a show of intentness upon the matter in
hand, but thinking more of the way in which her actions
may impress possible or actual spectators. The one unself-
conscious, the other eminently self-conscious. At puberty,
too, embarrassment first becomes a serious item in consciousness, and embarrassment is positive evidence of self-
consciousness. When it arises from inadequate external
provocation, it shows excess of self-consciousness. The
external evidence of embarrassment is the blush ; and hence,
at this period of life, blushing, if it do not first occur,
becomes a far more frequent and pronounced phenomenon
than either before or afterwards.

Among the other manifestations of increased self-consciousness is the craving for sympathy and fellowship that comes so prominently to the front at puberty. The child, whose thoughts are all externalized, and deal with circumstances and events without, enjoys the society of its fellows, and is by nature gregarious ; but it looks on its playmates with far different eyes from those with which the lover *in posse* looks on his or her companions. The child regards its playmates and associates as, like itself, in pursuit of objects, and engaged in interests, that are external to both. The adolescent woman seeks, not community, but mutuality of interests. She desires that there shall be, not a common interest with herself in some external object, but an interest in herself which she can mutually reciprocate. Such an interest is one of the primary features of sexual love, and at the period of the first appearance of sexual love the craving for this interest appears. As with so many of the other phenomena of puberty, owing to causes already considered, this craving readily becomes disordered, readily becomes excessive. If it fails to find the normal and legitimate outlet in the affection and interest of an individual of the other sex, then, as with other activities similarly placed, it becomes pent up, accumulates, and tends to find disorderly and excessive expression. Accordingly, running through all the disorders of hysteria, we find the craving for sympathy always present and always exaggerated. Often it is exaggerated to such a degree that no ordinary manifestation of interest or sympathy would satisfy it ; and hence, to obtain satisfaction for the craving, recourse is had to stratagems and devices of various kinds. The most usual occasion for an increase of the interest and sympathy with which people are commonly regarded is that of bodily illness, and the more severe the illness, the greater the sympathy shown ; while the more unusual and remarkable the illness, the greater is the display of interest. For these reasons hysterical persons are extremely apt to display signs of bodily ailment ; and the ailments whose signs are thus assumed are commonly either of great severity, or of bizarre and extraordinary character. How far the assumption and display of the signs of bodily illness are consciously and deliberately invented, manufactured, and shammed, and how far they involuntarily and unconsciously impose themselves on the patient as an indirect outgrowth and consequence of the craving, are questions which can never be satisfactorily determined ; and undoubtedly the two elements vary, not only in different cases, but from time to time in the same case. Some cases, at some times, are cases almost entirely of deliberate imposture ; other cases at some times are cases in which the patient is wholly misled, and imagines that the pains and inabilities that she undoubtedly feels and believes in, have an existence apart from the craving for interest and sympathy which, unknowingly to herself, has brought them into being. In the majority of cases, a mass of vague, voluminous, universally diffused, uneasy feeling, which we term, when thus formless and general, a craving, comes to a head locally, becomes intensified in some one direction, bursts out, as it were, at some local rent, and then becomes the hysterical joint, the hysterical back, the hysterical tumour, the hysterical paralysis, or what not. Instead of a general diffused feeling of uneasiness, there is a concentrated feeling of similar character, which is localized here or there. This uneasy feeling is referred to bodily disease, and thus at once establishes a claim for the payment of that sympathy which is so sorely craved for. Now appears a chance of getting this urgent need in some degree satisfied, and the patient would be scarcely human if she did not utilize the chance thus given, and, by emphasizing the expression of that discomfort which she really feels, put forth a stronger claim for sympathy than she is on that ground entitled to. From the trifling overacting of the languor due to a transient headache, there is every degree up to instances of wilful and elaborate imposture, extending over months and years, and involving, it may be, ultimate mutilation of the patient by painful operations.

The protean character of the manifestations of hysteria have long been a standing source of marvel to physicians; but it seems to me that if their origin is in that craving for interest and sympathy, which, it is admitted, invariably accompanies them, the varied forms that they assume are to some extent accounted for. It is obvious that the claim to interest will depend not so much on the seat of the malady as on its extraordinary and bizarre character; and that the claim to sympathy will rest, not on the seat or nature of the disorder, but on its gravity, its painfulness, and the extent to which it produces disablement. Hence we find that all the manifestations of hysteria, extraordinarily various as they are, are distinguished by certain common features. They are either of extraordinary and sensational character, or they are accompanied by manifestations of severe pain or by disablement. In the former category are the cases of abstinence from food, of horribly loud and discordant cough, of loss of voice, of loss of sight, of phantom tumours, of inability to swallow, to speak, to stand, to walk, of rigid maintenance of certain postures, of trance and ecstasy, of vomiting of blood or maggots or pins. In the latter are the cases of hysterical joint affection, the hyperæsthesia of the senses, so that the skin cannot be touched without manifestations of agony; so that the patient lives entirely in a darkened room, because the access of light to the eye gives rise to spasm and all the signs of pain ; so that not even a whisper can be tolerated ; so that flowers must be banished from their room because their odour is intolerable.

The most common and most pronounced symptom of hysteria is the hysterical "fit," an occurrence of very marked and peculiar character. The fit is a sort of grotesque caricature of an epileptic fit. The patient falls, but she falls gently, so as not to hurt herself. No hysteric ever fell into the fire, or cut her head severely in falling, as epileptics so frequently do. Then there follows a quantity of aimless sprawling and floundering about, with spluttering at the mouth, graspings of the hand, and gurgling in the throat, and after a time the patient gets up none the worse.

The fit is a manifestation of irregular and uncontrolled activity. It never occurs in people who lead busy lives and have abundant occupation for all the activities of their minds and bodies. It often occurs among those who live idle lives, but most frequently affects those who are moderately active, but whose activities are but one-sided and partial, and leave part of their nature unsatisfied. In idle people the activities are quiescent all round, and tend to cease from want of use ; but in people who maintain some forms of activity, their whole nature remains capable of and needing activity, and if any activities be unsatisfied, they will be apt to set up disorderly and excessive manifestations. "Seldom," says the oldest and shrewdest of alienists, "should you see an hired servant, a poor handmaid, though ancient, that is kept hard to her work, and bodily labour, a coarse country wench, troubled in this kind ; but noble virgins, nice gentlewomen, such as are solitary and idle, live at ease, lead a life out of action and employment, that fare well, in great houses and jovial companies, . . . of weak judgment, able bodies, and subject to passions (*grandiores virgines*, saith Mercatus, *steriles et viduæ plerumque*) such for the most part are misaffected and prone to this disease. I do not so much pity them that may otherwise be eased, but those alone that out of a strong temperament, innate constitution, are violently carried away with this torrent of inward humours, and though very modest of themselves, sober, religious, virtuous, and well given (as so many distressed maids are) yet cannot make resistance, these grievances will appear, this malady will take place, and now manifestly show itself, and may not otherwise be helped." Having availed myself so freely of the wisdom of my predecessor, it is but right that I should give the rest of a quotation so specially appropriate to the occasion. "But where am I?" he cries, "Into what subject have I rushed ? What have I to do with nuns, maids, virgins, widows ? I am a bachelor myself, and lead a monastic life. . . . *næ ego sane ineptus qui hæc dixerim.* I confess 'tis an indecorum."

The intimate connection of hysteria with the craving for sympathy, interest, and fellowship is shown very clearly by the effect of the display of sympathy towards the hysteric. Nothing is more certain or more striking than the aggravation of the symptoms produced by such a display, nothing better proved than the amelioration of the symptoms that follows a judicious display of indifference. The girl who has been in bed and unable to move for years under the care of a silly, fussy, indulgent, weak-minded mother, will recover in a fortnight when taken away from her home and placed under the care of a firm, kind, judicious, strong-minded woman.

The intimate connection of hysteria with insanity is well-recognized. It is not merely that the manifestations of hysteria major graduate into insanity by insensible gradations ; that in certain cases we are puzzled to say whether the patient is insane or hysterical ; that in some cases the same individual is at one time plainly hysterial, and at another plainly insane, that when at her best she is hysterical and when at her worst, insane ; the connection shows itself not only in such instances as these, but also in the close alliance with insanity that most manifestations of ordinary hysteria display. In every case of hysteria of ordinary severity there is some disorder of conduct. The patient either lies in bed without the disablement of bodily illness, or has fits of prolonged and excessive laughing or weeping, or outbursts of "temper," of screaming, or outbreaks of destructiveness, or cruelty, or other conduct that is not adjusted to her circumstances. At the same time, there is evidence of disorder of mind. The craving for sympathy and interest, which is natural to the time of life at which hysteria first appears, is, in all cases of hysteria, present in exaggerated degree. The manifestations of emotion, which are so prominent a feature in the conduct, indicate, there is no doubt, disorderly and excessive phases and tides of emotion occurring in the mind. Anger, vindictiveness, pity, especially self-pity, religious, and other emotions, are present in excess, and out of proportion to the circumstances of the individual : in other words, they are disorderly. Intelligence, too, is often disordered in some degree, although the disorder of this side of mind is rarely prominent, rarely conspicuous, and is consequently often overlooked and disregarded ; and this is the reason why there is often so much difficulty in recognizing the positive nearness of relationship between hysteria and insanity. If we find a person acting strangely and in a way that is manifestly unadjusted to her surroundings, and if yet we find her able to reason with average acuteness, having regard to her sex and age, and to give plausible explanations of her conduct, we are apt to conclude that there is no intellectual disorder ; but there remains often this residual defect. She does not herself perceive the defect in her own conduct. Conduct is the external expression of intelligence. Conduct is acted thought ; and disorder of conduct necessarily implies disorder of the thought of which it is the expression.

The close connection between hysteria and insanity is displayed again in the similarity between the received methods of treating them. The first thing to do with a case of acute recent insanity is to effect a complete change in the surroundings. The patient is taken from home and placed among strangers under novel and unusual circumstances, and this is the first step and the first condition to recovery. In hysteria also, the readiest, speediest, and most reliable means of cure is to remove the patient from her home, and place her in new conditions of life. In the one case as in the other, what is termed " moral treatment " is among the most powerful recuperative agents.

Close as the connection of hysteria with insanity undoubtedly is ; and definitely as that connection has always been recognized, yet at the same time it has always been held as a matter of course that hysteria, although it may be associated with insanity ; although it may graduate into insanity ; although it may display the disorder of conduct, of feeling, and of thought, which together constitute insanity ; yet it is itself something different from insanity. Closely allied as the two undoubtedly are, and puzzling as it often is to distinguish between them, yet it is common to meet with cases of hysteria which it would be felt to be an outrage to call insanity. The question arises, What is this subtle difference which distinguishes things so closely allied in nature and appearance ?

The difference is, that while in insanity the part of the nervous system that is affected is the very highest of all— the topmost layers of the topmost strata ; in hysteria the seat of disorder is in layers immediately below the topmost. If we imagine the highest region of the nervous system to contain several layers of slightly different degrees of altitude, then in insanity the highest of these layers are affected. It may be that the lower layers are affected also, but in any case the most superficial stratum, the actual surface layer, is disordered. In hysteria, on the other hand, however much and however widely the highest nerve regions may be affected, there always remains, so long as the case is one of hysteria alone, above the disordered layers, a stratum, however thin, of nervous arrangements which still continue to carry on their functions normally. Beneath this superficial film there may be several layers, all belonging to the highest stratum, all pertaining to that system of centres, to that region which regulates conduct, and whose activity is accompanied by vivid, active, high-level consciousness, but yet not the highest of all—still having above them a superior authority which co-ordinates, as well as it can, their erring activities, and provides that the highest manifestations of all shall be adapted and adjusted to circumstances. Sometimes it will happen that the disorder in the lower levels increases, becomes yet more uproarious, and invades the highest level also ; and in such cases the hysteria will merge into actual insanity ; but more commonly the disorder remains limited to the layers just below the highest, and the manifestations are those of hysteria alone.

The evidence in support of this view appears convincing. The disorder of feeling—of feeling of elaborate and elevated character, of the more elaborate and late-developed emotions —indicates without a doubt that the region of the nervous system involved in the disorder is a very elevated region. The disorder of conduct proves that it is the highest stratum of nervous arrangements that the physical disorder affects. But there are other manifestations which show that above the disordered region there are some arrangements yet intact, which assert some authority, and endeavour with more or less success to control and regulate the disorderly action beneath them. The paroxysm of excessive laughter or excessive weeping is described as " uncontrollable," clearly indicating that the necessity for control is appreciated. Efforts are evidently made to suppress the excessive manifestation. Sometimes these efforts are successful, sometimes they are not ; but the fact that they are made is sufficient proof that the controlling authority, that is to say, the highest nervous region, still exists, still acts, and even if its action be ineffectual in controlling its mutinous subordinates, yet so far as that action goes, it is normal and healthy.

The considerations dealt with in this chapter lead us to the following conclusions. At the period of puberty new activities are added to the body ; a new phase of development occurs. This development takes place rapidly, and on that account its products are apt to be unstable. The mental changes that take place at puberty are in the main additions to the cœnæsthesis or consciousness of self, and are chiefly three ;—increase of self-consciousness ; craving for self-sacrifice : and craving for sympathy and interest ; all of which are factors in, or modifications of, sexual emotion. Owing to the disturbance produced by the rapid addition of these new faculties, the nervous system is prone at puberty to suffer disorder ; and when disorder occurs, it usually manifests itself in some excessive or bizarre expression of one or other of the newly-added faculties.

CHAPTER IX.

THE CAUSES OF INSANITY (*Continued*).

Indirect Stresses of Internal Origin (continued).

THE stress of puberty tells with special severity, as we have
seen, on the female, and the same is true of all the stresses
connected with the reproductive function. The assumption
of the reproductive function is in all organisms a period of
storm and stress. When the function, from being potential,
becomes actual, further changes occur, and the changes are
of a twofold nature. On the one hand, the gaining of an
outlet for activities is always *ipso facto* beneficial. Activities
that find no outlet must of necessity produce disorder, and
are the direct occasion of unhappiness and harm. The un-
fettered exercise of activities is always a source of satisfaction
during their exercise, is always of beneficial effect to the
organism at large, and leaves behind it an abiding feeling of
contentment, which is the mental reflexion of an enhancement of the general well-being. What is true of activities
generally is especially true of the reproductive activity. If
it is denied its natural and proper outlet, the organism
suffers. Either it finds expression in unnatural and im-
proper ways, or it breaks out disorderly, or it is transmuted,
as it were, into other activities, whose exercise is less beneficial to the organism, and still leaves something unsatisfied ;
leaves the organism incomplete, undeveloped, one-sided.[1]

[1] Burton had a very keen insight into the evils of sexual abstinence:
" As I cannot choose but condole their mishap that labour of this infirmity,
and are destitute of help in this case, so I must needs inveigh against them
that are in fault. . . . How odious and abominable are these superstitious

On the other hand, the function of reproduction has by its very nature a disintegrative, deteriorating influence upon the organism in which it occurs. Down at the bottom of the scale of life, in the simplest organisms, reproduction is effected by fission—by the division of the simple being into parts, each of which takes on a separate life and becomes a complete individual. The gregarina consists of an almost homogeneous jelly enclosed in a sac or body-wall. When the time for reproduction arrives, the body breaks up and divides into a number of spindle-shaped masses, which remain enclosed in the sac. Then the sac bursts, and each spindle develops into an adult gregarine. Here, in this simplest and most fundamental instance, the performance of reproduction is attended by the entire destruction and disappearance of the parent. The individual ceases to exist as an individual, and exists only in its offspring.

In the higher animals and in the human race, in which reproduction is such an immensely longer and more elaborate process, it has still the same essential nature. The parent still persists, as an individual, it is true, after the birth of the offspring. The individuality of the parent is not entirely dissipated and lost in the process of reproduction ; but still that process is not effected without cost. The whole life of the parent is not lost it is true, but a part of it is lost. With each reproductive act the bodily energy is diminished ; the capacity for exertion is lessened ; the languor and lassitude that follow indicate the strain that has been put upon the forces of the body, the amount of energy that has been abstracted from the store at the disposal of the organism. Now, the seat of the reservoir

and rash vows of Popish monasteries ! so to hind and enforce men and women to vow virginity, to lead a single life, against the laws of nature, opposite to religion, policy, and humanity, so to starve, to offer violence, to suppress the vigour of youth by rigorous statutes, severe laws, vain persuasions, to debar them of that to which, by their innate temperature, they are so furiously inclined, urgently carried, and sometimes precipitated, even irresistibly led, to the prejudice of their soul's health, and good estate of body and mind."

of energy is the nervous system, and any drain upon the energies of the body is a drain on the nervous system, whose highest regions will, on the general grounds already familiar, be the first and most affected. Hence the reproductive act has an effect on the highest regions of the nervous system which is of the nature of a stress, and tends to produce disorder.

With a normally constituted organism the stress of the reproductive act is not sufficient to produce disorder, unless it is repeated with undue frequency ; on the contrary, by providing a natural and legitimate outlet for surplus activity, its influence is distinctly beneficial. But in an organism whose energies are naturally defective, the tendency of the reproductive act will be to increase the deficiency ; and in an organism which is inherently below the normal stability, the tendency of the stress of the reproductive act will be to produce disorder. This tendency will be especially severe when indulgence in the sexual act is begun at too early an age.

Hence we find that a certain number of cases of insanity, amounting to about $2\frac{1}{2}$ per cent. of the total number that occur annually in this country, are attributed to sexual excesses. In this estimate there is, however, a source of error, for the tendency of the normal organism is to spread its expenditure evenly throughout all the avenues of escape provided for it. Hence, if one of these channels is more favoured than is due, and is permitted to draught off more than its due proportion of the common store of energy, it indicates either that the facilities for escape through this channel are unusually copious, or that the organism possesses an inherent tendency to dissipate energy to excess in that direction. Cases in which the facilities for, and temptations to, unduly excessive sexual indulgence do occasionally occur, and, if yielded to, do produce deleterious results ; but the majority of cases in which sexual excess can rightly be attributed as a cause of insanity, are cases of the second class. Such excess is not commonly indulged in unless by inherent defect, or vice in the constitution of the organism, there is a decidedly undue proneness for the expenditure of energy in this direction ; and in such cases the inheritance of this tendency must be regarded as a factor in the production of the insanity of equal importance with the stress.

The variations which occur in the tendency for energy to be directed into this channel are normally very wide. In some individuals it is insignificantly small, in others again it is very powerful. Now, whenever a faculty, function, or structure, is found to undergo wide variations within the limits of the normal, it is always found that such a faculty tends frequently to exceed the normal. The tendency to vary, which always exists, will occasionally be excessive. An organ or a function which maintains, throughout the majority of individuals, a nearly constant ratio to the rest of the structures or functions, will seldom be found developed to excess ; but one which, within the limits of health, largely exceeds the average in some people, and falls short of it in others, will be liable, in a small minority of cases, to development that is excessive, or disorderly, or both. For instance, the salivary glands, by whose secretion the mouth is kept moist and the food is lubricated, are remarkably constant in size and activity. They grow uniformly with the growth of the body, they attain in every person to similar dimensions, and their activity in all is about the same. Consequently, we find that it is very rare for these glands to attain an excessive development—to grow to an excessive size—and rare for them to take on disorderly development—to become the seat of tumour or of cancerous growth. On the other hand, the breast, a gland of precisely similar structure and nature to the salivary gland, varies greatly in size and activity both in different individuals and in the same individual at different times. In men it is altogether absent. In some women it is almost absent ; in others it is greatly beyond the average in size. In all women during and after pregnancy it is greatly increased in size and activity. In some women its activity is great and its supply of milk copious ; others have not sufficient milk to nourish their offspring. Correspondingly with these wide limits of variation within the normal, we find that the limits of the normal are often exceeded. Not infrequently the development of the breast is so excessive as to amount to a veritable deformity, and even occasionally to necessitate amputation ; and of all the seats of cancer the breast is the most common. In the same way, the tendency to the expenditure of energy through the satisfaction of the sexual passion, as it normally varies within wide limits, both in different individuals and in the same individual at different times, is specially subject to variations which exceed the limits of the normal. This is the explanation of the occasional occurrence of those wretched beings whose whole attention is absorbed and whose whole time is occupied with this one aim and object. Cases so extreme are not met with outside the walls of lunatic asylums, but cases in which the tendency is excessive in a minor degree are moderately common ; and the indulgence in this proclivity is a fruitful source of that deterioration of the higher powers of the nervous system which is the foundation of insanity.

It has been said in a previous chapter that the function of the male element in the process of reproduction is to give to the germ an impetus sufficient to carry it on through the long process of development. The actual material addition made by the male to the mass of the offspring is insignificant. The whole and sole utility of the union of the male element with the female is the additional impetus thereby imparted to the process of development. This being so, it will appear clear that while the main contribution of the female to the joint result, to the constitution of the offspring, is the *matter* of which the body is composed, the contribution of the male is the *energy* which animates the matter.

Hence, excessive indulgence by the female in the sexual act is comparatively harmless to her unless it results in unduly numerous and frequently occurring offspring.

Hence the danger to the female—the draught upon her vitality, the circumstance which renders the reproductive function a danger to her, is in part the loss of energy, and in part the subtraction of matter ; while in the male it is the dissipation of energy only that is to be feared.

For this reason we find that undue frequency of sexual congress is not attended in the female by the same ill results that follow it in the male. In the latter, the repeated loss of energy eventuates at last in a state of anergy, apathy, lethargy, and dementia. The tension of energy in the nervous system is reduced to the lowest ebb, and all the manifestations of the existence of this energy are wanting or are exhibited in feeble and perfunctory shape. The condition is one of dementia—there is the want of mind, the inability to perform mental operations of even moderate difficulty, the dulness and slowness of feeling, the loss of all the higher emotions and of many of the lower ones also, that characterize dementia. There is the deficiency of movement, the absence of muscular exercise, the inability to make exertions that are at all prolonged or continuous, the general degradation of conduct, the loss of all the higher attributes of humanity, and the retention of only the lower and more animal characteristics. Such are the results of the indulgence of the sexual passion in great excess. When the indulgence is less excessive, the degradation is less profound, but in every case there is degradation, and in every case the deterioration is of the nature of dementia, that is to say, it is a manifestation of deficiency in the amount of the stored energy.

In the female the circumstances are different. While her contribution to the offspring is in part one of energy, it is chiefly material. From her the offspring derives its bulk, its mass, the material ingredients of its composition ; and to provide these is the chief office of the mother. Hence the female does not, as a rule, suffer greatly from undue repetition of the sexual act, even when the indulgence is very prolonged and excessive. The stress upon her is not in the sexual, but in the reproductive act. It is not from sexual congress, but from child-birth, and its attendant circumstances, that danger to her arises.

We have seen how far more important the assumption of the reproductive function is to woman than to man ; how much more numerous, more bulky, and more important are the alterations and additions to her bodily structure at the time of puberty than are those to the structure of the male, and correspondingly how much greater the disturbance that attends their development. This greater prominence and importance of the reproductive function in the female is continued throughout her life. It occupies a far larger proportion of her life than it does in the male. Not merely has she, on each occasion on which she produces offspring, to provide for three-quarters of a year the whole materials for its growth ; not only has she to pass through on each occasion the storm and stress of delivery ; not only has she for a further nine months to supply it still at her own cost with materials for nutrition and growth ; not only has she to suffer under this prolonged period of stress on each occasion on which she produces offspring : but during every month she undergoes a miniature pregnancy, and at each menstrual period she passes through a miniature delivery. Her whole life, from puberty to her climacteric, is passed either in producing and nourishing offspring, or in preparing for the production and nourishment of offspring.

As has been said, the female, in giving life to her offspring parts with a portion of her own. Just as the gregarina breaks up its entire self into a number of separate young individuals, and in giving life to them loses her own ; so the higher animal, in separating off from itself a portion of its being as a new individual, loses thereby a portion of her own. The loss in the latter case is much less complete than in the former, and, unlike the former case, the loss is in the latter capable of reparation, so that, after a lapse of time, little or no detriment remains ; but none the less is there at the time an actual loss of a portion of the life—of a portion of the power and capacity of living. For the time, the amount of life existing in the female, the degree of vitality, the power of dealing with circumstances, the ability to throw off injurious influences, is reduced. The loss is evidenced by her weakness, her prostration, her incapacity for exertion, her increased obnoxiousness to damaging influences, to the poisons of fever, to the stress of anxiety, to the ill effects of exposure and privation. The debility of the parturient woman, and her increased liability to suffer from noxious influences, are sufficiently notorious. In short, the whole reproductive process is in woman an occasion of stress, of diminution of the normal energies. And the stress is not a local stress it ; affects the organism at large and generally. Hence the highest nerve regions, which represent the organism at large, are specially liable to suffer. The main weight of the stress bears on the nervous system, and especially on the higher regions of the nervous system ; and hence the performance of the reproductive function is in woman always attended by a liability to failure of the highest nervous arrangements. In women whose nervous systems are constituted with normal stability, the stress is productive of weakness, of diminution in the power and energy with which the nervous system should perform its functions. It is not enough in them to produce great disorder, and the minor defect from which they suffer is soon repaired. Yet even in the healthiest women pregnancy is attended by certain slight manifestations of disorder—by longings, by irritability, by emotional displays that are excessive and are for them unusual. Every woman in child-birth displays exaggerated manifestations of emotion which, if occurring frequently and at other times, would certainly be considered insane. But in women whose nervous systems are less stably constituted, in women who have derived from heredity an undue instability of tissue, the consequences are graver. The incidence of so urgent a stress upon a nervous system of less than normal stability is liable to produce a degree of weakness that quite disables it from performing its highest functions—to produce that definite and positive disorder that is evidenced in insanity. Hence in women who are by heredity predisposed to insanity the process of reproduction is attended with special danger. Hence, in a considerable proportion of the cases of insanity that occur in women, the insanity appears for the first time during pregnancy, or at, or immediately after, child-birth. In nearly 10 per cent. of the women who become insane, the insanity occurs at this period.

It has been said that, at each menstrual period, a woman passes through what is practically a miniature delivery. Whatever stress attends the process of child-birth occurs in a much milder and less aggravated degree at each menstrual period ; and hence at these periods we should expect to find evidence of stress—evidence of some slight defect in the working of the nervous system in those in whom that system is of normal stability ; evidence of graver defect in those whose nervous systems are inherently below the normal standard. And such evidence we do find. Every woman at her menstrual period is less active than at other times. She suffers more or less from languor, from apathy, from disinclination for exertion ; she is at such times less prone to be energetic, and more easily fatigued. She is unusually irritable, more readily moved to tears. That is to say, her nervous system is acting less efficiently than usual. In women of naturally unstable nervous organization, the effects and signs of stress at the menstrual periods are much graver and more conspicuous. The hysterical woman is especially liable to fits and other marked manifestations of hysteria at her menstrual periods. The insane woman is specially liable to exaggerations of her insanity at her menstrual periods. More than one case has been recorded in which a woman became insane at each menstrual period, and was sane in the intervals.

While the greatest stress connected with the reproductive function attends the actual process of child-birth, the entire

17

process from the beginning of pregnancy to the cessation of
suckling is a strain upon the resources of the organism, is
a source of stress to the nervous system, and is a cause of
disorder in those whose nervous systems are inherently
faulty.   Of the 10 per cent. of insane women whose insanity
dates from the process of reproduction, $7\frac{1}{2}$ per cent. date
from the time of child-birth, $2\frac{1}{2}$ per cent. occur during
suckling, and 1 per cent. during pregnancy.

Throughout the fertile period of her life, woman is subject
to the periodic recurrence of stresses of varying intensity,
arising from the activity of her reproductive function;
beginning with the stormy period of puberty, rising in
minor culminations at each monthly period, and reaching
at each successive child-birth a degree which disorders for
the moment even the strongest and stablest nervous system,
and produces in those which are inherently defective, a
disorder which is profound and prolonged, or slight and
transient, according to the character of the nervous system
on which it acts.   Even when the fertile period of life
reaches its close, the cessation of the reproductive function
is attended by stresses that are inferior to those only which
accompanied its development.   At her climacteric, between
the ages of forty and fifty, woman undergoes a process of,
as it were, inverted puberty.   The organs and functions
which she acquired with so much disturbance, and which
have been throughout her life so fertile a source of trouble
and danger, now undergo involution.   They subside once
more into the quiescence from which at puberty they
emerged; but even when they go, they cannot go quietly.
When the devil was cast out of the deaf-and-dumb boy, he
did not go quietly, but cried, and rent him sore, and left
him as one dead; and when the reproductive functions
depart from a woman, they make their exit, as it were,
unwillingly, and with a demonstration of rage.   They
give their possessor a parting kick.   In other words,
the process of involution is like the process of evolution,
attended with stress and difficulty.   The rapid loss of

functions, no more than the rapid addition of functions, can take place without disturbing the general balance, the equilibrium of the distribution of energy. When activities and potentialities for activity are added to a person's nature, the addition is necessarily accompanied by disturbance, which is great in proportion to the amount of activity that is added, and to the rapidity with which the addition is made. And conversely, when activities and potentialities for activity are withdrawn, the withdrawal is accompanied by disturbance, which is great in proportion to the amount withdrawn, and to the rapidity with which that amount is abstracted.

Hence it is found that in women in whose nature and in whose life the sexual and reproductive functions have absorbed a large proportion of the total activities, the disturbance that attends withdrawal of these activities is greater than in those in whom these functions have been less active ; and when the involution and loss of the climacteric take place rapidly, they produce more disturbance than when the change is spread over a longer period of time. Hence we see, not only why some women become insane at the change of life, but also why the vast majority pass through this period, not indeed without evidence of disturbance, but without the disturbance attaining the gravity of actual insanity. To produce this extreme effect there must be a concurrence of favouring conditions. The nervous system must have been inherently unstable ; and the change must have been unduly grave, or unduly rapid, or both.

Bearing in mind the principles already enunciated, it will not appear strange that the climacteric period, which is in all women a period of stress and of danger, and which is in some women the occasion of an outbreak of actual insanity, is the signal in others for the disappearance of an insanity which existed so long as the reproductive functions were active. If the organism has never been able to so rearrange its energies as to adapt them to the new conditions brought about by the addition of the reproductive functions, and if in consequence there has been disorder during the time of activity of these functions, then it is easy to understand that when the reproductive functions cease, and the disturbing element is withdrawn, the equilibrium of activities may be re-established, and the disorder may settle down once more into normal action. Whatever the explanation, it is an indisputable fact, that a certain proportion of insane women do recover from their insanity upon the establishment of the menopause.

Of the indirect stresses of internal origin, those which accompany the general commotions that occur in connection with the reproductive functions are the most important and the most frequently occurring. Other stresses, there are, however, of this class, produced by general commotions pervading the entire organism, but not directly connected with the reproductive functions. When a person suffers from a fever or other general malady affecting his whole organism, insanity is apt to occur, as we have seen, from the direct stress of the poison in the blood upon the superior nervous system. But in addition to this mode of action, fevers may, acting in quite another way, produce insanity. In fever the entire mass of the blood is vitiated by the contained poison. The blood is supplied by its vessels to every part of the organism. The entire mass of the tissues are continually bathed and soaked in the blood, and if the blood contain a noxious ingredient, this ingredient is distributed to every part of every tissue of the body. The noxiousness of the new ingredient in the blood in fevers depends, not so much on its action on the blood itself, as on its action on the tissues to which the blood carries it. The blood goes to the tissues to nourish them, and to carry away their waste. It is at once the commissariat and the scavenger of the body. If it contains an ingredient which is capable of modifying the process of nutrition, it is evident that the process of nutrition throughout the whole body will be modified. Amongst the tissues so modified are those of the nervous system, and the copiousness with which the blood is supplied to them, and the high degree of activity which is normal to the nutritive process in the grey matter, will ensure that whatever modification nutrition undergoes in the body generally, will be felt with especial severity in the superior nerve regions.

That fevers and other "constitutional" or general maladies do affect in some way the nutrition of the whole body, is rendered evident by certain signs that follow them. The affection of nutrition that is now dealt with is a different matter from the direct poisoning of the superior nerve centres that occurs upon the invasion of a fever, and that has already been dealt with among the direct stresses. The process of nutrition in the nervous system has a two-fold aspect. A continuous supply of blood from moment to moment is necessary to enable the nervous arrangements as they then exist to continue in action. If the blood supply is suddenly cut off, as by failure of the heart in fainting, the action can no longer continue. The nervous system ceases to act, and the individual falls paralysed and un-conscious. If, instead of ceasing altogether, the blood supply is vitiated by the addition of a poison, the nervous system does not cease to act, but its action is defective and dis-ordered. At the same time that the temporary changes which constitute the functional activity are going on, there are also going on changes of a more permanent nature—changes whereby the tissues are maintained in their integrity in spite of the wear and tear of action ; changes by which the modifications of structure that result from functional activity, are dealt with, and either fixated or deleted ; changes of maintenance and repair. We may compare the two sets of changes with those that go on in a steam engine during its working. On the one hand, the stokers are continually adding fresh coals to keep the machine going ; on the other, the engineers are always on the alert, tighten-ing a bolt here, removing rust there, adding oil in another place, repacking a valve, or renewing a bearing. The one is a change in the way of working, the other is a change of

structure. Now if the quality of the blood that is supplied
to the nervous system is altered, it is obvious that, not only
will the first set of changes, which affect the functional
activities from moment to moment, be altered, and the
altered results be immediately seen in altered manifestations ;
but the second and more permanent set of changes will be
altered likewise. The nourishment of the brain will be
altered ; its structure will be modified ; and this modification
of structure will exhibit itself in an alteration in the way
of working that persists long after the change in the blood
has passed away and been forgotten. When pigs are fed on
madder their bones become coloured ; and long after the
madder has been discontinued in the food, and long after it
has ceased to be a constituent in the blood, the colour
remains in the bones. Weeks or months after a person has
suffered from fever, or other general malady, the nails are
found to have ridges on them, the hair falls off, the skin
desquamates, the growing teeth are found to take abnormal
shapes. And similarly, when the nervous system is fed on
vitiated blood, the effect of the faulty nutrition will remain
in the brain long after the blood has been freed of its
mischievous ingredient.

Hence we find, not only that the invasion and acute
period of fever are accompanied by delirium, but that, after
the fever is over, and during the period of convalescence,
the mind is always a little below the normal, and is often
perceptibly weakened. In this, as in all other cases, we find
that an effect which is always present in a slight degree,
assumes, in certain cases in which the stress was unusually
great, or the conditions unusually favourable, much graver
proportions ; and just as it occasionally happens that the
debility of body, that is left after a fever, is so extreme as to
result in a general break down, and, for instance, to lead
directly to consumption ; so it occasionally happens that the
debility of mind, that is concomitant with the bodily weakness, exhibits itself in extreme form, and becomes actual
insanity.

If we bear in mind the fact that every process that goes on in the body has normally a representation in the highest regions of the nervous system, modifies in some degree the nerve currents which go to these regions, and so impresses itself to some extent on the mode and degree of their action, and indirectly modifies the mental states which are the accompaniment of their action ; it will be easy to understand that a general alteration in the way that the tissues throughout the body have been nourished must produce a sensible modification in the currents going from the whole body to the higher nerve regions, must give rise to stress upon them, and must tend to disorder their action. Thus we see that there are three ways in which the occurrence of a fever tends to produce insanity. First, by the direct stress of the action of the poison in the blood on the highest nervous arrangements during their working, which is analogous to the action of a man throwing sand into the bearings of a machine while it is working. Second, by the alteration of the tissue of the brain by its assimilation of the poisoned blood ; which is analogous to the action of a dishonest watchmaker who takes out some wheels of a watch and replaces them by wheels of inferior workmanship. Third, by the reflection, in the highest regions of the nervous system, of the altered nutrition of the tissues throughout the body.

The fact that the vast majority of people who are attacked by fever exhibit some derangement, even if only trifling, of the action of the higher nerve regions, during the time when the action of the poison is most intense, shows how powerful is the action of this direct stress ; and the fact that the vast majority of people who suffer from fever, show no permanent deterioration of mind, shows the remarkable stability of that condition of mobile equilibrium which has been already referred to as obtaining throughout the nervous system. As in other cases, so in this. The escape of the majority from ill consequences, together with the non-escape of a few, shows that the ordinary process of fever alone is insufficient to produce insanity. When insanity follows fever, it is either because the alteration of nutrition that always takes place in fever has in this case lain with unusually heavy stress on the higher regions of the nervous system ; or because the stress, arising from the general alteration of nutrition throughout the body, has acted, with perhaps exaggerated force, on a nervous system of less than normal stability.

What has been said of fevers applies also to other general maladies—to rheumatism, to gout, to ague, to erysipelas, syphilis, and other diseases.

The last of the indirect stresses of internal origin is that which arises from the altered innervation produced by some bodily malady whose seat is local. It is occasionally found that a strictly local malady—such, for instance, as an ulcer of the intestine, or a flexure of the womb, a catarrh of the stomach or of the bladder—may be accompanied by insanity ; and the cure of the local malady may be attended by simultaneous recovery from the insanity. In such cases the concomitant variations of the two sets of symptoms—those of the local malady, and those of the disorder of the highest nerve regions—forbid us to dissociate them entirely. In such cases as the following there can be no reasonable doubt as to the existence of a connection between the one malady and the other.

A patient, whose case is recorded by Schroeder van der Kolk, had catarrh of the bladder, and at the same time had violent nervous symptoms, with hallucinations, both visual and auditory. At first the nature of the bladder trouble was mistaken, and so long as the mistaken treatment continued, neither the local nor the general malady improved. At length, however, appropriate local treatment was adopted, the symptoms of catarrh of the bladder were quickly alleviated, and at the same time the patient awoke as out of a dream. He recognized the falsity of his previous notions, and was practically well. After a time he had a slight recurrence of the catarrh, and immediately the mental symptoms recurred also ; his hallucinations returned. On the cure of the bladder trouble the mental trouble permanently disappeared.

Niemeyer relates that he "treated a very wealthy man for chronic gastric and intestinal catarrh, who, during the disease, thought he was near bankruptcy, and left unfinished a great building he had begun because he thought he had not sufficient money to continue it. After spending four weeks at Carlsbad, his old strength and feelings returned, he finished his house with great splendour, and has been well ever since."

Two cases have been recorded by Dr. J. A Campbell, and I have had two under my own care, in which local abdominal disease (ulcer of the intestines in three of the four cases) was associated with insanity, and the manifestations of the insanity had direct relation to the bodily disease. In each case the patient had the delusion that his bowels were entirely obstructed, and that nothing ever passed through him, and persisted in this delusion in spite of daily evidence to the contrary. It is very significant that Dr. Campbell's patients were brothers, a fact which speaks very strongly for the existence of a previous tendency by heredity to insanity, a tendency which was converted into actuality by the stress of the bodily malady, and received from the latter its local colour.

CHAPTER X.

THE CAUSES OF INSANITY (*Continued*).

Indirect Stresses of External Origin.

THIS class of indirect stresses arise from the action on the higher nerve regions of the circumstances in which the individual is placed. It has already been explained how conduct, the aggregate of the movements of the organism as a whole, is actuated by the highest nerve regions; each phase of conduct depending on the action of a special portion of these regions. And it has been explained how conduct is determined, both from moment to moment, and in its longer excursions, by the impression that is made upon the organism by circumstances. The impressions that determine the minor features of conduct arise from limited portions of the circumstances, and those that determine more important phases arise from larger and larger aggregates of circumstances. The particular moment and place at which it becomes necessary to touch a horse with the whip are determined by the particular impressions made by a limited group of circumstances—the pace and disposition of the horse, the lie of the ground, or the position of surrounding objects. The choice of the time and occasion of setting out on the journey is determined by a larger group of impressions, made by a larger group of circumstances : by the need of visiting a certain person, at a certain distance, for a certain purpose. The resolution to " set up " a carriage is determined, again, by a larger group of impressions, proceeding from a wider group of circumstances: by the recurrence of needs of travelling certain distances in certain times to supply certain needs, by the general state of prosperity, and so forth.   In each case it is the complex impression made by an aggregate of various circumstances that determines the conduct ; and the impressions, which are received proximately by the special sense-organs, and are co-ordinated and combined in the lower and intermediate centres, produce their special effect in determining conduct only when they impinge upon, and alter the disposition of, the highest centres.

It is the normal function of the impressions made by circumstances to impinge on and to produce an alteration in the highest nerve centres.   It is easy to understand, therefore, that if, from any cause, the impressions are excessive in intensity, the alteration that they produce in the highest nerve regions may be excessive.   Normally, this alteration is limited to the setting in activity of centres already organized or in process of organization, and to producing new combinations of centres, by forming new connections between them, in the way indicated in the opening chapters.   Speaking in terms of molecules, the function of the impressions made by circumstances is to produce discharge of certain extensive groups of molecules, and re-arrangement of certain other groups.   Now, supposing that the in-going wave produced by the impression is of undue volume and intensity, it is easy to understand that the discharge of the molecules might be continued to complete disorganization, and the rearrangement might be so extensive as to result in confusion.   Either of these conditions, and à fortiori a combination of both, would be sufficient to dissolve the organization of the highest nervous regions, an organization which, as we already know, is feebly compacted, unstable, and easily disarranged.   The highest nerve regions, whose function it is to produce those elaborate and prolonged combinations of bodily movements in adaptation to circumstances that we call conduct, are not only of feeble stability, and loosely compacted organization, but they are, as we have

seen, far less definite in their limitations than the lower
centres. When a lowest centre is destroyed, a certain part
of the body, a muscle or a limb, loses its function completely,
while adjacent parts suffer little or not at all. When a
middle centre is destroyed, a certain part of the body, a
limb or part of a side of the face, suffers much, but retains
some function, and the adjacent parts—other limbs or the
rest of the side of the face—suffer somewhat. In the highest
centres the delimitation is still less sharply defined. When
one of them is destroyed, the whole body suffers somewhat,
though certain parts suffer more than other parts.

As an accompaniment of this absence of strict delimitation
of the function of the highest nerve centres there is a similar
absence of delimitation of their structure. They are not
rigidly defined, but merge into one another on all their
confines. An excessive discharge started in a lower centre
does not as a rule spread far. An excessive discharge started
in a middle centre spreads down to its subordinates before it
begins to spread laterally to its equals in rank; and hence we
find that an epileptiform seizure, beginning in the hand,
spreads to the arm before it begins to involve the face or
leg. But an excessive discharge, beginning in a highest
centre, has as much tendency to spread laterally to its
coevals, the other highest centres, as to spread downwards
to its inferiors. Hence we find that, when a very voluminous impression is made on the organism, a very widespread
wave of discharge spreads all over the highest regions, and
arouses in a nascent form a vast complex of activities and of
slumbering forms of expression that had previously been
registered there. Such a widespread wave of discharge is
accompanied by a mental state, a mental state consisting of
a vast complex of indistinct confused memories of multitudinous activities and impressions previously experienced ;
and this flood of vague memories is termed an emotion.

The physical accompaniment of thought is, as we already
know, the formation of new connections between centres.
Such a process is in its very nature orderly and little prone

to excess. But the physical accompaniment or basis of an emotion, which is a diffused tumultuous wave of general discharge from many widespread regions, can, it is obvious, easily become excessive, and, when excessive, tends much more strongly, by excessive exhausting discharge, to produce disorder, than does the orderly, localized and gentle process of forming connecting channels between one centre or region and another. Hence the impressions that tend to produce disorder in the highest nerve regions are those whose access is attended by emotion, and those impressions which merely are occasions for increase of intellectual activity are not of a dangerous character. It is, therefore, in emotion-producing impressions that we seek those sources of stress that endanger the stability of the highest nerve regions, and rank as causes of insanity.

The inferior potency of this class of indirect stresses as causes of insanity is seen ;in this ; that, while the direct stresses will, if sufficiently potent, disorder the most thoroughly hale and stable nervous system sufficiently to produce manifest and unmistakable insanity ; and while the internally arising indirect stresses, which are harmless to nervous systems of great stability, will, in those of average stability, produce some disorder,—the indirect stresses are powerless, even when of great intensity, to produce insanity in a person of average nervous stability. In order to occasion insanity, the indirect stress must act on a nervous system which is hereditarily constituted with stability distinctly inferior to the normal.

The stress on the highest nerve regions will be severe in proportion to the volume and intensity of the emotion ; and the character and magnitude of the emotion will depend on the character and gravity of the circumstances which give rise to it. Different sets of circumstances produce different emotions, of which some are attended by far greater stress than others, but common to them all are the features that— (1) The greater the emotion, the greater the stress ; and (2) the more sudden the emotion, the greater the stress. The emotion corresponds in character with the circumstances which give rise to it, and thus the two elements which determine the amount of stress which the highest nerve regions have to suffer, are, the magnitude of the change in the circumstances in which the organism is placed, and the suddenness with which the change takes place.

Take, for instance, the stress of adversity. Suppose that a man sustains losses in his business, in his means of subsistence. The amount of stress that the change in his circumstances imposes on him depends—(1) On the amount of his loss. The greater the loss, the greater his anxiety, the greater his grief, the greater the body of unpleasant emotion that he suffers. But (2) the amount of stress also depends on the suddenness with which his loss occurs. If he loses, say a third of his income, in small instalments spread over a period of several months or years, the stress is less intense than if he loses the same amount at one blow, in a single day. Similarly, the loss of a dear friend, after a prolonged and lingering illness, is less severely felt than if he had been brought home dead from an accident. The suddenness of the change in circumstances is an important element in determining the magnitude of the stress. If we remember the characters of nervous action as explained in the earlier chapters, we shall see that susceptibility to suddenness of change is a fundamental character of constitution of nervous tissue. It was there pointed out that the application of a continuous stimulus to a nerve produced no effect. It is only when the stimulus is applied, and when it is removed, that a current passes through the nerve. Or, when a continuous stimulus is being applied to a nerve, if its intensity be increased or diminished, then at the moment of alteration a current is produced in the nerve, and the magnitude of this current depends partly on the *amount* of the increase or decrease in the intensity of the stimulus, and partly on the *rapidity or suddenness* with which the increase or decrease is made. In other words, to produce discharge in nerve tissue, there must be a provocation, and this provocation must be of the nature of a *change* in the conditions to which the tissue is subjected. The amount of the discharge is proportionate to the magnitude of the change which produces it, and in the magnitude of a change there are two elements. One element is the difference between the state from which and the state to which the change is made. The greater this difference, the greater the change. The other element is the rapidity or suddenness with which the change is made. The more rapid the transition from the one state to the other, the greater the change. When a nerve is gradually warmed, by warming the glass plate on which it lies, no contractions, or only a few trifling contractions, take place in the muscle to which the nerve is supplied. When the same nerve is rapidly warmed to the same extent, by placing a rod of hot metal upon it, a vigorous contraction of the muscle at once occurs. The amount of change in the nerve is the same in the two cases, but in the one case the change is made slowly and the result is small, and in the other the change is made suddenly and the result is great. What is true of this very simple case of nerve action is true of more complicated, and of all cases. The gradual rise in prosperity by a lifetime of toil and prudence is productive of no emotional disturbance. But if the same prosperity is attained suddenly, by drawing a prize in a lottery or receiving an unexpected legacy, the emotion aroused is great, and may, in an unstable nervous system, be accompanied by disorder. On the other hand, if the legacy comes to a man who is already wealthy, the change is not so great as if it comes to one who is living in penury ; and, correspondingly, it is less liable to produce disturbance in the former case than in the latter. The two elements in the change, the amount and the suddenness, have to be estimated and allowed for in every case in which indirect stress is produced by the action upon a person of his circumstances. Bearing this in mind, we may go on to consider the nature of the circumstances whose changes may be productive of stress.

The entire aggregate of circumstances in which a human
being exists falls naturally into six groups, as has been explained elsewhere,[1] and in each group circumstances may
occur of such a nature as to give rise to disordering stresses
upon the higher nerve regions of the organism that is placed
in them.

The first group of circumstances are those constituting
the physical environment, that is to say, those which directly
affect the bodily health.   Such circumstances are the climate
and soil, the quality of the air, the nature of the food and
drink, the dryness or dampness of the dwelling, the whole-
someness or unwholesomeness of the occupation, and circumstances of a like nature.   With respect to the circumstances of this group, it is evident that they are, with one
exception, not of a character to give rise to intense stresses
of the indirect form.   Malaria in the air, the poison of
typhoid in the water, lead in the substances handled in
earning the livelihood, may each of them be sources of
stress, but the stresses so arising are of direct application,
and act, by their presence in the blood, directly upon the
nerve elements in the way already indicated.

The exceptional case, in which circumstances belonging
to the physical environment do give rise to indirect stress,
arise when the circumstances are such as to place, or to
appear to place, the individual in bodily danger.   Under
such circumstances there arises the powerful emotion of
fear ; and if the circumstances arise suddenly, so as to add
the important element of suddenness to the gravity of the
change, then the emotion aroused is one of fright, and is
attended by a stress of exceptional severity.

So prominent a position is, rightly or wrongly, assigned to
fright in the causation of nervous maladies, that it will be
advisable to examine with some care the nature of the stress
that is connected with it.

In the first place, it is necessary to bear in mind that
when nervous maladies follow a shock of fright, the fright

[1] "The Nervous System and the Mind," p. 152.

itself is not the cause of the malady. Fright is a mental state, an emotion of considerable volume and of great intensity; and being a mental state, it cannot, as has been already so fully explained, have a material origin or produce material effects. It has, however, a material accompaniment, and one of great importance. When a shock of fright disturbs the mind, a violent and widespread molecular commotion disturbs the working of the higher nerve regions. What occurs is this: In the long history of our ancestry, innumerable occasions have occurred on which the then existing representative of the race has been exposed to danger. On each such occasion a strenuous effort of some kind has been made to escape from, or to avert, the danger. Sometimes the danger has been of one form and sometimes of another; and the nature and direction of the effort have varied with the form of danger; but common to all such occasions have been an impression made by dangerous circumstances, and a strenuous effort made to avert or escape the danger. According to the laws of nervous action already explained, these occurrences will have left in the structure of the nervous system traces of their past existence; and these traces, these modifications of structure, will have been inherited, passed on from generation to generation, each generation adding, in partially organized form, its own contribution to these connections between impressions of danger and strenuous activity of some form. The activities have been different in the different cases, but they have all been widespread activities—activities involving many muscles in many combinations—and the activity in each case has been of very high intensity. It is this high intensity of the activity that insures the permanence of the " trace " left in the nervous organization by the event. We have already seen that the permanence of a nervous connection depends in part on the intensity of the original process of forming the connection, and in part on the number of times that the connection has been traversed. In the case of high and wide activity

following exposure to danger, the nerve currents passing
from the receiving area to the motor area are in every case
of high intensity ; and hence tend strongly to become
permanent. As, however, occasions of imminent danger
are not, on the whole, very common events in the life of any
one individual, the channels so formed will not be often
traversed, and therefore will not retain a high degree of
permeability, although from the intensity of the pressure
under which they were originally formed, they will remain
slightly permeable. Traces, vestiges of their existence, will
remain. The general result will be that from the area of
grey matter, at which are received impressions made by
circumstances of danger,[1] there will radiate very numerous
channels of very slight permeability, over virtually the
whole motor area of the cortex. When circumstances of
danger suddenly present themselves, this receiving area is
suddenly started into intense activity. It discharges intensely, and the discharge spreads as it best can, in the
directions in which resistance is least ; that is to say, it forces
itself simultaneously through every channel of which a
vestige remains, and arouses into nascent action a great
number of different activities, all widespread, all tending
to move the whole body, all involving many groups of
muscles in many combinations. Now it is obvious that
all these movements cannot occur at once. The organism
cannot move simultaneously in several different directions.
But still all *tend* to occur ; all begin to occur ; all become
nascent. Until they have, as it were, fought it out among
themselves, and one has risen into unquestionable superiority,
asserted itself, and become actual, there will be an equal
tendency for many activities to occur at once ; and the effect
of this will be a sudden bracing up of all the muscles
throughout the body. If the impression of danger is sudden

[1] I do not believe that there is a localized area at which such impressions
are received—a danger centre, as some might term it—but for the purposes
of illustration, and to make the explanation clearer, it may be supposed for
the moment to be localized.

and intense ; if, for instance, it is a loud crash near the ear ; the nascent discharge of the numerous motor areas will be sudden and intense ; the bracing up of the muscles will be sudden and intense ; and there will be a violent start of the whole body.

After a sudden and severe fright certain other effects are noticed. The start is followed by a prolonged expiration, a long puff of breath, a " sigh of relief," which indicates that at the moment of the start, a deep inspiration was made. The breath was drawn in, and the chest fixed, as always happens before a strenuous effort of any kind is made. Now the chest movements are movements of fundamental character, and any discharge which modifies them must be not merely widespread, but must stir the lower strata of the nervous system also. Furthermore, it is noticed that after the start, and after the sigh of relief which follows it, the whole surface of the body breaks out into a sweat, which is another sign of the profoundity of the disturbance which the nervous system suffers. The whole phenomena of the starting in fright, indicate that there is, throughout a very wide area, and to a very great depth in the nervous system, a sudden and excessive, if brief, discharge.

Now, whenever a mechanism is started suddenly, and especially when it is suddenly started into excessive action, it is liable to be disordered. A clumsy coachman, starting his horses with a loose rein, will be apt to break the traces. An engine driver never starts his engine by pulling his lever over to the full extent, and getting full steam on at once. He knows that if he does so, he will certainly break or disorder some of the mechanism. What he does is to start gently, and gradually to increase the pressure as speed is attained. It is the same in the nervous system. If the nerve elements are to work orderly and safely, they must start into action gradually. If they start suddenly, and especially if they start suddenly into violent action, they will be liable to become disordered. The whole pheno-mena of "a fright," show that it is a sudden "start" into violent action. The nervous system, throughout a very wide area, and to a very great depth, is suddenly started into great activity; and the shock of such a start is eminently calculated to produce disorder. Hence we find that manỳ cases of nervous disorder make their first appearance after a fright, and are doubtless correctly attributed to the stress that accompanies the fright. Among the disorders so produced is insanity, and every year a small proportion, amounting to about fifteen in every thousand of the persons who become insane in this country, have their insanity ascribed to fright and nervous shock.

Many thoroughly well-authenticated instances of the efficacy of this form of stress in producing nervous disorder have been recorded. The cases adduced in a previous chapter of the changes of colour in the hair and skin are cases in point. The disorder showed itself indeed in dis-colouration of the skin, and greyness of the hair, but it was of course produced by nervous action. Gowers records the case of a girl who had four attacks of chorea, each excited by the shock attending a fright. Of epilepsy he says that the most potent exciting causes are mental emotion, fright, excitement, and anxiety, and the most frequent of these is fright. Bucknill and Tuke mention the case of a young woman who was assaulted and violated. From that hour she never spoke ; she speedily became completely demented, and so continued till her death. Dr. Savage records a case in which a fire in the house was the occasion of an attack of acute mania. I am acquainted with a case in which a fright given to a child by a nurse-maid in a foolish practical joke, was followed by such a derangement in the nervous system of the child that it stammered ever after.

The group of circumstances constituting the Vital environ-ment is that in which indirect stresses most frequently arise. In this group are included all those circumstances which affect the livelihood or means of subsistence. In these circumstances are included the nature of the occu-pation, the scarcity or abundance of employment, the rate and kind of remuneration, the degree of dependence or independence, the character of employers, of official superiors, the tenure by which office is held, the precariousness or certainty of the means of subsistence, the state of markets, the demand for commodities, the facilities for and obstacles to commerce, the vagaries of fashion, the amount of leisure that the vital occupation leaves, the proportion of the total energies that it absorbs. There are but four elements in this large group of circumstances that are sources of stress on the higher nerve regions. These elements are (1) exhausting nature ; (2) deficiency ; (3) fluctuation ; and (4) precariousness of the means of livelihood.

Means of livelihood are of an exhausting or " trying " character when they absorb an undue proportion of the total energies. In a normal existence the process of obtaining a livelihood does not absorb the whole or nearly the whole of the energies. After the livelihood is gained, there should remain a considerable residuum of leisure time and spare energy for family and social and political activity, for recreative and æsthetic employment. These secondary fields of activity are neither so extensive nor of so exhausting a character as the primary field of livelihood ; and moreover, the very fact of changing the field and character of the activity, is of itself of the nature of a rest. It brings into play new activities, developes new sides of the character, and allows a period of rest and recuperation to those activities which are directly concerned in earning the livelihood. When the means of livelihood are of so exigeant a nature that they absorb the whole of the energies, and leave neither time nor energy for employment in other ways ; when, for instance, a man has to work fourteen, sixteen, and seventeen hours a day at his occupation, it is evident that his nature cannot develop itself in other directions. A portion of his activities will be exercised to exhaustion, and another portion will be unemployed, and will become pent up, will accumulate under pressure, and will tend to break out in disorderly action. In this way, too prolonged hours

of work are productive of stress. Besides the undue prolongation of work, another cause of stress exists in work of unduly
absorbing character ; work which requires unremitting care,
attention, and precision. In the daily occupation of the
vast majority of people, by far the greater part of the work
is routine work, is work that has become habitual, and that
can be carried on correctly without great concentration of
the attention. The navvy in excavating, the labourer in
ploughing and sowing, the coachman in driving, the cook
in concocting a dish, is doing over again, with only slight
and infrequent variations, that which they have done many
times before. Now to do a thing which has been done
many times before, involves but little strain upon the attention. Attention becomes necessary only when variations
have to be made, when new proceedings have to be executed,
when something unfamiliar has to be done. In the same
way, a doctor in seeing his patients, sees in the majority
of cases, combinations of symptoms which he has witnessed
in the main many times before, and the ways of treating
them recur to him with little effort. Only occasionally
does he meet with a case displaying unfamiliar symptoms
or unfamiliar combinations of symptoms ; and only in such
cases does a special mental effort become necessary. The
same is the case with the lawyer. The great majority of his
work is routine work ; the names and the other details of
the cases differ, but the main features of the case that he has
now to deal with resemble the main features of cases that
he has dealt with before ; the ways of dealing with them
arise in his mind without effort and without strain. In
every business the main part consists of routine work, of
operations which have become habitual, and are attended
with but little activity of the very highest nerve regions.
Now it is in activity of these very highest nerve regions that
stress arises. It is easy to understand that so long as the
activity that is going on is mere habitual activity—is activity
proceeding in well-worn, well-organized channels, there will
be little tendency for the process to become disorderly. But

when the activity consists in forcing new channels in directions hitherto untraversed, the process is in its nature a more exhausting one. It absorbs and uses up a greater quantity of energy to force a new channel than to traverse an old one, and hence activity on the higher levels tends sooner to exhaustion, and to the pathological effects of exhaustion, than activity on lower levels. Moreover, when activity on the higher levels is unduly sustained, the exhaustion may easily become extreme. Hence, in any occupation in which routine work is reduced to a minimum, and continuous close attention becomes necessary, the stress on the highest nerve regions is great, and the possibilities of disorder are increased. Hence it is found, that while overwork is not a fertile cause of insanity, yet in cases in which the work has been of a nature to require a close and prolonged application of attention, the stress so produced is occasionally sufficient to produce disorder ; so that a prolonged process of preparation for examination is the most fertile source of disorder under the heading of overwork. If we can find two bodies of men who are subjected as far as possible to the same conditions in other respects, but whose work differs in respect of the amount of continuous and close attention that it demands ; we ought to find, if the foregoing discussion is valid, that that body whose work demands most attention, and is therefore attended by most stress, should furnish the largest number of cases of insanity. Such an instance is furnished ready to our hand by railway servants. Serving the same masters, living in the same mental atmosphere, subject to the same conditions with regard to the security, &c., of their livelihood, all classes of railway servants are circumstanced pretty much alike, with the exception of the drivers and stokers, who, circumstanced alike in other particulars, are subjected to far greater stress from the prolonged, continuous, close, and vigilant attention which their work necessitates. Among all other classes of railway servants, cases of insanity occur at the rate of about 5·5 in 10,000 per annum. But out of every 10,000 of drivers and stokers, no fewer than seventeen, or more than treble the proportionate number, annually become insane.

It is not contended that attentive and intelligent work is necessarily a cause of insanity, even when pushed to a degree which absorbs a very large proportion of the time and energies. The contention is that, among the causes of stress that will provoke an outbreak of insanity in a person hereditarily predisposed to become insane, is that of a too prolonged, too continuous demand for close and vigilant attention. It must be admitted that the stress of over-work is not a common occasion of insanity.

The amount of labour, the number of hours of continuous exertion, of which so very many persons prove themselves capable under necessity, is very great and surprising. The researches of the Sweating Committee have shown that it is frequent for people to work for sixteen and seventeen hours a day, with the closest application, for six and even seven days a week, and, among the people who do so, insanity is not especially common. But then it is to be remembered that the work these people do is of the merest routine and mechanical character ; it is sewing button-holes, or making shirts or trousers. It is done to a very large extent automatically, and does not involve a strain on the highest nerve regions.

Then, again, it is remarkable how men, who are naturally hard-worked in their own proper professions, will undertake a large amount of gratuitous and unnecessary labour in addition to that which they are obliged to do. After spending a whole day in their office or chambers, they will pass the evening in political or charitable or artistic work, and will perhaps rise early in the morning to take a ride or a swim before going to business. And these are not the people who show signs of stress. They are the most healthy, vigorous, and happy of men. They are happy because they are healthy and vigorous ; and it is because they have inherited such splendid constitutions, because they have within them so great a store of energy, that they seek so many outlets for this energy, and can maintain so many different forms of activity concurrently. Exertion which is undertaken in order to satisfy and expend the buoyant spontaneity of a man's nature is never harmful. It is only when the energies are drained by exertions that are made, not spontaneously, but in answer to urgent and repeated demands—demands that may not be refused—that the reserve store of energy is lowered to a dangerous extent, and stress arises. It is to be noticed, also, that spontaneous exertion is always varied in form. It is now mental, now athletic. The objects of pursuit are many and various, the activities displayed in each pursuit are different, and while one is active the remainder are resting. But the exertion that is made in response to an imperative demand is, as a rule, a continuous exertion of the same class of activities, and is therefore more exhausting.

The stress arising from over-exertion is unquestionably of rare occurrence. In order to be productive of stress, the attention must be occupied with a closeness and vigilance, and over a period of time, such as are not often called for even in exacting occupations. I fully agree with Dr. Wilks that "if both sexes be taken, the opposite is nearer the truth ; and that more persons are suffering from idleness than from over-work. . . . The persons who apply to the doctor are not the Prime Minister, the bishops, judges, and hard-working professional men, but merchants and stock-brokers retired from business, Government clerks who work from ten to four, women whose domestic duties and bad servants are driving them to the grave, young ladies whose visits to the village school, or Sunday performance on the organ, is undermining their health, and so on." There is a common saying that "hard work never hurt any one," and, like most common sayings, it expresses one half of a truth. Mere laboriousness of occupation probably never did hurt any one, provided that it was accompanied with a sufficiency of food and of sleep. When, however, to laboriousness of occupation is added a demand for close and vigilant attention, the occasion is much more exhausting ; and exertion upon this higher level of the nervous system is apt to be accompanied by sleeplessness.   The activity evoked in the highest nerve regions is so great and so widespread, that it is with difficulty, and only after prolonged absence of stimulus, that it subsides into the quiescent state that obtains during sleep, and that, in fact, constitutes sleep.

2. The scantiness or abundance of the means of livelihood has little influence *per se* in inducing indirect stress on the higher nerve regions. The possessors of great wealth are, indeed, prone to dilate upon the cares and responsibilities that great wealth brings with it, but that these cares and responsibilities ever attain such proportions as to constitute a source of stress there is no evidence to show.   Undoubtedly cases have occurred in which a sudden accession to great wealth has been the occasion of an outbreak of insanity ; but in such cases it is the gravity of the *change*, and not the affluence of the circumstances, that has brought about the result. Such cases fall to be considered under the next heading.

Neither does the opposite condition of scantiness of the means of livelihood appear to be *per se* a source of such severe stress as to be an important factor in the production of insanity. It is not found that insanity is especially prevalent among the very poor, although doubtless the standard of intelligence among that class is lower than in the rest of the community. The poverty is, however, more a result than a cause of the lack of intelligence. When means of subsistence fall so low as to verge on starvation, then the higher nerve regions get badly nourished, and the signs of alienation resulting from the direct stress of imperfect nutrition begin to show themselves ; but short of actual starvation, the struggle of penury against necessity, urgent as it often is, does not appear to be attended by specially severe stress of the kind we are considering. When the stress arising from "adverse circumstances" is a factor in the production of insanity, it is always found that the adverse circumstances have not been the normal state. In such cases there has always been a fall from a more prosperous to a more adverse condition, and the stress is more properly ascribable to the change in circumstances than to the poverty itself.

3. In the case of worldly prosperity, as in every other agent that affects the nervous system, it is this element of change that is the most important factor in the production of stress ; and, as in other cases, the gravity of the stress is measured by the magnitude and the suddenness of the change.

Stress is least urgent when the change is from a less prosperous to a more prosperous condition ; and to produce ill effect, a change in this direction must be of great gravity—must be both sudden and of great magnitude. That such a stress, however grave, will not produce disorder unless it act upon a nervous system of undue instability, is of course understood. When all the conditions are favourable for its occurrence, disorder does occasionally occur upon this pro-vocation ; and cases are on record in which a sudden accession to fortune, by a person previously in poor circumstances, has been immediately followed by an outbreak of insanity. In one instance three members of the same family—a mother and two daughters—became insane upon a sudden accession to fortune : two of them upon being informed of the change in their circumstances.

The reverse change—from a more to a less prosperous condition—is a more fertile occasion of insanity, and this no doubt for two reasons : first, because the change in this direction is much more common than in the other ; and, second, because in this change the stress is naturally so much greater. As in the previous cases, the gravity of the stress will depend in part on the magnitude of the change, on the amount of the vicissitude of fortune that is suffered, and in part on the suddenness with which this change occurs.

A person who lives always on the verge of penury ; whose means of subsistence suffice, at the best of times, to procure for him only the bare necessaries of life ; who seldom enjoys the satisfaction of having quite enough to eat ; whose clothing in winter is seldom substantial enough to be a full protection against the weather ; whose dwelling is at the best of times destitute of all comforts, and of many things which are regarded by the majority of people as necessaries ;—such a person will suffer less stress from a complete withdrawal of his scanty means of subsistence, than will another person who is accustomed to live in the lap of luxury, and who, from loss of the greater part of his fortune, is compelled to remove from a lordly mansion to a cottage of six rooms. Although the condition of the first man, who is reduced to sleeping under a haystack, and who knows not, when he awakes in the morning, whether or no he will taste food that day, is absolutely worse than that of the second, who has a neatly furnished cottage, and enough saved out of the wreck of his fortune to provide him with a living for the rest of his life ; yet the amount of vicissitude experienced by the first is not so great as that experienced by the second. He has landed at a lower depth, it is true, but he has not fallen so far. The change from penury to destitution is not so great as that from luxury to poverty ; and the stress that is experienced in the first case is less severe than that experienced in the second.

With regard to the suddenness with which adversity comes, it is unnecessary to repeat what has been already said on that subject. It is obvious that the sudden and un-expected loss of fortune is productive of much more intense stress than a loss going on by driblets, long foreseen, and extended over many years. That the suddenness with which a calamity occurs increases the gravity of the stress that it occasions, is recognized in the prevalent practice of " breaking " ill news. The intelligence of disaster is com-municated to the person whom it most affects, not at once and in the mass, but gradually and by instalments. In this way it is considered, and rightly considered, that the force of the stress is dissipated, broken, and diminished.

It is remarkable that although a single vicissitude of fortune is attended by so great a stress that insanity not very infrequently follows, yet repeated vicissitudes are less dangerous, and the reason seems to be that the first occasion is the occasion of the greatest shock—of the greatest change —and that subsequent vicissitudes act upon an organism which has become to some extent habituated to them—to whom they are, therefore, changes of less novelty and less gravity, and so are attended by diminished stress.

4. If actual vicissitudes of fortune are attended by intense stress upon the higher nerve regions, impending vicissitudes are attended by a stress which, if less intense, is more enduring : and especially dangerous is the long-continued and varying stress which attends *precariousness* of the means of livelihood. In this case, again, the stress is less upon those who live upon the margin of the self-supporting community, who for part of the year are able to earn their own subsistence, and for another part regularly seek the shelter of the workhouse. In such cases, indeed, the means of living are not really precarious, for they are sure all the year round of some subsistence, and of subsistence which does not vary much in amplitude whether they are inside or outside the " House." The intensest stress lies upon those who live in comfortable, or, it may be, luxurious circumstances, but who cannot calculate with certainty on the continuance from day to day of their standard of living. To such people the failure of the means of subsistence means much more than to the other class. It means not merely a far greater change in the mode of living, but it means more or less disgrace ; it means a fall in the estimation of their fellows ; it means the loss, not only of livelihood, but of most of the things which make life worth living. Those who live in comfortable circumstances, but whose living is precarious, live under a perpetual load of care. They are subject to the incessant stress of recurring anxieties, and such a stress has all the evil quality of that already dealt with as arising from too close and too prolonged attention, together with an additional element of stress in the intrinsically lowering, depressing influence of the anxiety.

There is one other circumstance, connected with the means of livelihood, that is apt to produce stress in those who are subjected to its influence ; and that is the sudden cessation of work by one who has been for many years accustomed to a uniform course of toil. The disappointment that is in store for those who have been looking forward, during a lifetime of toil, to the period of golden leisure that they shall enjoy in the evening of their days, has become a stock subject for the moralist for many generations. All have heard of the soap-boiler, mentioned by Dr. Johnson, who, after selling his business, begged of his successor to allow him to come up on melting-days and witness the operation ; and the anecdote illustrates a state of things which is extremely common. A man who has all his life been in active employment, who has not only always had abundant outlet for all his activities, but who has, by long habit, so modified, and moulded, and trained his nervous system, that a certain amount of activity is forthcoming every day, suddenly relinquishes his employment, and stops up the channels by which these habitually accumulating energies were habitually expended. What must happen is clear. The activities will not suddenly cease. The man may voluntarily relinquish the habitual modes of employing himself, but he cannot, at a few days' notice, so modify his nervous system as to cause it to abandon habits which have been the growth of a lifetime. The activities still continue to be felt. The energies still continue to be generated ; but, cut off from their normal and habitual mode of expression, they accumulate ; they become pent up ; and, unless outlet is found for them, they will infallibly produce disorder. Hence we find that when a man in the evening of life, or about the time that was considered by the ancients his grand climacteric, retires from his business, he is subject to stress ; and if by this time his energies have not much diminished, but are still very active ; and if he has no alternative occupations in which he can find outlet for his unemployed activities ; this stress is extremely likely to produce disorder. Within six months I have been consulted about five gentlemen, all of whom were becoming, or were, insane from this cause. All of them were men of great bodily and mental activity, all about the same age, all had recently retired from active business, and here is the significant fact—all of them were destitute of mental resources. Not one of them ever opened a book; not one of them had a hobby; not one of them cared for music or any form of recreation, with the sole exception of one who occasionally played golf, and one who occasionally played chess. Not one of them took any active part in social, municipal, or political life. It is remarkable that the cases of insanity arising from this cause usually exhibit the same symptoms. In all the above five cases the patients were very wealthy men, and each one, upon relinquishing his business, sank into melancholia, and cherished the belief that he was miserably poor. One tried to take his own life with the intention of relieving his family of the burden of supporting him; another entered his sumptuous carriage and told his coachman to drive to the workhouse, saying it was the only place he himself was fit for. It is cases of this class which show perhaps most clearly that the seat of the disorder is in the *process* of adjusting themselves to their surroundings.

The next group of circumstances from whence stress may arise, is that constituting the Family environment; which includes the circumstances as to parentage, marriage, offspring and other relatives; the degree of dependence or independence existing among them; the help or hindrance that they afford to the individual in his struggle for life; and the customs and laws which regulate his dealings with them. The circumstances in the Family environment that may be productive of stress are those which arouse emotion, and the stress that they produce is severe, according as the emotion aroused is intense, is voluminous, and is long continued. It will be convenient to consider the stresses in the order of the relationship of the persons whose conduct gives rise to them.

The conduct of parents towards their children is not often conducive to insanity in the children, and this is probably because in childhood, when the relation of the parents is most important, and their influence predominant, acquired insanity is extremely rare ; while in adult life, when insanity is more readily acquired, the influence of the parents as producers of emotion is not very powerful. There is, however, one case in which this influence is directly productive of insanity, and that is the case of an hysterical girl with a foolish, weak, indulgent, fussy, anxious mother. The mothers of hysterical girls are often of this description, and their influence upon their children is noxious in a high degree. The girl whose salvation depends upon being "taken out of herself ;" upon having her attention withdrawn from her own cœnæsthesis, and concentrated upon externals ; upon being induced and compelled to interest herself, not in her own feelings, but in what is going on in the world around her ; is taken in hand by an over-solicitous mother ; put to bed ; shut off as far as possible from commerce with varied scenes and external interests ; and taught by continual inquiry into "how she feels," by continual expatiation to friends and visitors upon her delicacy and precarious condition, to concentrate and intensify the interest that she is naturally predisposed to take in her own sensations ; and is thus urged and worried into a condition which always partakes of the nature of insanity, and which occasionally culminates in a definite outbreak of mania.

The relationship towards brothers and sisters does not include many occasions of stress. The chief occasion so arising is when one or two or several brothers or sisters of an individual are already afflicted with insanity. In such cases the members of the family who still remain sane are subjected to a very definite stress of considerable intensity. The fear of following in the footsteps of their relatives, and of themselves becoming insane, is so urgent, and is attended by so great a stress, as sometimes of itself to bring about the very disaster which is dreaded. It would of course be untruthful to deny that persons so related are exposed to greater chances of becoming insane—are more obnoxious to the influence of stresses tending to produce insanity—than are the majority of other people ; but, on the other hand, it is the height of folly to suppose that, because a person has one or more brothers or sisters who are insane, therefore that person stands in imminent or urgent danger of himself becoming insane. The operation of the laws of heredity, as explained in a previous chapter, secure that the tendency of each individual to develop in the direction, in the manner, and to the extent of the average individual of the race from whence he springs, is so powerful, that it will assert itself against conditions the most unfavourable ; so that parents, who differ very widely from the usual standard of the race, commonly produce children who approximate to that standard very closely ; and even if they produce one, or two, or more children who inherit their peculiar divergence from this standard, the chances are quite as great that the remaining children will follow the usual course of development, and grow into normal average individuals, as that they will follow the development of their parents, and inherit their instability. If persons situated in the way supposed, that is, related to insane brothers and sisters, and on that account worrying about their own sanity, were aware of the immense number of perfectly normal people who are in the same predicament as themselves, they would find their fears considerably allayed.

In comparison with other family relationships, that of marriage is a fertile source of stresses that favour the production of insanity ; and the reason of this greater fertility is apparent. In adult life the relation to parents or to brothers and sisters is not an extremely important one ; does not, as a rule, largely influence the life, the conduct, thoughts, and emotions of an individual ; but the same cannot be said of the relationship towards husband or wife. In the case of a man, the disposition, character, and health of his wife form very important considerations in determining his

conduct and mode of life, and are potent elements in direct-
ing his thoughts and arousing his emotions ; while in the
case of a woman, whose profession and business it is to be
her husband's wife, the character and conduct of the
husband exercise an even more important and powerful
influence on the life, the physical and mental well-being.

Among the circumstances of this relationship that are
productive of stress, the most potent is doubtless conjugal
unfaithfulness in the other party. While not absolutely a
frequent cause, it is, relatively to other family circumstances,
the most frequent cause in this group. A case has been
related in an earlier chapter, and more than one case of
the kind has come under my own notice. The stress is
simply that commotion of the nervous molecules which
attends intense, violent, and continued emotion ; and does
not call for further examination as to its nature.

The complementary circumstance of unfaithfulness, not
in the other party, but in the individual, is sometimes
an occasion of stress that becomes a factor in the production of insanity, as in the case of Lady Mordaunt,
who became insane upon being made respondent in a
divorce suit. In that case there were, of course, the
additional stresses arising from the public exposure of
the trial, &c. Without unfaithfulness in either party,
stresses occasionally arise from the relationship of marriage. The marriage with an individual who is found to
be extremely unsuitable, who offends against every instinct
and proclivity, may produce enough stress to cause insanity
in the individual so offended. Or, without any such manifest unsuitability, the marriage with one person, when the
whole affection has been given to another, may be an
efficient cause ; or even, it is probable, the mere fact of
marriage with a person for whom no affection is felt.
The case of Lady Durham, tried before Sir James Hannen
in March, 1885, is in point.

This consideration leads directly to those cases in which
the stress which occasions the insanity is the loss of a

lover. Such cases are frequently referred to in songs, and occasionally in romances ; and undoubtedly such cases do occasionally happen, but they are not common. The craving of human nature about the period of adolescence is for some object to lavish its affections on. The object fixed upon may be appropriate or it may not ; but in either case, if it be lost, its place does not, in the vast majority of cases, remain long vacant. The craving is too powerful to remain unsatisfied, and as the majority of the qualities which constitute the appropriateness—that is, the excellence—of the loved object exist, not in that object but in the imagination of the lover, an apparently suitable object is easily found, and the affections are transferred with a readiness which often causes some surprise, and even some humiliation, to the transferer.

In the relationship to children stresses may arise which favour, if they do not by themselves produce, the occurrence of insanity ; and I have had under care a case of insanity which was ascribed to the anxiety and worry produced by the excesses and enormities of a spendthrift, graceless son.

Besides the stress arising from the misconduct of children, there is that arising from anxiety as to their means of subsistence. The onset of poverty and adversity, which could easily be borne if the individual alone were concerned, may become a source of dangerous stress from the fact that it will involve the offspring also ; and anxiety as to their fate under such circumstances may be attended by an amount of stress sufficient to produce insanity. In September, 1883, William Gouldstone was tried at the Central Criminal Court for the murder of his five children. He was a sober, hard-working man, in the receipt of 25s. per week. In three years he had had three children, and in six months more his wife was confined of twins. It is noteworthy that his means of subsistence remained the same, but the extra drain upon these means of subsistence, arising from the addition of two more children to his family, was a circum-

stance sufficiently adverse to produce stress enough to cause
insanity. He was found guilty by the jury, but subsequently respited on the ground of insanity.

In addition to those which have been mentioned, there
are certain other family relationships that may give rise to
stress. Among these the most frequent and the most
severe is the case of seduction, and the giving birth to
a child by an unmarried girl. In such a case a number of
causes combine to produce the stress to which the insanity
is due. There is the overwhelming and intense emotion
of shame at her position. There is the prospect of her
life being blighted by inability to obtain employment, to
marry, the enhanced difficulty of supporting herself thereafter. There is the additional burden upon her resources
of a child to support. There is very often the additional
stress caused by the loss of her lover, a circumstance which
is alone sufficient in some cases to induce insanity. Then,
in addition, there are the powerful internally-arising stresses
of pregnancy, childbirth, and suckling to aid and reinforce
the other forms of stress. Under the circumstances it is
not to be wondered at that a considerable number of cases
occur annually of insanity in young unmarried mothers.

The next division of the environment that we have to
consider as a source of stress, is that which comprehends
the social and political circumstances in which the individual lives. Man is by nature gregarious, and the gregarious
instinct, though not a very prominent one, is an instinct
of enormous volume and powerful sway. There are two
ways in which the gregarious instinct affects the sanity
of the individual.

In the first place, for this, as for all other activities, there
must be an outlet, if the organism is to remain in health.
The desire for companionship of our kind is a craving as
urgent, although not so immediate, as the desire for food ;
and just as the bodily health suffers when the individual
is deprived of food, so the mental health suffers when he
is deprived of companionship. We do not so often see

instances of this deprivation in man, but we have abundant evidence of the strength of the instinct in other gregarious animals. Practical dairymen know that a cow placed by itself will never give as much milk, put on flesh as fast, or be as profitable in any way as one which has the companionship of its fellows. A horse which occupies its stable in solitude, and runs alone, will never do as much work as one which has a companion in the neighbouring stall and runs in double harness. When a hunter is put out to grass, it will break down, or surmount, almost any obstacle to get into another meadow in which other horses are. Put two or more animals of any kind on a common to graze, and they will always be found near together. So it is with man. The man who lives without the companionship of other men of similar tastes and similar mental calibre, lives a mutilated, unsatisfied, unwholesome existence; and he who lives in solitude cannot long preserve his mental health. Hence the system of solitary confinement for long periods in prison has had to be abandoned on account of the large proportion of the prisoners who became insane. Hence tenders of lighthouses and light-ships are very prone to melancholia. Hence men who tend sheep in the solitudes of Australia will walk incredible distances and undergo intolerable hardships for the sake of getting once more into human companionship; and if this companionship be inaccessible, they become insane. " This alone kills many a man, that they are tied to the same still, as a horse in a mill, a dog in a wheel, they run round, without alteration or news, their life groweth odious, the world loathsome, and it embitters their highest pleasures that they are still the same."

The second way in which the gregarious instinct affects the conditions of sanity is by the influence upon the individual of the particular *grex* in which he lives. Every member of a society is influenced, to an extent of which he himself is seldom conscious, by the character, the action, the opinions of the society of which he is a unit. It is in their simplest and most separate forms that all phenomena are most plainly exhibited ; and if we notice social phenomena in their simplest examples, we see, very conspicuously displayed, the influence of all upon each. If we watch the flight of a flock of starlings, fieldfares, or even pigeons, we shall see that their movements are actuated by a unanimity which is not approached, *pace* Mr. Puff, even upon the stage. A great flock, consisting of many hundred birds, may be seen to wheel, to turn, to rise, to approach the ground, with a simultaneity which gives to the whole flock the appearance of being moved by a single impulse. Similarly a shoal of small fish may be seen to alter the rate and direction of movement in such a way that, while each individual alters its movement to the same extent, each remains at the same distance from its neighbours, and the general outline of the shoal is unaltered. In these phenomena we see two principles exemplified. In part they are no doubt due to the similar action of similar circumstances upon similarly organized beings, and are good examples of the stringency of the subjection of Conduct to Law. But in part also they are examples of the tendency of every individual of a society to follow the conduct of the majority of the members. All the members of the flock or of the shoal are not subjected to quite the same conditions, and yet the conduct of all is virtually identical, so that a large proportion of the effect must be set down to this second factor. The tendency of each individual to act as the rest act is so strong that no alternative seems possible. An exception, a rebel, a case of individual, independent judgment, is never witnessed. For one of these animals to turn in a contrary direction to the rest, would be as impossible as for a tradesman in ancient Egypt to change his occupation, or for an English country squire to vote for a Radical. The conformity of conduct is the result of no external coercion. It is the outcome of an organized mechanism that has become so thoroughly adapted to combined or conventional action, that independent action is inherently impossible—is in the line of greatest resistance, internal as well as external.

While we recognize the power of this inherent tendency, in every member of a society, to follow the example of the rest, we must not omit to notice that, in order there may be an example to follow, some individuals must take the initiative. There must be in some individuals a tendency, not to follow, but to lead ; not to imitate, but to initiate. Yet if we observe the movements of the flock or of the shoal, we see among its members such an almost perfect simultaneity of action, as, taken together with the sameness in direction and the equality in the amount, renders us certain that, since the actions are so closely alike, the motives also that prompt to action must be closely alike in all. These motives we have seen to be the tendency to imitate others, and the tendency to initiate new lines of action. Since it is unlikely in the extreme that, in individuals so closely alike in other respects, there should be a difference so great as that one should be wholly imitative and another wholly original, we are led to the conclusion that every individual in a society possesses in some degree both of these tendencies to action—the tendency to conform, to imitate the acts prevalent in the society in which it exists ; and the tendency to originate, to initiate new actions, to revolt, to rebel. In every individual these two tendencies exist, but in no two individuals are they combined in precisely the same proportions. Upon the strength of the initiative or conforming tendency is founded the whole power of Mrs. Grundy. Her dominion rests upon fear— upon the fear of doing that which is not customary, which does not conform to the customs of the majority. According to the degree in which this tendency preponderates over the tendency to originate, in so far is the individual conservative in his tastes, opinions, and acts. He desires to go on doing what the majority are doing. Any departure from the uniformity of action of all the members of the society to which he belongs, is irksome to him ; it offends against a deep instinct of his nature ; it impresses him as a species of treachery ; as militating against the stability of the social organization. If all the birds in a flock were to fly at random, the flock would disperse ; if all the fish in a shoal were to swim at random, the shoal would be scattered ; and if all the members of a human society were to discard uniformity of action, the society would fall to pieces. It is the dim perception of this fundamental truth which makes the conservative so tenacious of his conservatism, and so bitter in his opposition to the party of progress.

On the other hand, the possession of a greatly preponderating amount of the initiative or originating faculty makes a man by nature a rebel. Perceiving the defects of the system under which he lives, and unrestrained by the coercive agency of the conforming tendency, he desires to loosen the bonds of the social organization in order that its elements may be rearranged. In all his departures from customary proceeding he is met by a determined opposition from the conforming party. It is in vain that he displays the manifest benefits that must result from the change that he advocates. It is in vain that he appeals to past experience, and shows the advantages that have resulted from similar changes. Arguments are powerless against instinct, and it is an instinct that he has opposed to him. When once his reform is carried ; when it has become familiar ; when it has become a part of the customary order of things ; then the same instinct will mount guard over it, and will defend it against the innovations of another generation.

It is upon the variations of these two tendencies that the existence of the two parties of Conservatism and of Progress depends. Since the tendencies have their foundation deep down in the constitution of humanity, we should expect their manifestations to be widespread and multiform, and that is what we find. Not only do we find that in every nation the two parties of Conservatism and Progress are opposed to one another, but we find the same opposition in every minor aggregate of which these great societies are composed. When first Macadam proposed to improve the roads of England, and substitute a firm roadway for the sloughs in which the waggons had been wont to get embedded, a pamphlet was published which had for its burden the question, "What shall we do if we leave the old ruts?" The opposition to steam locomotion is a matter of history, and in every trade a new process is looked upon with a disfavour which is great in proportion to the novelty of the proposal.

The interest which these tendencies possess for us who study insanity is twofold. In the first place, as with all other tendencies to feeling and conduct, their excess is itself insanity; and secondly, where the conforming tendency is very powerful, and the individual so endowed is placed in an insane environment, he may become insane by the mere force of his imitative tendency.

The influence of the Religious environment in causing insanity is not very easily computible, for so much more depends on the individual upon whom the religious circumstances act than on the circumstances themselves. The close connection between religious fervour and sexual passion has already been adverted to. In connection with normal development a large body of vague and formless feeling arises, and until experience gives it shape, the possessor remains ignorant of the source and nature of the feeling. If the circumstances are appropriate for the natural outlet and expression of the activities, they are expended in affection, and are a source of health and strength to the possessor. But if no such natural outlet exists, the vague, voluminous, formless feelings are referred to an occasion that is vague, voluminous, and wanting in definite form—they are ascribed to the direct influence of the Deity, and assume a place as religious emotion. In all this the religious environment takes but little part; but when the tide of emotion has once been directed into the religious channel, then the particular manifestations

in which it finds outlet are determined by the nature of
the religious environment ; so that one girl becomes a nun,
another a district visitor, and a third a hallelujah lass.
Some of those who seek these occupations do so because
they happen to have been brought up in a convent and
have had no inducement to leave it, or because no other
occupation presents itself, and they happen to have been
thrown in the way of the particular employment which
they follow ; but those who actually seek out these particular modes of life, do so because in them the religious
emotion is unusually powerful or prominent ; and the fact
of any emotion being unusually powerful or prominent
is itself an indication that that particular nature is not
evenly balanced, and that in it disorder will be more readily
provoked than in the normal. With such natures it depends upon the character of the religious environment
which acts upon them whether they remain sane or
whether they become insane. So long as the circumstances of their environment are such as to provide
abundance of employment with little provocation to
emotion, so long they will remain sane ; but let them
be subjected to inactivity, so that their energies have
time to accumulate, and let their circumstances be highly
provocative of emotion, so that the accumulated energy
tends to widespread, intense, and unregulated discharge,
and the occurrence of insanity becomes a question only
of time and of the degree of excitement that the circumstances are capable of producing. Let persons of such
nature be taken from their daily avocations and subjected
to the highly exciting circumstances of a religious " revival,"
and their insanity will be inevitable, provided the excitement is sufficiently intense and long continued. Thus
every "revival" is attended by its crop of cases of insanity,
which are the more numerous as the " revival " is more
fervent and long continued.

CHAPTER XI.

THE FORMS OF INSANITY.

If, in considering the causes of insanity it has been found necessary to depart from the usual practice and to regard them from new points of view and in new lights, still more is this necessary when the forms of insanity have to be dealt with. The number of different classifications of insanity is the same as the number of writers on the subject, each individual author having proposed his own, which differs in some point or other from all the rest. Most of these classifications are founded upon a general principle, but it has not been found possible to apply any one principle uniformly throughout. At some point it fails, and another principle has to be brought in ; so that the classification comprises, as separate and mutually exclusive, such groups as Mania, Epileptic Insanity, General Paralysis of the Insane, Puerperal Insanity, Dementia, Idiocy, &c. ; which is much as if a librarian should classify his books into histories, books bound in cloth, novels, works of fiction, octavo volumes, periodicals, and books published in London. The difficulties of the subject are certainly extreme, for even if we consider only the symptoms, the same individual may at different times present the features of several of the forms of insanity which are generally recognized as distinct ; while if we consider both symptoms and causes, as is often done, we may have to classify the same case in several different groups, and find that for another case there is no group provided. The more and more numerous the cases of insanity that I have had to deal with, the more strongly the fact has impressed itself upon me that it is fruitless to endeavour to draw up an elaborate scheme of classes, orders, and genera, into which cases of insanity are to be grouped. No such divisions exist in nature, and to create them would be a highly artificial proceeding, and one that would not accurately represent the facts. Certain it is, that there are wide differences between different cases, but equally certain is it that the differences are not abrupt, and that any scheme of division, that shall correspond with the facts, must separate the cases into but a few broad and comprehensive groups, and must recognize that between these groups no exact line of demarkation can be drawn. Cases will always occur partaking pretty equally of the nature of two adjoining groups, and other cases will occur which exhibit at one time the features of one group, and at another time those of another. Nevertheless, it is certain that cases of insanity do differ widely among themselves, and that the majority of cases resemble, in a greater or less degree, one of a few well-marked types. A very common mistake has been to confuse the division of *forms* of insanity with the division of *cases* of insanity. To suppose that every case of insanity exhibits a single form, and persists in exhibiting that form, is a mistake. The same individual may at one time display one form and at another time another. In the following consideration of the forms of insanity, regard will be had only to the nature of the symptoms displayed, and it will be understood that the description applies, not necessarily to the whole course of a case, but to the phenomena that characterize a case at any given time.

The artificiality of current divisions becomes apparent when we find that one group of cases of insanity is included under the head of Mania, another under that of Epileptic Insanity, another as Puerperal Insanity, and another as Senile Insanity. Now nearly every case of insanity in which epilepsy is a frequent and regular occurrence, and which comes therefore under the head of Epileptic Insanity, exhibits maniacal outbursts from time to time, and then becomes a case of mania. Moreover, almost every case of mania which goes on to its natural termination, and is not cut prematurely short by some intercurrent disease, exhibits at one period or another of its course an attack of epilepsy. Most cases of senile insanity are subject to maniacal outbursts, and many have epileptic attacks. All cases of puerperal insanity are more or less maniacal in the early stage of the malady. So extraordinarily varied are the manifestations of insanity, that it has been said, and said truly, by the father of alienism, that there are "scarce two of two thousand that concur in the same symptoms. The Tower of Babel never yielded such confusion of tongues as the chaos of madness doth variety of symptoms. There is in all madness *similitudo dissimilis*, like men's faces, a disagreeing likeness still ; and as in a river we swim in the same place, though not in the same numerical water ; as the same instrument affords several lessons, so the same disease yields diversity of symptoms. Which, howsoever they be diverse, intricate, and hard to be confined, I will adventure yet in such a vast confusion and generality to bring them into some order." [1]

Regarded from the point of view merely of the symptoms that they present, and without reference to the occasion on which they occur, or to their accompaniments, the forms of insanity are not numerous. They are few and broadly distinguished rather than numerous and strongly marked. By confining ourselves strictly to the symptomatic point of view, we are precluded from regarding puerperal insanity, epileptic insanity, phthisical, religious, or gouty insanities, as distinct varieties or forms. We recognize that different cases of insanity may have the puerperal state, phthisical lungs, epilepsy, or gout, as antecedents or accompaniments, but we do not find that the antecedent or the accompaniment gives to the manifestations of the insanity an individuality sufficient to allow us to infer from them the nature of the antecedent or accompaniment. We recognize that the antecedents, or occasions, or provoking causes of

[1] Burton.

insanity are various and numerous ; but we are compelled to admit that the form in which the insanity manifests itself, the symptoms that it displays, do not depend exclusively, nor even largely, upon the nature of the stress that provokes it. What the circumstances are which determine the form that the insanity takes we shall presently consider ; for the moment it is enough to point out that among these circumstances the provoking cause is not an important factor.

It has been shown in an earlier part of the book that the amount of intelligence that a person displays depends upon the degree of development of his higher nerve regions. It has been shown how, according as the process of development starts with a vigorous or a feeble impulse, it is carried forward to a high degree of elaboration, or becomes exhausted when a comparatively low level of organization is reached. The highest nerve regions, being the last and highest effort of the process of development, the flower of the unfolding organism, are the parts which are most sensitive to any defect in the vigour of the developmental process. If any part fails to reach its full completion owing to the premature exhaustion of the developmental forces, that part will be the highest nerve region. If any part becomes erroneously developed, owing to a bias or fault in the developmental process, that part will be the highest nerve region. These, we have seen, are the two prime developmental factors in the production of insanity—deficiency and error in the process of development—and the first great division of the forms of insanity rests upon this difference in the developmental cause.

Where the process of development has come to a premature end, and the higher nerve regions have never attained to the average development of the race, there exists congenital mental deficiency, the *dementia naturalis* or *fatuity a nativitate* of jurists. According to the degree in which mental capacity is deficient, this defect is styled by alienists weakness of mind, imbecility, or, in its most marked degree, idiocy ; but the latter term is made to include all degrees, both in law and by non-specialists generally.

Where the process of development has proceeded to the average extent, so that the individual has attained an average degree of intelligence ; but yet has become defective in its later stages, so that a proneness to insanity is left, which tendency has been made actual by the incidence of some stress ; in such cases there is insanity proper, the *dementia accidentalis vel adventitia* of jurists.

Thus it will be seen that in idiocy and weakness of mind, the process of development has not been carried *far enough ;* while in insanity, the process has been carried far enough, but has diverged into the *wrong direction.*

In weakness of mind there is every degree. At one end of the scale is the person who is not quite up to the average ; who is found by his friends to be a little dull ; who was in a lower class at school than others of his age ; who, in spite of assiduous study, got plucked at his examinations ; who is slow to appreciate humour ; who is incapable of entertaining ideas of a moderate degree of abstractness or complexity ; who, if he reads novels, reads those only which deal with incidents and adventures ; who, if he admires pictures, selects those which portray a definite act. Such men, if they possess industry and power of application, often attain a degree of success in life which surprises those who know the narrowness of their intelligence ; the fact being that their interests are so circumscribed that their application to the object they have in view is not apt to stray ; and the attainment of an end depends more on steady, continuous application, than on brilliance of mental ability.

Beneath this class come those who are recognized as being definitely " deficient ; " as being not merely below the average, but below the normal ; as being more or less imbecile. The line that divides the dull or weak-minded man from the imbecile is the ability to earn a living. A man who can earn his own living, whose services to the community are of sufficient value to enable him to maintain the standard of living proper to his station in life, may be a dull man, a stupid man, a man of feeble, limited intellect, but he cannot be called an imbecile. Not until his intellectual defect is so grave, that by reason of it he is unable to earn his livelihood, does it become imbecility.

The distinction between imbecility and idiocy is less clearly marked. All agree that the latter is a more intense degree of the same defect as the former, but there is no precise criterion by which the one can be distinguished from the other. An old legal definition, as quoted by Bucknill and Tuke, does indeed say, "He that shall be said to be a sot and idiot from his birth is such a person who cannot count or number twenty pence, nor tell who was his father or mother, nor how old he is, so as it may appear he hath no understanding or reason what shall be for his profit, or what for his loss ; but if he have sufficient understanding to know and understand his letters, and to read by teaching and information, then it seems he is not an idiot." It is doubtful how far this definition would be accepted at the present day. There is an old proverb which, so far from regarding as idiotic a person who cannot do so, regards as endowed with exceptional wisdom the child who knows his own father ; and if the inability to tell his own age is to render a person liable to be considered idiotic, I know of at least one person who is unable to withstand that test, and is yet considered of average intelligence by his acquaintances. A distinction between imbecility and idiocy may, however, be drawn, and that which I shall propose has the additional advantage of proceeding upon the same lines and belonging to the same system as that already drawn between imbecility and mere weakness of mind.

In the preceding chapter a description was given of the various classes of circumstances to which this human organism has by its activities to adapt itself. The greater the store of energy which the organism contains, the more completely does it effect its adaptation to all these classes of circumstances. A thoroughly healthy, vigorous man will be able to compass, not only those activities by which he avoids direct physical dangers; by which he earns his livelihood; and by which he rears, feeds, clothes, and educates his off-spring; but will be able also to take his part in social functions, to enjoy social meetings, to partake in political movements, and still will have energy to spare which he can expend in recreating himself, and in the pursuit of art, or of some hobby. If, however, the organism is somewhat lacking in vigour and energy, it will no longer be able to fill out the entire sphere of these activities. Some of these circumstances will fail to evoke the activities which answer to them, and by which the organism adapts itself to them. When energy is thus lacking, it is obvious that those activities will first be relinquished which are least essential to the support of life, and that those which will be adhered to most tenaciously, and will be the last to be relinquished, are those which are the most immediately essential to existence. Now the least important group of activities is no doubt that which satisfies the recreative and æsthetic cravings, and hence when energy begins to fail, this is the point at which economy is effected. Less active forms of recreation are adopted, less energy is expended in this direction; a quiet evening over a pipe takes the place of a long walk or of a game of cricket or football. As the feebleness increases, first the social and political activities are discontinued, then comes inability to maintain the wife and children, then the ability to earn a livelihood fails, and finally the power of avoiding physical dangers is lost. If we look at the reverse process, and notice the order in which activities are acquired by the growing organism, we shall find the order is precisely the reverse of that just considered. The first thing the child learns is to avoid physical dangers—to keep from falling downstairs, to get out of the way of moving bodies, to avoid being knocked down and run over, to escape falling into the water, running against obstacles, burning and cutting itself, and all forms of physical injury. When this class of circumstances has been so thoroughly complied with

20

that danger is no longer to be apprehended from ordinary risks ; when the activities answering to this class of circumstances has been thoroughly acquired, then, and not till then, begins the acquisition of those activities by which the livelihood is to be earned.   Then begins the formal process of education, which is the first step in fitting the individual to get his living.   When this has been done, when sufficient time has been spent daily in the acquisition of these activities, then what remains over can be devoted to recreation and other purposes.

It is obvious, upon the foregoing considerations, that when an individual fails to reach the full development of the race, the failure will be first noticeable in the activities that are left over after the livelihood has been gained ; hence we find that in the first degree of weakness of mind the individual is able to earn his own livelihood, but that when this is done his energies are exhausted.   He does not shine socially, he has no "resources," no hobby, no employment for his leisure time.   Wife and children he may have, but he takes no part in the education or bringing up of the latter—he lets them find their own way about.

In the next degree of weakness of mind—in imbecility— the standard of activity has sunk one degree lower.   The imbecile is unable to earn his own livelihood.   That is the test and that is the criterion of imbecility.   He may be capable of doing odd jobs, and of executing simple work under supervision, but his services have not sufficient market value to bring him in enough to support life.   He cannot, unassisted, adapt himself to what I have termed his Vital Environment.   His activities are not sufficiently developed, and this degree of deficiency of development is imbecility.

In idiocy the deficiency is still greater. The imbecile fails to adapt himself to his Vital Environment, he fails to complete the second step in his intellectual development; but he surmounts completely the first step, that which enables him to adapt himself to his *physical* environment.   He can be trusted to go out by himself without running the risk of being knocked down by passing vehicles. He can be trusted to cut his own food without cutting his fingers. But the idiot fails to effect even these simple adjustments to his circumstances. He is not only incapable of earning his own living—of adapting himself to his Vital Environment—but he is incapable of preserving himself from the risks of physical harm that are present in his ordinary Physical Environment. So incapable is he of conserving himself against ordinary risks that he cannot be left alone. Although of adult age, he has not proceeded further along the path of development than a young child, and like the young child he requires constant attention. If left by himself he will set himself on fire, or fall into the water, or cut himself, or get entangled in a machine, or come to some actual physical harm which could have been avoided by the exercise of rudimentary intelligence. He fails to adapt himself to the simplest of all the sets of circumstances with which he has to deal, and this extreme degree of failure constitutes idiocy.

If the doctrine here advanced is true, and if the idiot differs from the person of average intelligence in the fact that the former has not proceeded so far along the path of development as the latter, then, in addition to the evidence of function, we shall expect to find evidence in the structure of the idiot showing that development has stopped short before reaching completion. We shall not expect to find evidence of defect in the early stages of development, for the impetus gained at conception was sufficient to carry the organism through its early stages successfully ; but, as the latest stages were not reached, we shall expect to find that the latest acquired structures are wanting. It has already been explained that the latest acquired structures—the flower, as it were, of the animal organism—are the highest nerve regions ; and it is the want of these regions which constitutes the main physical defect in idiocy. Now the highest nerve regions are situated in the convolutions of the

A

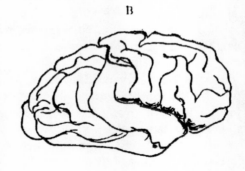

B

C

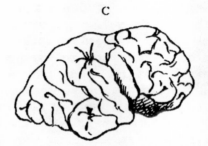

FIG. 16.—Side view of right cerebral hemisphere. A, normal
adult ; B, adult idiot ; C, new-born child.

A

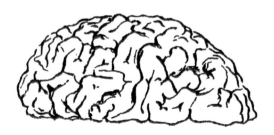

B

C

FIG. 17.—Left cerebral hemisphere seen from above.　A, normal
adult ; B, adult idiot ; C, new-born child.

brain, and hence when these regions are greatly wanting in development we shall expect to find—(1) That the convolutions of the brain are less bulky, contain a less amount of material than normal; (2) That the convolutions are less elaborate and less complicated in structure than normal; and (3) That the adult brain which has failed to take on the later stages of development, resembles the brain of an infant, to whom the period for assuming these later stages of development has not yet arrived. A comparison of the Figures 16 and 17 will show how far these reasonings are borne out by the facts.

Although the main feature in idiocy is a premature failure in the process of development, by which the intellect of the idiot is permanently arrested at the childish stage, yet there is a considerable difference between the conduct and general mental condition of the idiot and that of the child. This difference is accounted for by the fact that the adult idiot is older than the child; that is to say, that although the nervous structure has not increased in elaborateness beyond the childish stage, yet, since the age of childhood was passed, the tissues have been altering with the increased age of the individual, and these alterations of tissue have of course been reflected in the nervous system, and especially in those regions which are, in the imperfect individual, the highest. The nervous system, too, in so far as it is developed, undergoes with advancing years the same process of consolidation and settlement that takes place in that which has reached the full stature of normal development; so that the idiot, while similar to the child in the simplicity and rudimentary character of his nervous system, of his conduct and of his mind, yet lacks the buoyancy, the spontaneity, the freshness of childhood, and presents a strange mixture of childishness and maturity which is painful to see, and which is at once recognized as abnormal.

In the idiot, as in the person of full mental competence, the revolution of puberty takes place. It occurs later, it is true, and is less complete, less thorough, and often more gradual ; but it occurs, and corresponding alterations take place in the imperfect nervous system of the idiot which are unknown in that of the child. The higher regions of the nervous system being undeveloped, and the lower regions having reached a degree of development which is comparatively much further advanced, it .results that the due and proper balance between the higher and the lower regions is not maintained. That control which it is the function of the higher regions to exercise over the lower is inefficient, and the lower regions tend to overact—to act too strongly and too continuously. Hence we find that among idiots and imbeciles the lower appetites and propensities are unduly displayed. They are greedy for food and drink, their sexual passions are seldom at rest, if of sufficient intelligence they are usually thieves, and they are subject to outbursts of rage upon trifling provocation.

Occasionally a case of imbecility presents itself, in which, while the general intellectual powers are markedly deficient, one isolated group of faculties is of average, or even more than average, development. Such are the cases in which persons, otherwise imbecile, show a talent for music or for calculation. In such cases we must suppose that the deficiency in cerebral development is not uniform, but that in some directions the development has proceeded to the normal extent, while in the remainder it has failed.

While the failure in the last stages of development is always most conspicuous in the higher nervous regions, whose development occurs wholly in the latest stages, yet, if the failure is considerable, and has begun before these last stages are reached, it will exhibit itself, not only in defect of the higher nerve regions, but also in defect of other attributes of the organism which appear towards the completion of its development. Among the attributes which are late in appearing are the attainment of the full stature and bulk of the adult, and when the process of development fails prematurely, before the adult stature and bulk are acquired, they are never afterward reached, and consequently we find

that most imbeciles and all congenital idiots are much under
the average in stature and weight.

Since the higher nerve regions remain undeveloped, the
total amount of nerve tissue at the service of the individual
is below the normal. Comparison of the Figures 16 and 17
will indicate how conspicuously the nerve masses of the
idiot are deficient in bulk. But the great nerve masses, the
brain and spinal cord, are the great reservoirs for the
storage and supply of energy to the body ; and hence, if
these nerve masses are conspicuously deficient in bulk, the
amount of energy at the disposal of the organism must be
conspicuously deficient. Hence we find that idiots and
imbeciles are always inactive : given to sitting and lolling
about, disinclined for even such simple modes of activity as
they are capable of, lethargic and indolent.

Doubtless those who are familiar with the peculiarities of
idiots and imbeciles will demur to the generality of the
foregoing statement. While admitting that the majority of
the individuals so afflicted are indolent and lethargic, they
will point to here and there an exception. Dealing here
with the broad outlines of the subject, and being unable to
go into detail to explain exceptional cases, it will be enough
to say that the description here given is true of those cases
in which the process of development has come to a premature end by reason of its own exhaustion—because of
deficiency in the original impetus' which set it going—
because it has, as it were, run itself out. But it may happen
that the developmental process, instead of dying a natural
death in this way, may be brought to a violent end. An
injury to the head, an intracranical inflammation, undue
pressure, the presence of a poison in the blood, or other
cause acting in very early life, may so distort, disturb, and
arrest the development of the brain as to produce idiocy ;
and in such cases, which are common, the symptoms will
differ from those of the classical type ; but these differences
it is not worth while to pursue here.

In every deep there is a deeper depth, and even in idiocy

there are degrees of defect, some being less and some more severely affected. An extension of the test already applied serves to distinguish them. While idiocy differs from imbecility in the incapability of performing adjustments to a simpler set of circumstances in the environment, the different grades of idiocy are distinguished by the more and more fundamental and necessary character of the adjustments which alone can be made. The idiot who can dress and undress as well as feed himself, is superior to him who can perform the latter act but not the former ; he who cannot feed himself, but can stand and walk, is less idiotic than the wretched being to whom even these simple acts are impossible.

Leaving now the consideration of those forms of unsoundness of mind which are due to original defect in the *extent* of the developmental process, we may go on to consider those in which development proceeded to the normal extent, but the later stages were wanting in stability.

CHAPTER XII.

THE FORMS OF INSANITY (*Continued*).

THE whole of the foregoing discussion has been conducted under the guidance of a single fundamental principle : the principle that no disorder of organic processes is the result of the importation of an entirely new element into their working. We have recognized throughout that every case of disorder was but the exaggeration of some normal mode, constituent, or element in the healthy working of the bodily processes. There is no phenomenon that can be produced by disease, however bizarre, startling, and marvellous it may appear, which has not its counterpart in little in the healthy organism. Disease does not create, it merely exaggerates.

Keeping fast hold of this principle, which has served us so well hitherto, it is natural to ask whether the manifestations of insanity, startling, bizarre, and marvellous as they are, have not some less exaggerated counterpart in the normal manifestations of mind and conduct in sane people ; and whether, by identifying these counterparts, we may not be able to trace the disorders of insanity to their source, and discover where and how they diverge from the processes of health. In working upon these lines, it is manifest that we must not begin with those manifestations which are most extravagant and most divergent, but rather with those which are less strongly marked, and present the least striking differences from the normal.

Regarding the phenomena of health from the point of view of their proximity to insanity, we find that there are at least two sets of phenomena which tend naturally and inevitably to occur in the life-history of every individual, and which exhibit an unmistakable kinship to insanity. The first of these is sleep, and the second is the decadence that occurs in old age. There is a third group of phenomena which does not actually lie within the normal, and yet is not far distant from it ; which reproduces with absolute accuracy all the features of insanity ; which is, in fact, so long as it lasts, unquestionable insanity ; and yet from the ease with which it can be produced, from its transient duration and manifest cause, is not considered insanity ; which connects the wholly normal phenomena of sleep and of old age, with the wholly abnormal phenomena of insanity. This is the group of phenomena produced by alcoholic intoxication. Thus we have in sleep, old age, and intoxication, a series of approximations to insanity.

Normal sleep is a temporary and complete dementia. It is, in fact, the last and complete stage of dementia which is known as coma. The higher nerve regions are placed completely out of action, they cease altogether to emit energy, and are occupied solely in molecular redintegration, and in storing up energy for future use. Since the higher nerve regions are the actuators of conduct, when these regions cease to act, conduct is abolished ; and hence during sleep there is no conduct ; the organism remains motionless. The action of the highest nerve regions is attended by feeling and thought ; and hence, when these regions cease to act, feeling and thought are abolished ; and during sleep there is no consciousness. Normal sleep is therefore a sudden, complete, physiological or healthy, extreme dementia, occurring normally once in twenty-four hours.

Since the higher nerve regions exercise control over the lower ; and since at the onset of sleep the higher regions are placed out of action, it might be expected that this suspension of the action of the higher regions would be accompanied by an over-action of the lower, due to the removal of control ; but this does not usually occur ; and the reason of its non-occurrence is this : that the suspension of function affects, not the highest regions only, but the whole of the nervous system from top to bottom. The whole system is affected simultaneously, but not uniformly. The function of the highest regions is completely obliterated; that of the middle regions is greatly diminished, without being quite obliterated; and the operation of the lowest regions is rendered slower and weaker, but is less affected than that of the middle. So that while conduct, the function of the highest regions, together with its accompaniments, thought and feeling, are completely obliterated; movements, the outcome of the action of the middle regions, while greatly diminished in number and frequency, do occasionally take place during sleep; and the action of heart, lungs, and viscera, regulated by the lowest centres, still continues, although decidedly diminished in vigour and intensity. Although, therefore, by the cessation of the action of the highest nerve regions, control is removed from the lower, and hence there arises a tendency for the lower to over-act, on the other hand this tendency is nullified by the simultaneous diminution of the activity of the lower centres.

Except in childhood, the normal course of sleep is not often maintained in perfect integrity. The obliteration of function no longer takes place with perfect uniformity. Instead of the whole of the higher regions being gradually, uniformly and equally submerged beneath the flood of inactivity, islets are left outstanding, which still retain more or less of irregular activity, while all the regions surrounding them are at rest. In the common case, the amount of activity in these isolated regions is not sufficient to set in action the lower centres, and to produce actual movements of the body, but it is enough to have accompaniments, more or less vivid, of feeling and of thought; and these isolated scraps of feeling and thought, accompanying the activity of islets of the higher nerve regions unsubmerged beneath the tide of sleep, constitute the phenomena of dreams.

The activity of these isolated regions varies in intensity. Where it is but weak, the dreams are of but faint intensity;

where it is considerable, the dreams are vivid. In rare cases it happens that the activity of these isolated regions reaches so high a degree that it sets in action the lower centres, that it spreads downwards to the muscles, that it produces movements—conduct—of a kind corresponding with the limited amount of brain involved in producing it, and in such cases are displayed the phenomena of somnambulism.

Somnambulant actions differ from normal actions in displaying a partial adjustment only, to the circumstances in which they occur. The somnambulist finds his way about his house, avoids obstacles, goes upstairs and downstairs, unlocks the door and gets out into the street. He can adjust his acts to circumstances which are simple and well-known ; but put him in a strange room, and he will open a cupboard door and try to make his way out through that ; or let him get upon a strange landing, and he will be likely to fall down the stairs. A portion only of his higher nerve regions being at work, and that portion not including any of the highest of all ; the whole of the impressions made by circumstances are not received. A large part of the currents produced by these impressions go to parts of the brain which are inactive, which do not respond, and are, for the purposes of guidance, lost. Since the circumstances are imperfectly perceived, the adjustment to them must be imperfect. Then, too, of the adjusting apparatus, only a small part is in action ; and for this reason also the adjustment must be defective.

Thus from the study of sleep we gather the following conclusions : 1. That a periodical cessation of action of the higher nerve regions, with diminution of action of the nervous system generally, is a normal and healthy habit. 2. That the cessation of action, while normally uniform and simultaneously progressive over the whole of the higher nerve regions, yet in the vast majority of cases departs somewhat from this uniformity, so that certain regions and areas are commonly later and less affected by the subsidence into inactivity than the remainder. 3. That in some cases the amount of activity retained by certain areas is enough to

actuate simple forms of conduct, and to produce imperfect
adjustments of the individual to his surroundings.

It not unfrequently happens that at the time that should
be devoted to sleep, sleep is not obtainable. For some reason
the nervous molecules do not subside into the quiescent condition, that accompanies and gives rise to sleep, but maintain their function of emitting energy at a time when they
should be wholly, or almost wholly, employed in storing it.
When this is the case—when, in spite of inactivity of the
body, the recumbent posture, and the absence of spontaneous
exertion, sleep fails to occur, and the cerebral molecules still
emit streams of energy instead of confining themselves to the
reception of energy for future expenditure, certain peculiarities of action are observed. The expenditure of energy,
although proceeding from a wide area, including the highest
nerve regions, is yet of extremely low tension. The natural
diurnal tides in the tension of the nervous energy have
already (p. 95) been described. The lowest ebb of these
tides is in the small hours of the morning, and, whether
sleeping or waking, the ebb still takes place. If the molecules
of the higher nerve regions become wholly quiescent over
the whole area, the condition is one of dreamless sleep. If
they become generally quiescent, but leave small isolated areas
of activity outstanding, the condition is one of sleep with
dreams. But if there remains activity over wide areas, then
there is wakefulness—a vigil both of consciousness and of
bodily function. But the condition of the nerve function in
nocturnal vigil is not the same as in the activity of the daytime.
Although the full daylight of consciousness may exist in each
case, and although equally wide areas of the highest nerve
regions may in each case be active, yet the activity is not alike
in the two cases. In the daytime, not only is there a wide
area of discharging grey matter, but this wide area is discharging at high tension, and all the nerve channels are filled
to repletion with abounding copious currents of energy,
everywhere pressing against their boundaries and everywhere
trying to escape. But in nocturnal vigil, although the area

of activity is equally wide, the intensity of the activity is very greatly inferior. The currents of energy permeate, indeed, as many channels, or nearly as many, as in the daytime, but they pass along the channels in driblets. So far from filling the channels to repletion, they trickle through them in runlets of little pressure and little intensity. What will be the consequences and what the accompaniments of this reduction of intensity in the nerve currents? The consequence will be that movements—the movements which make up conduct —will be few, feeble, and sluggish. The conduct will be sunk in lethargy. Little will be done, and that little slowly, feebly, and with difficulty. The other movements, too, which all owe their activity to that of the nerve currents, will be similarly affected. The molecular movements of nutrition will be feeble and sluggish ; the modifications of nutrition— the processes of secretion and excretion—will be similarly inactive. The visceral movements, the action of heart, lungs, and intestines will all fall to a very low phase of activity. Concomitantly with this inactivity of body, the mental states will be less vivid ; but the chief alteration in consciousness will be that diminution of the feeling of well-being which always accompanies a reduced tension of the nervous energy. Nothing is more characteristic of nocturnal vigil than the feeling of wretchedness which accompanies it. As we lie awake in the small hours of the morning, the horror with which the situation inspires us surprises us even then, and is a matter of amazement in the subsequent light of day. Then, in those dark hours, all our mistakes, all our follies, rise up in a black legion to menace and taunt us. The long-forgotten sins of our youth push themselves forward, and demand to be recognized and remembered. The difficulties of our daily life swell and grow to impossibilities. If we look back we are confronted by remorse ; if we look forward we are met by despair.

Turning now to the phenomena of old age, we notice that the most obvious and striking characteristic of the onset of this period of life is a general diminution of activity. The impetus, that was given to the organism at conception, has

carried it on through the process of development to manhood, has sustained it in activity throughout a long life, but
with each year that has passed a portion of the initial
velocity has been dissipated. The friction with the world
has tended constantly to bring the organism to rest, and as
its career approaches termination, it moves more and more
slowly. The bones of the child are composed largely of
gristle, the earthy matter in their composition is comparatively little ; they can be cut with a knife ; they can be
bent without breaking; their weight is light; they easily yield
to the stresses of weight and of muscular action, and become
altered in shape. In the old, the bones are stony hard, they
are brittle, heavy, rigid, and unaltering. As with the bones
so with the other tissues. The nervous system of the child
is impressible, plastic, easily moulded, easily altered, is continually the seat of new combinations and new development.
In the old man the nervous system is stirred with difficulty.
The movements of the molecules are sluggish ; new combinations are slow to form ; widespread commotions are
difficult to effect. The structure becomes rigid, so that the
slight alterations that are impressed upon it are readily
effaced. Forced for a moment into new combinations, the
rigidity of the tissue prevents these combinations from
becoming permanent. The old forces soon resume their sway,
and the molecules fall back into their old positions.

The diminished mobility of the molecules of the nervous
system is evidenced most conspicuously by the general
diminution of the bodily movements in old age. The chief
characteristic of youth is its buoyant, spontaneous, eager
activity ; old age presents the antithetical condition of
quiescence, repose, inactivity. The corresponding peculiarities of nerve tissue are, in the young, a copious store of
energy, freely expended and readily renewed ; in the old, a
diminished store of energy, requiring stronger stimulus for
its arousal, and renewed but slowly after expenditure. In
these characteristics the brain of the old man resembles that
of the young after labour and at the approach of sleep.

This diminution in activity that occurs in old age does not weigh equally upon all the regions of the nervous system. It pervades indeed throughout, but is not quite uniform throughout. The highest regions are the most affected, the middle regions less, and the lowest least; so that while the intellect is dull and the emotions are feeble, while conduct becomes both less strenuous and less elaborate, the bodily movements remain fairly efficient, and the heart's action is not greatly impaired. In this, again, the quiescence of old age resembles the quiescence of sleep.

Another striking peculiarity of old age is its inability to assimilate new impressions. The nervous structure is no longer plastic, the molecules of the ground substance are settled in their places, and oppose increased inertia to the efforts of errant currents endeavouring to force channels through them. The diminution in the amount of free energy, by lessening the intensity of the currents, ensures that this increased resistance is acted on by diminished forces; and hence new combinations are made slowly and with difficulty, and the more slowly and laboriously, the more of novelty they contain. It is an old and accurate observation that "you cannot teach an old dog new tricks." A lad of twenty may easily change his occupation in life and take up one entirely new, but a man of sixty must continue in the profession that he has followed all his life. Send a boy to a foreign country, and in a few weeks he will speak the language passably well; but an old man in the same circumstances still needs an interpreter.

Even when new impressions are assimilated, and new combinations of nerve elements made, the changes so induced have not the thoroughness nor the permanence of those which take place in early life. The structure has lost its plasticity. The molecules are rearranged with difficulty, and are apt to fall back into their former places. Hence we find that the memory of recent events, which depends of course on recent changes in brain, is apt to fail. The changes becoming easily effaced, the memory, which is their

21

mental counterpart, is effaced also. But memories of events which happened in early life, and which impressed themselves on a plastic nervous system, remain. That very rigidity of structure which opposes the modification of tissue by newly-made impressions, tends to conserve the modifications that were effected long ago ; so that we find that, while memories of recent events elude the mental grasp of the old, memories of events long past are reproduced with all their former vividness, and something more than their former frequency.

These changes in the mode of action of the nervous system have, of course, their representatives in the modes of mental action. The diminished activity of the nerve-molecules has its bodily equivalent in diminished energy of movement, and its mental equivalent in diminished activity of mind. New projects are not readily undertaken, new thoughts do not readily present themselves ; the whole process of thought is less vivid, less rapid, less active. As with thought, so with feeling. In the child, emotions are easily aroused and easily allayed. In the youth, the emotions are predominant, are active, voluminous, powerful, vivid. As old age advances, this part of the nature also becomes steeped in lethargy. The affections wane. New attachments are not formed, anger is not easily stirred. The jealousies and heartburnings of early life subside into placidity.

Such are the concomitants of the onset of old age in all people. In the great majority of people a real old age is not attained. They are cut off by some quasi-accidental malady, some fever, some inflammation of the lungs, some fibroid degeneration of liver or kidney, before the process of life dies out from sheer exhaustion. The candle of their life is blown out or extinguished, it does not burn completely away. It comparatively seldom happens that we get an opportunity of witnessing the expiry of life from natural decay—from the gradual and complete exhaustion of that impetus which the life of the individual received in the act of conception, which has carried it on, with constantly diminishing velocity, through the development of childhood and youth, and the activity of adult age, and which must, sooner or later, be brought to an end by the friction of surrounding circumstances upon the advancing organism. When, however, we do have an opportunity of witnessing the advance of an individual into an extreme old age, and his final decease from "decay of nature"—that is to say, from the exhaustion of the forces which have kept him alive—we notice a uniform series of phenomena. It should here be stated that old age in the sense here spoken of is not measured by years alone. One man may die at eighty from that exhaustion of his power of living which is here described, while another may live on, hale and hearty, to ninety, or a hundred or more, and then die of inflammation of lungs, or some other intercurrent and quasi-accidental malady. I speak now of those only who die, at whatever age, from the complete expenditure of their vital impetus.

When we watch the closing years of such a person, we notice that the signs of diminished activity and diminished plasticity of the nervous molecules are exhibited with continually advancing distinctness, and continually increasing emphasis. We see that the bodily activity steadily declines, the walks get less and less extended, until they are limited to the garden, and to an infrequent visit to a near neighbour; then even this amount of activity is not reached, and the old man just gets about the house and, when he leaves it, has to avail himself of the aid of a bath-chair. His bedroom is removed to the ground floor because he is no longer capable of mounting the stairs; he just totters between his bed and his fireside, and at last is altogether bedridden.

With this continuous decrease in the quantity of conduct goes a continuous subsidence in its elaborateness. The more important parts of his business have been for some time in younger hands. He still lingers as long as possible round the scenes of his old labours, but his actual part is limited to routine work; and at length, incapable even of this, he retires altogether. The whole sphere of activities comprised in his business relations is altogether relinquished; the activities necessary for the rearing and maintenance of offspring have long been uncalled for, his daughters being married, and his sons providing for themselves. There remain to him only the simple activities requisite for the immediate conservation of life, and after a time even these are imperfectly performed. His food must be prepared for him; then it has to be cut up for him; and at last he must actually be fed. His clothes must be ordered for him; and at last he has to be dressed and undressed. No longer capable of conserving himself from the ordinary risks of every-day life, he must be carefully watched and tended to prevent some accidental circumstance from extinguishing the feeble glimmer of life that still remains to him.

Together with the steady declension of conduct, goes a continuous declension of thought and feeling; and as with conduct, so with mind, the most complex and elaborate processes are the first to fail, and the simplest and most fundamental remain to the last. On the more important and higher branches of his business, on the general policy of the business, he exercises no influence, but he is still consulted as a matter of form upon the general routine of the office. Then, when he retires altogether from business, his children, or those who have care of him, consult him as to the disposition of the day, the time of his drive, the fare at his dinner, the alteration of his garden, and so forth. As his decadence progresses, even these simple matters become beyond his capacity to decide, and he is managed and "done for" like a child. He is amused with simple anecdotes, but he can give attention only to the most direct and concrete interests. He can appreciate what this man said, and what that man did, but the movements and opinions of masses of men are beyond his capacity to comprehend. The peculiar defect of memory we have already considered. At length a time comes when he ceases to interest himself in anything save the simplest and most concrete matters. He appreciates that his food is not ready when he wants it, and his daughter's absence from his room is a trouble to him ; but beyond this he does not interest himself. His own condition and inclinations may be discussed in his own presence without arousing his intelligence or attention about the matter.

The decadence of feeling proceeds, *pari passu*, with that of conduct and intelligence. When an old man's other faculties begin to fail, he becomes incapable of feelings of a high degree of elevation. On the occurrence of a *cause célèbre* he fails to rise to the feeling of justice, but takes the feminine view that it would be cruel to punish the offender. He loses his appreciation of humour, and it needs the coarse stimulus of broad farce to arouse his sense of the ridiculous. As his decadence proceeds, he ceases to feel sympathy with the sufferings of others, his anger degenerates into peevishness and fretfulness ; occasions of grief, the loss of near relatives, move him only to slight and transient sorrow. Finally, even the more rudimentary feelings fade away, and he sits huddled in his chair doing nothing, noticing nothing, feeling virtually nothing.

The failure of action in old age is, however, not only in the nervous system. While the brain has been growing old, the rest of the body has not remained young. The altered structure of the bones has already been referred to, and corresponding changes take place in every tissue. What remains of the hair turns grey ; the skin is withered and wrinkled ; the *arcus senilis* appears in the eye ; the muscles waste ; all the viscera, every part of the body alters, and alters not only in structure, but in the activity, and in the very nature of the processes that takes place in it. We have already seen that the activity and the nature of the processes that go on throughout the body, give rise to a continuous set of voluminous nerve currents which flow upwards and break upon the shore of the highest nerve regions, whose action is influenced, modified, and coloured by their agency. The existence and the nature of these currents has, as we have seen, a reflexion in the mental state. Upon them depends the character and permanence of the subject-consciousness, of the consciousness of self, of personal identity. When these currents become changed, as, upon alteration of the processes which initiate them, they must do, the consciousness of self must and does change; and when the currents alter in intensity, the feeling of well-being undergoes alteration. Hence it is that as the body grows old, the individual feels aged ; not by deliberately counting up the years that he has lived, but by the mirrored representation in consciousness of the changes that the body has undergone. Hence, as the body changes by addition or subtraction of functions, as at puberty and the menopause, so the individual changes by the addition or abstraction of faculties—of elements of character. Hence a high state of vigour in the nutrition of the body is mirrored in buoyancy of spirits, and imperfect tissue changes in mental depression. In the dementia of old age, the vigour of the nutritive processes is greatly slackened and diminished, and hence in this condition buoyant and abounding spirits are unknown. As, however, the slackening of the nutritive processes, and therefore of the viscerally derived nerve currents, is in proportion to the general diminution of activity of the entire nervous system, the diminution of the sense of well-being is not out of proportion to the actual diminution of the bodily energies, and amounts merely to a placid absence of high spirits rather than to any actual feeling of depression. Apart from the alteration in activity, the change in the nature of the nutritive processes is such, that in consciousness of self the old man is a different being from the young one. Circumstances, in themselves the same, impress him differently, as explained in a previous chapter.

From beginning to end the process is a continuous, gradually progressing loss. Conduct, intelligence, feeling, and self-consciousness gradually diminish, and at last cease to exist ; the loss affecting, first and most, the highest faculties, and leaving till the last those that are simplest, lowest, and most fundamental. The decadence of old age is, in fact, a *dementia*, a deprivation of mind. It is a normal and physiological dementia, the natural and inevitable result of the gradual subsidence of the molecular movements of the nervous elements into stillness ; the natural outcome of the exhaustion of the initial impetus which started the organism upon its course of life and kept it going ; the natural expression of that dissipation of energy which accompanies the integration of matter in the process of evolution. It is by this gradual subsidence to rest of the process of storing and expending energy, that life tends to terminate. The prolongation of the average length of life, that has taken place with advancing civilization and sanitation, has not resulted from any perceptible increase in the vigour and staying power of the human race. It has resulted from the diminution of the causes of intercurrent maladies which tend to cut life short before its initial impetus has been wholly expended. By this lessening of the causes of intercurrent maladies ; by the greater skill that they are dealt with ; and by the greater and more intelligent care with which the later stages of man's career are nursed, and his friction with circumstances diminished ; it has resulted that more individuals survive to the extreme end of their career, and that those who are cut off before the vital energy wholly fails, reach, on the average, a later stage before they succumb, than was formerly the case. But however perfect our sanitation may become, and however careful a valetudinarian race may be of the air they breathe, the water they drink, the clothing they wear, the amount of exercise they take, of the thousand-and-one things that the lugubrious prophets of health enjoin or forbid them to do, the effect upon the natural termination of life by lapse of energy, as distinguished from its artificial termination by disease, will be inappreciable. If, indeed, long-lived families were carefully chosen and bred together under favourable conditions, there is no reason why in time a longer-lived race of men should not be created ; but there appears no prospect of such a process being started at present, and for generations to come we shall have to be content with a duration of natural life approximating to that which now obtains, with, it may be, some slight increase due to the healthier and more vigorous condition that wiser ways of living may induce, in the generality of parents, up to the time of procreation.

We have traced the organism from the time of conception, when it receives the original impetus to which its existence is due, through the course of its growth and development, to the condition of maturity; and then through its decline into quiescence as the original impetus becomes spent. We have yet to notice the final scene of all, and to observe the way in which the ultimate failure of energy brings about the subsidence from dementia into death.

It has been shown how the higher faculties are the first to fail, and how they fail most completely while the lower faculties still retain some degree of efficiency. If we imagine this process of degradation carried to extremity, we shall find a state of things in which the whole of the higher faculties are lost, and nothing remains but the lowest and most fundamental of all. Such a state of things exists in the condition known as coma. In coma there is deep insensibility. The patient lies motionless. Conduct is altogether abolished. There can be no conduct, for there is no movement. There is no movement because the whole body is more or less paralyzed. The paralysis of the body is due to the loss of function, not only of the highest layers of nervous arrangements, but of the middle and part of the lower layers also. The process of degradation has proceeded very far. Conduct is abolished; voluntary movement is abolished; only the most fundamental movements of all— those of the heart and of the breathing—remain; and even these are altered.

Since conduct and voluntary movement are abolished by the abolition of function of the higher and middle nervous arrangements, of course feeling and thought, which are the accompaniments of the action of these arrangements, are lost also. In coma the whole man is paralyzed; he is also insensible. Speak to him and he does not answer; shake him and he makes no response. Hold a bright light to his eye and he does not wink; pinch or prick his skin and he does not retaliate, nor even withdraw his limb. The loss of function has extended almost to the lowest strata of the nervous system; those functions only remain which are essential to the mere preservation of life. Such is the condition of a man who is stunned by a severe blow on the head; such the state of a man whose brain is compressed by the bursting of a blood-vessel inside his skull; and such is the condition of a man who is in the very last stage of a life that is expiring from failure of the energy necessary to to carry it on. If the process of degradation is carried but one step further, if the abolition of function proceeds so as to affect those processes that still remain; the nervous apparatus that actuate the movements of breathing and the movements of the heart become still more affected, the breathing gets more and more embarrassed, the intervals between the several acts of inspiration become longer and longer, until at last the breathing ceases altogether, and the heart, after vainly struggling for a time to carry on its function with unaerated blood, also ceases to act, and death ensues. Such is the natural termination of life; the termination that all would suffer were it not for the intervention of some inflammation or other positive malady, which, in the great majority of cases, cuts men off before their sands have completely run out. Such is the natural termination of the dementia of old age.

It now remains to examine the third occasion in which insanity occurs in the normal organism—the insanity that is due to alcoholic intoxication. It has been shown how the alcohol that is taken into the stomach is absorbed into the blood, and carried by it into actual contact with the nerve elements, upon which it acts as a direct stress of very urgent and powerful character.

It must be understood that, in speaking of alcoholic intoxication as a form of insanity, the expression is not used as a figure of speech : it is strictly and literally true that when, and in so far as, a man is intoxicated by alcohol, then and to that extent he is insane. Seeing that the cause is so obvious, the condition so temporary, and that the manifestations of the insanity as a rule differ somewhat from those in insanity due to other causes, and have a general resemblance to other cases due to the same cause, the insanity due to acute alcoholic poisoning is not usually looked upon as insanity. It is called by a different name, and is considered a different thing ; but in essential nature the two are identical. If a man disorders his higher nerve functions by a few doses of alcohol taken at dinner, and appears after dinner to be in liquor; if, under these circumstances, he becomes uproarious and commits an unprovoked assault, he is looked upon, not as being insane, but as being drunk. But if, after a prolonged course of drinking extending over years, he becomes habitually uproarious, and habitually prone to commit unprovoked assaults, he is looked upon, not as being drunk, but as being insane. Usually, drunkenness is distinguished from other instances of insanity by the peculiar character of the mental condition, which we call " elevated," and by the bodily defects which go with it—by the thickness of speech, the reeling gait, the clumsy and inefficient movements of the hands. But, in the first place, there is a form of permanent insanity—general paralysis of the insane—with which we shall presently have to deal, which exhibits, not only precisely the same kind of elevation of mind, but precisely the same thickness of articulation, the same reel in the gait, the same clumsy inefficiency of the digital movements, that characterize ordinary drunkenness ; and in the second place these characteristics are by no means invariably present in the insanity of drunkenness itself. When the drunken man is a man of ordinarily strong and stable constitution, the manifestations of drunkenness take the ordinary form ; but when a man who inherits an undue instability of nerve tissue gets drunk, the manifestations are very different. In such a case the bodily defects of articulation and gait may be wholly absent. Not a trace of unsteadiness or hesitation may be observable ; and, on the other hand, the disorder of conduct may amount to a violent outbreak of maniacal delirium ; so that the drunkard, instead of reeling home in a state of maudlin besottedness, raves, screams, smashes the furniture, strips himself naked, jumps through the window, murders, or tries to murder, an inoffensive by-stander, and is taken to a lunatic asylum as a dangerous maniac, which he is. In the course of a few hours, the alcohol is disintegrated and passes out of the system, the higher nerve regions resume their function, the drunkard becomes sober, and it becomes difficult to believe that the quiet, rational being of this morning was the furious maniac of last night. Such cases are not very uncommon, and few persons who have had asylum experience have failed to see them. If persons whom drink affects in this way are wise, and have sufficient self-control, they entirely abjure the use of alcohol after an experience of this kind, and so long as they keep from it they are useful members of society. If, however, they are deficient in determination, and cannot keep from the bottle, they pass their lives going in and out of lunatic asylums. Every drunken debauch constitutes such a man a maniac ; he is taken to an asylum, and in a few days his enforced abstinence from drink cures him of his insanity. Being sane, he is discharged, and in a few weeks he is back again with all his old symptoms upon him.

However the manifestations of drunkenness may vary in different cases, we still find that, in all cases, the action of alcohol on the nervous system follows the same law that has been so often stated. It abolishes the function of the nerve regions in the order of their succession from above downwards. The highest suffer first and most, the lowest last and least. Let us trace the course of an ordinary case, and note the completeness with which this law is observed, as evidenced by the parallel and simultaneous failure of conduct and mind.

Ask a man who has just left a city dinner to settle with you the lease of a house, or a deed of partnership. He will naturally refuse. If you press him, he will say that it is not a proper time to transact business ; and, if pressed further, will explain that to take him now is unfair, for to such an important and delicate matter one must come with a clear head. The admission is that the mind is not now as vigorous as it will be to-morrow morning. There is a slight enfeeblement. Partly from the fatigue of the day, partly from the effect of the dinner in drafting off a part of the blood-supply from the brain to the stomach, but chiefly from the benumbing effect of the alcohol that he has imbibed on his highest nerve regions, his mind is not as clear nor as vigorous as it is wont to be. The confusion is not great, he can make an after-dinner speech of average intelligence, can reckon his legal cab fare, and so forth, but he will not trust himself to settle a delicate matter of negotiation. He feels that the keen edge of his intellect is blunted. It is the very highest of all his intellectual faculties that have been dulled. Similarly on the bodily side—he can walk perfectly straight, can light a cigar without bungling, and button his overcoat with facility ; but when he tries to play billiards he finds " his hand is out." He is not certain of his strokes. He can no longer regulate his movements with the nice precision that is required for success. Of bodily, as of mental capabilities, he has lost the most elaborate, the most delicate, the most precise. At the same time that he shows these signs of defect in his highest nerve arrangements, he shows some sign of over-action of somewhat lower arrangements. By the annulling and placing out of action of the highest, control is removed from those just below the highest, which are consequently " let go " and tend to over-act. The staid and self-enclosed man of business becomes an expansive, jolly companion. He gets on back-slapping, rib-punching terms with his convives. He tells little anecdotes about his past career, with winks, and wheezes, and warnings that they are not to be repeated to his wife. His discretion and reticence are diminished by the loss of his highest centres, and he exhibits a phase of character inferior to his usual standard. No one would call this state of things insanity ; but for all that it is the beginning of a process which, if continued, would become insanity. It is the point at which divergence from the processes of health begins to occur. It is not insanity, but it is the rudiment of insanity. Let us trace the process further and see what it develops into.

Let us suppose that the toper has taken distinctly more than is good for him ; that instead of the thin film taken off his highest centres, a paring of appreciable thickness has had its function removed by the alcohol. The consequence of this loss is that his conduct becomes more conspicuously defective. He is excited into a quarrel by a provocation which would have no such effect on him in his normal condition, and he conducts the quarrel in an unseemly manner. He uses language which he would never permit himself to use when sober, and displays his passion before strangers and servants in a way that would horrify him at other times. Here there is, on the one hand, deficient regard of his surroundings, and deficient control, due to the removal of his highest faculties ; and, on the other hand, there is the positive excess of action, the violent language, and so forth, which is due to the over-action of the centres below the highest, which are now uncontrolled in their action. With this disorder of conduct go parallel disorders of mind. His higher feelings of decorum and self-respect are weakened or lost, and his lower feelings of anger and resentment are present in excess. His appreciation of the regard and respect of his companions is diminished, and his appreciation of the provocation he has received is exaggerated.

At this stage is introduced a new phenomenon. It has been shown that the highest centres suffer first and most ; and at this stage the highest layers of the highest regions are those which suffer most ; but they are not the sole sufferers.   Besides the failure in conduct, which is due to failure in the highest regions, there is a failure in the apparatus by which conduct is executed.   Not only has the driver lost his way, but the horse is lame also.   The motor apparatus which carries out the directions of the highest centres through the intermediation of the inferior centres, is acting imperfectly.   The articulation is thick and hesitating ; the movements of the hands are shaky and uncertain ; the gait is unsteady.   In other words, not only are the highest centres affected, but the middle group are affected also ; and in this group the same law still holds good ; that is to say, when the middle regions become affected the highest portions of them are the first to go.   The movements of articulation, which are the most precise, delicate, elaborate, and complex, suffer first and most ; those of the hands next ; and those of locomotion last.   Within each of these minor groups the same law holds good ; the distinct enunciation of syllables is lost before the varied cadence, and the variations of cadence sink into uniformity before the voice is altogether lost.

At this stage, or at a stage a little in advance of this, the insanity of the toper is no longer in doubt.   Suppose that instead of the evening it were the morning ; suppose that the previous indulgence in alcohol were not known and were not recognizable ; suppose that the condition, instead of being temporary, were permanent ; what would be said of a respectable merchant who should quarrel violently with a chance acquaintance upon insignificant provocation, and who, in the presence of strangers and servants, offered to take off his coat and fight ?   What would be said if he remained for several days or weeks in this condition, now maudlin, now quarrelsome, incapable of understanding or conducting the affairs of his business, and disgracing his family by his conduct ?   Would not his friends consider that beyond all question the man was insane ?   Would not they take steps to restrain him from putting himself outside the law, and damaging his business ? Unquestionably they would. And if this condition is one of insanity when prolonged and proceeding from no obvious cause, none the less is it one of insanity so long as it lasts, when it is of brief duration, and when a manifest cause can be assigned for it. The causation and duration do not affect the nature of the malady, however much they may determine its gravity. The insanity may be the transient insanity of drunkenness or the permanent insanity of general paralysis ; but if the manifestations of drunkenness are identical with those of insanity, it cannot be denied that the drunkard, so long as he is drunk, is mad.

That the resemblance of the manifestations of drunkenness to those of insanity means a real identity in nature between the two conditions, and is not merely a far-fetched analogical resemblance, is shown by two circumstances : first, that there is a well-marked and distinct variety of insanity which reproduces with minute faithfulness the characteristic signs that ordinary cases of drunkenness display ; and second, that every form of insanity is reproduced with accurate simulation by some case of drunkenness. Although, in nineteen cases out of twenty, the drunkard is jovial, noisy, restless, stuttering, and unsteady, we have already seen that in a certain proportion of cases he manifests no thickness of articulation, and no unsteadiness of hands or legs, but exhibits a maniacal fury. We have now to record that this is but one of the unusual manifestations of drunkenness. In others of these atypical cases, the drunkard is sullen, morose, suspicious, and revengeful. In others he is subject to delusions of various kinds. In others he has definite hallucinations ; he hears voices commanding him to certain acts ; he sees spectral forms of men or animals about him. There is no form of insanity that may not be simulated by a case of drunkenness ; and when it is not known, from other sources of information, that these manifestations are due to drink, no expert in the world, however skilful, could distinguish between the insanity that is due to alcoholic poisoning and the insanity that is due to other causes.

As if to place the matter beyond all sort of doubt, it occasionally happens that the effects of a drunken debauch do not pass away in a few hours or days, but persist for weeks. In such a case the manifestations are usually different from those of ordinary cases of drunkenness, and resemble those of other cases of mania ; and in such cases the patient very often finds his way into a lunatic asylum, where he is recorded and treated as a case of "insanity caused by drink." When the drunken debauches have been frequent and long-continued, the condition of insanity becomes permanent, and remains after the drink has long been discontinued. In such cases the transition from the insanity of drunkenness to ordinary insanity is complete.

Finally, the last stage of drunkenness and the last stage of insanity are identical and indistinguishable. We have seen that the natural termination of life is by coma. The progressive loss of all the higher nerve functions leaves at length none but those which actuate the breathing and the circulation. Then a continuation of the same degradative process stills the breathing ; the circulation fails, and the result is death. Such is the natural termination of the dementia of old age, and such also is the natural termination of other cases of dementia—of every case of insanity. All insane people, who die of their insanity, and not of any intercurrent disease, die by coma. Such also is the termination of every case of drunkenness. It is well known that if a man goes on drinking after he has had enough and more than enough, he will at length drink himself into a state of insensibility ; he will at length fall on the floor, and lie there snoring and incapable of being aroused. He is said to be asleep, but if he be examined it will be found that he is not in ordinary sleep, but in coma. He cannot be aroused ; his limbs are paralyzed ; his breathing, his heart's action, the condition of his skin, his eyes, &c., are those of a person in coma. From this condition he usually recovers ; but he does not always recover. Cases occur from time to time in which a man passes from the sleep of drunkenness to the sleep of death. Such an event is a not infrequent result of "sucking the monkey."[1] The dose of poison that he has taken is found to be enough to paralyze, not merely his highest nerve region, not merely the highest and middle, but to still the action even of the lowest, the most obdurate, and the least obnoxious to the influence of the drug. Thus, from beginning to end, a case of drunkenness is a case of insanity.

There are, therefore, three ways in which the normal and healthy organism undergoes a decadence of conduct and mind amounting to insanity : in the natural obliteration of nervous function that occurs in sleep ; in the natural and more prolonged obliteration that occurs in old age ; and in the obliteration artificially produced by the action of alcohol and other narcotic drugs. Seeing that in these three ways the mind and conduct naturally tend to err, and bearing in mind the principle that all abnormal states are but exaggerations of the normal, it is not unlikely that the main forms of insanity might be founded on—might be the abnormal counterparts of—these natural modes of decadence. Failure of function will naturally tend to follow the course which it has been accustomed to follow. If there are definite ways in which the nervous system is accustomed to fail under normal stresses, these will be the ways in which it will tend to fail under abnormal stresses. The failure will be more complete as the stresses are more intense ; but the starting-point and direction of the failure will be alike in the two cases. A prolonged and extensive study of insanity shows that the ways in which the functions of the nervous system fail in that disorder, do resemble, in the main, the several ways in which it fails physiologically.

It will have been noticed that each of the several physiological forms of insanity has its distinguishing peculiarities. The dementia of old age, which is the type and example of

---

[1] This term is applied to a practice pursued by dock labourers, of boring a gimlet-hole in a cask of spirits and applying the lips to the orifice.

all insanities, is distinguished by the *equable, proportional, and gradual* failure of every portion of the nervous system. The failure of the highest regions is most conspicuous and prominent, it is true ; but while the highest regions are failing, the middle and lower regions are also failing to an extent, which, while not *the same* as the failure of the highest regions, is strictly *in proportion* to their failure ; that is to say, in proportion as the highest regions lose their power of initiating forms of conduct, the middle regions lose their power of initiating forms of movement, and the lowest regions lose their power of maintaining the nutritive processes. *Pari passu* with the diminution in the vividness and comprehensiveness of the knowledge and appreciation of surroundings, occurs a diminution in the vividness and completeness of the consciousness of self. All the faculties, both of mind and body, decay regularly, equably, and proportionally to one another, and the decay is gradual and uniform in its progress. Feeling, intelligence, self-consciousness, conduct, movement, and nutrition, undergo gradual, simultaneous, and proportional diminution.

In the other forms of physiological dementia this equable, proportional and gradual form of the process is departed from ; and the several varieties that they present depend upon the amount of the departure from the regular course, and on the element in that course in which the departure takes place. Thus, when the defect presses with disproportional intensity upon the visceral moiety of the nervous system, there is alteration in the consciousness of self, which is out of proportion to the alteration in the consciousness of surroundings. Then the leading manifestation of the insanity is a condition of melancholia or mental depression, accompanied by a torpor in the bodily processes. When the defect weighs with greater intensity on the other moiety of the nervous system, there is a condition of dementia without a proportional diminution or depression of self-consciousness.

We have already seen (Chap. III.) that consciousness consists of two parts. One, the cœnæsthesis, or consciousness of self, is the reflection, in the mirror of the mind, of the processes set up in the higher nerve regions by nerve currents originating in the interior of the body, currents which are started by the molecular movements of the process of nutrition, and which are vigorous or feeble, voluminous or attenuated, as nutrition is active or languid. Some part of this upward flow of nerve energy comes from the muscles, whose bulk is great, but whose nutritive changes are comparatively same and uniform, and do not, therefore, offer conditions very favourable to the production of energetic nerve stimulation. The great bulk of the internally originated nerve currents are derived from the viscera, and especially the abdominal viscera, whose immense surfaces, whose copious nerve supply, whose great variety of function, and whose wide and rapid fluctuations of activity, render them especially apt to give rise to voluminous and energetic nerve currents. The cœnæsthesis, the "conscious ego," the consciousness of a pervading and abiding self, which underlies, forms the background of, and gives colour to, the conspicuous and definite changes which occupy the foreground of consciousness, is therefore mainly a reflex of the state and activity of the processes that take place in the abdominal viscera.

Those crapulous philosophers who maintain that happiness lies in the integrity of the digestive powers, are therefore not without justification. The enormous influence of the abdominal processes upon the condition of the conscious self is seen in many instances quite outside the range of ordinary insanity. If a man receives from a swinging boom a blow on the leg which is severe enough to break the bone, he suffers from the shock of the injury, but he experiences no special and peculiar depression out of proportion to the gravity of the injury that he has received. But let the same man receive a much slighter blow in the abdomen, and the effect upon his sense of well-being is terrific; he sinks to the ground, not merely shocked, but collapsed; his eyes are sunk, his nose is peaked, a cold sweat breaks out all over him, his heart's action is feeble and fluttering, his pulse almost imperceptible, he gasps for breath, and his consciousness is one of awful and unutterable misery. A minute ago he was an active, vigorous being, buoyant with a feeling of health and well-being ; now he is sunk in misery so great as to be altogether indescribable. Death is longed for as a welcome relief from a state so intolerable. Let a man suffer from a toothache or the pain of an abscess, and his uneasiness is great. He moans and suffers ; but, great as the pain is, it is bearable, and through it all he looks forward to the time when it shall cease, and he shall be himself again. Severe it may be, but it does not altogether incapacitate him. If he is brought a paper to sign, he can still look it through and decide whether or no he shall affix his signature. But let the same man suffer from colic, and what a difference there is in his consciousness ! There is no looking forward now ; nothing but a blank despair, an annulment of energy, a feeling of utter misery. It is no use bringing him a paper to sign, or asking him to transact business ; he is too much occupied with his own wretchedness to have attention for anything else ; his energies are too reduced to allow him to make any effort necessary for a business transaction.

If such be the effect of sudden and acute disorders of the abdominal viscera, we may be sure that disorders which are less acute in character and more prolonged in duration, will have a mental accompaniment that is similar in kind, but that presents modifications corresponding with those of the bodily disorder. And that is what we do find. General physicians, who have great experience in the observation of abdominal disorders, are emphatic in their declarations of the lowering of the mental tone and the prevalence of a melancholy turn of mind which commonly accompany abdominal disorders. There is a peculiar expression of mingled anxiety and misery which so generally accompanies abdominal diseases that it is known as the *abdominal facies*. Most persons have been gratified by the relief that has been gained from a fit of unaccountable depression by the operation of a brisk purge ; and the vendors of the quack nostrums, so largely advertised, depend on this physiological law for the continuation of their sales and the success of their business.

The same connection between the sense of well-being and the working of the abdominal viscera is seen in many other occurrences. When a child is whining and fretting, its mother says that its " stomach is out of order," and gives it a purge ; and her opinion is commonly justified by the event. The horror and wretchedness of a nightmare are held to be sufficiently accounted for by an indigestible supper. The chronic dyspepsia from which Carlyle suffered is adduced in apology for his morose disposition. Dysentery and diarrhœa are the scourge of armies, but much more of defeated armies. When subscriptions are to be collected for a charity, the donors are first warmed into a generous and expansive mood by the administration of a good dinner ; and the effect is seen in the fact that the subscriptions following a charity dinner often amount to thousands, while those elicited by the most persuasive sermons, which are commonly delivered to fasting stomachs, rarely exceed a very few hundreds.

The activity of the abdominal visceral processes, and therefore the effect upon the state of nervous tension, and so upon the sense of well-being, depends on two factors : first, the structural integrity, and second, the innervation. If there be any structural malady, as a catarrh of the mucus membrane of the stomach or intestine, a dilatation of the stomach, an ulcer or constriction in the intestinal tract, a gallstone, or other disorder of the liver ; or if there be disordered working from the irritation of indigestible food, or emetics, or what-not ; then there is alteration of the visceral nerve currents going to the brain, and then there is a diminution of nerve tension generally, and a feeling of depression. But this depression does not sensibly surpass the limits of the normal. It is not pro-

found ; it is not associated with delusion. It is a mere
depression of more or less transient duration. But when
there is torpor of the abdominal organs owing to defective
innervation—that is, to deficiency in the volume and intensity
of the nerve currents, which set going and regulate the
processes—then the depression is of more serious character.
In such a case the fact that the innervation is defective
indicates a derangement of the central nervous system.
That part of the higher nerve regions which represents the
visceral motor processes is not working efficiently. The
tension of its energy is below normal, and the currents
which it emits are of subnormal tension. Consequently
the abdominal processes are inefficiently and sluggishly
conducted, and the reverse currents—the currents returning
to the superior nerve regions — are greatly reduced in
intensity ; hence in these cases there is a vicious circle of ill
effects. The primary defect, inefficient action of the higher
nerve regions, representing the body generally, produces an
inefficiency in the innervation of the whole body ; hence a
lack of muscular activity, and a sluggishness in the movements of nutrition. The weight of this inefficiency falls
with specially onerous burden on the abdominal viscera, and
diminishes their activity. This diminution of activity is, of
course, represented in the diminution of the upward currents
which they transmit to the brain ; and the higher nerve
regions, lacking their normal stimulus, are confirmed in
the inefficiency of their action. The mental reflexion of
this diminution of activity in those highest nerve regions in
which the visceral and nutritive processes are represented, is
diminution of the feeling of well-being, or mental depression.
It may be that the inefficient working is confined for a time
to these particular regions of the highest nervous arrangements, and that for a time the condition is one of simple
melancholy without delusion, but this condition can be only
temporary. Seeing that the primary and initial defect was
in the highest nervous arrangements, which represent the
whole organism, and adjust the organism to its surround-

ings, it can hardly be that the representation of the organism can be altered and disordered without its adjustment to surroundings being altered and disordered likewise; and hence, although the cœnæsthesis suffers first and most, and the consciousness of self is most disturbed, it will soon follow that the relations of self to surroundings will suffer, for the self, being wrongly represented, must also be wrongly adjusted.

Then not only may either of the chief moieties of the nervous system be affected with preponderant gravity, but, within each moiety, similar irregularities of distribution of the defect may obtain. It has already been shown how, in sleep, the obliteration of function may proceed irregularly, so as to leave islets of tissue outstanding, unsubmerged beneath the tide of inactivity; and how the activity of these unsubmerged and disconnected islets has its mental counterpart in the phenomena of dreams. It has been shown, too, how the activity of these isolated portions is sometimes of sufficient intensity to spread downwards and set up action of the middle and lower regions, producing actual movements, the defective conduct and imperfect consciousness of somnambulism. The same state of affairs may exist as a more permanent condition, with differences in the amount and distribution of the areas thus left outstanding, and then the patient exhibits a form of insanity accompanied by delusion. Persons who are thus affected are virtually in a condition of permanent somnambulism. The state of their brains is virtually the same as that of the brain of the somnambulist, and the delusions of the one resemble the dreams of the other, not merely in their general nature but often in their particular form also. Thus, many people have dreamt, at one time or another, of witnessing, as bystanders, their own death, or of attending their own funerals. I have at present under care a patient who is tormented by the continual necessity of attending his own funeral procession. So, too, we are all familiar with the colour which is given to our dreams by impressions reaching

us from without—how the exposure of the legs to cold by
kicking off the bedclothes may give rise to a dream that
we are wading in cold water ; or the clanging of a bell may
start a dream of an alarm of fire, and so forth.   In precisely
the same way, the delusions of the insane are coloured by
the events that are passing around them.   The sight of
three or four people talking together in the road will start
the delusion that they are conspiring against the patient ;
the wind whistling in the chimney will be interpreted as
voices calling to him ; the floating specks in the humours of
his eye will appear to him as rats or mice, or birds flying
about him.

Such are the results of irregularities in the distribution of
a defect that is confined to the higher nerve regions ; but
defects are not always so confined.   It may be that there are
defects throughout the whole hierarchy of nerve regions,
but that throughout they are irregularly distributed, and
that not only are the several regions disproportionately
affected, but the several parts of each region are also affected
disproportionately.   Thus, for instance, we have seen that
in drunkenness the middle and lower centres are often
affected disproportionately to the higher, so that, while the
head is comparatively clear, the power of walking, or the
movements of the hands or the ability to articulate clearly,
are much affected.   Similarly we find that in general
paralysis, which is the permanent counterpart of drunkenness, it occasionally happens that the movements are greatly
affected while the mind remains fairly clear, while in others
the mind is much impaired with little defect in the bodily
movements.

Secondly, the form of the insanity depends largely upon the
rapidity with which the failure occurs.   The rule is that the
more rapidly the higher apparatus is put out of gear, the
more prominent, the more excessive, is the overaction of
the apparatus immediately below the part so abolished.   In
other words, the more suddenly control is removed, the
more rampant is the overaction of the parts which have

been freed from control. In this particular the nervous system conforms to a law which is not peculiar to itself, but prevails universally throughout activities, both animate and inanimate. The efficiency of a spring in projecting a projectile depends largely on the suddenness with which it is released. There is an explosive substance used in mines which cannot be exploded unless the cohesive force which binds its molecules together is suddenly removed. Set fire to it and it burns quietly away, but hammer a percussion cap upon it and it bursts out with explosive violence. So, when a lad, who has been kept at home under very rigid discipline, is suddenly turned out into the world and made his own master, he is far more apt to plunge into dissipation and excess than one who has been prepared for his freedom by a gradual relaxation of parental authority. So when a nation which has been ground down under a burden of tyranny is suddenly released, it indulges in wild excesses of license, as did the French at the first Revolution ; while one which has obtained its freedom by the gradual relaxation of its bonds, retains at each increment of liberty its self-control. So it is with the nervous system ; the more rapid the removal of the control of the higher regions, the more excessive is the overaction of the lower.

It will be remembered that the fundamental property of nervous matter is its susceptibility to change. It is change alone that will set going a nervous discharge. When a continuous current of electricity is applied to a nerve, no discharge is produced ; but let the current be altered in any way and at once a contraction is produced in the muscle to which the nerve is distributed. When the current is increased there is a contraction ; when the current is diminished there is a contraction ; when the current is first applied, and when it is arrested, contractions take place. The cause of the discharge through the nerve is a *change* in the conditions under which the nerve is placed. Now we have already seen that in the gravity of a change there are two elements, magnitude and suddenness. The greater the

difference between the state to which, and the state from
which, the change is made, the more decided is the change ;
and the more rapid is the passage from the one state to the
other, the more decided is the change. In every change
these two elements of magnitude and suddenness are the
prime factors in determining the effect that the change
produces. What is true of the component parts of the
nervous system is true of the whole which they compose.
If the electric current that is applied to a nerve be very
slowly and cautiously diminished, and at last be gradually
turned off altogether, it may be, if the operation is conducted
with sufficient care, that no current of discharge may be
produced in the nerve, and no contraction may take place in
the muscle to which it is distributed. But if the most
perfect graduation be not maintained, if a jerk or a jolt or
even a variation in rapidity occurs in the process, then a
discharge is set up and a contraction is produced. In the
same way the deletion and obliteration of the highest nerve
regions, if it go on very slowly, may be accomplished without
any effect of letting loose being produced on the centres
below. But if the process be rapid, if it be irregular, and
more especially if it be sudden, then an outbreak of discharge
will inevitably occur from the centres below, and this outbreak will be grave in proportion to the suddenness with
which the control has been removed.

Although the most frequent condition of overaction is the
letting go of an inferior centre by the sudden removal of the
control exercised by its superior, yet this is not the sole
occasion of excessive action of nerve tissue. The nervous
tissue of no two people is quite alike in the readiness with
which it parts with its accumulated energy. Some are
naturally, even from boyhood, lively, mercurial, and effer-
vescent ; others are staid, solemn, and lethargic. In some
people, owing to some fault, some defect in the stability and
cohesion of the nerve molecules, discharge of energy breaks
out from time to time in great excess and with great
suddenness, and occasions the phenomena of epilepsy. In

other people, in whom the nerve molecules are not
abnormally unstable, the direct application to them of some
liberating agent may unlock their stores of energy and
produce an unusual outpouring. Such is the case when
from any cause a great flush of blood occurs to the brain or
to any part of it ; and hence we find that the part of the
brain in the neighbourhood of actively growing tumours is
especially liable to epileptic discharges ; hence, too, we find
that in that more chronic inflammation of the brain which
is the basis of general paralysis of the insane, epileptic fits
are common. Such directly-actuated discharges are not
always, however, so sudden and so excessive as to produce the
terrible phenomena of epilepsy. When they are of more continuous duration, and, while excessive, yet less tremendously
excessive, they give rise, not to epileptic seizures, but to a
generally heightened state of the tension of energy throughout the whole or throughout large areas of the nervous
system. Such a condition of heightened tension of nerve
energy obtains throughout the course of general paralysis,
and is only raised to the intensity necessary for an epileptic
discharge upon occasion and at intervals. Such a condition
of heightened tension follows also upon the rush of blood
supply that takes place in drunkenness.

Lastly, the form of the insanity varies with the nature of
the person who becomes insane. It is obvious that if insanity
is the removal of the higher nature of the individual, the
manifestation of the insanity must depend upon the character
of what is left when this veneer of higher or more lately
developed qualities is removed. It is an old observation
that *in vino veritas :*—that when a man is drunk his true or
underlying nature and disposition show themselves unclouded
and unhidden by the accumulation of superficial qualities
that he has superadded in the course of his life. Hence we
find often a surprising alteration in the disposition of a man
when he is in his cups. The miser becomes generous, the
amiable man quarrelsome, the advocate of purity becomes
lecherous, the retiring and modest man boastful and arrogant.

So when a man becomes insane there is often an entire change in his disposition and character—a change which is to be accounted for, not by the addition of any new ingredient to his nature, but by the uncovering and exposure of underlying qualities which were always present in him, but which were overlaid, obscured, and suppressed by qualities of later acquisition.

When we consider how infinite may be the variations in the extent and distribution of the areas of the nerve regions whose function may be removed ; how many grades and degrees in the rapidity of the loss ; how great the differences in the degree to which the nervous tension may be raised or lowered ; and how various the dispositions left exposed by their removal ; we can well understand how indefinitely various are the manifestations of insanity ; and a consideration of the number and varieties of ways in which these factors may be combined, will give us an idea of the way in which the several forms of insanity merge into one another, of the indistinctness of their boundaries, and of the way in which the same patient may exhibit a combination of two or more forms. At the same time, the nature of the factor which gives to the case its most prominent characteristic provides us with a principle of classification by which we may group together the cases which have most in common and separate them from those that they resemble least.

So classified, we shall find that the forms of insanity group themselves as exhibited in Table I. It is evident that a little shuffling of the cards will produce the modified classification of Table II. ; and which of these methods is chosen is not of great importance. The main principle to recognize is, that the form of insanity varies with the region and the extent of the nervous system most affected, and varies also according as the affection is a loss of function, or an increase or decrease in the tension of the circulating energy.

Since the several portions of the nervous system are not isolated from one another, but are interwoven in intricate combinations, it will be rare for disorder to affect gravely

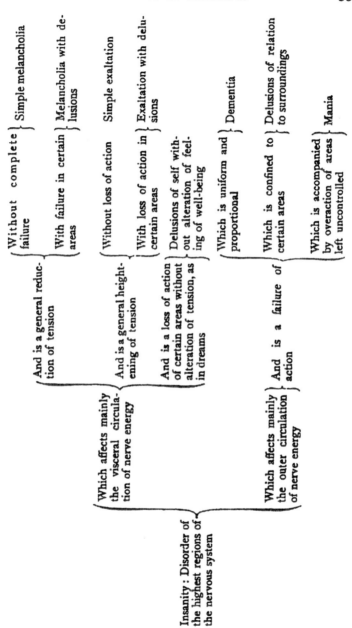

TABLE I.

Insanity: Disorder of the highest regions of the nervous system

Which affects mainly the visceral circulation of nerve energy

And is a general reduction of tension

Without complete failure — Simple melancholia

With failure in certain areas — Melancholia with delusions

And is a general heightening of tension

Without loss of action — Simple exaltation

With loss of action in certain areas — Exaltation with delusions

And is a loss of action of certain areas without alteration of tension, as in dreams — Delusions of self without alteration of feeling of well-being

Which affects mainly the outer circulation of nerve energy

And is a failure of action

Which is uniform and proportional — Dementia

Which is confined to certain areas — Delusions of relation to surroundings

Which is accompanied by overaction of areas left uncontrolled — Mania

TABLE II.

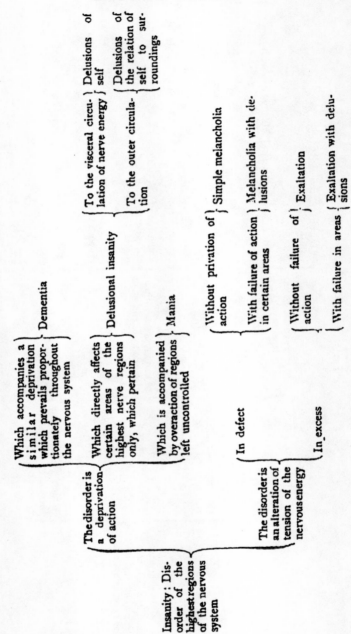

Insanity: Disorder of the highest regions of the nervous system

The disorder is a deprivation of action
- Which accompanies a similar deprivation which prevails proportionately throughout the nervous system } Dementia
- Which directly affects certain areas of the highest nerve regions only, which pertain } Delusional insanity
  - To the visceral circulation of nerve energy } Delusions of self
  - To the outer circulation } Delusions of the relation of self to surroundings

The disorder is an alteration of tension of the nervous energy
- In defect
  - Which is accompanied by overaction of regions left uncontrolled } Mania
  - Without privation of action } Simple melancholia
  - With failure of action in certain areas } Melancholia with delusions
- In excess
  - Without failure of action } Exaltation
  - With failure in areas } Exaltation with delusions

one portion while all others are unaffected, and it will be common for several or many portions to be affected at once. Hence that loss of action in certain areas of the inner circulation of nerve energy, which is the foundation of delusions of self, will often be combined with similar losses in areas of the outer circulation, which have for their accompaniment delusions of the relation of self to surroundings.

As loss of function in areas of the highest nerve regions indicates that some deteriorative process has attacked these regions, it will often happen that this process either begins, or at some time in its progress assumes, a rapidly destructive character. When the destruction proceeds rapidly, over-action takes place in the regions beneath those destroyed, and hence it happens that mania is a frequent accompaniment of the delusional form of insanity.

While the manifestations of insanity, in so far as they are manifestations of insanity only, depend on disorder of the highest nerve regions, it will frequently happen that the deteriorating process to which disorder of these regions is due, by no means confines its action to these regions, but affects the whole of the nervous system throughout all its extent. The external signs of disorder of the middle and lower regions are of course not those of insanity, but are disorders of movement, defects of sensibility, and faults of muscular action. When the deteriorating process extends throughout the nervous system, such disorders of movement, &c., on lower levels, accompany the insanity, though they do not constitute part of it; and the case presents an *ensemble* of insanity and bodily disorder which has to be considered clinically as a whole, although from a psychological point of view the bodily disorder is a mere excrescence on the insanity, which has to be considered separately. Such a combination of bodily defect with insanity occurs in dementia, and conspicuously in general paralysis of the insane.

CHAPTER XIII.

THE FORMS OF INSANITY *(Continued)*.

Melancholia.

THE first form of insanity that presents itself for consideration is that in which the weight of the defect lies with
especial severity upon the visceral nervous system, and
affects secondarily, and with less urgency, that moiety of
the system which operates the adjustment of self to surroundings.

The working of the visceral and nutritive portion of the
nervous system may be disordered in one of three ways :—

1. There may be simple defect of activity.

2. There may be simple excess of activity.

3. There may be defect of activity more or less extensive,
with isolated areas left outstanding in which activity is
normal or in excess.

Each of these errors in working may be associated with
errors in the working of the major circulation of nerve
energy.

When there is simple defect of activity, and a low state of
tension of energy in the visceral and nutritive moiety of
the nervous system, two concomitant and parallel sets of
phenomena are observed. In the first place, the processes
which are served, maintained, and regulated by this portion
of the nervous system, are lacking in vigour, activity, and
intensity ; and in the second place the consciousness of self,
which is the mental accompaniment of the activity of this
part of the nervous system, is lacking in buoyancy, and in
the feeling of well-being.

We find, therefore, that in melancholia there is evidence of want of vigour in all the bodily processes. The hair grows but slowly, the nails seldom want cutting, the mouth is dry, the digestion is sluggish, the bowels are constipated, the pulse is feeble, the breathing is shallow, the muscles are flabby, the bodily activity is diminished. Together with these bodily manifestations goes a depression of spirits which varies in degree from a trifling want of buoyancy to the profoundest misery and despair.

We have seen that in the normal organism there are diurnal fluctuations of the nervous tension, with corresponding fluctuations in the activity of the bodily processes and in the buoyancy of the temperament. We have seen how in the forenoon, when the nervous tension is highest, the bodily activity is greatest, the intellect is keenest, the highest order of feelings become predominant ; at the same time the viscera are most actively performing their functions, digestion, secretion, excretion, intestinal movements are most vigorous ; and correspondingly the sense of well-being is at its maximum. There is in the morning a buoyancy of mind, a flow of high spirits, a general hopefulness and enthusiasm which is unknown at other times. As the day wanes, all these signs of activity diminish ; conduct becomes more languid, consciousness is less intensely vivid, the processes of nutrition and the visceral functions are less active ; and correspondingly the flow of high spirits, the eagerness, the gaiety of mind subside. As the time goes on, and the small hours of the morning are reached, the tide of energy reaches its lowest ebb ; exertion becomes difficult, almost painful, the intellect is dull and sluggish, the visceral and nutritive processes are inactive, the tide of nerve tension is at its ebb, and the general feeling of well-being is supplanted by a feeling of misery. Such a feeling at such a time is in no respect abnormal, unless it is very excessive in degree ; but if this low tide of nervous energy, with its accompanying inactivity of conduct, its torpor of visceral and nutritive processes and its feeling of misery, persist the whole twenty-four hours round, and continue day after day, then the state of things is no longer normal ; then the modification of mind, of conduct, and of nutrition amount to positive disorder, and the case becomes one of insanity—of that form of insanity which is known as melancholia.

The symptoms or manifestations of melancholia are nothing more than a persistence, in more or less exaggerated form, of those which every one experiences in some degree who is wakeful between three and four o'clock in the morning. The most marked and conspicuous feature of the malady—the leading symptom—is the depression of spirits which always characterizes it. This feature in never absent. In some cases it is extreme in its severity, in others it is comparatively little ; but whether severe or trifling, it betrays its origin, and indicates its relation with the normal, by invariably being worst in the early morning. In slight cases the melancholy is perhaps present only in the early mornings, midday being a time of almost normal cheerfulness. In cases in which the depression is so great as to lead to attempts at suicide, the tendency to make these attempts is greatest in the early morning; and it is well known to those who have the conduct of asylums that it is in the early morning hours that the most vigilant watchfulness is required. In slight cases, the melancholy amounts only to a feeling of dissatisfaction, of diffidence in their own powers, and general vague unhappiness ; but in severe cases this is the most dreadful malady that can afflict a human being. In such cases the patient has a most miserable expression of face, his head droops on his breast, his arms hang listless by his sides, his forehead is puckered into innumerable wrinkles, his eyes are sunk, he weeps either constantly or frequently, his mouth is a picture of woe, and his whole attitude and expression are suggestive of misery and despair. Question him, and he does not answer; urge your question, and he groans and wrings his hands ; still urge him, and he cries, and says in a feeble monotone that he is the most

miserable and most wicked of men—that he is accursed of
God and man—that he has committed the unpardonable sin,
the sin against the Holy Ghost—that his wickedness is un-
speakable—that he is unfit to live.

In some cases the overwhelming feeling of misery is mani-
fested in the most striking ways : the patient sits all day,

FIG. 18.

rocking himself backward and forward, moaning and wailing
in intolerable distress. In one case recorded by Dr. Savage
the patient never opened his lips except to repeat the single
phrase, "Dead and damned." He "spoke only that one
phrase, as if in that one phrase his soul he did outpour."

When the lack of nervous tension is not very great, and the
feeling of misery not very profound, there may be little or no

evidence of disorder of the other great moiety of the nervous
system—that which adjusts self to surroundings.   In such

cases there is simple depression—a feeling of unhappiness,
which is not justified by the circumstances of the individual,

and for which he is unable to account. But when the disorder of feeling is profound, it is always accompanied by more or less disorder of intellect—by more or less marked delusion. The delusions of melancholia arise in two ways, or rather have a twofold cause, each moiety of which corroborates and enforces the other. In the first place, the profound feeling of misery naturally sets its unfortunate possessor casting about to discover a cause for it. Normally a feeling of misery is the state which corresponds with some untoward relation of our surroundings towards us. Consequently, when a feeling of misery is experienced, there is a natural tendency to seek for circumstances which would justify and explain it. If no such circumstance is immediately apparent, the tendency will be to think "It must be so and so"—a judgment of God for a sin committed, or an impending financial disaster, or what not. From the idea that it must be so to the idea that it is so is not a long step, and is a step which we are occasionally actual witnesses of, the lapse of a few days or a week being sometimes enough to transform the one declaration into the other.

The other cause of the delusions of melancholia is in the actual disordered working of the mental processes, concomitant with the disorder of the working of the highest nerve processes, which is inevitable from the low tension of the nervous energy which obtains there. If we remember that these highest nerve regions are a most intricately constituted plexus of intercommunicating channels—some of which are wide and freely permeable, while others are small, but half excavated, and permeable only with difficulty—it will appear evident that they can only be filled and thoroughly permeated by the currents of energy when the tension of that energy is considerable. When the tension is reduced, the less permeable channels, the channels in which the energy passes with difficulty, under friction, and under pressure, will fail to be traversed. Those only will have the passage through them effected, which are widely and freely permeable. Hence will result an irregular, inefficient working of

the higher nerve regions ; and the concomitant of irregular
and inefficient working of these regions is irregular and
inefficient mental action.   It is not only true of isolated
channels here and there that they are with difficulty permeable to strong currents, and not permeable at all to feeble
currents ; but it is true also of whole areas in the higher
nerve regions that they are thus constituted, if and when they
are of recent formation.   Hence, when the nerve tension is low,
these areas will not be supplied, their withdrawal from the
general activity will disturb the balance of that activity, and
will thus be directly productive of delusion.

Whether the rationale of the delusions of melancholia is
or is not as stated, certain it is that the ill-feeling of melancholia, when at all pronounced, is always accompanied by
delusion ; and usually the delusions bear such a proportion
to the feeling of unhappiness, that if they were founded in
fact, instead of being delusions, they would justify an amount
of unhappiness pretty near to that which is actually felt.
Thus we do not usually find that a very profound degree of
misery is accompanied by a delusion of some trifling injury,
nor that a light degree of melancholia accompanies a delusion
about eternal damnation.   If a patient has but a slight
degree of melancholy, he has a delusion that he suffers from
some comparatively slight misfortune—as, for instance, that
he is afflicted with the itch, or that he has a weasel inside him.
If his depression be of a more severe character, his delusion
is that he is suffering from a greater misfortune, as that he
has lost his fortune and is coming to the workhouse.   While
if he is buried in profound gloom, his delusion is that he is
the unpardonable sinner, that he has forfeited the mercy of
God, and will suffer eternally in hell.

We have seen that the depression of spirits has for its
physical basis a low ebb of tension of the nervous energy,
and that this same physical condition has its physical effect.
If the energy is emitted from the molecules of the nervous
system in greatly diminished intensity, its effect upon the
muscles and other structures to which it is distributed will

be greatly diminished. Now, the effect of the nervous energy upon the muscles is to produce movement, and its effect upon the other structures to which it is distributed is to promote activity of function. Hence we find that in melancholia, with a diminution of tension of nerve energy there goes a diminution of bodily movement, and a slackened activity of function throughout the body.

The melancholic person invariably exhibits an undue lack of bodily activity. That is a rule without any exception. There is no authentic case on record of a lively, active person being melancholy, or of a melancholy person exhibiting abounding activity ; the stories of Grimaldi and of other acrobats are *ben trovato*, but they are not sufficiently authenticated for belief, in the face of the universal experience of an opposite character of all alienist physicians. Doubtless there are men of abounding activity whose mental complexion is shaded with sadness and unhappiness, but that is because there are circumstances in their lives, in their relations with their families, their social surroundings, or their environment generally, which produce and justify such feelings. The sadness of a man who has lost half a dozen promising children from diphtheria, or who is ostracised from society because of the drunken and violent habits of his wife, is a normal sadness. The melancholy which, it is asserted, is never accompanied by a high degree of bodily activity, is a spontaneous and autogenic melancholy, having no explanation or justification in the circumstances in which the melancholy man is placed.

As a rule, the defect in the bodily activity corresponds pretty nearly with the depth of the melancholy. Those who are but a little sad, are languid, slow in their movements, disinclined for exertion and easily fatigued. But they do of their own accord undertake their duties, and strive to fulfil them as well as their enfeebled energies will allow. Those whose melancholy is more profound, relinquish altogether their daily duties. They can manage to get about, but they stroll languidly and indifferently. What they do, they do slowly and feebly ; but still they fulfil the commoner and more fundamental duties of their lives. In melancholia of the deepest kind the torpor is profound. The patient does not dress nor undress himself, does not even feed himself, becomes a useless log, and has to be cared for like a child.

With this depression of spirits, with this disorder of intelligence, with this deficiency of conduct, there goes invariably a torpor, not of the muscular movements only, but of all the bodily processes. The defective intensity of the currents of nerve-energy shows itself not only in deficiency of the muscular movements, but in deficiency of all the processes that are maintained in activity by nervous influence. Hence we find that secretions are diminished, the skin is dry, the hair is harsh from deficiency of the glandular secretion which in health keeps it moist and supple, the secretions of the mouth and of the whole gastro-intestinal tract are deficient. In addition, the muscular movements of stomach and intestines are of course defective. For both these reasons digestion is imperfect. The deficiency of saliva, of gastric and intestinal juices, cause the chemical changes of digestion to be imperfectly performed. The proper solvents of the food not being applied to it in due quantity, the solution of the nutritious parts of the food is of course retarded and diminished. The movements of stomach and intestine being deficient, their contents are not sufficiently stirred about, the deficient solvent does not get the usual chances of acting equally on all parts. For these reasons the digestion of melancholics is always disturbed, and an invariable accompaniment of the disorder is constipation.

Since digestion is so imperfect, we should expect the lack of nourishment borne by the tissues to express itself in a feeling of hunger, but this is not the case. Melancholy persons are never hungry ; and the reason is obvious. Hunger is the feeling which accompanies that state of the body in which nourishment is required ; that is to say, in which the stores of nutrient material present in the body have been used up in the repair of waste and the maintenance of the integrity of the tissues. But in melancholics this process of nutrition, of the repair of waste, of the maintenance of the integrity of the tissues, is itself greatly interfered with. Regulated as it is by the nerve currents, the slackening and diminution of these currents involves the slackening and diminution of the process of nutrition throughout the body. Hence the materials are used up but slowly, the want of new pabulum is not felt, and hunger is not experienced. The loss of appetite is one of the most striking and conspicuous features of melancholia, and it is as invariable as is the melancholy feeling itself. No case of melancholia has ever been placed on record in which constipation and loss of appetite were not present.

Since appetite is impaired, but little food is taken ; and since digestion is impaired, the full amount of nourishment is not extracted from this diminished quantity of food ; and hence it happens, not only that the tissues throughout the body are inactive in repairing the normal waste of their substance, but that the material at their disposal to effect these repairs is lessened in abundance and deteriorated in quality. Hence the repairs are but imperfectly and inefficiently executed, and, as the waste of the tissues is not fully supplied, they diminish in bulk, they dwindle, and the body wastes. Loss of weight is an invariable accompaniment of melancholia.

There is one other occurrence which it is necessary to notice in order to complete the picture of melancholia. We have stated that this disorder is an exaggeration, and a morbid counterpart, of the depression of spirits and the diminution of bodily function that normally take place when the early morning hours are sleepless. This extreme diminution of the tension of the nerve energy does not usually occur during sleep. In sleep there is always, of course, some running down of the tension, some considerable diminution of activity of the nervous molecules ; but when sleep is obtained, the upper layers of the nervous system are placed altogether out of action, and the middle layers act but feebly and upon occasion. Hence whatever energy is at the disposal of the organism is concentrated in the lowest regions of the nervous system, which govern and actuate the visceral movements and the processes of nutrition, and hence for this reason these movements and processes are, as a rule, rather more than less active during sleep, and their mental reflection, the cœnæsthesis, or sense of the condition of the body, is not reduced. So far as we are conscious during sleep we are not usually unhappily conscious, but rather the reverse. But if after the exertions and fatigues of the day we do not obtain sleep ; if during those hours in which the highest centres are calling for repose, repose is denied to them ; there is still the diminution of pressure, the running down of the tension, but this diminished head of pressure, instead of being concentrated in a small area in which it would still be capable of doing good service, is distributed over all the regions of the nervous system, and affords to each a miserably inadequate supply. Hence it is that, for the production of this feeling of wretchedness under normal circumstances, wakefulness is a necessary condition. And hence it is that melancholia, being but an exaggeration, prolongation, and intensification of these normal circumstances, is invariably accompanied by wakefulness. Night after night, and night after night, these unfortunate beings get either no sleep, or a sleep which is measured rather by minutes than hours, and which, even when gained, is of the lightest character, involving in its quiescence not a great depth of the nervous system, but a few only of the higher layers, and leaving the remainder in futile and exhausting activity. The wakefulness has not the accompaniments of restlessness and noise that accompany the wakefulness of mania, and is therefore less prominent and less frequently recognized, but it is constant in its occurrence.

Depression of spirits, delusion, torpor of conduct, torpor of nutrition and bodily processes, and wakefulness—such are the classical manifestations of melancholia, and all of them may be accounted for by considering the condition an exaggeration of that which accompanies every wakeful night, by regarding them as the outcome of a diminution in the tension of the nervous energy.

Such being the nature of melancholia, the treatment appropriate for it becomes obvious. We must endeavour to procure sleep, to accelerate and re-vivify the process of nutrition, and to raise the tension of the nervous energy.

The measures that should be taken to procure sleep are too long to set forth here in full. This much may be said : no attempt should be made to procure sleep by means of drugs ; certainly not until all other means have failed. Sleep so procured has never the efficacy of sleep that is brought about by more natural methods ; usually, large and even dangerous doses of soporific drugs have to be given before sleep can be procured, and it not unfrequently happens that by no amount of the drug that can be given will sleep be obtained. I have seen more than one patient, the sufferer from persistent, obstinate insomnia, dosed with opium, and more opium, and still more opium, until he has died with the symptoms of opium-poisoning without ever going to sleep. The way to procure sleep is to observe the hygiene of sleep ; to get the body into such a state, and to place it under such conditions and circumstances, that sleep is a natural and inevitable result ; but not to give dose after dose of narcotics. I have seen patients who had not slept for many days, and who had taken incredible quantities of morphia, bromide of potassium and chloral, fall into a sound sleep in a few hours when all these drugs were stopped, and what I call the hygiene of sleep had been observed, and sleep for sixteen hours at a stretch.

If in a case of melancholy we can procure natural sleep, we at once arrest the expenditure of energy in the higher nerve regions and promote the process of re-storage ; hence when the patient awakes he will wake with his nervous system in better condition, with more energy in store, with a

greater tension of energy, and generally in better condition.
It is essential, of course, that the sleep should be accompanied not only by a suspension of expenditure of energy,
but by a renewal and invigoration of the process of storage.
This we cannot do directly, but we can do much indirectly
by taking measures to promote the activity of nutrition
throughout the body, so that in this general renewal the
cerebral molecules may share.   In melancholia the blood
is always impoverished.   Since, owing to the languid character of the nutritive processes, hunger is not felt, or but
little felt, food is taken in but small quantities or not at all,
and hence the blood is always poor in nutriment.   It will
occasionally happen that melancholic persons die of starvation, not from wilfully refusing their food with suicidal
intent, but simply because they never feel hunger, and never
represent to themselves the consequences of abstinence, until
the brain has become so wasted and atrophied from deficient
nourishment that no representation of consequences is any
longer possible.   If, under such circumstances, we compel
the individual to take food ; if we cram him with an
abundance of nutritious material, the blood which bathes
his tissues becomes rich in pabulum, and of the pabulum
so presented the tissues cannot fail to assimilate some.   Now
if we enforce a measure of exercise, we place the tissues
in a state in which, physiologically and naturally, they have
an increased inclination to assimilate pabulum from the
blood ; and if we insure that, after this enforced exercise,
the hungry tissues have a rich store of pabulum presented
to them in the blood, they cannot fail to assimilate some.
The process once started, the unaccustomed habit of
feeding once again resumed by the wasted tissues, it is not
difficult to maintain the habit and to restore their integrity.
With increased activity of nutrition going on throughout
the body, with increased power in the heart's action, increased pressure in the blood-vessels, increased richness in
the blood circulating in them, the tissue of the brain is subjected to so strong an impulse toward re-invigoration that

it can scarcely resist. Its molecules also begin to share in the general redintegration, and when once the process gets a start it is continued with less difficulty. The resumption of activity in the nutritive processes tends in two ways to remove the symptoms of melancholia. By restoring to the cerebral molecules their normal powers, it produces directly an increase of the tension of the nerve currents, and this increases the activity of the body; and this general increase in the activity of all processes throughout the body is reflected, in the manner already set forth, in the highest nerve centres, and is consequently accompanied by a modification—an exaltation—of the cœnæsthesis. The feeling of misery gives way to a feeling of well-being. So marked and so strong is the connection between the improvement of nutrition of the body generally and the disappearance of the melancholy, that it has been recognized from time immemorial. A thousand years ago Rhazes, an experienced physician, wrote as the result of his experience, "Make a melancholy man fat, and thou hast completed the cure."

There is one other matter which must be referred to in connection with melancholia, and that is the tendency to suicide which so often accompanies it. Suicide is so complete and violent a reversal of the strongest and most fundamental of instincts—the instinct of self-preservation—that its origin, and the frequency of its occurrence, are extremely puzzling. It seems as if in this instance our faithful master-key would fail to unlock the mystery—as if no germ of such an action could exist among the normal tendencies of the healthy organism; no principle of action whose exaggeration could produce such a result; and certainly the explanation is very difficult.

It is often assumed, not only by the verdicts of coroners' juries, but in the writings and speeches of thoughtful men, that a person who commits suicide must necessarily be insane at the time of the act. In this opinion I do not share. It seems to me that a man's circumstances may be such that he may, upon careful and comprehensive review of them, deliberately conclude that life is not worth living, and that it is better to seek annihilation, or to take the chance of happiness or unhappiness in a future life, than to submit to certain and extreme misery in this.   Suppose that a man is subject to a combination of adverse circumstances, that his wife has run away from him, his daughters disgracèd him, his sons have robbed him, that his business is a failure, and that he is afflicted with some horrible and incurable disease.   Who will say that, for a man so situated, to shorten the poor and miserable remnant of life remaining to him is an act of insanity?   He has to take his choice of evils.   Even granting that by choosing to put an end to himself, to throw down his fardel and refuse any longer to grunt and sweat under a weary life, he chooses wrongly and unwisely, yet does the wrong and unwisdom of such a course amount to insanity?   Surely not.   If, then, there be circumstances which may render the act of suicide a natural and ready way out of intolerable misery, it is easy to understand that there may arise in melancholia a state of mind which is in every respect equivalent to that which would normally exist in such circumstances ; and that the way out of a misery which is autogenetic, and does not correspond with or depend on adversity of circumstances, may be the same as that out of a misery, the same in degree, which is justified by the circumstances in which the organism is placed.   There may be no justification in his circumstances for the misery which the melancholy man experiences, but his misery is as acute, as real, as profound as that of the man whose circumstances are extremely adverse ; nay, there is no such misery as that of melancholia ; and under the pressure of this feeling suicide may be the natural and quasi-normal course to take.   Here, then, a large class of suicidal cases receives an explanation on grounds which import no new principle of action into human motives, and which harmonize with the general course of human nature.

It must be admitted, however, that a large proportion of the persons who are suicidally disposed do not exhibit the signs of extreme misery. All of them, indeed, are melancholic to a certain degree or at certain times, but in many cases the taint of melancholia is so slight, or so seldom present, that it is very difficult to assign the act to extremity of misery. In a certain proportion of cases, the suicide, while associated with melancholia, is yet not directly the outcome of the feeling of extreme misery, but is the logical consequence of some delusion. Thus, I have known a man of wealth, who upon quitting business became subject to acute melancholia with delusions of poverty, commit suicide in order to save his relatives from the burden of supporting him. In many cases a delusion will be found if diligently sought for, but in some cases the motive of the suicide remains inexplicable. Of all the tasks of the alienist physician none is more difficult, of all his heavy responsibilities none is more onerous, than that of determining when the tendency to suicide in any individual case has so far subsided as to allow of the patient being restored to home, to friends, to society, and to liberty. A patient is admitted to an asylum in deep melancholia ; he improves in health, he becomes cheerful, he becomes active, his delusions subside ; he says that he feels better, that his former fancies have departed, that he recognizes their falsity. He is watched for days and weeks, and as his improvement is maintained and he seems quite recovered, he is allowed to go home. Next morning he is found hanging from a gas-bracket. Such, with variations in non-essentials, is the history of scores of cases. Nothing is more difficult than to tell when the tendency to suicide has faded out. The patient seems well, seems cheerful, happy, and active. His friends are clamouring for his discharge. The basest and most sordid motives are attributed to his medical custodian for his caution and prudence. At length he yields ; the patient is discharged, and forthwith commits suicide. Then is the wrath of his friends more bitter than ever against the doctor who, at their own persistent solicitation, gave the patient the chance of de-

stroying himself. Then a coroner's jury gravely censures
the doctor for his want of care, forethought, and skill.
Cases have occurred in which it has appeared that a patient
has actually been able to *sham* a recovery, to assume a
cheerfulness that he did not feel, in order to gain his
liberty, and with his liberty the means of destroying
himself.

How are we to account for such cases—for the persistence
of the tendency to suicide, which is an outgrowth and, as
it were, a non-essential excrescence on the fungus of melancholia, when the more constant and more fundamental
manifestations of melancholia have disappeared ? The problem is an extremely difficult one, but its solution will
probably be found in the following considerations. The
recovery from melancholia is often interrupted by fits of
depression, which occur at varying intervals and with
varying degrees of severity. The suicidal impulse may
arise during an unexpected relapse of this nature, which,
but for the untoward termination, would have been of a
temporary character. This explanation is an obvious one,
and I am bound to say that it is one which is not very
satisfactory, for the fits of depression which interrupt the
recovery from melancholia are not usually extremely severe.
The true explanation is probably to be found in considerations of a very different character.

The following cases were related by Dr. Hughlings
Jackson in his recent Address in Medicine to the British
Medical Association :—A man was clasping a vessel containing an explosive, when the vessel exploded and blew
his hand off. As is often the case, he retained a phantom
hand ; that is to say, he had feelings as if the hand were
still there ; and this phantom hand appeared to be always
in the position of grasping the vessel. Another man had
a sudden attack of brain disease, by which he lost his speech.
The only words which he remained able to utter were,
" Come on," or " Come on to me." He was a signalman,
and it is presumed that in the course of his duty he was

uttering, or was about to utter, these words when his seizure took place. A soldier, while " numbering off," had a fit. Afterwards he had many fits, and in each one he would begin to count. In another case, a woman fractured her skull while laying oilcloth ; and during the stupor that preceded her death, she kept manipulating the counterpane of her bed as if laying oilcloth, and would desist for a time when told that it was properly laid. All these cases resemble one another in this : that in each there was either prolonged persistence, or more or less frequent recurrence, of a form of activity that should have been temporary only ; and in each case the activity was renewed without any appropriateness to the circumstances in which it occurred. Hence we are impressed with this quality in the nervous system—the quality of gaining a habit of renewing a certain activity, without reference to the appropriateness of that activity to the circumstances. It is possible that the tendency to suicide may in the same manner be fixed, and be impressed with a habit of recurrence at odd times and without provocation from circumstances. It is true that in all the four cases, the fixation of the temporary state was brought about by a sudden shock of some kind to the nervous system, and that in the cases of recurring suicidal impulse no shock is traceable ; but we do not know that shock is the only fixing agent that can produce this result on the nervous arrangements. It seems probable that this principle will account for the apparently causeless recurrence of the suicidal impulse in those who have to all seeming recovered from melancholia. But there remain a number of cases still unaccounted for, cases in which suicide is attempted by persons who are not very deeply sunk in melancholia, or by persons who are rather demented than melancholic, who attempt suicide without appearing to be fully aware of what they are doing ; or by persons whose malady ordinarily partakes more of the nature of mania than that of melancholia. The explanation of such cases is at first sight extremely difficult, but the difficulties fade

24

away when we regard such acts as exaggerated instances of acts that, if not quite normal, are at least very common.

The tendency to self-injury is very widely spread in the human race, and must therefore, no doubt, be very deeply seated. The spirit of self-sacrifice, to which allusion has already been made, is but self-injury on a higher level than that of actual physical mutilation. The principle on which it depends is precisely the same, although the manifestation takes a different form. We have seen how this spirit of self-sacrifice is intimately connected with the sexual function, of which, indeed, it is an essential and integral part; and hence we are not surprised to find that suicide, a gross and brutal form of self-sacrifice, is frequently due to sexual promptings. When a silly girl jumps into the water because her lover has wearied of her, it is not the mere disappointment and grief that prompt her to the deed. By the fact of being in love she signifies that the willingness—nay, the longing— to allow herself to suffer injury for the ultimate produc- tion of offspring, has descended to her from an interminable line of ancestry, throughout which the example of the gre- garine has been followed, in principle, from generation to generation without a single exception. Offspring cannot be produced by any organism without some sacrifice on the part of the parent, especially of the female parent, and the readiness to submit to sacrifice is an integral part of the sexual attitude. This readiness to sacrifice varies much in different individuals, though present to some extent in all ; and we have already seen that a quality which varies much within the limits of the normal is especially prone to ex- ceed the limits of the normal both in excess and in defect. From the fact that the amount of self-sacrifice of which lovers are capable varies so widely in different cases, we might be confident à priori that cases would occasionally occur in which the proneness to sacrifice self would be in excess.

Self-sacrifice occurs in two forms. One form is when it is undertaken as the only means of conferring benefits on others, as, for instance, when a landed proprietor deprives himself of the rent of a plot of land in order to give his poorer neighbours the benefit of a park and a playground ; or when a Winkelreid gathers the points of his enemies' lances in his own breast, in order to make a breach for his comrades to enter ; or when a Father Damien voluntarily cuts himself off from society, and devotes himself to a lingering and loathsome disease, in order to minister to a forlorn and neglected section of his fellow-creatures. Such forms of self-sacrifice, in which the amount of hardship inflicted on self *is no more than is necessary to obtain the benefits desired for others* are altogether normal, praiseworthy, and admirable, and are examples of the highest development to which human feeling and human action can attain.

Far otherwise is it with the other class of cases, which are common enough, in which self-sacrifice is inflicted and endured, not to enable others to obtain benefits, but for its own sake,—for the satisfaction derived from the consciousness that suffering is being endured. Such cases, far from being examples of piety, of patriotism, or of benevolence, are simply cases of perverted sexual instinct. That at the root of the function of reproduction lies the necessity of self-sacrifice has already been demonstrated, and that the sexual desire to sacrifice self, when denied its legitimate outlet and gratification, will, after blind strivings and gropings, find its expression in some form, however strange and superficially remote from sexuality, has also been shown. When a mother goes without sugar in her tea in order that her child may have a double portion, she is sacrificing herself for the sake of her offspring ; she is following her gregarine ancestor afar off ; she is satisfying a normal parental instinct in a normal way ; and her conduct is altogether praiseworthy. But when she deprives herself of sugar, not for the sake of giving it to another, but merely that she may experience the self-righteous feelings of martyrdom, she is gratifying an abnormal feeling of sexual origin in an irregular manner. She is prompted by the same motives that wield the flagellum of the monk and that raised the pillar of Stylites ; and more than this, her motive is precisely that of the suicide. She desires to injure herself for the sake of injuring herself, in order to satisfy her sexual instinct of self-sacrifice. Self-sacrifice for self-sacrifice sake, whether it take the form of unsweetened tea, of monastic vows, or of a cut throat, is always of sexual origin, and is merely an aberrant manifestation of the tendency to injury of self which accompanies the production of offspring. Among the forms in which this sexual desire of self-sacrifice finds expression is that of suicide.

Hence we are not surprised to find that a large proportion of cases of suicide are directly connected with the sexual function. The subjects of them are lovers, either actual or potential ; that is to say, they are young people who have been disappointed in love, either by the desertion of their lovers, or it may be by the non-appearance of a lover. At any rate, they are persons of the age at which love is most fervent—adolescents. Another large contingent of suicides are those whose tendency is connected with the sexual function indirectly through religion. They are the subjects of religious mania, and practically come into the same class as the last.

There is another class in which the act of suicide has a different origin. It has to be remembered that, rare and morbid as the act of suicide is with us, there are people with whom it is comparatively common, and in whom it is comparatively a natural and normal act. Among the Chinese, if a man wishes to inflict upon his enemy a deadly injury, he disembowels himself on that enemy's doorstep. The act of inflicting an injury upon one's self in order to be revenged on some one else is common among various lower races, but that it is not confined to these the following cases will show :—When I was house-surgeon at the London Hospital it happened on several occasions that a woman came in with a more or less severely lacerated hand ; and on being asked the usual questions as to the origin of the injury, she would explain that she and her husband were having some words and that he aggravated her so that she put her hand through the window. Upon inquiry I was never able to ascertain whether the act of dashing the hand through the glass was done with the intention of injuring herself, or of annoying her husband by putting him to the inconvenience and expense of the broken glass. Such inquiries evidently appeared to the patient foolish and uncalled for. They could give no account of the motive of the act, and evidently wondered that any motive should be sought. To them it was as natural and facile a mode of retaliating upon the provocation, as if they had pulled the husband's hair or scratched his face. If they had done either of these two things, the fact that they had been provoked to do it would have been a sufficient explanation ; and to them the same explanation was equally sufficient of the act of putting the hand through the glass.

The fact seems to be that the normal expression of rage is to injure some one. If the person who aroused the rage is handy, then to attack and injure him gives the satisfaction needed. If he is inaccessible or not obnoxious to attack, then the rage may find expression in the injury of a third party, as in the classical cases of Captain Absolute and Mr. Fag in "The Rivals." But it seems that when the appetite for destruction is once aroused, it will find satisfaction in the injury of anything—even of inanimate things, or of the enraged individual himself. Thus, one man in a rage will attack the person who has injured him, another will smash the furniture, and a third will put his own hand through the glass, or cut his throat, or disembowel himself.

The act of suicide, then, may originate in one of several ways—may be prompted by one of several motives. It may be the expression of a feeling of misery so intolerably severe that it can be no longer borne—that death is deliberately preferred to so miserable a life. It may be the outcome of a delusion which, if it were true, would go far to justify the act, as where a man kills himself in the belief that his wife and children are dead, and that their spirits are urging him to join them.   It may be an exaggeration to the extreme of the desire for sacrificing self, which is one of the fundamental characters of sexual activity ; or, finally, it may be an expression of blind rage, the outcome of those destructive activities with which we shall have more to do hereafter. Whichever of these origins the act may have, the immediate occasion of it may be a delusion or an hallucination ; *e.g.*, the suicide may have imagined that the Deity has commanded him to sacrifice himself, or may have heard an imperious voice exhorting him with irresistible vehemence to do so.

CHAPTER XIV.

THE FORMS OF INSANITY (*Continued*).

Exaltation.

THE second alteration of self-consciousness occurs when the tension of the energy that circulates in the visceral and nutritive moiety of the nervous system, is not diminished, but increased. Under such circumstances the symptoms will be in all respects the contrary of those described in the last chapter. Exaltation will be substituted for depression, and exaggeration for diminution.

When the tension of the nervous energy is reduced, the reduction in the tension is not usually confined to the visceral moiety of the nervous system, although it often affects this moiety with preponderant severity; and the same is the case when the tension is increased. The heightened tension is not usually confined to this part of the nervous system, but it does usually affect one part more prominently than the other. So that in some cases the main symptom is exaggerated activity in the conduct, while in other cases the main symptom is exaggerated activity of the nutritive processes; but whichever symptom is the more prominent, some degree of the other usually accompanies it.

Exaggeration of the tension of nerve energy to a morbid entent occurs in practically only two conditions—in drunkenness and in general paralysis of the insane; which latter has all the appearance of a permanent, progressive, and incurable drunkenness. While defect in the tension may exist without appreciable loss of function in any local area, and hence a simple depression of mind may exist without the accompaniment of any delusion, or even of any appreciable impairment of the integrity of the other mental processes ; exaggeration of the nervous tension, as a clinical fact, occurs seldom, and then briefly, without some impairment of intelligence. It may be, in the very early stage of drunkenness, when as yet there is only an increased flow of blood to the higher nerve regions, and before the benumbing effect of the alcohol has had time to make itself felt, that the increase of blood supply causes an increased emission of nerve energy, and so a heightened tension in the regions affected, without any appreciable loss of function in even the highest regions. When this occurs, there is for the time, and usually it is for but a short time, not only an exaltation of the sense of well-being, but an actual increase of intellectual power. The individual is not only jovial and companionable, self-satisfied and happy, but he is then even witty ; his conversational powers are exalted. The hesitating man becomes fluent, the dull man bright, the slow man quick, the serious man sees a joke with an unwonted readiness of appreciation. So, too, in the earliest stages of general paralysis it occasionally happens that the patient gives evidence, not only of enhanced self-complacency and increased vigour, but of actual increase of ability over his usual standard.

Such periods of simple exaltation are not, however, of long duration. Soon the very increase in the blood supply which produces the heightened cerebral activity of the man who is elevated by drink, provides additional facility for the action of the alcohol, which is present in the blood, to act on the higher nerve regions ; and soon the flush of blood, which is the earliest phenomenon in inflammation, is succeeded by the deterioration of tissue that inflammation produces ; the highest nerve regions succumb to the damaging influence, and while the enhancement of tension and the exaggeration of action continue, they are conducted on lower levels, and result in manifestations of increased vigour, it is true, but of vigour misapplied and misdirected.

The way in which the enhancement of tension manifests itself depends on its extent and on its seat. When it preponderates in the visceral circulation of nerve energy there results an enhancement of the vigour with which the bodily processes are carried on. Digestion, secretion, assimilation, nutrition, are all conducted with increased efficiency. The improvement in digestion, which is brought about by the consumption of wine with dinner, is well known. Many persons of weak digestion are unable to digest their food unless it is accompanied with wine ; and in such cases the wine acts by enhancing the tension of the nerve energy going to the abdominal viscera.

Nothing is more remarkable in the state of the general paralytic than his splendid muscular condition. Although, owing to the defect in his highest nerve regions, his conduct may have deteriorated so much as to be almost abolished ; although, owing to defect of his middle nerve regions, his movements may be so much impaired that he cannot lift his food to his mouth without spilling it, nor stand without support ; yet, from the continuous flow of high tension currents into his muscles, they are maintained in as high a state of nutrition, as hard, as firm, and as vigorous as if he were in training for a race.

With this enhancement of tension of the energy in the higher regions of the visceral circulation, goes a corresponding enhancement of the feeling of well-being, which is the mental accompaniment of the action of that portion of the nervous system. After a few glasses of wine, the bashful man loses his diffidence and becomes self-confident. His self-confidence is based upon the enhancement of his appreciation of his own qualities, consequent on the increase in his nervous tension. The braggadocio in which so many tipsy men indulge has its root in the same circumstance. Feeling an enhanced consciousness of their own abilities, and having lost, by the removal of the highest layers of their external circulation, the due appreciation of the fitness of expressing themselves modestly and with reticence, they give full expression to their enhanced self-appreciation, and brag to excess. That their self-laudation is the honest expression of their own belief in their own powers, appears from the fact that they will back themselves to perform prodigious feats, and will even attempt them. At such a time a man will offer to jump over the table, to fight overwhelming odds, or to write a poem.

In general paralysis, as the enhancement of the nervous tension is so much more exaggerated, so the vagaries of self-consciousness are much more extravagant. While the tipsy man will content himself with the claim to be considered the strongest man in the room, the general paralytic considers himself the strongest man on earth. While he is lying bedridden, helpless, incapable of dressing, feeding, or helping himself, he will boast of his prodigious muscular power and ability : that he can lift a house, drink the sea dry, beget a hundred children in a night, and that his arms and legs are miles in length.

As in the case of defect, excessive nervous tension is seldom confined to one system of nervous circulation, and is usually combined with local losses of function in both. Hence, in conditions of exaltation, we usually find delusions of self combined with delusions of the relation of self to surroundings. The general paralytic believes not only, in spite of his manifest infirmities, that he is " all right," in splendid health, and capable of boundless activity ; but also, in spite of the sordid surroundings of a workhouse, he believes himself to be in a palace, that he is the possessor of untold wealth, that he owns " millions and millions and millions," that he can " pave the streets of London seventeen feet thick with diamonds," and so forth.

Of course it is not every case of general paralysis which presents delusions so exaggerated as these, and there are many cases in which no actual delusions can be elicited; but in even the least exaggerated case there is a quiet contentment, a buoyancy of mind, a general state of happiness and feeling of well-being, which are in striking contrast with the utter wreck of bodily and mental faculty, and which render this malady one of the saddest to witness, as it is undoubtedly the least painful of all to endure.

The increased vigour of the nutritive processes, and the corresponding enhancement of the feeling of well-being, are, as might be expected, not the sole evidences of increase in the tension of the nerve energy. When, as usually happens, this increase of tension obtains in the outer, as well as in the inner, circulation of nerve energy, there follows an increase in the vigour of the action of the individual upon his surroundings, which is great or little according to the amount of increase in the nervous tension, but which is usually considerable. Nothing, not even the marked self-complacency and arrogance of the incipient general paralytic, is more strikingly conspicuous than his eager, restless activity. His hours of sleep are abbreviated, and his waking hours, longer though they are, are more fully employed, are more crowded with activity than ever before. His bearing and demeanour are eager and restless. He is constantly in motion, and his walk is rapid and hurried. He meddles with everything that he comes across ; he writes dozens of unnecessary letters ; he talks with undue vehemence, rapidity, and frequency, and at undue length. He laughs immoderately and on insufficient provocation. There is an entire absence of repose about him. The manifestations of the heightened tension of the nervous energy are of endless variety, depending as they do for their form upon the amount and distribution of the areas of the higher nerve regions which are left uncontrolled and unco-ordinated by loss of the regions above them.

The peculiarity of all these cases is that, as a rule, the character and degree of the delusions have a general relation with the other evidences of heightened tension. The greater the activity of the visceral nervous processes, the higher the self-appreciation ; and when we are able to reduce the one, a corresponding reduction takes place in the other. Thus to a patient with a glorious exaltation, of a most jovial and smiling aspect, and of eager and incessant activity, who claimed to be the Almighty Himself, I administered a large dose of bromide of potassium, with the effect of reducing his bodily activity to comparative quiescence, of replacing his jovial expression by one of mere placidity, and of lowering his claim for honours from those due to the Deity to those due to the Prince of Wales.

While delusions of grandeur occur most commonly in association with heightened nervous tension and increased feeling of well-being, they occasionally occur without these accompaniments, and every asylum contains quiet, orderly, well-conducted men and women, whose activity is not in excess, whose appearance and demeanour are not suggestive of any exaltation of self-consciousness or unjustifiable feeling of well-being, who, upon a short acquaintance, would pass as sane beings, but who cherish delusions of personal grandeur. Of such people, some lay claim to royal honours. One is Prince of Wales, another is her Majesty, another is a Royal Duke and Emperor of Universal Dominion ; others aim higher still, and are satisfied with nothing short of the attributes of the Saviour and of the Deity. For some of these cases the explanation is that given in the previous chapter to account for certain cases of suicide. They are not evidences of exalted nervous tension now existing, but remanets from a former state of that nature which has now passed away. They are the cicatrices of old sores. They are conditions which, in the ordinary course of things, should have been temporary, but which, owing to some variation in the nature of the morbid process, have become permanent. Other cases of this nature fall into the following class.

The third variety of alteration in the cœnæsthesis occurs when, without any important alteration in the general nervous tension, changes take place in the highest regions of the visceral nervous circulation, of the same character as occur in the other moiety of the nervous circulation in

ordinary cases of delusion of the relation of self to surroundings. We have seen how, in dreams, a partial and perturbed
activity of some of the highest nerve regions proceeds simultaneously with the suspension of activity in the remainder ;
how the suspension of activity, beginning in the highest
regions of all, spreads downward with an irregular progress,
leaving, here and there, areas outstanding which still remain
active ; and that the uncontrolled, unbalanced, unco-
ordinated, uncombined activity of these isolated areas, has
for its mental counterpart the phenomena of dreaming, and
finds its outward expression, when it is of sufficient intensity
to spread downward to the middle regions and produce
outward expression, in somnambulism and somniloquence.
So long as this irregular remainder of active areas is confined to that part of the nervous system which regulates
the adjustment of self to surroundings, so long the delusions
have relation to this adjustment, and fall to be dealt with
presently ; but when the areas acting thus irregularly
belong to the highest regions of the visceral and nutritive
circulation of nerve energy, then the corresponding alteration of consciouness is an alteration of the cœnæsthesis, and
then the delusions that result are delusions, not primarily of
the relation of self to surroundings, but are delusions of the
nature of self. Often this irregular failure of the higher
nerve regions of the visceral circulation is associated with
alterations in the nervous tension, which give to the manifestations their predominating character, and then the case
falls in one of the categories, already considered, of melancholia with delusions, or exaltation with delusions. But
occasionally there is a simple failure without conspicuous
modification of tension, and then there are delusions of
self without exhilaration or depression.

The conditions upon which delusions of self depend are,
however, more complicated than has been described. The
alteration in the highest regions of the visceral circulation
produces an alteration in the distribution of the nerve
currents flowing to the viscera,—an alteration in the distri-

bution of the volume and pressure of the nerve energy.
This alteration in the nerve supply produces, of course, an
alteration in the manner and in the activity with which the
nutritive processes are severally carried on ; and this alteration of the nutritive processes in its turn modifies the flow
of the return currents to the highest nerve regions, and is
mirrored both in their action and in the state of the
consciousness of self which accompanies their action. Thus
there is a vicious circle of morbid errors. The altered
nervous supply acts on the tissues and modifies their nutrition ; and the altered tissues react on the nervous system
and alter its working. Every alteration in the nutrition of
the body is mirrored in the higher nervous regions, and has
its attendant alteration of consciousness; but not every such
modification of nutrition is attended by delusion. Only
when the higher nerve regions are independently disordered
does there arise delusion, which then takes its form from,
and is referred to, the locality of any alteration of nutrition
which happens to be going on at the time.

At the outset of a fever, during the invasion stage, there
is a profound alteration of the cœnæsthesis. The processes
of nutrition going on within the body are greatly altered.
The nerve currents set up by these processes, and flowing
to the highest nerve regions, are greatly modified ; and the
cœnæsthesis, or feeling of self, which is the mental accompaniment of the wash of these currents on the shores of
the highest nerve regions, is profoundly altered. Almost
every one knows the feeling of malaise, of languor, of " being
ill," which attends the invasion stage of a fever, and can
testify as to the profound alteration which then takes place
in his ordinary feelings of health and well-being. But yet
this alteration of cœnæsthesis is not necessarily accompanied
by delusion. The feeling is attributed correctly to its actual
cause, and no delusion arises. In order for a delusion to
arise, there must be some other change—some additional
factor. Supposing that a man attribute his feeling of malaise,
not to the invasion of a fever, but to possession by a devil :

the feeling, we suppose, is the same, and is due to the same alteration of bodily processes, but the ascription of this feeling to an imaginary and impossible cause, is due to some other disorder of nervous processes, over and above that arising from the altered incoming currents. It is necessary to insist upon the existence of this additional factor, because the existence of a lesion, at the place to which a delusion is referred, is sometimes considered to be a complete and adequate explanation of the delusion. If, for instance, a man has a delusion that his bowels are completely stopped ; and, upon post-mortem examination, an ulcer of the bowels is found, it is considered that the ulcer accounts for the delusion, and that no further explanation is called for. If this were so, it would be impossible to account for those numerous cases in which an ulcer exists without any such delusion. Manifestly another factor must be present, and this factor is disorder of the highest nerve regions or some of them.

When, however, there is disorder of the highest nerve processes, and in addition there is an alteration in the nutrition of the body, either as a whole or in some localized position, then it is highly probable that the modified visceral nerve currents will so act upon the disordered nerve regions as to give a permanent bias to their action, and then it is probable that on the mental side the modification of coenæsthesis will take the form of a delusion of self.

Delusions of self thus arising are of two forms, general or local, according as the modification of nutrition which gives form to them is general or local. When the disturbance of nutrition extends throughout the body, and the alteration of coenæsthesis is general, then the delusion will have the same character of generality, and the patient will believe that his total individuality is in some way altered. When the modification of nutrition is local, the delusion will have reference to the locality so affected.

Delusions of the whole self are well classified by Professor Ribot into three groups. One in which the new self is substituted for the old ; one in which the new and the old self prevail alternately ; and the third group including the curious cases in which the new and the old self exist side by side, and simultaneously.

To the first group belong those cases in which the patient believes that he is dead, that he is possessed by a devil, that he is transformed, that he has no body, that he is some one else, that he is unnatural, that he is preternaturally large or small, hard or soft, that he is a cat, a horse, a cow, a sheep, a chair, a teapot, or even a *pâté de foie gras*.

Of the second class, in which the new individuality alternates with the old, several cases have been recorded. Although they are rare, they are of so extraordinary a character that they have attracted much attention, and are therefore tolerably familiar. After some critical event— a long sleep, or a convulsive attack—a woman awakes with a complete forgetfulness of her whole past life and with a great change in her character. She lives for some time in this new state, and then, after another sleep, she wakes with a normal memory of all the experiences of her life before her first sleep, and with her former character restored ; but with a complete oblivion of everything that happened in the new state. Another sleep reverses the condition of things. She has now resumed her altered character, remembers all the occurrences of her former new state, but is completely oblivious of all the occurrences of the rest of her life. The old state and the new state may alternate for an indefinite number of times, the experiences of each being remembered, and the character appropriate to each being retained, only in the periods of its own recurrence.

The third general alteration of the individuality is when the old state and the new state subsist side by side. These are the cases of double personality—cases in which an in- dividual believes himself to be two, and, as in a case reported by Dr. Hack Tuke, looks for himself under the bed, or, as in another case, ascribes his ill doings to another self which occupies the left half of his body.

Local or partial delusions of self are much more common. When the disturbance of nutrition which gives form to the delusion is in the skin, the patient imagines that his skin is made of velvet or of horn, or that he is swarming with vermin, or that he is uncleansably dirty. If it be in the body he may think that he is inhabited by a rat, a wolf, a dog, a cat, a weasel, a crab ; that he has no inside ; that he or she is pregnant (for this delusion is by no means confined to the female sex) ; that his bowels are completely stopped, and so forth. If the disturbance of nutrition be in the limbs, he thinks that they are made of glass, of brass, of iron, of putty ; that they are absent, are too large, too small. If in the head, his brains are boiling, they have been taken out and his head is empty, or another person's brains have been substituted for his own ; his head is bursting, there is no back, no top to it, and so forth.

CHAPTER XV.

Dementia.

SIMPLE dementia is, as we have seen, the natural condition of man in his declining years. It is a stage that has to be passed through on the road to death, if death takes place by the natural expiry of the forces of life, and not by violence or by the quasi-violence of disease. Normally, dementia is a process of simple enfeeblement and decadence. As the bodily powers diminish, the mental horizon contracts. Little by little, there steals upon the organism an inability to concern itself with matters that are far removed from its own immediate welfare. Little by little, its attention becomes more and more concentrated on the things which are passing immediately around it, and which affect it most directly. The ability to deal with abstractions fails, and there remains at last only the vestige of the mental, as of the bodily strength. In extreme old age—a period which, as before explained, is to be reckoned, not by years, but by the degree to which the power of living has ebbed away—the individual sits doubled up in his chair, his head sunk forward on his breast, his eyes staring straight before him, his jaw dropped, his arms hanging uselessly by his sides, his hands resting inactive, his legs with the knees either resting against each other or fallen apart, his ankles bent sideways, and his feet lax. Speak to him, and he answers only the simplest questions, and not always these. Scarcely ever does he initiate a remark, save perhaps to ask for food or drink. He can neither dress nor undress himself. He has to be fed like a child. Often he is dirty in his habits, and has to be cared for like an infant. Such is the end of life in every one in whom life goes on to the end.

Now it sometimes happens that, owing to the incidence of some one or more of the stresses already considered, this failure of energy, which is due to occur at the end of life, sets in prematurely. It has been said that old age cannot be estimated altogether by years. If we set a ball rolling, its speed will not begin to slacken appreciably until the impetus that we gave it begins to be exhausted; and the stronger the initial impetus, the further the ball will go, and the longer it will run, before it comes to rest. So with the living organism; all lives receive at conception an impetus which is to carry them forward to the end, but the impetus is not equally powerful in all, and hence in some it is exhausted at sixty or seventy, while in others it suffices to carry the organism over the century. It may happen, however, that owing to the exceptionally rough nature of the ground, the velocity of the ball is materially diminished at an early stage in its career, and that it comes to rest prematurely; and similarly it may occur to the human organism, that, owing to the incidence of some stress, dementia sets in prematurely; and we may have, in a young man or woman of forty-five, forty, thirty-five, or even at an earlier age, a state of things precisely similar to that in the senile dement. The same enfeeblement of body, the same loss of initiative, the same emptiness of the storehouse of energy, the same decadence, almost to the point of absence, of mind, that naturally occur in old age, may set in in earlier life, if the life have been subject to some severe drain upon its energies. Thus, it will occasionally happen that after very severe exertion, either bodily or mental, undertaken by a person who had no very copious store of energy to fall back upon, he may fall into a condition of dementia virtually identical with the dementia of old age. The chief and most searching source of exhaustion of the nervous system is,

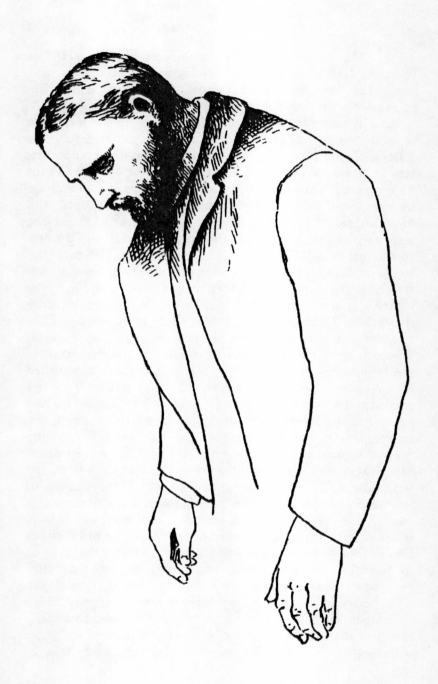

however, an outbreak of mania, and the commonest occasion of premature dementia is an antecedent mania. Every case of mania ends in dementia. Doubtless this fact has another aspect, as we shall presently see. From one point of view the exhaustion of the mania may be looked on as a cause of the consequent dementia; from another point of view, the mania may be regarded as an incident or a bye-product of the process of dementia; and both views would be correct. At present, however, we confine ourselves to the first of these aspects.

It has been said that mania is the commonest antecedent of premature dementia; it has now to be said that dementia is an invariable consequent of mania. Every case of mania, unless it is cut short in its maniacal stage by physical accident, or by the accident of disease, goes on into dementia. The generality of this statement will no doubt be startling to those who have had experience in the care of lunatics, and will arouse much antagonism. " What ! " they will say, " Every case of mania end in dementia ! Do not scores and hundreds of cases of mania recover every year ? Nonsense." To which I reply, Certainly, numerous recoveries from mania take place every year ; but this does not invalidate my position. By dementia as ordinarily understood, is meant a permanent condition, but dementia is not necessarily permanent. Doubtless, the dementia of old age is permanent and progressive; doubtless, also, many cases of mania end in a dementia which is permanent; but this character of permanence is not a necessary attribute of dementia. Every alienist of experience will remember cases of mania which have gone on into dementia, and which, after a longer or shorter period, have emerged again from the dementia and recovered ; and, when it is thus put to them, I doubt not that every alienist will admit that every case of mania, which has recovered under his care, has passed through a stage of greater or less mental enfeeblement between the subsidence of the maniacal excitement and the restoration of mental health. Of course it may be said that this intermediary stage of mental enfeeblement is not dementia ; to which I reply that if by dementia is meant a permanent condition, then, no doubt, it is not dementia. But permanence is not a necessary or invariable character of dementia. Every one will admit that cases of dementia occasionally recover. In young people recovery from dementia is not uncommon. If the dementia from which such a recovery takes place has been consecutive on an attack of mania, then we have the type of the sequence which is always followed in recoveries from mania. In some cases the consequent dementia is more prolonged, in others it is more transient, in some it remains permanent ; but in every case, dementia of more or less duration is the necessary consequence of an outbreak of mania ; and the dementia is more or less prolonged and profound, in proportion to the severity and duration of the outbreak of mania.

Seeing that the pathological condition of dementia is an emptiness of the storehouse of energy—an exhaustion of the grey matter—it is evident that anything which produces an excessive emptying of these stores may produce dementia. That the enormous drafts that are made upon them by the excessive and long-continued activity of a maniacal outbreak, should produce this exhaustion, is easily understood ; and it is equally clear that any other source of depletion, if equally prolonged and equally excessive, will produce the same result. Hence it occasionally happens that excessive study, overwork of various kinds, and even very excessive physical exertion, brings about a subsidence into dementia. The commonest source of excessive drainage of energy from the nervous system is, however, undoubtedly sexual excess. It has already been shown how powerful is the drain upon the resources of the organism which the sexual act involves, and how much more severe is this drain upon the energies of the male than is that of the sexual act, apart from the reproductive process, on those of the female.

Hence it is in males chiefly that are exhibited the ill-consequences of excessive sexual indulgence ; and in the male sex a very large proportion of cases of dementia are either due to, or are aggravated, enhanced, and prolonged, by undue sexual indulgence. Besides those cases in which the dementia so produced is sufficiently pronounced to incapacitate the wretched individual for the duties of life, and to render it necessary to commit him to asylum care, there are an enormous number of cases, forming together a considerable proportion of the total population, in which premature decadence of the mental powers, premature exhaustion of the energies, premature inability for vigorous and active exertion, result from excessive sexual indulgence in early life. The young man, full of vigour, boiling over, as it were, with energy and activity, recently let loose from the restraint of school or college, unaccustomed to control himself or to deny himself any gratification, launches out into excesses which at the time appear to be indulged in with impunity. But sooner or later comes the day of reckoning. He has felt himself possessed of abundance of energy, and he has dissipated it lavishly, feeling that after each wasteful expenditure he had more to draw upon ; but he is in the position of a spendthrift who is living on his capital. Had he husbanded his resources and lived with moderation, the interest on his capital would have sufficed to keep him in comfort to old age ; but he has lavished his capital, has lived a few short years in great profusion, and before middle life he is a beggar.

On the other hand, the origin of the dementia may be, not in excessive expenditure of energy, but in diminished activity of the process of storage. If from poverty of the blood, from the condition called anæmia, the nervous system is not properly nourished, it does not receive into store the normal quantity of energy. Its stores are always much below the normal level, and hence less is ordinarily expended ; and if any extraordinary draught be made upon the diminished store, the amount is reduced far below the normal, and the evidences of defective energy become conspicuous. In every case of anæmia, as we have seen when dealing with the stresses that help to produce insanity, there is a certain mild degree of dementia. There is a certain under-activity both of mind and body, and there is evidence that the highest faculties of the mind are especially deficient. There is increased irritability, showing deficiency of controlling power ; there is loss of the higher and better qualities of feeling and of thought. There is, in fact, a certain mild degree of dementia.

As to the symptoms of dementia pure and simple, there is little to add to the description, already given, of the natural dementia of old age. The whole nervous system acts sluggishly and anergically, and its topmost strata are altogether out of action. The patient is slow, sluggish, and inert. He moves but little, undertakes, in advanced cases, no employment ; in less marked cases, employment only of a simple kind. He does not speak unless addressed, and then answers not directly, but after an interval, in monosyllables, and is relieved at being left alone. In his mind the finer and higher feelings are extinguished. Affection, regard for the feelings, comforts, convenience of others, is lost. Nothing remains but the appetite for food and the desire for tranquillity. In advanced cases, even the former is lost. Mind and conduct are alike reduced to the lowest denomination. Such are the symptoms of advanced cases ; but all cases are not advanced. Often the symptoms are present in but slight degree and the cases but mild, as in the case of anæmia just instanced. There is, in fact, every possible stage and gradation of dementia, from the underaction of mind and body which comes with fatigue at the close of day, to the purely vegetative existence of the confirmed dement who has to be dressed, undressed, and fed, and who fails to recognize his own children.

In all the cases hitherto dealt with, the affection has been a simple loss. There has been diminution in the amount, and degradation in the character, of the activity of mind and body ; and that has been all. But there is a large proportion of cases of insanity in which this is not all. In every case of insanity there is, it is true, a degradation in the character of the activity of both body and mind ; but not in every case is there a diminution in the amount. The nerve centres have, as we have seen, three simultaneous and co-ordinate functions—the function of initiating, the function of controlling, and the function of combining in due proportion the activities of their subordinates. When the centres are damaged, when their activity is diminished, these three functions suffer of course equally and simultaneously. It may happen that the whole of the hierarchy of the nerve centres is affected simultaneously and proportionally, and in that case initiative will be lost, from top to bottom, simultaneously and proportionately with control and combining power ; and the effect will be that that we have just described, a simple dementia, uniform diminution, and degradation of activity of mind and body. But it may happen, on the other hand, that the higher nerve centres, which always receive the main weight and incidence of the damage, are affected, not only more than the inferior centres, but disproportionately more ;—that they are severely damaged while the inferior centres are comparatively un-affected. In such a case the organism will lose those activities which were represented by the damaged highest centres, and will be incapable of the elaborate and complex activities which those centres actuated. It will, however, retain the activities represented by the rest of the nervous system, and from the removal of the control which the highest centres exercised, these lower activities will, if the removal have been rapid, be present in excess ; and, owing to the loss of the combining or co-ordinating power of the highest centres, the lower ones will act, not only excessively, but disorderly.

It is found in experience that it is almost as frequent for the nerve regions to lose their functions in the one of these ways as in the other. That is to say, that while the normal course is for the activity to cease in all the grades of nerve centres proportionally, so that there is a uniform weakening of mind and body ; it yet happens very often that the weakening is not quite uniform ; that the higher centres fail not only more than the lower, but disproportionately more ; and that the weakening, while really existing throughout, is conspicuous only in the working of the higher regions, and that the action of the lower regions is both in excess and disorderly.

It is very often noticeable that old people, when they have reached such a degree of dementia that they have to be looked after and cared for, become not only weak in mind and inactive in body, exhibit not merely a loss of ability to perform the highest mental operations and to carry out the most elaborate forms of conduct, but display also certain positive signs of disorder ; they become fretful, they become irritable ; their tempers are less under control than formerly; little things excite them to anger, and arouse a display of passion disproportionate to the offence received ; they are easily grieved ; they take again, after an interval of many years, to weeping ; and their tears are elicited by comparatively insignificant matters. In all these manifestations we have evidence of loss of control. The display of emotion, that would normally be held in check by the controlling influence of the highest nerve regions, fails to be inhibited, and occurs from the excitation of trifling causes. Thus the higher nerve regions are disproportionately weakened, and the lower are taking advantage of this weakness to assert themselves with undue emphasis. In the term " second childhood," which is so generally applied to this state of things, we see recognized the fact that it is a degradation, a reversing of the order of evolution, a return to a more elementary and undeveloped state of things. The dotard who has lost his highest controlling regions is actually in much the same condition as the child whose highest controlling regions are not yet developed. In each case the absence of the control allows of a greater instability, a more ready provocation to activity, than is permitted when the controlling centres are present.

If the overaction of the lower nerve regions is more pronounced, the exaggeration of conduct is more conspicuous. When the lower nerve regions are here mentioned, it is not meant that none of those elevated strata which actuate conduct are left in activity. What is meant is that of these highest regions, the highest of all, it may be a mere film from the surface, is taken off; and the disproportionate weakening of any higher region, however limited, allows of overaction of those which it is the duty of that region to control. The conduct, therefore, which is in excess, may be of a considerable height of elaboration, but yet is excessive, because the region which actuates it, is liberated by the removal of a still higher controlling region.

The fretfulness and irritability that so often accompany the dementia of old age, need but a little exaggeration to become actual mania. If an old dement begins to whimper because his posset is not ready at the usual hour, he would be looked on as betraying the childishness of old age. If he became on the same provocation irritable and angry, and declared that he was neglected and nobody cared for him, he would still be looked on as a childish old man, but his aberration would scarcely exceed the normal. Suppose, however, that the conduct is somewhat more exaggerated. Suppose that he screams aloud for his posset, and creates an uproar; suppose that, when his daughter brings it him a few minutes late, he assails her with foul language; suppose that he proceeds to actual violence, and strikes her, overwhelming her at the same time with low abuse; in such a case there is something more than dementia—than mere weakening of mind and conduct. There is now overaction of lower forms of activity left uncontrolled by the dementia. Such an outbreak would very nearly amount to mania; and if it were a little more exaggerated; or if, without being more pronounced, such an outbreak were to become frequent; or if, from occurring upon slight provocation, it were to occur without provocation; then it would amount to actual mania, and then the case would present the usual characters of a case of "senile insanity."

What happens so often in the dementia of old age may equally happen in the dementia which sets in, before old age is reached, by reason of some stress, such as was considered in the last section. In either case, if the failure of the nerve region takes place proportionally, the highest most, the middle less, and the lowest least, then the case is one of simple dementia, senile or other as may be. But if the highest nerve regions, or rather the highest strata of the highest nerve regions, fail very much the most ; the other strata of the highest regions but little ; and the middle and lowest regions scarcely at all ; then, not only is the activity of the nervous system, as a whole, diminished, but the proportion of activity in the several parts is disturbed, and the result is that there is an exaggerated amount of a low order of activity.

Hence we see that many cases of dementia, as already noticed, begin with an outbreak of mania. The obliterating process that deletes the functions of the nervous system seldom proceeds quite regularly. It attacks the highest regions first, and the first sign of an approaching dementia may be an outbreak of maniacal violence. The removal of the control of the highest regions, not only lets go the region beneath and allows it to overact, but removes, at the same time, that normal restraining influence, which, as we have seen in an early chapter, causes a centre to return to rest when the immediate provocation to action subsides. A centre which is let go in this way tends, therefore, not merely to overact, but to go on overacting until it is completely exhausted. Not only does it tend to exhaust itself, but, as it acts through inferior centres, it tends to exhaust them also, and proportionally to its own overaction. Hence, while an outbreak of mania may be the first symptom of an irregularly-invading dementia, it tends very powerfully to assist the dementing process, and to make the dementia regular and complete.

The amount of overaction that will prevail in an outbreak of mania from this cause, will depend, not on the quantity or depth of the stratum which is peeled off, as it were, from the surface of the cortex, but in the *suddenness* with which it is removed.

For this reason we find that if a man slowly soaks in his liquor during the whole of an evening, he gets gradually more and more stupid, and at last is hopelessly drunk, without having at any time been uproarious. But a man who gets drunk by drinking off a tumbler of brandy for a wager, gets uproariously drunk. In the latter case, the higher strata are altogether removed, and rapidly removed, before - the spirit has time to produce its full effect on the lower ; and these latter are, therefore, suddenly set free, and actuate the uproarious conduct. After a time, when the lower centres are reached, he subsides into stupor, and then into coma.

Hence we find also that all cases of very violent mania—by which is meant, not necessarily mania with manifestations of violent, dangerous, or homicidal conduct, but mania in which the movements are very excessive and very violent— arise very rapidly. The insanity may have been there before ; some amount of mania may have existed before ; but when an attack of violent mania occurs, it always begins rapidly. It is never led up to by a continuously increasing violence of conduct. This, at least, is always the case in ordinary cases of mania, in which the violence of conduct is due to overaction from loss of control. In the rarer cases, in which there is a gradually increasing violence, there is always other evidence showing that the overaction is due not mainly to loss of control, but to direct stimulation of the nerve elements, as already explained. It is frequent in cases of mania from loss of control, for the violent outbreak to be preceded by lesser outbreaks ; and these lesser outbreaks may be of increasing severity; but occasional attacks, preceding a violent outbreak, are different from a gradually increasing mania culminating in a violent outbreak. It may easily happen, and does not unfrequently happen, that an occasional slight breakdown of the highest nerve centres takes place before the main breakdown. Under increasing strain a bit gives way here, and a bit gives way there, before, at last, the strain becomes so great that the bottom falls out.

The violence of an outbreak of mania depends, then, on the suddenness with which the higher centres are deprived of their function. Different cases of mania differ from one another, however, in other respects besides the violence of the maniacal manifestations. The variety in the manifestations is almost infinite. It is a very common supposition among the laity that every madman entertains a delusion, and the existence of a delusion is regarded as the essence, the criterion, and the test of insanity. It will be apparent to every reader who has got thus far, that this is by no means the case. In point of fact, the lunatics who entertain delusions are in a minority, and not a very large minority, of the whole number. In dementia, which is unquestionable insanity—unquestionable failure of the process of adjustment of self to surroundings,—there is commonly no delusion. There is merely a weakening, degradation, and narrowing of mind, so that the patient becomes incompetent to manage himself and his affairs, simply because he is no longer able to appreciate and understand his affairs, or to estimate truly his own wants. In that modification of dementia, which we call mania, there may be no delusion. There is still weakening, degradation, and narrowing of mind, but this enfeeblement of mind is not accompanied, as in simple dementia, by a proportionate weakening of body. The higher layers of the higher centres alone are affected. The middle and lowest strata of nervous arrangements are intact ; and hence, while conduct is disordered, the bodily movements, of which conduct is composed, are as powerful and frequent as in the normal state, or are, perhaps, of exaggerated strength and frequency. The lunatic is still able to get about, to run, to walk, to play cricket, to ply his trade ; but the more elaborate nervous arrangements, which actuate the higher phases of his conduct, being disordered, he cannot effect these higher phases of conduct normally. It does not necessarily follow that his mind his distorted and his conduct biassed by delusion. There may be simply mental enfeeblement, that is to say, the higher processes of his mind are bemuddled. When he attempts to think out an elaborate course of conduct, he falls into a state of confusion. When he attempts to carry out an elaborate course of conduct he gets astray ; he does things wrong, he makes mistakes, he fails to appreciate the force, and to estimate the comparative value of circumstances, and his acts are wrongly directed, confused, and muddled ; but, throughout it all, there is none of that definite distortion of mind that we call delusion. We cannot lay a finger upon any one point and say, " This is a delusive belief ; that is a delusive idea." We can only find a general state of mist and fog and bemuddlement. We find vague expressions of confusion, but no definite, sharp cut, fixed belief, that we can call a delusion. Consider such an utterance as the following, taken from a letter that I received this morning :—

" Knowing the only chance to escape from such awful nuisance for ages of delusions besides all ladies' honour concerned for upon that marriage of Lamb had depended triumph of faith crave happiness just had been heartless way preventing such deluded ladies to have such picture in their reach all cry shame were such faith revealed the scores in Bible which shall bring that marriage seen Messiah's Kingdom teach woman's heart that divine love." It is insane enough ; but it exhibits no definite delusion. It is a farrago of incoherent nonsense. The erroneous ideas that are prevalent with regard to the mental operations of the insane depend largely, of course, upon ignorance, but largely also upon want of the dramatic faculty—want of the capacity to take upon oneself, as it were, another person's individuality, and realize vicariously their mental condition. The person who wrote the passage given above does not entertain any delusion. The lower strata of his highest nerve regions are in good order. So long as he is dealing with concrete facts he is not only sane, but clever. He is a capable artizan, a skilful fly-fisher, a good shot, a brilliant billiard player, and a good chess player. For all these concrete employments his mind works well and clearly. But when he tries to deal with abstractions ; when he tries to bring into operation the highest faculties of his mind, the highest strata of his brain ; he falls at once into confusion. The truth is, that the highest strata of his brain are seriously and permanently damaged, and that, although he can set to work the fragmentary remains of them, they can no more turn out a complete and coherent piece of work, than can a blunted chisel cut a clean groove in wood, or a damaged loom weave a fair piece of cloth. With the damaged chisel you may cut a groove—of a kind ; and from the damaged loom you may get cloth—of a sort ; and from the damaged nerve centres you may get conduct—of some description. If the defect in the instrument is localized and definite—if the chisel is sharp, but has a notch in it ; or if the loom is well constructed, but has certain threads of warp missing—then there may be a definite defect running through all the work that instrument does. And similarly if the damage to the highest nerve strata is definite and localized, then there may be a definite delusion colouring all the operations of mind, and biassing all the phases of conduct. But if the chisel be merely blunt, without being definitely notched, the groove it cuts will not have a definite fault, but will be generally rough, ill-defined, and irregular ; and if the loom be not wanting as to the attachments of the warp, but be loosely and ill-constructed, there will be no single, definite defect running throughout, but the threads in the cloth will be at irregular intervals instead of being regularly placed, and the whole piece of cloth will be defective, with a diffused, irregular, general defect. So if the defect in the highest nerve regions is diffused and general, the manifestations will be vague and general.

The second difference in the manifestations of mania will therefore, depend upon the diffusion or localization of the damage to the highest nerve regions. In the former case the

mind will, in its higher operations at least, be merely confused, and conduct will be erroneous in vague, unaccountable ways ; while in the latter, mind will be coloured by a
fixed delusion, and conduct will err in ways having reference
to that delusion. Let me again repeat that the former class
of cases is much the larger, and that lunatics exhibiting
definite delusions are a minority.

The characters of the delusions that are entertained by
insane people are almost infinitely various, there being only
one class of circumstances to which they never refer, viz. :—
circumstances unconnected with the deluded person. Insanity being disorder of the adjustment of self to surroundings, it is evident that delusion, which is a part of insanity,
must implicate self. There are an almost infinite variety of
delusions, but we never find a delusion which refers wholly
to outside circumstances, and has no reference to self. A
man will entertain the belief that he is Emperor of China,
but he will never entertain the belief that another person is
Emperor of China, except he believe that the person so
exalted gains by his exaltation a power of interfering in
some way with the deluded person himself. Maclean, who
was tried for high treason in 1882, had a delusion that
almost everybody was dressed in blue, but he also believed
that they dressed in this colour in order to annoy him.

Delusions fall naturally into three classes :—Delusions of
self ; delusions of the relation of self to surroundings ; and
delusions of the relation of surroundings to self. The first
class we have already dealt with ; the remaining classes,
which depend on alterations of the other moiety of the
nervous circulation, have also been dealt with in part.

Delusions of the relation of self to surroundings vary
according as the relation in which self is supposed to stand
to surroundings is one of enhanced or diminished welfare
and consequence. To the former division belong the
delusions of power, of grandeur, and of wealth, which
commonly accompany exaltation of cœnæsthesis ; and to the
latter belong the delusions of diminished welfare and conse-

quence, which have been considered in connection with melancholia.

All the delusions of self and of the relation of self to surroundings have this feature in common—that the conduct to which they prompt is very rarely directly hurtful to others. They often prompt to direct injury to self, and to suicide, but only rarely to injury to others.

In the third class of delusions the alteration is in the relation in which circumstances are believed to stand to self. The difference between the delusions of this class and those of the last is very distinct. In the delusions of the class just considered, the alteration is in the way that the self acts, has acted, or may act on his surroundings. The delusions of the present class are concerned with the way in which circumstances act on self. The peculiarity of these delusions is, that the action of circumstances, to which the delusion refers, is almost always considered to be unfavourable. Persons with delusions of this character are the objects of fancied machinations and conspiracies. Their wives and children are endeavouring to injure them ; people are laughing at them, talking, whispering, thinking about them. People are thinking their thoughts, controlling their thoughts, putting vile ideas into their minds ; speaking to them, or acting on them, or influencing their minds from great distances, in occult ways, by mesmerism, by electricity, by telephones, by wires, through the gas, the water, the air, the sunlight. People are in a conspiracy against them. Spirits are influencing them, working upon them, playing upon them. People follow them about, point at them, and whisper about them. Or they are tormented by spirits. Horrible suggestions and promptings are made to them. They hear voices or see writing reviling them, or commanding or suggesting to them to do this or that. They are persecuted ; the police are after them ; they are to be tried, hanged, burnt, boiled in oil, roasted alive, starved, disembowelled. They have been robbed, swindled, cheated. Their wives are unfaithful ; their children, relatives, friends, acquaintances—the whole world is in one vast conspiracy to do them harm.

Delusions of this third class differ from those of the two preceding classes in the fact that they are very prone to prompt to conduct that is dangerous to others. From the belief that one is being injured, to the attempt to retaliate upon the injurer, is but a very short step ; and as the injurious agency is readily shifted in imagination from one person to another, the ill deeds may be ascribed to any one whomsoever. Oftenest they are ascribed to relatives, friends, or acquaintances—to people who have a direct relation of proximity to the patient. Not seldom the injurious agency is ascribed to some prominent personage—to the Queen, the Prime Minister, to a judge or a local magnate. Occasionally the attempt at retaliation is made against an entire stranger, one who is unknown to, and has never been seen before by, the insane person. Lunatics who entertain delusions of this character are never safe to be at large. The commission of some deed of violence by them is a matter simply of time, and sooner or later they are sure to become dangerous. It is not merely by direct retaliation that such persons become dangerous. It is common for them to commit some deed of violence on a person in prominent position, for the purpose of drawing attention to their grievances, with the vague idea that, once attention is drawn to them, they will be remedied. Such persons have commonly wearied out the patience of their friends by their continual complaints, which, at first combatted and reasoned against, are at last regarded with indifference, and passed by as a matter of course. This kind of demeanour, towards a person who is subject to delusions of this character, does not answer. To him his grievances are very real, and his sufferings very painful. When he finds that his complaints are habitually disregarded and ignored, he will seek some method of bringing them prominently before the public eye and compelling attention to them. Commonly he has carried his complaints before some public official. He has invoked the assistance of the police against his persecutors ; if a soldier, he has demanded redress from the commander-in-chief. He has applied to minister after minister, official after official, and all his complaints have been disregarded. Not only are his grievances not redressed, but they are not even inquired into, and he becomes exasperated by a double sense of injury. As his spiritual foes cannot be reached, or as all the members of the gigantic conspiracy against him cannot be punished, he will at any rate select some one whom he can reach, and whose danger and injury will compel the attention of the community to his intolerable grievances. It was on this motive that the Queen was shot at by Maclean ; that the Master of the Rolls was shot at by Dodswell; that President Carnot was shot at by Perrin ; and many other instances will present themselves to the memory of my readers. I again repeat, that persons who suffer from delusions of persecution can never safely be allowed at large.

The character of the delusions that an insane person entertains, depends in part upon the area and nature of the nervous strata which have been removed, or rather upon the character of those which remain. Upon this factor depends the determination of whether the delusion is to be one of self, one of the relation of self to surroundings, or one of the relation of surroundings to self. Then the colour of the delusion — its reference to increased or diminished welfare and consequence of the individual— depends on the condition of the tension of the nervous energy as high or low. The general features of the delusion being thus determined, its individuality will be settled, in part by nature of the person in whom it occurs, his history and experience ; and in part by impressions made upon him by passing events.

Thus a person who is naturally suspicious will have his suspicions morbidly exaggerated ; a person who is naturally vain of the impressions he makes on the opposite sex will believe that he is persecuted by their attentions ; a person who is naturally religious will believe himself the direct depositary of the commands of the Deity. Again, a man who has all his life been engaged in business, and whose whole attention and energies have been absorbed in his occupation, will have delusions in some way referring to it—delusions, either, generally, of poverty and failure, or of conspiracy among his customers, or of frauds made upon him, or more particularly of the machinations of business rivals and malign influences brought to bear by them. The uxorious man will believe his wife un-faithful ; the mathematician will believe, as in a case related by Dr. Clouston, that twice two are not four, but four and a quarter. The sportsman who suffers exaltation will have delusions of his own prowess, of the range and accuracy of his shooting, and the number of head of game that he has killed.

The impressions made by passing events will frequently give colour to a delusion. In the case of a man who believes that this or that eminent person exercises influence for good or evil over him, the particular person to whom the influence will be ascribed, is the one who is at the moment most prominently before the world. A series of political speeches reported in the papers will lead to the ascription of the influence to the leading political orators. A royal marriage will transfer the influence to the bride and bridegroom. The sight of an agricultural engine will colour the delusions so that the indescribable ill-feelings are ascribed to the action of steam. The description of a new invention in the newspapers will determine delusions to the telephone, the microphone, the phonograph, the electric light machine, and so forth.

Important as delusions undoubtedly are, as manifestations of insanity, let me, however, again impress upon the reader that the existence of a delusion is by no means of universal or regular occurrence, but that, on the contrary, in the majority of cases of insanity no definite delusion exists. In the majority of cases the condition of the mind is one of

enfeeblement or of confusion; and this condition of enfeeblement or confusion may extend throughout all the mental
operations, or may affect only a restricted and elevated
portion of them. It may be conspicuously prominent at
all times, or it may at some times be imperceptible, at
others elicitable, and at others manifest. While it is easy,
upon evidence of manifest delusion, to come to the conclusion that a person is insane, it is extremely fallacious and
dangerous, from the absence of such evidence, to conclude
that a person is sane. If there has arisen, within any recent
period, *prima facie* reason to think that a person is insane,
no prudent man will venture, upon a single interview, to
pronounce positively that that opinion was not justified by
the facts.

With this statement of the nature and significance of
delusion we may terminate our review of the facts of
insanity. No attempt has been made to enter upon a
detailed exposition of those facts, for, even if the space
at disposal were sufficient, such an exposition in detail
would not serve the purpose for which this book is intended
—that of giving a general view of the facts, and a statement of the laws to which the facts conform.

INDEX.

UNWIN BROTHERS,
THE GRESHAM PRESS
CHILWORTH AND LONDON.

Printed in the United States
17798LVS00003B/34